The Diplomatic History of

WITHDRAWN

Winner of the prestigious Yoshida Shigeru Prize 1999 for the best book in public history, this book presents a comprehensive and up-to-date overview of Japan's international relations from the end of the Pacific War to the present. Written by leading Japanese authorities on the subject, it makes extensive use of the most recently declassified Japanese documents, memoirs, and diaries. It introduces the personalities and approaches Japan's postwar leaders and statesmen took in dealing with a rapidly changing world and the challenges they faced. Importantly, the book also discusses the evolution of Japan's presence on the international stage and the important – if underappreciated – role Japan has played.

The book examines the many issues which Japan has had to confront in this important period: from the occupation authorities in the latter half of the 1940s, to the crisis-filled 1970s; from the post-Cold War decade to the contemporary war on terrorism. The book examines the effect of the changing international climate and domestic scene on Japan's foreign policy and the way its foreign policy has been conducted. It discusses how the aims of Japan's foreign relations, and how its relationships with its neighbours, allies and other major world powers have developed, and assesses how far Japan has succeeded in realizing its aims. It concludes by discussing the current state of Japanese foreign policy and likely future developments.

Makoto Iokibe is President of the National Defence Academy of Japan. He has served as advisor on foreign policy to several Prime Ministers, and is Emeritus Professor of Kobe University, Japan. His publications include *Japanese Diplomacy in the 1950s* (also published by Routledge).

Robert D. Eldridge is Associate Professor in the School of International Public Policy, Osaka University, Japan. His many publications include *The Origins of the Bilateral Okinawa Problem* (also published by Routledge); and a translation of Miyazawa Kiichi's memoirs *Secret Talks between Tokyo and Washington*.

The Diplomatic History of Postwar Japan

Winner of the 1999 Yoshida Shigeru Prize

Edited by
Makoto Iokibe

Translated and annotated by
Robert D. Eldridge

Routledge
Taylor & Francis Group

LONDON AND NEW YORK

First published 2011 by Routledge
2 Park Square, Milton Park, Abingdon, Oxon, OX14 4RN

Simultaneously published in the USA and Canada
by Routledge
270 Madison Avenue, New York, NY 10016

Routledge is an imprint of the Taylor & Francis Group, an informa business

Sengo Nihon Gaikoshi 2nd edition by Iokibe Makoto
Copyright © 1999, 2009 Iokibe Makoto
All rights reserved.

Originally published in Japan by Yuhikaku Publishing co., ltd., Tokyo
English translation rights arranged with Yuhikaku Publishing co., ltd.
through The Sakai Agency

Copyright © 2009 English Translation and annotation by
Robert D. Eldridge

Typeset in Times New Roman by
Taylor & Francis Books
Printed and bound in Great Britain by
CPI Antony Rowe Ltd, Chippenham, Wiltshire

British Library Cataloguing in Publication Data
A catalogue record for this book is available from the British Library

Library of Congress Cataloging in Publication Data
Sengo Nihon gaikoshi. English
   The diplomatic history of postwar Japan / edited by Makoto Iokibe ;
translated and annotated by Robert D. Eldridge.
       p. cm.
   Includes bibliographical references and index.
   1. Japan–Foreign relations–1945-1989. 2. Japan–Foreign relations–1989-
I. Iokibe, Makoto, 1943- II. Eldridge, Robert D. III. Title.
   DS889.5.S463 2009
   327.52–dc22
                          2009010037

ISBN 978-0-415-49847-0 (hbk)
ISBN 978-0-415-49848-7 (pbk)

Contents

Figures

Preface to the English edition

The original edition of the Japanese version of this book was published in 1999, at the end of the twentieth century. To the great surprise of the chapter contributors and the editor, the book was awarded the Yoshida Shigeru Prize for history, which is unusual for an edited volume.

It is the first comprehensive history on Japanese diplomacy, and thanks to the interest of educators throughout Japan, is regularly used as a text at numerous universities. I was happy when the contributors to the project agreed that we should also publish it abroad in English, as well as in Chinese and Korean, in order to share with the world academic and policy communities our insights into the path that Japan has taken in the sixty-plus years of the postwar period. Dr. Robert D. Eldridge, my former student, kindly agreed to translate it into English and annotate it as necessary for a non-Japanese audience. An early draft of the translation was used as a text in seminars at Harvard University, where I was a visiting scholar from 2001 to 2002. I am grateful for the strong support shown to me by the Reischauer Center and especially to professors Iriye Akira and Ezra Vogel and then Ph.D. candidate Rustin Gates.

In this age of globalization, people are coming more and more into contact with others, whether they desire it or not, but unfortunately all too often, there is a lack of appropriate understanding about other countries and their cultures. Due to this "deficit in understanding," globalization, rather than bringing about happiness to all, sometimes has tragic consequences. The contributors to this book hope that it will be helpful in explaining Japan's foreign relations to those interested abroad.

At the time, we thought the end of the century was an appropriate cut-off point for analyzing Japanese diplomacy. However, shortly after, in the beginning of the twenty-first century, the 9/11 terrorist attacks took place causing great changes in the international environment. Moreover, Japanese diplomacy underwent major changes under the Koizumi Junichiro administration (2001–6). Although the wars in Afghanistan and Iraq and their aftermath remain unresolved, we felt that half-way through the first decade of the twenty-first century was probably a good time to publish a revised edition, particularly as we could now see the general direction in which Koizumi's diplomacy was taking Japan.

The book was revised in the following three ways. First, it now covers Japanese diplomacy and international affairs through the end of 2005. In other words, the concluding chapter in the earlier edition, "Japanese Diplomacy after the Cold War," which described the 1990s, now covers a period of fifteen years, instead of nine. This is done in a new separate chapter, Chapter 6.

Second, the end of the concluding chapter in the earlier version had a short section entitled, "Issues for the Twenty-First Century." This was scrapped in the new version in favor of a new concluding chapter, "What was Postwar Japanese Diplomacy?" It is an attempt to provide a systematic overview of the postwar. It also includes discussions of the political scene at the time, and how domestic politics affected the longer-term diplomatic interests at the time, and vice versa, which are sometimes difficult to work into the individual chapters.

Third, the declassification of diplomatic documents by the Japanese government has been moving along, as has the publication of memoirs by former officials. These two trends have led to a dramatic increase in diplomatic history studies. In light of this situation, each chapter has been updated to reflect the latest research which was published in Japanese in 2006.

I hope the revised edition will be read as faithfully as the original one was by those interested in Japanese diplomacy, both in Japan and elsewhere, and that it will be a reference point in our journey through the twenty-first century.

December 31, 2008
Iokibe Makoto, editor
(revised March 2009)

Preface to the original edition

This book is about the history of postwar Japanese diplomacy. Several works have been written in Japanese to date on the history of modern Japanese diplomacy since the Meiji Restoration in 1868. These histories, however, deal with the postwar period almost as an afterthought, attached like an appendix to a larger work dealing primarily with the modern prewar era. Until now, no book by a Japanese author has been written on the overall history of postwar Japanese diplomacy.

More than fifty years of the postwar era have passed, and we have now entered the twenty-first century. Not only has enough time elapsed to provide sufficient material on which to write, but more significantly, an important story has emerged. Rising from the defeat and ruins of World War II, postwar Japan, as an economic state rejecting a military role, was able to return to the community of nations as a member of the Western camp amid the harsh international environment of the Cold War, navigate the rough waves of the rapid international changes of the 1970s following the high economic growth period of the 1960s, and successfully reemerge on the international stage by the 1980s, playing an important global leadership role as an economic power along with the United States and Europe. Looking back, 1989, the year the Cold War ended, can be said to have been the high point for Japan as an economic power. With the Gulf crisis the following year, the foundations of postwar Japan began to shake and the country entered a period of lull and confusion as the bubble economy collapsed in 1991. In the wake of these challenges, Japan has been searching for ways to rebuild its political and foreign policy. Japan's postwar diplomatic history is thus not a subject that can be treated simply as a sequel to a prewar history that ended in defeat. The history of postwar Japan, in which the country became a significant actor in international society as an economic power, rivals the drama of its prewar history of modernization during the Meiji era (1868–1912) and subsequent path of military-dominated imperialism.

For this reason, we believed that a work that discusses the entire history of postwar Japan was needed. With the dismantling of the Cold War structure and its domestic counterpart, the so-called 1955 System, postwar Japan moved from economic maturity to the brink of collapse. A new framework in politics and diplomacy, not to mention the economy, was necessary. This serious situation highlights the need to clarify the historical path of postwar Japan. How can Japan, moving—no, actually rushing forward—in the present without thinking about its own postwar experience, face the challenges of the future? It is necessary for Japan to be aware of its own postwar history and earlier diplomatic traditions—both its successes and its failures—in order to prepare itself for a new voyage in the twenty-first century.

The contributors to this volume are all historians who stress working with primary documents. In order to describe Japan's more recent history, for which access to ordinary documents is inherently limited, great efforts were made to re-create as carefully and clearly as possible Japan's diplomacy during each respective period. By writing about the history of Japan's foreign affairs and the international context, the authors hope that the overall history of postwar Japan will become more comprehensible to students of every field of Japanese studies. In particular, we earnestly hope that this book will provide the younger generation with a new perspective on the history of modern Japan and its relations with the rest of international society.

This book could not have been produced without the efforts and enthusiasm of Seikai Yasushi of Yuhikaku Publishing in Kyoto. His almost daily contact with (and prodding of) the authors during the writing of this book will be something remembered and cherished in later years.

April 10, 1999
Iokibe Makoto

About the contributors

Iokibe Makoto, the author of the Introduction, Chapter 1, Chapter 6, and the Conclusion and the overall editor of this book, graduated from the Law Department of Kyoto University in 1967, and received his master's degree from there in 1969. In 1987 he earned his Ph.D. After holding positions as research assistant, lecturer, and associate professor in the Law Department of Hiroshima University, he joined the faculty of the Law Department at Kobe University as professor, specializing in Japanese political and diplomatic history. During that time, he was also a visiting scholar at Harvard and London universities. Dr. Iokibe is the author of numerous articles and books, including *Beikoku no Nihon Senryo Seisaku* (America's Occupation Policy of Japan), winner of the 1985 Suntory Academic Prize; *Nichibei Senso to Sengo Nihon* (The Japan–U.S. War and Postwar Japan), winner of the 1989 Yoshida Shigeru Award; and *Senryoki: Shushotachi no Shin Nihon* (The Occupation Period: The Prime Ministers' New Japan), winner of the 1997 Yoshino Sakuzo Award. In August 2006, he became the 8th President of the National Defense Academy in Yokosuka, and a professor emeritus at Kobe University.

Sakamoto Kazuya, the author of Chapter 2, graduated from the Law Department of Kyoto University in 1979, and in 1981 received his master's degree from there. He earned his Ph.D. in 2002. From 1982 to 1985 he studied at Ohio University, after which he served as a research assistant in the Law Department at Kyoto University and as an associate professor in the School of Humanities and Social Sciences at Mie University and the Law Department at Osaka University. Currently he is a professor at Osaka University, specializing in international politics and diplomatic history. Dr. Sakamoto is the author of numerous articles and recently authored *Nichibei Domei no Kizuna* (The Bonds of the Japan–U.S. Alliance), winner of the Suntory Academic Prize in 2000.

Tadokoro Masayuki, the author of Chapter 3, graduated from the Law Department of Kyoto University in 1979, and in 1981 received his master's degree from there. In 1983 he received a second master's degree from the London School of Economics, after which he served as a research assistant in the Law Department at Kyoto University, a visiting scholar at Johns Hopkins University, a visiting professor at the University of Pittsburgh, and an associate professor at Himeji Dokkyo University before joining the faculty of the National Defense Academy as a professor of international politics. Currently he is a professor of international relations at Keio University in Tokyo. He earned his Ph.D. in 1998. Dr. Tadokoro is the author of numerous articles, book chapters, and most recently of *"Amerika"o Koeta Doru: Kinyu Gurobarization to Tsuka Gaiko* (The Dollar That Goes Beyond the United States: Financial Globalization and Monetary Diplomacy).

Nakanishi Hiroshi, the author of Chapter 4, graduated from the Law Department of Kyoto University in 1985, and in 1987 received his master's degree from there. From 1988 to 1990 he studied international history in the graduate course of the History Department of the University of Chicago. In 1991 he joined the faculty of the Law Department at Kyoto University as an associate professor of international politics and has been a professor there since 2002. Professor Nakanishi is the author of numerous articles and book chapters including, "Can Japan Play a Role in Northeast Asian Security?" *Gaiko Forum*, English edition (Winter 2001); "Japan's Century in the Twentieth Century," *Japan Review of International Affairs*, vol. 15, no. 2 (Summer 2001); "Japanese Relations with the United States," in *The Golden Age of the U.S.–China-Japan Triangle, 1972–1989*, edited by Ezra F. Vogel, Yuan Ming, and Tanaka Akihiko. His most recent publication, *Kokusai Seiji to ha Nani ka?* (What is International Politics?), won the Yoshino Sakuzo Award in 2003.

Murata Koji, the author of Chapter 5, graduated from the Law Department of Doshisha University in 1987. Following graduate work at Kobe University, Murata studied at George Washington University from 1991 to 1995. He served as an assistant professor and then associate professor in the Faculty of Integrated Arts and Sciences, Hiroshima University. Currently he is a professor of international relations at Doshisha University, specializing in American Diplomacy and Security Affairs. He earned his Ph.D. in 1998. Dr. Murata is the author of numerous articles, translations, and books and recently authored *Daitoryo no Zasetsu* (President Carter's U.S. Troop Withdrawal Policy from South Korea), which won the Suntory Award in 1999.

Robert D. Eldridge, who served as the translator of this book, graduated from the International Relations Department at Lynchburg College in 1990, after which he participated in the Japan Exchange and Teaching Program, serving two years. In 1994 he entered the Graduate School of Law at Kobe University, specializing in Japanese political and diplomatic history, earning his master's degree in 1996 and his Ph.D. in 1999. From 1999 to 2000, he held a postdoctoral fellowship with the Suntory Foundation, followed by a research fellowship with the Research Institute for Peace and Security in Tokyo from 2000 to 2001, after which he joined the faculty of the graduate School of International Public Policy at Osaka University as an associate professor. Dr. Eldridge is the author of numerous articles and books in Japanese and English, including *The Origins of the Bilateral Okinawa Problem: Okinawa in Postwar U.S.–Japan Relations, 1945–1952* (Garland, 2001), the Japanese edition of which won the 15th Asia-Pacific Award and the Suntory Prize for History and Civilization in 2003; *The Return of the Amami Islands: The Reversion Movement and U.S.–Japan Relations* (Lexington, 2004); and a translation of the memoirs of Miyazawa Kiichi entitled *Secret Talks between Tokyo and Washington* (Lexington, 2007). His most recent work is *Iwo Jima to Ogasawara o Meguru Nichibei Kankei* (Iwo Jima and Ogasawara in U.S.–Japan Relations) published by Nanpo Shinsha in 2008.

Introduction

Japanese diplomacy from prewar to postwar

Iokibe Makoto

As an island country sitting off the eastern coast of the Asian continent, Japan has preserved its independence by learning from Chinese and then Western civilizations. In the prewar period, Japan pursued both "cooperation" with the Great Powers and "expansion" as an Imperial Power in its own right. It became difficult to pursue both goals simultaneously as the international environment changed after World War I and Japan ended up choosing "expansion *at the expense of* cooperation." Following World War II, Japan was reborn as a country pursuing economic "expansion *through* cooperation."

The diplomatic tradition of modern Japan

Civilized response and Herodism

In the vocabulary of Japanese politics after World War II, one finds many references to the "conservative mainstream" (*hoshu honryu*). Likewise, the phrases "Yoshida line" (*Yoshida rosen*) or "Yoshida Doctrine" are often used regarding the foreign policy of postwar Japan.[1]

Although similar phrases do not exist for the prewar period, two concepts do come to mind. One is "Herodism," which describes the approach that Japan took in developing its modern civilization. The other is "Kasumigaseki orthodox diplomacy" (*Kasumigaseki seito gaiko*), referring to Japan's Foreign Ministry in central Tokyo.[2]

"Herodism" was a word used by the historian Arnold J. Toynbee in his classic work *The Study of History*, analyzing the evolution of civilizations in world history. When a civilization is faced with a challenge from another more powerful civilization, how does it respond? Examining and generalizing the case of the ancient Jews challenged by Roman civilization, Toynbee pointed to two models: zealotry and Herodism.

Those who were filled with fanatical ethnic pride, who launched a determined resistance against hopeless odds and fought for three years even after the fall of Jerusalem, and who in the end committed mass suicide at the fortress of Masada, were the "zealots." In the context of modern Japan, the *joi-ha*, or the "expel the barbarians faction," who were against opening Japan to the West at the end of the Tokugawa shogunate, as well as the military groups calling for "fighting to the end," or *hondo kessen*, on the Japanese main islands at the time of World War II, were examples of this type of zealotry. Even today, anti-American nationalism, which occasionally comes to the fore, is an example of these types of "irreconcilables," or zealots. Zealots, in essence, have a pure but extreme sense of national pride, bordering on fanaticism. Controlled by irrational forces, zealots often bring about their own destruction.

Although the actual role of King Herod can be debated, Herodism here stands for a more rational and sophisticated policy line under extreme conditions, when Herod realized that any physical resistance to the Roman armies would have tragic consequences for the Jewish people. Herod chose to open the Judaic kingdom and accept domination by the Romans. But in doing so, he was left as king and thus saw to it that the Romans ruled only indirectly. His intention was, while ensuring the continuation of the Jewish race, to learn the secrets behind the strength of this more powerful outside civilization and, after mastering its skills, eventually to overcome it. Citing Japan as a successful example of Herodism, Toynbee gives it high marks for opening the country against the objections of the *joi-ha* exclusionists, achieving modernization quickly, and, having acquired the skills of Western civilization, defeating Russia in the Russo-Japanese War of 1904–5.[3]

Precedents existed in Japanese history for this successful interaction with foreign civilizations. In the past, ancient Japan had been faced with the incomparably stronger Chinese civilization. While learning from China through Korea and the dispatch of missions during the Sui and Tang dynasties, Japan, as an island country surrounded by the sea, used its geographical situation to its advantage and was able to prevent the loss of sovereignty. It can be said therefore that Japan already possessed its own way of interacting with foreign civilizations before the coming of the West in the mid-1800s.

In the modern era, Meiji Japan was even more successful than King Herod himself. A key figure at that time was Okubo Toshimichi, a member of the Iwakura Mission that visited the United States and Europe from 1871 to 1873 to learn about the West. Upon his return to Japan, Okubo expressed his opposition to the government's plans to conquer the Korean Peninsula (*seikanron*). Okubo's opposition prevented Japan from pursuing a self-destructive course and helped establish a path for Japan's modernization by giving priority to domestic reforms rather than potentially damaging outside adventures.[4]

In his "Objections to the Proposed Conquest of Korea," Okubo noted the difficulty a newly born state like Japan would have in defending its territory and people, and sounded the alarm against those who would bring about Japan's destruction by embarking on an unwise war against Korea out of national pride. He wrote that refraining from war "may entail shame, but it is to be endured; justice may be with us, but we are not to choose that course." He also insisted that leaders "must make a critical decision as our vital needs dictate, taking into account the importance of any problem and examining the political stream of the time."[5] Okubo's memorandum was essentially a blueprint for making modern Japan a successful example of Herodism. His antiwar argument was one based on realism. It was also a call to focus on "domestic reforms based on an actual knowledge of the outside world."

A quarter of a century after the Russo-Japanese War, however, Japan chose to adopt an autonomous style of diplomacy in the 1930s and pursue a brazen antiforeign militaristic policy that called for the creation of a "Greater Co-Prosperity Sphere in East Asia" rather than pursuing its goals in the framework of international cooperation and mutual benefits. In this atmosphere, the defeat of Japan, which occurred in the summer of 1945, became a preordained conclusion. Seventy-seven years after the Meiji Restoration, modern Japan had completed a full cycle—learning from an outside civilization, reform and rapid development, return to jingoism, and defeat. At that time, the Imperial Army called for a last stand in the main islands of Japan, the homeland. The country's most powerful domestic institution became the living embodiment of the zealots.

Cooperation and expansion: Kasumigaseki Diplomacy

The objective of Japanese diplomacy in the Meiji era during which Herodism held sway was expansion on the Asian mainland within the framework of cooperation with the major powers. The key words in this objective are "cooperation" and "expansion." "Expansion" meant not only widening and deepening economic and cultural interaction with neighboring countries but also expanding spheres of influence and acquiring rights and territories in Asia, often by military means. Born in the age of imperialism, Japan did not hesitate to pursue expansion on the Asian continent through power politics. The army actively sought a continental empire, and this goal was widely supported by nationalistic public opinion, or *taigai-ko* (strong stance against foreign powers), which was obsessed with perceived dangers and fears of humiliation in the world of imperialism.

Imperial diplomacy did not necessarily exclude "cooperation." In order to expand onto the mainland of Asia, understanding from the major powers was essential. Because it lagged far behind the Western powers in strength, Japan had to assume a cooperative stance in order to survive and not be divided up. The most pressing diplomatic matter for Japan at the start of the Meiji era was the revision of the unequal treaties of the 1850s and 1860s by which Japan had lost both the judicial power over the Westerners (extraterritorial rights) in Japan or its waters and the jurisdiction over tariffs. To achieve the goal of the treaties' revision, the trust and goodwill of America and the other great powers was crucial. In the late nineteenth century, however, a cooperative posture was not enough. In the end, it was not until Japan showed its mettle in the Sino-Japanese War a decade later and Russo-Japanese War (1904–5) that the unequal treaties were revised.[6]

Yet, force was not enough, either. The 1895 Triple Intervention by Russia, France, and Germany following the Sino-Japanese War dramatically showed the importance of Japan gaining the support of the other powers for its actions. Japan might take territory by force from a neighboring country, as in the case of China, but if the move did not meet with international approval, it would come to naught. This painful fact was something that Japanese diplomats had to learn the hard way.[7]

At the time of China's Boxer Rebellion at the turn of the century, Japan began to pay closer attention to international relations and regional order in the Far East, where Britain in particular had various special interests. Britain and Japan, both concerned with Russia's high-handed southern advances in the region, signed a treaty in 1902, the first alliance of its kind between a Western power and a rising Asian one.[8] This pact not only permitted Japan's victory in the war with Russia two years later, but made Japan's international place clear. Japan, an emerging non-Western nation, thus chose not to overturn the status quo by force, but to work with Britain, a strong supporter of international stability based on naval and economic might and which served as the center of information and finance. Now Japan's general policy of cooperation with the powers was at last given a framework with a concrete name: "cooperation with the powers centered on Britain." This later developed into an "Britain/U.S.-centered" foreign policy, and became known as "Kasumigaseki orthodox diplomacy." In Japan, those supporting cooperation with the two main Anglo-Saxon powers became dominant and included elite political leaders, such as Okubo, Ito Hirobumi, and Hara Kei, as well as many within the Foreign Ministry during the first three decades of the twentieth century.

Three approaches of diplomacy in the prewar years bear the names of individuals: Mutsu Diplomacy, Komura Diplomacy, and Shidehara Diplomacy. Both Mutsu Munemitsu (1844–97), who was foreign minister at the time of the Sino-Japanese War, and Komura Jutaro (1855–1911), foreign minister at the time of the Russo-Japanese War, were educated in the feudal clans as *samurai* and were members of the political and military elite in the Tokugawa period. Later in the Meiji era they became prominent diplomatic leaders. Both valued friendship with Britain and the United States, using these bonds as rudders to guide Japanese diplomacy through this crisis-filled age of violent power politics.

Cooperation or expansion? The 1920s and 1930s

After experiencing the unprecedented large-scale conflict known as World War I, the Western powers began to move away from the age of imperialism. The use of force lost credibility because of the enormous destruction and toll on human lives on both sides of the battle line. President Woodrow Wilson called for a "New Diplomacy" based on the international principles such as self-determination, justice, and democracy. This new thinking encouraged nationalism in Asia including China and Korea, and made it difficult for Japan to pursue both cooperation and expansion at the same time. In order to pursue cooperation with America, which was calling for self-determination for China and a policy of nonintervention, Japan would have to limit its military expansion on the Asian continent. Japan was now being forced to choose between the two objectives, expansion or cooperation.

The path Japan chose for the first ten years after World War I was to limit its expansion in China in order to preserve cooperation with the United States.[9] Prime Minister Hara valued close relations with America, and Japan actively participated in the Washington Conference of 1922, an international gathering organized to consider the limitation of naval armaments and other issues. Those representatives whom Hara chose to send to the conference, Navy Minister Kato Tomosaburo and Shidehara, then the Japanese ambassador to the United States, came to represent within Japan the cooperative foreign policy of the 1920s under the Washington system.[10] In other words, while Mutsu and Komura were the heroes of the pro-Anglo-American diplomacy of the imperial age, Shidehara in the 1920s led Japanese diplomacy based on pro-Anglo-American cooperation with a strong emphasis on pursuing mutual economic benefits and avoiding military expansion. Shidehara tried to establish a new course after imperialism, enabling Japan to develop without territorial expansion by military means.

Japan would come to adopt the opposite approach, however, following the 1931 Manchurian Incident, in which the Japanese military manufactured an incident in northeast China and clashed with nearby Chinese forces. In order to pursue expansion on the Asian mainland, Japan abandoned cooperation. The self-imposed limits on military expansion had been condemned by the Imperial Army and other extremist forces in Japan as an intolerable, weak-kneed style of diplomacy in which Japan simply followed the lead of the West. The extremists argued that Japan could lose the vested interests in China it had gained with much blood and sacrifice, and they began to criticize Shidehara's diplomacy as one in which Japan's national interests were being sacrificed simply to avoid conflict. In the 1930s, civilian control was forced to give way to the military on the political stage amid calls for a return to a Japan-first policy and an autonomous diplomacy that would bolster self-esteem. It was a time of nationalism accompanied by military might.

Tossing aside the framework for cooperation and embarking on efforts to unilaterally disrupt the status quo meant that Japan was choosing to defy the Anglo-American order in the global arena. It was uncertain whether Japanese diplomacy could survive under these changed circumstances. What is more, emerging Asian nationalism would plague Japan's efforts to develop its own empire in Asia. As pointed out by Konoe Fumimaro, prime minister from June 1937 to January 1939 and again from July 1940 to October 1941, even if the Anglo-American international order was deluding in that it favored those two countries, Japan's "New Order in East Asia" lacked even more legitimacy internationally.[11] Losing international support both in Asia and in the global arena and becoming increasingly isolated itself, imperial Japan stumbled into a war in which it had made itself an enemy of almost the entire world.

The defect in the Meiji System: dual structure

Cooperation and expansion, as well as the two methods of diplomacy and military force, are mutually at odds and thus need skilled and careful management. Interwar Japan switched dramatically from cooperative diplomacy in the 1920s to military expansionism in the 1930s, a reversal that signified Japan's crisis in governance as it sought to deal with the rapidly changing times. The choices were stark. The government's inability to achieve a sophisticated integration of the two revealed the shallowness of the foundation of Japan's modern civilization.

In the Edo period (1603–1867), the *samurai* class, as the governing elite, had monopolized the administrative structure of both civilian matters and military might and managed these affairs in a unidimensional fashion. In the modernization process following the Meiji Restoration, politics (*bun*, literally "civilian") and military (*bu*) were institutionally separated. After overcoming the crisis of the *Seinan-senso*, the civil war in southwestern Japan in 1877 that saw the last armed rebellion against the Meiji government, Okubo was assassinated. After this it was Ito, representing the political world, and Yamagata Aritomo, representing military affairs and the bureaucracy, who assumed central responsibility for institutionalizing the Meiji state. Although these two elder statesmen left impressive accomplishments, including the establishment of the Meiji constitution and the parliament, cabinet system and an efficient bureaucracy, they were also responsible for a fundamental flaw in the Meiji system, which became in essence a terminal illness for prewar imperial Japan—namely, the dual structure in government.

The system under the 1889 Meiji constitution made it difficult for the government to control the military. The prime minister was simply *dohaishachu no dai-ichi ninsha*, or "the first among equals" among his peers in the cabinet. He was not above them, could not give them orders, and did not possess the authority to dismiss them. The army and navy ministers, in contrast, by using the rule that only generals and admirals could serve as army and navy ministers, were able to bring about the downfall of cabinets by resigning and refusing to appoint a replacement. Moreover, with the creation of an independent imperial chief-of-staff in 1878, and the later codification of this position in the Meiji constitution in 1889, the imperial chief of staff was on a par with the army minister. The army minister could no longer give orders to the imperial chief of staff based on the will of the cabinet. The prime minister, army minister, and imperial chief of staff eventually developed a relationship of equality. They might consult each other about politico-military matters trying to reach agreement, but orders could not be given on a top-down basis. Civilian control did not develop in this environment.

The establishment of military professionalism in which military organizations have a strong sense of mission but take their orders from civilians and do not interfere in politics is a key element of civilian control that is necessary in democratic societies.[12] In prewar Japan it was impossible to rely on the self-restraint of the military to prevent its meddling in politics. With confidence earned from the successes in the Sino-Japanese and Russo-Japanese wars, the military expanded its sense of mission and viewed itself as the only group that could make unlimited contributions to the state, including dying for the country. When they became extremely active during the national crisis of the 1930s, it was next to impossible for any politician or civilian government to have powers on par with those of the military.

One may rightly argue that the government possessed a certain pre-eminence over the military, because in general politics symbolizes the whole and the military represents only a part of governmental functions. This position, however, was not clearly defined institutionally and thus the relationship could change for better or for worse depending on the situation. A strong politician like Prime Minister Hara was able to exercise leadership in a time of powerful antimilitary sentiment following World War I, and thus civilians gained the upper hand, but this did not last long. When the military's calls for expansion on the continent gained credence after the Manchurian Incident, the high point of party politics known as "Taisho Democracy" began to ebb.[13] The duality of the political-military system that formed the institutional basis of the Meiji state was decisive in undermining this structure. The authoritarian style of the Meiji state could not, paradoxically, in the end limit the Army's expansion of its influence because of the weakness of the powers of the prime minister. If the military was an arm holding a sword, then politics had to be the head controlling the movements of that arm (as well as of) the entire body. The fate of prewar imperial Japan instead was to see the paralysis of the proper function of government in preventing irrational choices by the military and the military's eventual usurpation of power.

What is difficult to ignore, moreover, is that at the time public opinion, instead of reproving the military for its excessive patriotism, often supported the more aggressive stance. Because the Japanese people were thrust into the imperial age after a long period of seclusion, they were not well informed about international affairs and ignorantly possessed an overly strong and mistaken sense of crisis. Although in retrospect no serious problems existed, some people asserted that a crisis existed, in effect creating one with their own jingoism. The strong racial pride of the Japanese also contributed to their oversensitivity to the international pecking order.

The continental state and maritime state

Japan is an island country, or *shimaguni*. If Japan were a territory connected to the Asian continent, it would always have been vulnerable to Chinese expansion or domination during the latter's imperial age. The Mongolians, who had conquered much of the Eurasian landmass and entertained designs on Japan's Northern Kyushu as well, were turned back in defeat in the seas off the coast. Island countries, such as Britain and Japan, and especially the United States, use the oceans surrounding them as natural moats for their protection. By further using ocean routes for trade and transportation to reach many points around the world, and by using the seas as an asset to project global influence, these countries have come to be called "maritime states," or *kaiyo kokka*.

Modern Japan, despite being an island country, imprudently walked not the path of a maritime state but rather that of a continental power. This course was probably not chosen by the leaders of Meiji Japan on the basis of any grand national strategy. Instead Japan, as a result of decisions that it unwisely judged unavoidable at the time, which in turn by chance led to victory on successive occasions, found itself on an unswerving march toward a continental empire believing itself invincible.

If one is looking for some sort of overall logic to suggest that walking the path of a continental power was a conscious decision, one might turn to Yamagata Aritomo's famous memorandum of 1890. In it, Yamagata attempted to define the difference between a "line of sovereignty (*shukensen*)" and a "line of interest (*riekisen*)." A line of sovereignty protecting one's country was, without argument, vital. Those important geographical areas with a close relationship to the line of sovereignty were what Yamagata labeled the line of interest. If the line of interest were imperiled or lost, the line of sovereignty would be endangered. Likewise, if a line of interest were gained or secured, then the line of sovereignty would be safe. Protecting this line of interest had to be, in Yamagata's doctrine, the core of Japan's foreign policy.[14]

Yamagata described the line of interest to Japan at the time as the "neutrality of the Korean Peninsula." If the Korean Peninsula were under the control of another power or became hostile itself, it would be like a "dagger pointed at [Japan's] head." In this approach the logic of the leaders who launched the Sino-Japanese and Russo-Japanese wars can be most clearly seen.

Yamagata's memorandum represented the general thinking of the leadership at the time and was supported by Japan's historical experience. The Mongols came down the Korean Peninsula and held the dagger, so to speak, to Japan's head. On the other hand, Japan during the Yamato dynasty in the seventh and Hideyoshi Toyotomi in the sixteenth centuries sent troops to the Korean Peninsula. Korea's geographical position as a corridor from the continent to Japan made it an unchanging "line of advantage" to both the Chinese and the Japanese.

In contrast to Sakamoto Ryoma, one of the architects of the Meiji restoration, whose richly imaginative *senchu hassaku*, or Eight-Point Plan, sought to make Japan into a trading state, Yamagata was not able to envision a maritime nation in which an island country would use the waterways for its protection and growth.[15] Instead, Yamagata based his views on an infantry-like approach to national defense policy, namely, that in order to deal with the possible threat to Japan's security that a continental power posed, it was necessary to expand and then defend at all costs one's territory. Yamagata's memorandum was the conceptual preparation for the start of the Sino-Japanese and Russo-Japanese wars, in which Japan's success set the direction of modern Japan's expansion as a continental empire.

International events during this time and Yamagata's own dominant position within the Meiji government meant that his memorandum significantly influenced Japan's becoming a continental state. There was also, however, a doctrine that viewed modern Japan as a maritime nation. Most representative of this vision was the more rational call in the private sector for a "small Japan" (*shonihon shugi*), led by the prewar liberal politician and postwar prime minister, Ishibashi Tanzan, which dismissed the need to expand onto the Asian continent and instead sought the creation of a modern economic state through trade with the wider world. Within the government, the views of Vice Admiral Sato Tetsutaro also deserve attention. He published his lecture notes from the Naval Academy as *Teikoku Kokubo Shiron*, or "A Historical Treatise on the Defense of the Empire", in 1908. From the perspective of diplomatic strategy, *A Historical Treatise* argued that Japan should not try to expand onto the continent, but should instead place greater emphasis on building up its maritime strength. Sato pointed out that England was able to direct political affairs in Europe only after it had lost its continental territory in 1066. When the English had territory in Normandy, they were diplomatically still vulnerable and their influence weak as their attention was on their scattered territories and not on the larger picture. Sato argued in his maritime state thesis that discarding Japanese holdings on the continent would give Japan more flexibility, allow it to take a larger view of its strategic affairs, and give it greater political influence with fewer costs involved. (Sato could not specifically call for the abandoning of Korea and Manchuria in his lecture notes at the military institution, but did so in another book published by a private company.)

This sort of debate was not made much of as a national strategy in the often jingoistic period of prewar Japan. Arguments for abandoning Manchuria, for which "100,000 heroes died," were difficult to make; one would have to be prepared for social rejection as well as the possibility of being at odds of the Imperial Army within the government. In the period of Shidehara diplomacy of the 1920s, a "small Japan or "maritime state" was still possible, blending pro-Anglo-American policies, the refusal to intervene militarily in Chinese domestic affairs, and a focus on economic development and commercial profit. However, the Foreign Ministry bureaucrat Shidehara was not able to undo the situation that protected vested interests. It was only in the postwar era that Sakamoto Ryoma's vision, theories on a maritime state, and the arguments for a "small Japan" were reappraised favorably and emerge as what later became known as the Yoshida Doctrine.

Overview of the book

This book is divided into chapters primarily based on decades. Following the first chapter, which deals with the 1940s including the making of U.S. occupation policy in Washington during the war and the five years of Japan's diplomacy following defeat, the second chapter looks at the 1950s. The next four chapters discuss the 1960s, 1970s, 1980s, and 1990s respectively. Chapter 6 also discusses events after the 9/11 terrorist attacks in the United States and the impact it had on Japan through the first half of the first decade of the twenty-first century.

One could argue the difficulty of capturing diplomatic history by dividing it into decades. The chapter on the 1950s, for example, represents one such dilemma. Normally, the occupation period is discussed until 1952, when the peace treaty went into effect, or the early postwar period is treated until the end of 1954, when Prime Minister Yoshida Shigeru, who was a fellow architect of the peace treaty and U.S.–Japan security treaty, resigned. While either approach is appropriate, this book has approached the postwar in general, and this specific period, in a different way. The negotiations on the peace treaty, begun in 1950 between Prime Minister Yoshida and the U.S. special representative, John Foster Dulles, were both negotiations to end the occupation policies as well as negotiations vis-à-vis a newly re-emerging independent country. Where the chapter could have been written to reflect a review of the past, it chose instead to look at it as the building of the foundation for the future. In other words, the United States wanted to avoid imposing upon Japan a forced peace like the one that was placed on Germany at the end of World War I, and undertook "diplomatic negotiations" with Prime Minister Yoshida, who represented Japan, which was about to recover its sovereignty and rejoin the community of nations. While the agreement reached between them could be called a product of the occupation in some regards, it was more than that in that it set the framework for Japan's foreign relations after its independence. In the sense that 1950 represented the year in which the starting point for an independent Japan began, Chapter 2 covers the decade from 1950 to the revision of the Japan–U.S. Security Treaty in 1960.

The other chapters probably do not need any explanation. The Security Treaty crisis of 1960 created a seasonal divide in the political climate by exposing the clash between the leftists and the ultraconservatives that had become prominent in the latter half of the 1950s. In its place came the age of economic growth of the 1960s, as advocated by the more moderate, mainstream, middle-of-the-road conservatives. The 1970s saw a number of crises, suggesting an era of international change. The 1980s saw a period of new conservatism that brought about a period of relative stability and internationalism. Following the end of the Cold War, the 1990s once again saw a period of drastic change in the international system. As seen by the shocks of 9/11, we have yet again entered a new age with the start of the twenty-first century, although its destination is far from clear.

In looking at this timeline for postwar Japan, the odd-numbered decades—the 1950s, 1970s, and 1990s—can be said to have been a period of rapid change and crisis in systems, while the even-numbered 1960s and 1980s were decades of relative stability and development. Of course each decade is not identical, and indeed each decade can further be divided into clear differences in the first and second halves.

Below follows a brief overview of each chapter in an attempt to introduce the layout of the book.

Chapter 1, "Diplomacy in Occupied Japan," is somewhat unique for its starting and ending points. Similar chapters would probably start with August 15, 1945, the end of the war. This one, however, begins by discussing the postwar planning for the occupation of Japan that took place in Washington during World War II. Even before the final victory over imperial Japan, the United States was busily preparing blueprints for postwar Japan. The U.S. component is crucial for understanding the immediate postwar history of Japan. This chapter thus focuses on the occupation of Japan from both sides of the Pacific. The final days of the occupation period—the negotiations over the peace treaty—are discussed in Chapter 2.

Japan, under occupation, surrendered all sovereignty, including its diplomatic rights. And yet, paradoxically, through engaging in repeated "negotiations" on an almost daily basis, the basic structure of postwar Japan was formed. Creating the new postwar constitution, which was technically a revision of the Meiji Constitution, and other occupation reforms developed as a result of diplomacy undertaken by a minor power vis-à-vis a major one.

Although the Foreign Ministry began preparations for the peace treaty at a very early point—in the fall of 1945—discussions over what sort of international political posture Japan should assume in the post-treaty period were affected by the larger and more turbulent international environment. Initially, while analyzing the severe demilitarization policies of the Allies being imposed on Japan, the Foreign Ministry was deeply concerned, from a traditional, realist perspective, whether Japan would be allowed even a minimum defense capability. But with the establishment of the pacifist constitution, the Foreign Ministry began to give consideration to international collective measures for Japan's security, such as those envisioned in the United Nations and regional organizations. Before this plan fully developed, however, the Cold War intervened in 1947, and the thinking within the Foreign Ministry moved back to the reality of power politics. Importantly, the shift was not to simple traditional power politics, but rather, attention was paid to the new dimensions of interdependency in international relations. As a result, Japan adopted the policies that were later described as the Yoshida Doctrine, namely, light rearmament, dependency on the United States for its security, and emphasis on economics and commercial development. This became the basic framework for postwar Japan.

Chapter 2, The Conditions for an Independent State, examines the establishment of the postwar system. The chapter begins with a discussion of the foreign policy decisions of Prime Minister Yoshida with regard to the peace treaty and the security treaty in San Francisco. Yoshida's choices were to have a long and controlling influence as the basis for postwar Japan.

The opposition that grew to Yoshida's strong temperament and style after the peace treaty is the theme of the second half of the chapter. After the merger of the conservatives in 1955 (forming the Liberal Democratic Party), prime ministers Hatoyama Ichiro and Ishibashi Tanzan, criticizing Yoshida's overly pro-American stance and calling for Japan to become a truly independent state, advocated a more autonomous diplomatic posture through the re-establishment of relations with the Soviet Union and China. Kishi Nobusuke sought to improve relations with the countries of South East Asia.

In the end, however, proponents of the anti-Yoshida line pursued during the mid-1950s did not succeed in abolishing the Yoshida doctrine of pro-American and economic-first policies. The "institutionalizing of the Yoshida line without Yoshida" became the pattern afterwards. Both prime ministers Hatoyama and Kishi had to give up their attempts to revise the constitution and pursue full-scale rearmament. Kishi, instead of bringing an end to the Yoshida line with the revision of the security treaty, in the end inadvertently played a leading role in strengthening it. Following the security treaty crisis of 1960, national attention turned to high economic growth under the leadership of Yoshida's protégé Ikeda Hayato, who proposed the Income Doubling Plan (*Shotoku Baizo Keikaku*). Economic growth had actually started in the mid-1950s amid the confusion of the political environment, but the 1960s saw the rise of a sort of "economic first-ism," or a focus on the economy.

The revision of the security treaty, which is the climax of the chapter, is shown by the author of this chapter, Sakamoto Kazuya, to be not so much the result of Kishi's vision, but instead the initiative of Ambassador Douglas MacArthur II, the nephew of General Douglas MacArthur, who had served as the Supreme Commander for the Allied Powers during the Occupation of Japan.

Chapter 3, "The Model of an Economic Power," discusses Japanese diplomacy in the 1960s, a time when Japan was blossoming as an economic power. The administration of Ikeda Hayato was born in the wake of the collapse of the nationalistic, high politics style of the ultra-conservatives in the latter half of the 1950s. Assuming a low posture with regard to politics, Ikeda spoke of "Tolerance and Forbearance" while at the same time positively addressing the desires of the people to become better off through his Income Doubling Plan. The historical significance of the Ikeda administration would lie in the fact that he was able to establish what Yoshida had originally proposed for postwar Japan—a prosperous, politically stable country with a respected place in international society. Moreover, during the Ikeda years, the intellectual community was generally freed of ideological domination by the Marxist Left and a more open environment for debate emerged, giving rise to academics more reasonable and objective in their analysis.

The political and diplomatic meaning of the "Ikeda line" in this case meant both the abandonment of the path calling for "true independence" through constitutional revision and rearmament, on the one hand, and the rejection of the ideas of the new socialist and neutralist camps, on the other. Prime Minister Ikeda led the early years of high growth in Japan. Diplomatically, he attempted to demonstrate that Japan was the third pillar of the free world through his visits both to North America and to Western Europe. Ikeda's pro-Western orientation was more economic, based on Japan's position as one of the free, developed economies. It was more sophisticated, beyond the simple context of the Cold War.

The Kennedy administration in the United States learned as much as the Liberal Democratic Party did in Japan at the time of the security treaty crisis of 1960, and strongly supported the continuation of the Ikeda line. In particular, the historian and leading Japan expert Edwin O. Reischauer, who became U.S. ambassador to Japan at this time, attempted to give a universal meaning to Japan's economic and political development by explaining it in the context of "modernization theory." The author of this chapter, Tadokoro Masayuki, generally praises the path that would lead postwar Japan to become a democratic nation politically and an advanced free-market-oriented society economically without having nuclear weapons, suggesting the possibility of a "Japan model" for the post-World War II world. He does not, however, overlook the liabilities that this success brought, criticizing postwar Japan—whose form emerged so clearly in the 1960s—for not developing the capability to judge and respond quickly to changes in international environment on its own.

The Sato Eisaku administration (1964–72) was able to realize the reversion of Okinawa through the strengthening of Japan's relationship with the United States, and the 1960s as a whole were the season of the blossoming and ripening of the Yoshida line. At the same time, it can be said that because the Yoshida doctrine was so successful, Japan later became too comfortable with it and dependent on it, eventually causing it to be slow to react to new challenges and crises.

Chapter 4, "Overcoming the Crises," examines Japanese diplomacy during the internationally unstable 1970s. America, which had prematurely entered a period of decline due to the disaster of the Vietnam War, attempted to change the international order to better suit its own situation through the harsh treatment of the Nixon shocks. To Japan, this came as a great blow, one in which its compass was badly damaged. When followed shortly after by the trauma of the 1974 oil crisis, postwar Japanese prosperity was in danger of disappearing altogether.

The reduction of U.S. forces from Asia and the international upheavals at the time, combined with the rise of Japan as an economic power, might have tempted Japan in the 1970s to begin to walk the path of becoming a military power in its own right. Although such predictions and fears lingered at the time, and even seemed somewhat borne out in Tanaka Kakuei's emphasis on oil (natural resources) diplomacy, an examination of the overall picture makes clear that it was not necessary for Japan to pursue a military path in light of the relaxation of tensions that developed between both the United States and the Soviet Union and the United States and China. Moreover, the Japan of the 1970s began to recognize its own weakness in the international environment and strongly felt the need for "comprehensive security" that would include reliable access to economic resources through mutually beneficial arrangements, and not simply military security alone.

The author of this chapter, Nakanishi Hiroshi, through looking at the Fukuda Doctrine and the expansion of Official Development Assistance, the progress of cooperative international relations in the Asia-Pacific region, and the role of the G5/G7 summits, acknowledges that Japanese diplomacy during the 1970s was able to succeed because Japan "developed into a major country in the world in which it played an important part in international cooperation" and combined autonomy and cooperation. In fact, it can be said that through its handling of the crises of the 1970s Japan, for the first time, established a global presence. At the same time, however, the author critically notes that "Japan was tactically able to develop a more autonomous form of international cooperation, but failed in the strategic sense," pointing out its failure to perform any substantial international roles outside those of the economic sphere or to build the domestic basis for such an international role.

Chapter 5, "The Mission and Trials of an Emerging International State," explores Japanese diplomacy in the 1980s, when Japan was searching to find its mission as an "international state" in light of the new prosperity realized after overcoming the crises of the 1970s. The invasion of Afghanistan by the Soviet Union at the very end of the 1970s decisively inaugurated an era of "new Cold War." Prime Minister Ohira Masayoshi made clear Japan's identity as "a member of the West" (*nishigawa no ichiin*), providing strategic aid. Ohira's successor, Suzuki Zenko, who placed great emphasis on liberal domestic policies, opposed the country's assuming such a large international role and showed that he did not fully understand the meaning of the word "alliance" and the commitments involved. Prime Minister Nakasone Yasuhiro, in contrast, created a close partnership with the United States, symbolized by the use of first names (the so-called Ron–Yasu relationship), and took the lead in discussions of security problems at the G7 summits, which until then had primarily focused on economic issues. The author of this chapter, Murata Koji, observes that the 1980s were a paradoxical period in which, on the one hand, the alliance functioned better, and, on the other hand, the bilateral relationship turned competitive, as seen by the trade friction at that time.

Chapter 6, "Japanese Diplomacy after the Cold War," discusses Japanese diplomacy during the 1990s. Losing international respect because of its slow response to the Gulf crisis and war, as well as a result of the collapse of the bubble economy immediately after the end of the Cold War, Japan rebounded by successfully cooperating in the Cambodia peace process and peacekeeping operations there, followed by facing the security crises of the nuclear weapons issue in North Korea and the Taiwan Strait missile firing by China. Japan and the United States subsequently strengthened their security ties in 1996. At the time of the Asia financial crisis in 1997, Japan extended support through the New Miyazawa Plan and other measures. As seen from the above, in response to the numerous crises following the end of the Cold War, Japan continually expanded its international role. This was true after 9/11 as well, when Japan dispatched its Self-Defense Forces to the far-away Indian Ocean and Iraq to support the War on Terror.

The concluding chapter, "What Was Postwar Japanese Diplomacy?", written for the revised edition, discusses sixty years of Japan's diplomacy following the end of World War II in the context of domestic politics. In postwar Japan, three political and diplomatic approaches emerged. They were the social democratic line, the economic-first line, and the traditional nation-state line. In postwar Japan, the mainstream approach was that led by Yoshida Shigeru, which emphasized making Japan an economic state focusing on the security and prosperity of the country as national objectives.

However, the liberal economics and pragmatism that made up the Yoshida Doctrine and the traditional realism of the "Normal State" have each broken up.

Notes

1 For a discussion of the "conservative mainstream," see Kitaoka Shinichi, *Jiminto* (Liberal Democratic Party) (Tokyo: Yomiuri Shimbunsha, 1995). The term "Yoshida Doctrine" did not exist when Yoshida Shigeru was in office. The role of Yoshida was reevaluated by the political scientist Kosaka Masataka in 1964 when he wrote the article "Saisho Yoshida Shigeru Ron" (On Prime Minister Yoshida Shigeru), *Chuo Koron*, vol. 79, no. 2, (February 1964). The term "Yoshida Doctrine" seemed to be first used by the international relations scholar Nagai Yonosuke in the 1970s.

2 "Kasumigaseki orthodox diplomacy" was the title of an article by Uchiyama Masakuma, "Kasumigaseki Seito Gaiko no Seiritsu" (The Establishment of Kasumigaseki Orthodox Diplomacy), in *Kokusai Seiji* (International Relations) 26 (1964), which later appeared as a chapter in his *Gendai Nihon Gaiko Shiron* (Contemporary Japanese diplomatic history) (Tokyo: Keio Tsushin, 1971).

3 Japan's "Herodism" in the late Tokugawa period was known as the "*kaikoku-ha*" or "Open the Country Faction," which was the position taken by *Bakufu* (Tokugawa) under the threat of the black ships. Opening the country was bitterly opposed by "*joi-ha*," sponsored by the powerful *han* (clans) of Satsuma and Choshu, Although the *Bakufu* fell out of power with the Meiji Restoration, the main theme of the new government led by Okubo Toshimichi (Satsuma) and Kido Koin (Choshu), was, ironically, modernization through opening and reforming the country.

4 For more about Okubo, see, for example, Masakazu Iwata, *Okubo Toshimichi: The Bismarck of Modern Japan* (Berkeley: University of California Press, 1964).

5 For a full translation, see Ryusaku Tsunoda, William Theodore de Bary, and Donald Keene, comps., *The Sources of Japanese Tradition* (New York: Columbia University Press, 1958), p. 658.

6 The unequal treaties fell into two categories: extraterritorial rights and jurisdiction over tariffs. The former was abolished in 1899 and the latter in 1911. For more, see Michael Auslin, *Negotiating with Imperialism: The Unequal Treaties and the Culture of Japanese Diplomacy* (Cambridge, MA: Harvard University Press, 2006).

7 The Shimonoseki Peace Treaty of 1895 recognized that China would render the territories of Taiwan, the Hoko Islands, and the Liaotung Peninsula, including Port Arthur and Dairen, to Japan. Desiring to obtain the warm-water port of Port Arthur, Russia invited France and Germany to intervene in the treaty between Japan and China, advising Japan not to take the Liaotung Peninsula. Japan was not able to stand up to the Triple Intervention.

8 Kibata Yoichi, Ian Nish et al., eds., *The History of Anglo-Japanese Relations, 1600–2000, vol. 1, The Political Dimensions, 1600–2000* (Tokyo: University of

Tokyo Press, 2000); Ian Nish, *The Anglo-Japanese Alliance: The Diplomacy of Two Island Empires, 1894–1907* (London: Athlone Press, 1966).

9 At America's urging, Japan and Britain did not renew the Anglo-Japanese treaty in 1922. In its place, the three Washington Treaties were signed, agreeing on (1) limitations on armament in the Pacific; (2) naval reductions; and (3) cooperation in China.

10 Concerning the Washington system in the 1920s, see Akira Iriye, *After Imperialism: The Search for a New Order in the Far East, 1921–1931* (Cambridge: Harvard University Press, 1965). Kato subsequently became prime minister in June 1922 but died in August 1923 while in office. His death permitted the expansion of influence within the navy of those in favor of an increase in naval capabilities and a harder line against America and England. See, for example, Asada Sadao, "Japanese Admirals and the Politics of Naval Limitation: Kato Tomosaburo vs. Kato Kanji," in Gerald Jordan, ed., *Naval Warfare in the Twentieth Century* (London: Croom Helm, 1977).

11 In a famous article written in 1918, Konoe called on Japan to "assert its position from the standpoint of justice and humanism." See Konoe Fumimaro, "Against a Pacificism Centered on England and America" (Ei Bei Honi no Heiwashugi o Haisu)," in *Nihon Oyobi Nihonjin* (Japan and the Japanese), December 15, 1918, pp. 23–26. A translated version is available in *Japan Echo* (Special Issue: Japan's View of the World) 22 (1995), pp. 12–14.

12 Samuel P. Huntington, *The Soldier and the State: the Theory and Politics of Civil–Military Relations* (Cambridge, MA: Harvard University Press, 1957).

13 In modern Japan there were three waves of democracy. The first was the liberty-civil rights (*jiyu minken*) movement in the Meiji era, which emerged after the armed rebellion of Seinan Senso in 1877 and saw the Meiji constitution and the opening of the Diet in 1890. The second wave came seven years after the Russo-Japanese War. In 1912, the Katsura cabinet led by the Choshu group was defeated under the pressure of a huge democratic movement demanding a constitutional party politics (*Taisho Seihen*), giving birth to the Hara cabinet in 1918. A more institutionalized party politics began in 1924, establishing a system of two major parties, the Seiyukai and Minseito, for eight years until the assassination of Prime Minister Inukai Tsuyoshi on May 15, 1932. The third wave came after the end of World War II.

14 Yamagata Aritomo, *Yamagata Aritomo Ikensho* (Policy proposals by Yamagata Aritomo) (Tokyo: Hara Shobo, 1966).

15 Sakamoto Ryoma was the most prominent strategist for the Meiji Restoration. He was the architect of the Satsuma–Choshu alliance against the Tokugawa Bakufu and induced the Bakufu to return its sovereign power to the emperor. After fostering this change, he wrote the "Eight-Point Plan" for the new nation. Immediately after that he was assassinated in Kyoto on the eve of the Meiji era.

1 Diplomacy in occupied Japan
Japanese diplomacy in the 1940s

Iokibe Makoto

While the occupation period is, on the surface, a time in which Japan lost its diplomatic rights after accepting the terms of the 1945 Potsdam Declaration and Instrument of Surrender, it was also a time in which highly skilled diplomacy took place between Japan and GHQ, an international organization of sorts that was based in the country, on a daily basis. The negotiations between Japan and the occupation forces over continuance of the emperor system and constitutional revision would have a fundamental and long-term impact on Japan. Moreover, although Japan was defeated, its handling of the negotiations for the peace treaty and the U.S.–Japan security treaty was quite impressive.

The formation of U.S. occupation policy

For modern Japan, the international environment has always been important. No external factor has had as deep an impact on Japanese society, however, as did the occupation period. Japan's extreme antiforeign, exclusionary, go-it-alone approach that had formed the basis of its expansionary wartime policies had in the end the opposite effect, causing the outside world to occupy and control Japan. The occupation policies, as external factors, were planted in the soil of traditional Japanese society, and what emerged was postwar Japan. It is necessary therefore to look at how these external factors—the occupation policies—were developed and how they were introduced into Japan.[1]

Postwar planning began before America's participation in the war

Occupation policy was formulated by the United States, the same country that played a central role in bringing about the surrender of Japan. The U.S. government began preparing for the postwar world at an early point, even before it was actually involved in World War II. With the outbreak of war in Europe in September 1939, more than two years before America's entry into the war in December 1941, Secretary of State Cordell Hull directed that studies be quietly begun on the future postwar world, establishing an advisory committee within the State Department as well as obtaining substantial support from the "War and Peace Study" conducted by the Council on Foreign Relations in New York.

For America, World War II was perhaps the most fulfilling moment in its history. Not only was it economically, technologically, and militarily all-powerful, but it earnestly hoped to use this influence positively to build a new, better world after the terrible destruction of total war.

In November 1940, after winning an unprecedented third term as president, Franklin D. Roosevelt stated that the United States would be the "arsenal of democracy," and in March 1941 Congress passed the Lend-Lease Act to permit the United States government to aid countries fighting Nazi Germany. In order to further help solidify support for the war, Roosevelt, along with British prime minister Winston S. Churchill, announced the Atlantic Charter in August 1941, calling for the creation of a new world order calling for freedom, equality, and peace.

The Japan hands and the drafting of occupation policy

Entering the war after the Japanese attack on Pearl Harbor, the United States simultaneously stepped up its planning for the postwar period. With Secretary Hull as chair, a new advisory committee for the president was established and the Special Research Division within the State Department was strengthened and expanded by bringing in many specialists from both inside and outside government, in essence creating a large internal think tank to plan for the creation of a new world after hostilities ended. A Far Eastern Unit was established in the summer of 1942, and two Japan hands, Clark University professor George H. Blakeslee, an authority on international relations and Far Eastern affairs, and Columbia University assistant professor Hugh Borton, a young specialist on Japanese history, were tapped to work on developing occupation policies for Japan.

The Atlantic Charter declared that "all States, great or small, victor or vanquished" would be allowed to participate in a postwar international economy on a nondiscriminatory basis. The Japan hands adopted this policy of egalitarianism as a guideline when drafting occupation policy. They tried to provide a chance to allow Japan to live as a peaceful economic state following its collapse as a military empire.

In order to realize this objective, the Japan hands believed that postwar Japan should be demilitarized and democratized and its territory reduced in size. At the same time, however, they argued that reforms and changes which were punitive in nature or sought to excessively intervene in the domestic affairs of Japan should be avoided. Instead, they emphasized the positive aspects of Japan's modern history: its efforts to learn from the West and its development of an indigenous democracy as demonstrated in the period of so-called Taisho Democracy. They believed that once militarism was done away with, internationally oriented Japanese liberals would re-emerge to become the driving force behind Japan's rebirth and reform.

Unconditional surrender

Roosevelt, however, was not willing to accept so generous a peace for an enemy like Japan. He believed that the failure to completely crush Germany militarily during World War I by accepting an incomplete armistice was one of the major reasons for Hitler's revisionist rise and World War II. In order to maintain peace in the postwar world, Roosevelt considered it necessary not only to destroy the aggressor completely but also to give the victor the right to alter the defeated country's mistaken beliefs and make whatever changes it desired in that country's internal makeup. This position was made clear in the "Unconditional Surrender" declaration announced in Casablanca in January 1943.

In addition to semi-permanently rendering the aggressors powerless, the major Allied powers would have to undertake the role of "world policemen" to maintain the postwar peace. In other words, Roosevelt believed in a perpendicular world order in which the main enemy states would be placed below ordinary states under the supervision of the great powers. Since this policy was widely supported by the American people, it was likely that the justice meted out to Japan would be severe indeed.

In the Cairo Declaration of November 1943, policies regarding the disposition of the Japanese empire, namely the reduction of its territory to what it had prior to seizing through "by violence and greed," were spelled out based on this line of thinking. Furthermore, the Teheran Conference of December 1943 emphasized the Allies' joint will to establish a postwar order and to protect that peace by the cooperation of the great powers—the United States, Great Britain, and the Soviet Union.

By 1944, as the likely defeat of Germany and Japan became more apparent, the U.S. government found it necessary to speed up its policy planning with regard to the disposition of the enemy states. In February a Postwar Programs Committee (PWC) was established in the State Department, and in April it began focusing its discussions on actual plans for the occupation of Japan.

The two burning issues for the PWC in 1944 were the future of the emperor system and the Japanese bureaucracy. The Japan experts who were in charge of drafting the policy papers for Japan favored retaining the emperor system as a symbol of a moderate and enlightened leadership, while higher-ranking officials in the department demanded the abolishment of the emperor system, seeing it as the core of Japan's militaristic nationalism. These officials instructed the PWC some five times to revise its drafts (PWC 93 series), but the Japan hands within the group argued that the emperor system could be an asset for America in both peace-making and occupation reforms. The PWC was not able to reach a final conclusion, and instead decided to continue to watch the situation. As for the Japanese bureaucracy, top officials in the State Department sought to suspend the powers of not only senior Japanese leaders such as the members of the cabinet and the Diet, the ministers and vice ministers of each ministry, which they called "policymaking organs," but also most of the bureaucrats as a whole that were in charge of implementing those policies. The Japan hands, however, countered that unless the United States prepared some 500,000 troops and other military personnel who were fluent in the Japanese language for the military government, the Allies would not be able to control Japan—a highly sophisticated but different society. In the end, the PWC agreed to utilize the Japanese administrative organs for occupation purposes. Thus it can be said that while the possibility of indirect control using existing Japanese agencies was not entirely eliminated, the United States continued at this time to seek the establishment of a direct military government in Japan under the occupation forces.

According to those discussions, wide-ranging reforms of Japan focused on demilitarization and democratization would take place under a U.S.-led Allied occupation. Not only the military machinery, but also the functioning of the cabinet and Diet among other main Japanese governmental organizations would be stopped during the occupation, and a military government would be placed in charge of all functions of government, including the administrative and legislative bodies. The Japanese government would cease to exist and a military government would take its place. Amid this debate, the Japan hands continued to argue that the decision as to whether to remove the emperor and end the emperor system should be postponed in order to watch how the situation developed, and that all of the Japanese government functions should not be ended but instead used by the occupation forces. Approximately two months before the end of the war in June 1945, the policy paper known as "SWNCC 150," calling for a direct military occupation, was drafted in June 1945 by the State-War-Navy Coordinating Committee, a coordinating body created in November 1944. The Potsdam Declaration in July subsequently overturned this policy.

The Potsdam Declaration and the revision of occupation policy

In April 1945, just as Germany was about to surrender unconditionally, Roosevelt suddenly died and was succeeded by Vice President Harry S. Truman. That spring, under the initiative of two senior statesmen intimately familiar with Japan, Under Secretary of State Joseph C. Grew and Secretary of War Henry L. Stimson, the United States considered relaxing its demands on Japan and its occupation policy. In June the U.S. government prepared the Potsdam Declaration, which moved away from the policies of unconditional surrender and direct military occupation. A number of important factors lay behind this.

First, from the time of the Yalta Conference in February of that year, the Soviet–American dispute over Poland and other issues became more pronounced, and the framework of U.S.–Soviet cooperation for German and Japanese unconditional surrender began to come apart. Second, there were voices within the U.S. government, including not only Japan hands in the

State Department but also those in military and intelligence circles, that called for more moderate surrender terms toward Japan in order to bring about a quick end to the war, where American casualties were very high in the battles of Iwo Jima (February–March) and Okinawa (March–June). Third, the incredible destruction in Germany was viewed as something that should not be repeated. After visiting Germany in April, Assistant Secretary of War John J. McCloy, in a report to Stimson, described what he saw as "Hell on Earth" and suggested that the "mistake made in Germany" under the doctrine of unconditional surrender should not be repeated vis-à-vis Japan.[2]

In light of the above developments, Under Secretary Grew at the end of May proposed that a presidential announcement to the Japanese be made that would include more moderate demands, including the retention of the emperor system. Grew wanted to bring Japan around to surrendering before the dropping of the atomic bomb and Soviet entry into that theater of the war. Stimson agreed with Grew on the need to avoid the complete destruction of Japanese society, pointing out the names of such pro-Western leaders in the 1920s as Shidehara, Wakatsuki Reijiro, and Hamaguchi Osachi. At the same time, he felt that any statement alone would not be enough to get the Japanese military to recognize and accept defeat. Stimson thus urged that the atomic bomb, which would have a huge psychological impact on the Japanese, should be used along with such a statement, and it was the combination of these two factors that brought about Japan's surrender.

Stimson passed the draft of the Potsdam Declaration to Truman on July 2. According to paragraph 12 of the declaration, "a constitutional monarchy under the present dynasty" was to be permitted in postwar Japan, "based on the freely expressed will by the people." However, the new secretary of state, James F. Byrnes, deleted that line, thus removing the open guarantee of the continuation of the emperor institution, which was Japan's primary concern.

At the same time, based on the opinion of the British at the Potsdam Conference, a decision was reached to make clearer the policy of an indirect occupation, which would allow for the continuation of the Japanese government. Paragraph 10 of the Potsdam Declaration, which stated, "The Japanese Government shall remove all obstacles to the revival and strengthening of democratic tendencies among the Japanese people," implied that the Japanese government would assume the responsibility for democratic reforms. As the inclusion of the word "revival" suggests, the declaration recognized that Japan had developed a democracy on its own in the prewar years. Furthermore, paragraph 11 spelled out the path for Japan to rebuild as a peaceful economy, stating, "Eventual Japanese participation in world trade relations shall be permitted."

Although tragically ignored (*mokusatsu*, literally "killed with silence") initially by the Japanese government, the Potsdam Declaration, announced on July 26, was eventually accepted by the Suzuki Kantaro Cabinet on August 14, following the dropping of atomic bombs on Hiroshima (August 6) and Nagasaki (August 9) and the entry of the Soviet Union into the war (August 8).

The German surrender in May did not include any conditions—the loser was simply forced to accept all demands to be made by the victor. In this unconditional surrender the victors had carte blanche over the vanquished. The Japanese surrender of August, however, can be said to have been a "conditional surrender" based on the acceptance of the provisions appearing in the Potsdam Declaration. Japan's "unconditional surrender" therefore could probably be best described as an "unconditional acceptance by the loser of conditions provided by the victor." In the text of the Potsdam Declaration, it was not the Japanese "nation" but only "all Japanese armed forces" that had to "surrender unconditionally."[3]

Overall, U.S. occupation policy for Japan, prepared during the war, was a balance of constructive measures—militarily disarming Japan and undoing the problems of prewar militarism, establishing democratic society in postwar Japan, and permitting Japan's economic return to the international community. It was not punitive or destructive in nature. It was not based on revenge or hostility. The Japan specialists involved in drafting the occupation policies possessed an understanding of Japan. While with the exception of Stimson, the senior leadership did not possess any knowledge of Japan, it did not prevent them from realizing that it was in the United States' national interest to strongly support Japan and develop it into a friend of the United States again.

The occupation of Japan by "Operation Blacklist"

Determining the role of the other Allies in the occupation of Japan continued to be a delicate question for the United States until the very end. The State Department as a whole eventually accepted the plan prepared by the Japan hands to share responsibilities with other Allies (joint occupation), but it wanted to ensure that the United States would maintain a controlling voice in occupied Japan (American supremacy) and avoid a division of Japanese territory (no partition of Japan). Some planners in the U.S. military, however, fearing the possibility of even stronger resistance by the Japanese in their homeland and believing that more than 800,000 troops would be necessary to occupy Japan, thought that it would not be desirable for America to undertake the occupation alone. As a result, in the belief that the burdens of the occupation should be shared, the Joint War Plans Committee (JWPC), calling for a large contribution of military forces from Britain, the Soviet Union, and China, completed the planning document JWPC 385/1 on August 16. This document in essence divided up Japan by placing Hokkaido and Northeast Japan (*Tohoku*) under a Soviet-led occupation.[4]

On the same day, Truman received a telegram from Soviet prime minister Joseph Stalin, requesting to be allowed to place the northern half of Hokkaido under Soviet control. After entering the war on August 9, the Soviet army had faced surprisingly little resistance from the Japanese army on the Asian continent. With much of its strength intact, Soviet forces began to prepare for the invasion of not only Karafuto and Chishima but Hokkaido as well.[5]

However, Truman refused Stalin's request on August 18, believing that there was no reason to accept Soviet troops in such a way as to divide Japan when the United States had received little help from the Soviet Union in the defeat of Japan. At the same time Truman approved SWNCC 70/5, drafted by the State Department, which ended the proposed division of Japanese territory.[6]

If Japan had continued to resist until December 1946, as originally predicted by U.S. military planners, it is very likely that the scenario spelled out in JWPC 385/1 would have become a reality no matter what the actual intentions of the U.S. government were by then. The fact that surrender took place before a "final battle on the main islands," coupled with America's policies for Japan, made it possible to have a unified occupation for Japan, unlike the situation in Germany—a country that would remain divided for forty-five years. Moreover, by accepting the Potsdam Declaration in the form of an "Imperial Decision" (*seidan*), the emperor played an important role at the time of the surrender, which in turn provided the basis for allowing for the continuation of the emperor system and Emperor Hirohito's reign.

JWPC 385/1 was in the end of no help in implementing the occupation of Japan. In its place, "Operation Blacklist," prepared by General MacArthur's headquarters in Manila, came to represent the plans for undertaking the initial occupation. This plan formed the preparations for the peaceful occupation of Japan in case of an early surrender by the Japanese government, at which point the entire Japanese archipelago would be placed directly under MacArthur's unified command.[7]

The substance of the occupation policies was prepared by the Japan hands within the State Department and formulated within the U.S. government, including the military, with revisions being made based on the Potsdam Declaration. The details of the occupation policies had yet to be fully discussed and prepared, however, and it was up to the General Headquarters (GHQ) of MacArthur, the Supreme Commander for Allied Powers in Tokyo, to respond to events and develop plans on the spot in an ad hoc manner after coordinating with Washington.

What was diplomacy in occupied Japan?

Diplomacy is the making of foreign policy and undertaking of negotiations by a sovereign state to secure national goals. Japan lost its sovereignty through defeat in the war and was placed under the control of the occupation authority. Because of this it can be said that, formally speaking, diplomacy did not exist until Japan regained its independence in late April 1952. Japan's representative offices abroad, such as its embassies and consulates, were all closed and its official diplomatic channels with other countries were all cut. With the start of the occupation, Japan was prevented from communicating with other countries and subordinated to GHQ.

On the other hand, GHQ, instructed from Washington to undertake indirect administration, preferred to work through the existing Japanese government.

Although its continued existence was conditioned on its usefulness for implementing occupation policies, the Japanese government was in any case permitted to carry on, acting as the representative of the Japanese people. Although the relationship was not an equal one between two mutually sovereign states and instead was more of a hierarchical one between the ruler and the controlled in which the ruler had the right to intervene at will, the Japanese government from the very beginning undertook significant, intense negotiations with MacArthur's headquarters. Even during the occupation, the Japanese government did not abandon its foreign policymaking and negotiating activities, interacting when appropriate with the representatives of China and the British Commonwealth, for example, although GHQ was the only "foreign country" Japanese diplomacy had to deal with until the spring of 1950.

These Japan–GHQ negotiations had great meaning because their results would form the basic structure of postwar Japan and Japanese society. Moreover, as the end of the occupation approached, the Japanese government had shown itself to be a responsible and important actor that could competently serve as the representative of a future independent country.

Japanese diplomacy during the occupation can be divided into four phases. The first phase was the initial stage, during which the Japanese government attempted to protect the basic occupation formula of indirect control, SCAP's exercise of power through the emperor and Japanese government. The most critical issue facing Japanese diplomacy during this period was to prevent a shift to direct rule by the occupation army. All energy was placed in convincing MacArthur and his staff that the Japanese government was supportive of occupation policies and could be put to good use. In addition, governmental leaders sought to preserve the emperor system as well as avoid the abdication of Emperor Hirohito. In this initial period following the surrender on August 15, 1945, until the February of the following year, the Shidehara Cabinet agreed with MacArthur on the need for the establishment of a democratic constitution with a symbolic emperor and a clause renouncing war. During this time, Japan accepted the occupation army without resistance, signed the Instrument of Surrender on September 2 aboard the USS *Missouri*, and managed to see to the withdrawal of the promulgation of the three directives, discussed below, that would have led to direct military government.

The second aspect of Japanese diplomacy during the occupation involved the negotiations over the various occupation reforms. Traditionally, the victor's demands would be forced on the vanquished state at the time of a peace conference in the form of dictated treaty terms such as was the case with Germany after World War I. What the United States actually did after the end of the second world war, however, was quite revolutionary—it occupied the enemy states for many years, during which it attempted to profoundly reform the enemy societies to make them into responsible international citizens. Because the reforms undertaken during the occupation were one step along the way to an early peace settlement and a return to the international community, the interactions and negotiations over the reforms were important to both sides, especially to Japan.

The third stage had to do with the rebirth of Japanese diplomacy regarding the manner of post-treaty security, which was triggered by MacArthur's call for an early peace for Japan in March 1947. However, the early peace conference was not held, and the occupation continued. During this time, Japan's economic recovery and social and political stability became the focus of the latter half of the occupation period.

The fourth aspect of Japanese diplomacy concerned the negotiations over the peace treaty and post-treaty security, from the spring of 1950 to the Peace Conference in September 1951. In late April 1950 Prime Minister Yoshida dispatched Finance Minister Ikeda Hayato to the United States to feel out America's intentions with regard to security policy, a move that bypassed and angered MacArthur.[8] During several rounds of meetings between 1950 and 1951 with John Foster Dulles, who had been appointed special advisor to Secretary of State Dean Acheson and then special representative of President Truman, Yoshida expressed Japan's views and in essence was able to "negotiate" the peace treaty and security treaty. Through this, Yoshida defined postwar Japan's international position and national identity. While relying on the United States for its larger security, postwar Japan would become an economic state under a free trade system and a liberal democratic society pursuing only limited rearmament—a policy that has continued through today.

Indirect Occupation through the emperor and government of Japan

The end of diplomatic rights

A chief objective for the Japanese government as the occupation began was to clarify the meaning of "surrender under the Potsdam Declaration." Did acceptance mean "unconditional surrender" or a "conditional surrender"? Even if supreme power were to reside with the occupation authority, how much administration would be left for the Japanese government? In other words, would it be an occupation of indirect administration and, if so, to what degree? Establishing the demarcation of authority for domestic affairs under the occupation was the biggest issue facing the Japanese government.

The problem of sovereignty over foreign affairs, or diplomatic rights, also existed. Japan surrendered to the countries with which it was at war, including, most importantly, the United States, Britain, and China, and submitted to their rule. Would Japan be able to continue foreign relations with the neutral countries that it had maintained relations with before and during the war?

That question was answered immediately. The Japanese government was shocked to learn that the U.S. government informed other countries on August 15 that all of Japan's foreign embassies, assets, and documents were to be confiscated, in effect ending diplomatic contact. In an August 16 telegram entitled "Regarding Japanese Diplomatic Agencies in Neutral Countries," the Japanese government objected that this demand "was not a part of the Potsdam Declaration" and, as a result, "could not be accepted."[9]

Regardless of objections Japan raised, the reality was that the vanquished were not equal to the victors. Such protest by the Japanese government caused some concern in Washington that GHQ might become involved in endless debate with the Japanese. On September 6, an executive order from the president was sent to MacArthur pointing out that SCAP's relations with Japan were not on a contractual basis, but based on the fact of "unconditional surrender." Therefore, SCAP could use the Japanese government insofar as was beneficial for occupation policies, but had no need to support it or be influenced by it.[10]

Defeat and the peaceful start of the occupation

Having had its relations cut off with other entities, what sort of diplomatic approach did the Japanese government take with GHQ?

The sole reason for the establishment of the Higashikuni Naruhiko Cabinet—the first ever by a member of the imperial family in modern Japanese history—on August 17 was the peaceful acceptance of defeat and occupation. If some of the zealots in the military decrying the "death of the empire" were to refuse to put down their arms and continue to fight the occupation forces, then that resistance would not only mean more unnecessary bloodshed, but would likely also remove any reason to allow the continuance of the emperor and the Japanese government. The Japanese government had to demonstrate SCAP, which had absolute power, its own value. If it did not, it was likely that GHQ would simply dissolve the government and institute a direct military occupation. It was impossible to envisage just how tragic direct control by outside powers would be for the Japanese people. In order for the people of Japan to avoid a situation in which their country would be lost, the Japanese government had to show that it could rule, on the one hand, and that it could be relied upon by the occupation authorities to support GHQ's policies and cooperate, on the other. Only by a combination of both could the Japanese government persuade GHQ to recognize its value.

The return of peace through the "Imperial Decision" was a critical first step, and the Higashikuni Cabinet followed that lead. First of all, through radio addresses and newspapers, the prime minister, Chief Cabinet Secretary Ogata Taketora (formerly vice president of the *Asahi Shimbun*), and Foreign Minister Shigemitsu Mamoru called upon the people to remain calm and to cooperate with the occupying forces. In addition, while suppressing any show of military resistance at home, Prime Minister Higashikuni sent Imperial Japanese Army Lieutenant General Kawabe Torashiro to Manila to negotiate the arrangements for the arrival of the occupation forces. Under the command of General Arisue Seizo, final preparations were made, and on August 30 Supreme Commander MacArthur was received at Atsugi Airfield near

Yokohama in Kanagawa. By demonstrating both its ability to govern and its cooperative stance, the Japanese government was able to protect its role in an indirect occupation.

The danger of direct military government

The Japanese government was encouraged by MacArthur's speech on the deck of the *USS Missouri* appealing for a better world. It was disturbed, however, when later that day GHQ issued the so-called three proclamations and called for their implementation by the Japanese government. They were: (1) SCAP would control Japan, using English as the language of the occupation; (2) a military tribunal would be established; and (3) military currency would be issued as the official currency of the occupation.[11]

Facing this shift toward direct occupation, the Higashikuni Cabinet dispatched Foreign Minister Shigemitsu to see MacArthur the following morning to request that he withdraw the orders.[12] Shigemitsu stated that the three proclamations went against the policy of the indirect occupation that Japan had understood to be the case when agreeing to surrender. He also reaffirmed that the Japanese government intended to cooperate with the occupation forces, and that this was in the interest of both parties. MacArthur changed the "three proclamations" to an "order to the Japanese government," and agreed that the Japanese government would be responsible for implementing them. The government survived the crisis over its very existence, and succeeded in maintaining its function within an indirect occupation.

MacArthur's GHQ had likely issued the initial directives that signified a shift to a direct military government because no plan existed in his headquarters other than Operation Blacklist. This document had been prepared in Manila on the assumption of the direct control of Japan, before the acceptance of the Potsdam Declaration, which abruptly changed U.S. policy to the new line of indirect control.

The above developments, in which the Japanese government was able to promote the idea of an indirect administration rather than a direct military government meant that Japanese diplomacy in the early postwar period was able to succeed in its main goal to protect Japan through an indirect occupation. In this process, the handling of the emperor held particular significance.

The status of the emperor

On September 17 MacArthur's headquarters moved from Yokohama to the *Dai Ichi Seimei* Building, across the moat from the Imperial Palace in Tokyo. On the same day, Yoshida Shigeru replaced Shigemitsu as foreign minister in the Higashikuni Naruhiko Cabinet, with Shigemitsu having lost the confidence of GHQ because of a comment he had made at a press conference publicly calling for the withdrawal of the three proclamations. Under Foreign Minister Yoshida, relations with GHQ went somewhat smoother, and on September 27 the first meeting between MacArthur and the emperor was held. Since the planning stages in Manila, MacArthur himself had been in favor of using the emperor, and through their meeting, MacArthur became convinced of the importance of this approach. MacArthur was apparently moved by the emperor's call for the fair treatment of his people while accepting his own responsibility for the war, confirming for MacArthur that the emperor could be an important partner in the Allied occupation of Japan. This meant that the policy of "indirect rule through the emperor and Japanese government" was not only firmly established but moved further along as well.[13]

However, even if MacArthur valued the emperor and his position, there was no guarantee that this approach would be accepted internationally. Within the United States, there were many influential people who demanded that the emperor be tried as a war criminal, and within Australia and the other allied countries, this feeling was even stronger. Although it was important for the U.S. government to treat the question of the abolition of the emperor system with great caution, particularly at the end of the war and the start of the occupation, it was widely believed among the victors that the emperor's stepping down was unavoidable. Even the emperor himself referred to this possibility some three times between his decision to end the war and his first meeting with MacArthur.[14]

Home Minister Kido Koichi and others close to the emperor tried to dissuade him from doing so, and MacArthur too, following their first meeting, was strongly against it. An October 2 memo by Brigadier General Bonner F. Fellers, an aide to SCAP, sought to support MacArthur's desire to retain the emperor as a partner in the occupation by calling upon the Japanese government to build a case that would clear the emperor of any war crimes. The result was the "Showa Emperor's Monologue (*Showa Tenno Dokuhakuroku*)," in which the emperor relayed his version of events to an aide. The main point was that if the government and military had come to an agreement, even if it went against the emperor's will, there was no choice for the emperor but to recognize it because the system was a constitutional monarchy and not an autocratic one. The emperor explained that the only times that policy was decided on the will of the emperor was at the time of the "2.26 Incident" when young officers in the Army led a rebellion in 1936 against moderate leaders in the military and government and the emperor ordered their suppression and in August 1945 in ending the war. Regarding the start of the Pacific War, MacArthur's headquarters and the Japanese government both agreed with the interpretation that Prime Minister Tojo Hideki was ultimately responsible. Following this line, it was possible to avoid having the emperor appear at the International Military Tribunal for the Far East (Tokyo Tribunal).[15]

In this way, while stressing its cooperation with the occupation, the Japanese government was able to further its defensive diplomacy in order to promote its continued existence. The emperor became the spiritual base of that diplomatic battle and at times led it. The reign of the emperor and retention of the emperor system symbolized the continuation of the nation and its autonomy, but it would not be until the revision of the constitution that this would be finalized.

Negotiations over occupation reforms

MacArthur's dual strategy

On October 2, 1945, GHQ did away with its Military Government Section and created the Government Section (GS) in its place. This action visibly suggested that SCAP had given up any plans to conduct a direct military occupation and instead decided to adopt a policy of indirect rule through the existing Japanese government. At precisely this time, however, GHQ's posture toward the Japanese government became even sterner. This was due to the fact that Col. Charles L. Kades, a New Dealer and an advocate of rapid and radical reform, became the deputy chief and led GS, thus putting into place the structure to thoroughly implement demilitarization and democratization.

The change occurred as part of the severe policies of Washington toward Japan. The U.S. government had become increasingly annoyed with MacArthur's antics at this time. Looking at the Japanese government's attempts to resist occupation policies with regard to third-country relations and diplomatic documents, as well as witnessing the withdrawal of the three proclamations, Washington became concerned that MacArthur was being tricked by the old guard in Japan. What particularly irritated Washington was MacArthur's statement of September 17 in which he highly praised the success of the occupation of Japan, declaring that "only 200,000 [of the then 400,000] troops" were necessary, although 800,000 U.S. forces had been initially believed necessary for the invasion and occupation of Japan. His statement, without the consent of the U.S. government, that many U.S. soldiers could return home by Christmas—no doubt news that was very welcome among the American people—clearly exceeded his authority and embittered the Truman administration. At some point it would become necessary to discipline MacArthur, who had forgotten his own position and acted as the monarch of a semi-sovereign country in which he had become the patron of the Japanese people.[16]

On September 22, the U.S. government publicly released the September 6 executive order, already secretly relayed to MacArthur, stating that GHQ's "relationship with the Government of Japan is not a contractual one, but one based on unconditional surrender." The "Basic Initial Post-Surrender Directive" for Japan was also publicized. This was in essence a message to show that Washington was the main player, and MacArthur was nothing more than the tool for the implementation of the policies decided on by Washington.

MacArthur in this way had to fight a two-front war against both Japan and Washington. The strengthening of his approach to protect the emperor through his successful meeting with him on September 27 made administering

Japan easier but it also made the struggle with Washington even more diffi-cult. Symbolically, at the forefront of this were the Home Ministry's attempts to prevent the publication of the photograph of the meeting between the emperor and MacArthur (in which the latter towered over the former), as well as the ministry's leaking of the contents of the meeting to a reporter from the *New York Times* in an attempt to make it appear as if MacArthur and the emperor were equals. For MacArthur, who was already fighting a battle with Washington, this was the equivalent of a mutinous action. On October 4, SCAP issued a "Civil Rights Directive," which purged Home Minister Yamazaki Iwao and some 4,000 officials from the Home and Justice minis-tries and police, abolished the thought police (*kempeitai*), and released hun-dreds of political prisoners. Regarding this as a vote of no-confidence in the government, the Higashikuni Cabinet resigned en masse the next day.

The Shidehara Cabinet's liberal reforms

The Shidehara Cabinet was born on October 9 amid, on the one hand, pres-sure by Washington on MacArthur to proceed with rapid demilitarization and democratization in Japan, and on the other, the creation of a framework within GHQ, led by Kades of the Government Section, to bring this about. At Shidehara's meeting with MacArthur two days later, MacArthur did not assume the usual posture of delivering his own sermon, but instead simply read from a memorandum calling for "Five Great Reforms"—the emancipa-tion of women, the promotion of labor unions, and the democratization of economic, legal, and educational systems – prepared by the Government Section based on a directive from Washington.[17]

Shidehara, who had served as foreign minister for five of the cabinets led by the Minseito (Popular Government Party) during the age of constitutional government in the 1920s when the two major political parties, Minseito and Seiyukai (Political Friends Party), alternated power and espoused the ideals of enlightened liberal reforms. Shidehara promised MacArthur his coopera-tion in implementing the five reforms, most of which he himself had hoped to accomplish in prewar Japan. However, Shidehara believed that it was not wise to immediately call for "American democracy." He convinced MacArthur that it was better to permit the further development of a "Japanese-style democracy," initiated and fostered by the Japanese themselves.[18]

Shidehara was already seventy-three years old by this point but he had not lost his facility in English, for which he had been without rival in the Foreign Ministry, or his talent for negotiations. In this first meeting with MacArthur, he not only convinced him on certain points but gained the general's con-fidence as well. The members of the Shidehara Cabinet, working from the experience of Taisho Democracy, decided to implement their own reforms, including a new electoral law that included the right of women to vote and a labor law that was considered progressive even by today's standards, under-taken even before GHQ handed down any detailed directives.

However, on the question of "liberal reforms of the constitution" that MacArthur had called for in their meeting, Prime Minister Shidehara may have at first underestimated the degree and pace of reforms that GHQ and the Allied powers hoped to see. Shidehara believed that from the perspective of preserving Japan's own initiatives and self-respect, it was inappropriate for its constitution, the basic law of the land, to be decided by foreign rule. Indeed, when the *Kenpo Mondai Chosa Iinkai* (Constitutional Problem Investigation Committee) was established at the end of October under the chairmanship of renowned civil-commercial law scholar, State Minister Matsumoto Joji, it was the shared understanding of Shidehara, Yoshida, and Matsumoto that deliberations would proceed carefully and slowly and that in fact no actual revisions would take place for a long time.

SCAP did not permit this deception to go on long. On October 4, MacArthur had already encouraged Konoe Fumimaro to take the lead in constitutional revision. However, when Konoe became the target of criticism over responsibility for the war, SCAP withdrew its support of Konoe in a statement released on November 1. Moreover, MacArthur also stated that he had directed Shidehara to undertake constitutional revision and that the Japanese government draft would be announced soon. Having no choice, the Matsumoto Committee was forced to proceed with revisions, however limited, of the Meiji constitution.[19]

With Home Minister Horikiri Zenjiro being responsible for the election law, Welfare Minister Ashida Hitoshi in charge of the labor law, and Agriculture Minister Matsumura Kenzo responsible for agrarian reform, there was much excitement in the air that a near ideal draft for postwar Japan would emerge from the enthusiasm and intellect of the drafters.[20] With regard to the most important reforms of the constitution, however, there were attempts at hedging and deception from the very beginning. While Prime Minister Shidehara and Foreign Minister Yoshida, who had been involved in diplomatic work, would come to recognize that the above approach would not succeed, Matsumoto, overly confident and often too authoritative to be an effective negotiator, did not change the basic approach of the committee that tried to preserve the Meiji constitution intact.

The purge and rebirth of the Shidehara Cabinet

Prime Minister Shidehara devoted Christmas Day at his cold residence to drafting the emperor's New Year's Day announcement, "Declaration of Humanity (*Ningen Sengen*)," in which the emperor would renounce his divinity. The next day, the prime minister collapsed after developing a high fever caused by pneumonia. After a request by Yoshida, MacArthur sent Shidehara penicillin, probably saving his life.

Symbolically, that *O-Shogatsu* (New Year's Day) was the worst in Japanese history, with demobilized soldiers gradually making their way back to Japan wandering about searching for their families amid the destruction and hunger in the cities. The prime minister himself remained ill and bed-ridden. On January 4, when the cabinet began work again, GHQ announced the purge of militarist and nationalist leaders in high positions during the war. In all more than 200,000 people were purged during the occupation.

Chief Cabinet Secretary Tsugita Daisaburo, Agriculture Minister Matsumura, Home Minister Horikiri Zenjiro, and Education Minister Maeda Tamon, all wise ministers in important posts in the Shidehara Cabinet, were subject to the purge. An extraordinary cabinet meeting, held when the prime minister was absent, decided that it would reshuffle the cabinet to replace the purged ministers. Shidehara, however, was becoming increasingly irritated with MacArthur's actions and informed the cabinet of the decision to resign en masse. The emperor and MacArthur both requested that Shidehara remain and continue the government after a reshuffling of the cabinet, but Shidehara would not listen.

Within the cabinet, Matsumura led those against resigning en masse, and, along with Chief Secretary Tsugita, visited the prime minister at his home. Matsumura challenged Shidehara by asking him rhetorically whom he planned to recommend as his successor at this critical time in Japanese history, when the fate of the nation was in his hands and when skilled diplomacy was needed. After a long silence, Shidehara broke into tears and agreed to stay in office.[21] He would come to play a critical role in the revision of the Meiji constitution.

The Shidehara–MacArthur meeting

On January 24, 1946, Shidehara, now recovered, visited MacArthur to thank him for the penicillin. This meeting is often looked at as the origin of the postwar peace constitution that emerged later that year. However, the exact contents of the meeting are still not certain. In his own memoirs published some twenty years later, MacArthur records the scene very dramatically.[22] But because MacArthur was skilled at portraying events in a way that made himself shine, the overall reliability of the account is doubtful. On the other hand, the only testimony of Shidehara is the "Odaira Memo," which was written up later when the daughter of Shidehara's good friend, Odaira Komazuchi, to whom Shidehara told everything about the meeting, asked her father about it. There is much uncertainty regarding this memo because it was a second-hand, if not third-hand, account.[23]

Shidehara began by telling MacArthur that "while bedridden, he had given much thought" to some issues and proceeded to raise to them. The first one was the continuation of the emperor system. Shidehara appealed to MacArthur to permit it, saying he could not die a peaceful death without knowing the emperor's position was assured. MacArthur also believed strongly in the maintenance of the emperor system and promised to work toward realizing it. Shidehara appeared hesitant as he raised the second issue. When encouraged to continue by MacArthur, Shidehara explained that he thought it would be a good thing for Japan to renounce war and adopt a national policy of becoming a peaceful nation. Surprised, MacArthur, when hearing this, reached out to shake hands with Shidehara, unable to hide the tears in his eyes.

Prewar "Shidehara diplomacy" was widely known for its opposition to the use of force on the Asian continent and for its calls for cooperation and nonintervention. Shidehara strongly believed in the peaceful pursuit of rational mutual economic interests. As a diplomat active during this period, Shidehara was no stranger to the thinking seen in the League of Nations and the antiwar 1928 Kellogg-Briand Pact. Moreover, Shidehara, in drafting the emperor's statement on humanity, had the emperor mention pacifism twice, in the phrases "realizing peace by both the people and leaders" and "firmly choosing peace for one's civilization forever." Likewise, Shidehara stated on New Year's Day his intention to see the "construct[ion] of a new state that is thoroughly democratic, peaceful, and rational." This call for pacifism did not come from an old man on his deathbed, but instead was part of Shidehara's deep-rooted rationalism in both the prewar and the postwar periods.

It is not surprising then that Shidehara would have proposed this call for pacifism at the meeting with MacArthur. Yet there is much that still remains unclear. First, did Shidehara speak of not only wars of aggression but also wars for self-defense? And second, when Shidehara spoke of making pacifism a national policy, was it he himself who proposed that it be included in the constitution? Many scholars have questioned these points, and some believe that the entire episode may have been a story created or at least promoted by MacArthur. It is true that former diplomat, Shiratori Toshio, who was convicted as a Class-A war criminal,[24] drafted an appeal for a new constitution that included a peace clause, which was passed from Yoshida to Prime Minister Shidehara, but there is no record as to how much influence that recommendation carried. Several scholars believe the correct understanding of this episode is the one put forth by Professor Tanaka Hideo—that Shidehara proposed "pacifism" and MacArthur, in strong agreement, then took measures to include it in the constitution.[25]

Why did MacArthur, a military man, show such warm support for an antiwar clause? In the prewar period, MacArthur, who served as Philippine President Manuel L. Quezon's military advisor, had helped to include the "renunciation of war" in the country's 1935 constitution. The spirit of the Pact of Paris (outlawing war) of 1928, proposed by U.S. secretary of state Frank B. Kellogg and French foreign minister Aristide Briand, and of the 1931 Spanish constitution, was included in the 1935 Philippine constitution. Likewise, MacArthur, who belonged to the conservative wing of the Republican Party in the United States, shared the strong belief that it was the mission of the United States to bring American culture and democracy to Asia, and thus did not see the planting in Asia of a democratic constitution with a renunciation of war clause as anything unusual.[26]

A more important motivation, perhaps, was the difficult situation in which MacArthur had found himself. International public opinion was becoming more and more critical of the emperor system. The U.S. government position paper, SWNCC 228, on the revision of the Japanese constitution, prepared on January 11, instructed MacArthur not to force constitutional reform on Japan. At the Foreign Ministers Conference in Moscow in December, the creation of a Far Eastern Commission (FEC) for the administration of Japan was decided upon, and it was believed that authority for constitutional revision would move to the FEC. In this situation, it was uncertain if it would be possible for MacArthur to establish, on his own authority, a constitution that would protect the status of the emperor system. There were some among an FEC delegation that visited GHQ on January 17 and met with Kades who strongly wanted MacArthur to draft a new constitution. Perhaps MacArthur was also inspired to do so by Shidehara's suggestion. If Japan itself were to propose a constitution that was completely peaceful and democratic in nature, perhaps the Allies would also accept a constitution that preserved aspects of the emperor system.

The biggest demand of the Allies toward Japan was the "pacification" of the country so that it would not commit an aggressive war a second time. In order to guarantee this domestically, the implementation of "democratization" was necessary. If the manifestation of this pacifism was so dramatic that it surprised the world, then the international level of acceptance for the emperor system would probably be high. MacArthur probably found a hint in Shidehara's words of a way to resolve this policy problem.

The MacArthur constitution

On January 25, the day after his meeting with Shidehara, MacArthur went ahead with his promise regarding the emperor system. In a telegram to Washington, MacArthur, following the interpretations in the Fellers memo, already mentioned, argued that on the basis of evidence there was no reason to try the emperor as a war criminal because he had acted in the manner of a constitutional monarch. Moreover, MacArthur explained in dramatic terms the political effects on occupation policies if the emperor were tried as a war criminal:

> His indictment [would] unquestionably cause a tremendous convulsion among the Japanese people, the repercussions of which cannot be overestimated. He is a symbol that unites all Japanese. Destroy him and the nation will disintegrate ... It is quite possible that a million troops would be required which would have to be maintained for an indefinite number of years.[27]

No matter how unpleasant these words were, the U.S. government could not easily counter the steadfast judgment of a field commander.

Around the same time, MacArthur directed the Government Section of GHQ to begin a legal analysis as to whether the supreme commander had the authority to undertake a revision of the constitution. The results of the study by Kades and others were given to MacArthur in a February 1 memorandum. It stated that once the FEC began operations, the decision with regard to constitutional revision would move to the FEC, but until that time all powers rested with him as SCAP.

On the same day, the *Mainichi Shimbun* ran a story (the so-called "Mainichi Scoop") on the Matsumoto Committee's constitutional revision draft. (It is now known that the draft was a partially completed one and did not represent the final Matsumoto version.) Examining a hasty translation, the Government Section concluded that the draft was extremely conservative in nature, being no more than a minor rewrite of the Meiji constitution, and that it would be a waste of time to accept it and then proceed with revisions.

On Sunday, February 3, Courtney Whitney, the chief of the GS, called together Deputy Chief Kades, Lt. Col. Alfred R. Hussey, and Lt. Col. Milo E. Rowell, principal officers in the section and individuals with law backgrounds, and directed them to come up with a constitution draft within the week. Whitney handed them a note with MacArthur's "Three Principles": (1) the emperor is at the head of the state; (2) war as a sovereign right of the nation is abolished; (3) the feudal system of Japan will cease.[28]

Under the direction of these officers, seven subcommittees, created on Monday, February 4, worked nonstop in secrecy during the week. However, Colonel Kades alone drafted the no-war clause. The second principle by MacArthur stated that "war as a sovereign right of the nation is abolished. Japan renounced it as an instrumentality for settling its disputes and even for its own self-defense." At that time, Kades removed the second clause "even for its own self-defense" in order to clarify the passage to mean "as an instrumentality for settling its disputes." Kades believed that denying the right to self-defense in light of the reality of the international situation was extremely unwise, and feared that if the constitution were viewed as unrealistic and as having been forced on Japan by the occupiers, then there was a danger that as soon as the occupation ended the entire constitution would be abandoned. MacArthur and Whitney approved the changes made by Kades. From this point on, the fact that the renunciation of war clause in the new constitution was strictly for aggressive wars was very clear to at least these three individuals.[29]

However, they did not mind giving the impression both domestically and internationally that postwar Japan would stand on complete pacifism that renounced all war. To do so was desirable because of the political ramifications.

On February 13, Matsumoto and Foreign Minister Yoshida met with GHQ officials, expecting to get an answer on the Matsumoto Committee's constitutional revision draft, but instead Whitney handed them the draft prepared by MacArthur's staff. Whitney suggested to them that if they wanted to preserve the emperor system, it would be wise to accept the draft. Matsumoto was shaking with anger, arguing that Whitney's approach was offensive and full of "threats." Moreover, the draft used terms that were "like those found in literature," such as the reference to the emperor as a "symbol," and not proper legal expressions.[30]

The cabinet meeting on February 19 witnessed a great uproar. In order to control the situation, Prime Minister Shidehara met with MacArthur again for three hours. At this meeting, Shidehara decided to use MacArthur's draft, upon which the Japanese government would make revisions. The next day, Shidehara appealed to the cabinet for its cooperation. The cabinet agreed to complete the democratic constitution based on the clauses for a symbolic emperor and war renunciation. The emperor subsequently announced his strong support of Shidehara's decision.[31]

MacArthur and the emperor, who had called on Shidehara not to resign and continue with the premiership some weeks before, again agreed on utilizing the prime minister to realize the drafting of the new constitution. Looking back on the chain of events set in motion from when Shidehara prepared the emperor's "Declaration of Humanity" statement of January 1, it can be said that key political decisions jointly made by MacArthur, the emperor, and Shidehara brought about the birth of the constitution. Through the acceptance of the constitution draft by the Shidehara Cabinet, Japan was accepted back into the international community and gained a respected place in it. Moreover, some 80 percent of the Japanese public expressed their strong support of the new constitution at that time. It was no longer possible for the emperor and the Japanese government to be disclaimed—they had a constitutional base and the recognition of the public and the international community. As Yoshida, who succeeded Shidehara as prime minister and was responsible for passing the revised constitution, had anticipated, the passage of the constitution was somewhat like a foreign treaty that was critical to Japan's effort to cope with a very difficult international situation. It can be said that the making of the postwar constitution was one of the central focuses of diplomacy during the occupation period.

Occupation reforms

Revising the Meiji constitution was as much a diplomatic issue as it was a domestic issue during the occupation years when GHQ was all-powerful. To some extent, the same can be said with regard to various other occupation reforms. The weight and meaning, however, changed with each reform.[32]

For example, the election law and labor union law already referred to were reforms in which the Japanese government took the lead and the occupation forces simply approved them after the fact. Of course, even in these situations, the political environment of control by reformist thinkers in the occupation army was a decisive factor in the ability of the Japanese government to initiate these reforms on its own. Nevertheless, it should be pointed out that no true diplomatic negotiations were necessary in making these particular reforms. Japan's own experience in the era since the years of the Taisho Democracy meant that the Japanese government possessed a certain reservoir of intellectual preparation, evident in that the draft reforms were enough to convince even the New Dealers in the occupation.

At the same time, there were many reforms that were realized only with the *gaiatsu*, or outside pressure, of GHQ because they were not desired by the Japanese government itself. For example, regarding measures of "economic democratization," such as the dissolution of the financial combines (*zaibatsu*) and the strengthening of antimonopoly laws, many officials in the government opposed the reforms because they feared that Japan's already weak economy would be weakened further. Likewise, the prewar Home Ministry, the most powerful ministry in the government, strongly opposed the police law reforms and the establishment of the local autonomy law for fear that they would weaken its power and that of the central government. As a result, some reforms had to be led by GHQ in order to be realized. Indeed, after applying pressure on the Home Ministry and making sure that the reform bills GHQ wanted to see were passed, the Government Section went ahead in 1947 and directed the dissolution of the ministry. The phrase "to be used, not supported" in the executive order to MacArthur from Washington on September 6 with regard to dealing with the Japanese side was applied verbatim to the Home Ministry.

Many reforms were a mixture of efforts by the Japanese government and GHQ. For example, the first agrarian reforms, led by Minister of Agriculture Matsumura, were seen by GHQ as inadequate and incomplete. Wolf I. Ladejinsky of the Natural Resources Section drafted the second set of reforms, which were realized through the cooperation of Matsumura's successor, Wada Hiro, in the Yoshida Cabinet. It goes without saying that in developing these "mixed" reforms, "diplomatic" negotiations were undertaken on almost a daily basis between the working levels of GHQ and the respective ministries and agencies in the Japanese government.

In the process, the division between GHQ and the Japanese government lost its form shape and a new paradigm began to take shape. Within GHQ, a deep, serious rift developed between the Government Section, which sought radical reforms, and the conservative G-2 (Intelligence), led by Maj. Gen. Charles A. Willoughby, which stressed the need for stability and anti-communism. Kades and others from the Government Section relied on Katayama Tetsu and Nishio Suehiro of the Socialist Party and Ashida Hitoshi of the Democratic Party to lead Japan's democratic reforms and formed close connections with them. Willoughby, in contrast, developed cooperative relations with conservatives such as Yoshida and Shirasu Jiro, as well as Hirano Rikizo, who was a member of the anti-Nishio forces in the Socialist Party, and sought to protect former Imperial Army officers like Hattori Takushiro. Midway through the occupation, moreover, when economic recovery became an important issue, the power of the Economic and Scientific Section (ESS) grew, and it strengthened its relations with the Finance Ministry and other economic agencies in the Japanese government. Within the ESS, the finance division and the labor division fought with each other and formed their own alliances with their Japanese counterparts.[33]

In this way, the dynamics of politics created various patterns of cross-national coalitions. "Coalition politics" were based not only on the simple difference in interests between countries, but also on divisions within sections over position and ideology. The occupation reforms represented the sum total of these dynamics and, in a complicated way, were a collaborative effort between Japan and the United States.

Occupation politics

It was not only in reforms but in politics as a whole that GHQ held absolute authority. Without the support and understanding of GHQ, the Japanese government would not even have been able to maintain its position, let alone implement its policies. There were several patterns of "GHQ diplomacy" during this time within the respective cabinets.[34]

First was the pattern of failure. Prime Minister Higashikuni, for example, was not able to develop cooperative relations with GHQ which resulted in the quick collapse of his cabinet. Similarly, Liberal Party head Hatoyama Ichiro's lack of understanding of GHQ invited his purge by the GS in May 1946 just before he was to be named prime minister following his party's victory in the first postwar general election the previous month.

Second, there was the pattern of GHQ diplomacy displayed by Shidehara and Yoshida. Both established friendships with the head of GHQ, MacArthur, and did not interact with other officers. This was probably due to the fact that both had been prewar imperial diplomats and were used to dealing with the heads of state, and also due to their concern that while GHQ was an occupying force it was a matter of honor that the prime minister should not have to deal with the working levels of GHQ. Not only could both of them discuss things with MacArthur directly in English, but they had been diplomats thoroughly familiar with England. Among the elite in England, there was a feeling that although the United States had indeed come a long way, it was still a young country and prone to make mistakes and thus there was a sense of superiority when looking at America. Both Shidehara and Yoshida had enjoyed exchanging such comments while in England and were thus unlike other Japanese, who felt timid when dealing with American authorities. Instead, they were prepared to deal with the United States on an equal basis—psychologically a very valuable asset.

The third pattern was that of those that worked closely with the Government Section, namely Katayama, Ashida, Nishio, and Narahashi Wataru. GS was not only the section within GHQ that was responsible for politics, but its chief, Whitney, had the absolute confidence of MacArthur and enjoyed the status of a political chief of staff within the GHQ. As such, he exercised a great deal of control over the Japanese government in the first half of the occupation. Moreover, because the influential Kades, who possessed a strong reformist ideology, was the deputy chief of the section, he was, to Katayama and Nishio of the Socialist Party, and Ashida of the Democrats, someone who was an important backer as they went about creating their centrist and left-of-center coalition governments. Kades openly intervened in the affairs of the Japanese government, attempting to exclude the conservatives and support the reformist, middle-of-the-road groups.

A fourth pattern was found in the many individuals and groups in Japanese government agencies who developed ties with their counterparts in GHQ on the basis of their areas of jurisdiction and expertise, such as with the ESS.

When the Liberal Party won a majority in the general elections on April 10, 1946, the Government Section purged its leader, Hatoyama, hoping to give an opportunity to the reformists. On the contrary to Kades' expectations, however, the conservative Yoshida eventually took control of the government. But in the general elections on April 25 of the following year, the Socialist Party won a relative majority and through the strong support of the Government Section, was able to form a coalition with the Democratic Party and the People's Cooperative Party (Kokumin Kyodoto). The Government section hoped to further occupation reforms by having a coalition government, made up of progressives and conservatives, actively pursuing reforms. When the Katayama Cabinet resigned in February 1948, Kades, working with Nishio, helped to establish the Ashida Cabinet the following month, essentially paying no heed to public opinion. When the Ashida Cabinet resigned en masse seven months later over the Shoden scandal,[35] Kades and others, in order to block the return of a Yoshida administration, supported the idea of a cabinet led by Democratic Liberal Party (Minshu Jiyuto) secretary general, Yamazaki Takeshi. (Yamazaki and others, like Shidehara, had left the Democratic Party in March 1948, and joined the Liberal Party which became the DLP.) In the end Kades was unsuccessful.

The direct support by the GS was a blessing to the centrist coalitions as well as a burden. First, because Kades sought to manage the political situation on his own, he made Nishio and Ashida and other cooperative Japanese officials dependent on GHQ, leading to the loss of their independence and their prestige among their colleagues and the public. Second, although the Kades alliances were based on mutually held principles of demilitarization and democratization, eventually they became partisan, and the ensuing political manipulation led by Kades became excessive and lost legitimacy.

Of course Yoshida maintained a partisan focus as well, being close to MacArthur. For example, he asked MacArthur to end a political strike against his government (February 1947) and to release business and economic leaders from the purge. However, not only were the counterparts in "diplomacy" different between groups two and three, so was the nature of their cooperation.

From MacArthur's perspective, moreover, he did not overly lean toward Shidehara and Yoshida per se. When Katayama and Ashida became prime minister, he warmly welcomed them and strongly supported them. MacArthur undertook his own sort of omni-directional diplomacy vis-à-vis each prime minister, but it was only Shidehara and Yoshida who often requested to meet with him. Not only did Yoshida meet with MacArthur more often than any other Japanese, but he also attempted to make MacArthur work on behalf of Japan's national interests.

For example, during the time of the food crisis in the spring of 1946, both Shidehara and Yoshida were successful in getting MacArthur to announce that "as long as [he was] commander, no Japanese would starve," making him a sort of sponsor of Japan. At the same time, Yoshida tried to mobilize MacArthur to control the radical leftist movement, suggesting that this would endanger order and Japan's economic recovery. Until this was accomplished by SCAP, Yoshida was slow to organize his cabinet in May 1946. When GS attempted to put Yamazaki instead of Yoshida in the premiership in 1948, Yoshida fought against it after contacting MacArthur to get assurances that SCAP was not against the formation of another Yoshida Cabinet. In addition, at the time of the peace and security treaty discussions, Yoshida generally did not hesitate to make MacArthur aware of his and Japan's views.[36] The one big exception, discussed earlier, was in the spring of 1950 when Yoshida dispatched Finance Minister Ikeda to Washington to tell the U.S. government it was willing to offer bases for the U.S. military in the post-peace treaty era without the knowledge of MacArthur. MacArthur was initially angry at the Yoshida, and after this, Yoshida learned that it was important to keep MacArthur informed.

Japanese security during the occupation

The establishment of the Peace Treaty Problems Research Committee

On March 17 MacArthur gave a speech at a press luncheon in Tokyo in which he described the three stages of the occupation as: (1) demilitarization; (2) democratization; and (3) economic recovery. The first stage had been completed and the second one was almost finished. The third stage, however, was beyond the ability of the occupation forces alone, MacArthur said, and he alluded to the need for an early peace treaty. This proposal was based on MacArthur's own views that the occupation should not last long. At the same time, the proposal was made in response to the movements of the State Department toward an early treaty, as seen by the visit of Hugh Borton, chief of Japanese Affairs at the State Department, to Tokyo at that time.[37] It seems that there was also a private motivation in that MacArthur was considering running in the 1948 U.S. presidential election, and the scenario he had in mind was a successful occupation of Japan followed by a peace treaty and then the presidency. MacArthur told Borton of his desire to see a peace conference held in Tokyo that summer.[38]

With MacArthur's proposals and Borton's own group at work, Washington began to make preparations toward an early peace conference during the spring and summer months. The situation was a serious one for Japan. Of course an early peace was something that Japan in general desired. But, if a peace treaty was written by the victors without Japan's involvement and was then forced on Japan, the nightmare of a dictated peace that befell Germany at the end of World War I would be repeated. In order for this not to happen, the Foreign Ministry had already begun studies for a future peace treaty. Indeed, the recognition of the need for these studies had been discussed as early as November 1945, with the actual studies begun in January 1946.

In addition, the first half of 1947 was a very delicate time internationally. On March 12 President Truman announced the so-called Truman Doctrine, stating that the United States would give support to Greece and Turkey in the context of their struggle against communism. In June, the East–West division of Europe became clear when the Soviet Union announced its decision not to participate in the Marshall Plan. In light of this situation, it was uncertain whether Article 9, the anti-war clause of the new constitution, was enough to ensure Japan's security. Recognizing the seriousness of this problem, Japanese diplomats began to take action. In a traditional sense, this meant Japan's recommencement of diplomacy as an independent state.

First, let us briefly examine the Foreign Ministry's preparations during the occupation. When Yoshida became foreign minister in the Shidehara Cabinet in the fall of 1945, two former Foreign Ministry officials, Shigemitsu and Ashida, called together the heads of the Treaty and Political Affairs divisions. Shigemitsu and Ashida argued that it was critical not to let Japan suffer the same fate that befell Germany with the Versailles Treaty. (Yoshida, Ashida, and Shigemitsu had all participated as diplomats in the Paris Peace Conference and witnessed Germany's unfortunate fate.) In light of their advice, the Executive Committee on a Peace Treaty Problems was established within the Foreign Ministry on November 21 under the direction of the Director of the Treaty Division.

Subsequently the Foreign Ministry pursued a four-stage plan concerning the peace treaty.[39] The first stage was one in which the Potsdam Declaration and the Allied occupation policies toward Japan were analyzed and their implications for Japan written up. The result was great concern over the attempts of the Allies to go ahead with the complete demilitarization of Japan. The question for Japan was how to "preserve a minimum amount of military power to defend itself" in order to "continue as an independent state."[40] The Foreign Ministry at this time looked at affairs from the perspective of a traditional sovereign state and took seriously a situation in which Japan was not allowed the ability to defend itself.

The second stage began with the announcement of the draft revision of the constitution in March 1946. Those working on the issue in the Foreign Ministry were forced to change their thinking. With Article 9 appearing in the draft constitution, it now became necessary to discuss Japan's future in the context of "permanent neutrality" and "collective security by the Far Eastern Commission." At this time, there still existed a strong hope that the United Nations would broker the postwar peace and that Japan's security might be guaranteed collectively by international society.

The third stage began with the start of the Cold War, when the world was awakened from the dream of a permanent peace following the horrors of World War II.

The fourth and final stage followed the outbreak of the Korean War in 1950, when the Cold War became hot near Japan and planning for the peace treaty crystallized under the leadership of Yoshida Shigeru.

The emperor seems to have been the first one to suggest that Japan's security could not be entrusted to an international security structure under the United Nations. The emperor, who was the peacemaker in August 1945 and a determined sponsor of the new constitution in 1946, was in 1947 now seeking a Japan–U.S. security arrangement. On May 6, 1947, the emperor, in his fourth meeting with MacArthur, stated that he believed that "as long as Japan had no military it was necessary to maintain hope with regard to its security in the United Nations, but the reality was that it would be difficult for the United Nations to function." In response, MacArthur expressed his hopes in the ideals of world peace and Article 9. The emperor did not agree and appealed to MacArthur, saying that "in order to guarantee Japan's security, it was necessary for the United States to take the initiative." MacArthur no longer stuck to general statements and responded that "the basic concern of the United States was to guarantee Japan's security, and on this point, Japan should remain assured."[41]

The plan in the Foreign Ministry at this time was not so much a bilateral security arrangement to the degree that the emperor seemed to call for, but was rather multidimensional and multilevel in nature. In particular, until the summer of 1947, the Foreign Ministry had a three-layered concept in mind: while receiving the international security benefits from joining the United Nations, Japan also envisioned a sort of Western Pacific regional security arrangement and the ability to handle internal security on its own.

The Ashida initiative

On the basis of this planning within the Foreign Ministry, Foreign Minister Ashida, who was also the vice premier in the Katayama Cabinet, attempted to influence U.S. and Allied thinking in the summer of 1947. His first motivation was to avoid a dictated peace as the planned peace conference approached, and for this, Ashida sought hints on how to negotiate with the Allies. Second, in light of the start of the Cold War, Ashida cautiously began to explore the possibility of modifying the policy of complete demilitarization adopted by GHQ up until that time.

Ashida met with MacArthur's political advisor George Atcheson, Jr., Government Section chief Whitney, and British Commonwealth representative in Japan W. McMahon Ball over the course of several weeks in late July and August, handing each of them a nine-point document regarding Japan's desires for a peace treaty. The document also expressed Japan's desire for its security to be guaranteed under an international security structure of the

United Nations, based on the Foreign Ministry's planning during stage two mentioned above. Both Atcheson and Whitney returned the document, however, explaining that accepting a written expression of Japan's desires would end up anger the other Allies.

If Foreign Minister Ashida had really made up his mind to "restart diplomacy," it might have been better to meet with General MacArthur and request his cooperation. In fact, when consulted, Shidehara had recommended this very step to Ashida. But Ashida did not follow the advice, perhaps thinking that it was better to lightly sound it out first with his contacts at the working level in SCAP. After he approached them, however, MacArthur became aware of his efforts and rejected them.

For the Japanese government, it was essential to avoid being blocked out from the peace treaty planning. Ashida next approached General Robert L. Eichelberger, commander of the Eighth Army in Yokohama who was set to return to the United States temporarily, and handed him a copy of the same nine-point document toward the end of the summer. A few days later, on September 13, Ashida prepared another document for Eichelberger which explained that in a situation where U.S.–Soviet relations worsened and it became impossible for Japan to rely on the United Nations for its security, Japan wished to "entrust its security to the United States" through a bilateral arrangement. The origins and spirit of the Japan–U.S. Security Treaty can be seen in this early document, the second "Ashida Memo." Unfortunately, it seems that Eichelberger did not pass these memos on to officials in the U.S. government, instead holding on to them for his own reference.

The "Emperor's Message"

Ashida's initiatives during this time thus failed to come to fruition. In contrast, the "Emperor's Message," relayed to Atcheson's successor, William J. Sebald, by Terasaki Hidenari, a Foreign Ministry official working for the emperor, on September 19 did in fact reach Washington. According to Terasaki's spoken comments to Sebald, the emperor desired for the United States to continue to militarily occupy Okinawa for another twenty-five or fifty years, but at the same time to allow Japan to retain sovereignty over Okinawa. In other words, the emperor offered a bilateral base-leasing arrangement. This type of method was needed to "convince the Japanese people that the United States has no permanent designs on the Ryukyu Islands," which appeared to have been the aim of the US and the Allies due to statements by MacArthur earlier that year.[42]

The "Emperor's Message" arrived just when the State Department and the U.S. military were clashing over the status of Okinawa and base rights.[43] Robert A. Fearey of the Division of Far Eastern Affairs had prepared studies premised on the United States being able to lease bases in Okinawa while leaving sovereignty with Japan. The U.S. military, however, which had come to occupy Okinawa only after the loss of much blood, refused to accept the

State Department's position, arguing that such an arrangement was "inadequate" and that it was necessary to acquire or at a minimum place the islands under a U.S. strategic trusteeship. It was George F. Kennan, head of the newly created Policy Planning Staff (PPS) under Secretary of State George C. Marshall, who was responsible for coordinating these opposing views and drafting an overall plan. Referring directly to the "Emperor's Message," Kennan reintroduced the possibility of a base-leasing arrangement.

The efforts for an "early peace," which the Japanese side took very seriously and which became an opportunity for the restart of diplomacy, eventually were aborted. Kennan and his superiors at State opposed an early peace, thinking in part that Japan was not ready for a peace treaty and that it was necessary to reassess U.S. policy in light of the Cold War context. Kennan criticized Borton's peace treaty draft (completed on August 5), as one that still sought to punish a former enemy state and lacked the perspective of rebuilding and developing Japan as a friendly state in the Cold War. In addition, the Soviet Union had proposed that a peace treaty should be discussed at the Foreign Ministers' Meeting, in which unanimity was necessary (and each country could exercise a veto). This proposal clashed with the plan of the United States and Britain, which called for a meeting of the FEC, in which only a majority vote was necessary. The start of the Cold War would have profound effects on the future peace treaty and security of Japan.

Efforts to see a return of diplomatic rights

In this way, after putting on hold both the problem of the peace treaty and that of the disposition of Okinawa, Kennan visited Japan and Okinawa in March 1948 and decided to develop new policies based of his investigations there. The result was the document, NSC 13/2, appearing in October that year, which called for the continuing of the occupation, while stressing the need to relax the occupation machinery and bring about economic recovery. Thus while Japanese diplomacy obtained some breathing room, Japan still did not know if it would be a true participant in the peace treaty negotiations.[44]

At the end of 1948, as if timed with the new policies in Washington emphasizing economic recovery, power returned to Yoshida, also a strong believer in economic recovery. Cooperating with the Detroit banker Joseph M. Dodge, who was sent to Japan to advise on economic policy, the second Yoshida Cabinet, formed in October 1948, confronted the problem of moving from a controlled economy under the occupation to a free-market economy. Moreover, the so-called "Dodge Line" retrenchment policies also helped reopen trade, using the fixed exchange rate of 360 yen to 1 U.S. dollar, and allowing the Japanese economy to return to the international economy.

The last effort made during this time was the dispatching of Finance Minister Ikeda Hayato to Washington in the spring of 1950. In Washington, Ikeda relayed Yoshida's offer to the U.S. government of the continued use of bases in Japan after the signing of the peace treaty. Although this direct approach to the U.S. government angered MacArthur, Assistant Secretary of State W. Walton Butterworth believed Japan's offer would make it possible to restart discussions with the military on a peace treaty for Japan. This direct approach had the effect of forcing the U.S. side to recognize that the Japanese government was an interested party with regard to any future peace treaty negotiations, and was likely made as an effort to prevent a repeat of the dictated peace of Versailles.

The complete return of Japanese diplomacy during the occupation—the fourth stage—occurred at the time of the Korean War, when Yoshida and Dulles were involved in direct negotiations over the peace treaty and security treaty. This will be taken up in the next chapter.

The meaning of diplomacy in occupied Japan

One after the other, battles outside the castle walls were lost until finally the enemy approached the main gates, and no reinforcements were to be found as they had already been defeated elsewhere.

This was the situation in which Japan found itself at the end of World War II. Surrounding the castle of Japan, the enemy called for Japan's leaders to surrender. The United States wanted to avoid needlessly sacrificing its forces in a final battle whose outcome was already determined. Japan responded that if there were confirmation that the monarchy (national polity) would be spared, it would surrender. If, as the Imperial Army called for, a "final battle" were to take place on the homeland, after untold destruction, it was likely that both the emperor and the Japanese government would cease to exist and the Allied forces would place the areas conquered under direct military government. U.S. forces were to land on the Pacific side, and Soviet troops would land in Hokkaido and on the Sea of Japan side. It was most likely that Japan would be divided between north and south. And perhaps would remain so.

In light of this, we can now understand that the decision of the Suzuki Cabinet to accept the Potsdam Declaration was an effort of last-minute diplomacy to maintain the national unity of Japan. Likewise, while preventing the outbreak of conflict by the diehards within Japan, the Higashikuni Cabinet was able to realize the peaceful arrival of occupation troops and protect the indirect approach to the occupation as one of indirect rule through the emperor and the Japanese government. It was defensive diplomacy for the sake of continued existence of the nation and its own government.

The research by the Foreign Ministry in January 1946 predicted that, unlike other peace treaties in the past that sought to be "a starting point for the postwar order," the peace treaty after the occupation of Japan would be "a finishing point for the postwar order" in that it would formally recognize the "existing facts" established during the occupation. In other words, the diplomatic negotiations involving the occupation and reforms were viewed as de facto peace treaty diplomacy.[45]

In this sense, while some apprehension and tension existed in the diplomacy exercised during the occupation, Japan cooperated with the occupation army and discovered that if under its aegis anti-Japanese sentiment "gradually and naturally disappeared," then a long occupation would not necessarily be such a bad thing. The Shidehara and Yoshida cabinets: (1) helped to create a constitution that could be accepted internationally; (2) eventually established connective cross-national coalitions between GHQ and the Japanese government; and (3) orchestrated a situation in which the outside controller was beginning to act as a defender of Japan's interests.

Just when a radically peaceful constitution was established and a variety of democratic reforms implemented, the international system began to change dramatically and a divisive structure at the world level gradually came into being—the Cold War. Having departed from traditional realism and established a plan for Japan's future relying on international institutions, the Foreign Ministry now faced the harsh international reality of a bipolar world. As a hot war broke out on the Korean Peninsula, special emissary Dulles requested that Japan rearm and contribute to the Western camp. Japan was the subject of "foreign pressure" to become a "normal state." Yoshida, however, chose to establish a path for postwar Japan based not on traditional power politics but on international cooperation and mutual economic benefit. In the long run this approach determined not only postwar Japan's politics and diplomacy but also the national characteristics of this island country.

Notes

1 Section 1 is based on Iokibe Makoto, *Beikoku no Nihon Senryo Seisaku: Sengo Nihon no Sekkeizu* (U.S. Occupation Policy towards Japan: The Blueprint of Postwar Japan), 2 vols. (Tokyo: Chuo Koron, 1985). Also see, Hugh Borton, *Spanning Japan's Modern Century: The Memoirs of Hugh Borton* (Lanham: Lexington Books, 2002). These memoirs were first published in 1998 in Japan by the Asahi Shimbunsha and edited by Iokibe.

2 Diary Entry for April 19, 1945, Henry Louis Stimson Diaries, Manuscripts and Archives Division, Yale University Library, New Haven, Connecticut. Also see the John J. McCloy Diaries, Archives and Special Collections, Amherst College Library, Amherst, Massachusetts.

3 For a longer discussion of the significance of the unconditional surrender policy for Japan, see Makoto Iokibe, "American Policy Towards Japan's 'Unconditional Surrender'," *The Japanese Journal of American Studies*, no. 1 (1981), pp. 19–53.

4 "JWPC 385/1, Ultimate Occupation of Japan and Japanese Territory (August 16, 1945)," Record Group 218, National Archives II, College Park, Maryland. Many of the essential U.S. diplomatic and military documents on preparations for the occupation of Japan were compiled and published in microfiche form. See Makoto Iokibe, ed., *The Occupation of Japan, Part I: U.S. Planning Documents, 1942–1945* (Bethesda: Congressional Information Service, 1987).

5 *Stalin's Correspondence with Roosevelt and Truman, 1941–1945* (New York: 1965), pp. 266–67. Also see Harry S. Truman, *Memoirs by Harry S. Truman, Vol. 1 Year of Decisions* (New York: Doubleday and Co., 1955), pp. 440–41. For a study based

on Soviet Archives declassified after the end of the Cold War, see Boris N. Sla-
vinsky, *Nisso Senso e no Michi* (The Road to War between Japan and the Soviet
Union, 1937–45) (Tokyo: Kyodo Tsushinsha, 1999).

6 "SWNCC Memo, August 11, 1945," and "SWNCC 70/5, National Composition of
Forces to Occupy Japan Proper in the Post-Defeat Period (August 18, 1945)," Record
Group (hereafter RG) 59 National Archives (hereafter NA), College Park, Maryland.

7 "Basic Outline Plan for *Blacklist* Operations to Occupy Japan Proper and Korea
after Surrender or Collapse," by General Headquarters, United States Army
Forces, Pacific, 3rd ed., August 8, 1945, MacArthur Memorial, Norfolk, Virginia.
"JWPC 264/9, Further Action as to Immediate Occupation of Japan and Japanese-
Held Areas (August 13, 1945), Appendix A," RG 218, NA.

8 For more on the significance of the Ikeda–Miyazawa trip, see Robert D. Eldridge
and Ayako Kusunoki, "To Base or Not to Base: Yoshida Shigeru, the 1950 Ikeda
Mission, and Post-Treaty Japanese Security Conceptions," *Kobe University Law
Review*, No. 33 (1999), pp. 97–126.

9 "Telegram No. 367, Foreign Minister (Togo Shigenori) to Envoy to Switzerland
(Kase Shunichi) Regarding Japanese Diplomatic Agencies in Neutral Countries
(August 16, 1945)," *Diplomatic Papers of Japan*, in Eto Jun ed., *Senryo Shiroku* I
(The History of the Occupation of Japan, vol. 1) (Tokyo: Kodansha, 1995), p. 677.

10 "Instruction to General of the Army Douglas MacArthur (Message no. 1)," *Foreign Relations of the United States, 1945, Vol. 6, The British Commonwealth, the
Far East* (Washington, D.C.: Government Printing Office, 1967), p. 712.

11 "Proclamation No. 1 to 3, September 2, 1945," in Eto, ed., *Senryo Shiroku*, pp.
271–76.

12 For more on this, see Mamoru Shigemitsu, *Japan and Her Destiny: My Struggle
for Peace* (New York: E.P. Dutton, 1958), pp. 375–77. The explanation by
MacArthur in his memoirs (*Reminiscences*, New York: McGraw-Hill, 1964, pp.
329–30) contains several inaccuracies.

13 Kojima Noboru "Tenno to Amerika to Taiheiyo Senso (The Emperor, America,
and the Pacific War)," *Bungei Shunju*, vol. 53, no. 11 (November 1975), p. 117. For
more on this meeting, see Toyoshita Narahiko, "Showa Tenno-MacArthur Kaiken
wo Kensho suru (Reexamining the Emperor-MacArthur Meetings)," *Ronza* no. 90
(November 2002), pp. 56–69. This article appeared following the declassification of
most of the contents of these meetings by the Imperial Household.

14 The emperor asked Kido Koichi whether the Allies would stop hunting Japanese war
criminals if he stepped down. Diary entry for August 29, 1945, *Kido Koichi Nikki 2* (The
Kido Koichi Diaries, vol. 2) (Tokyo: University of Tokyo Press, 1966), pp. 1230–31.

15 For more on Showa Emperor's monologue, see Terasaki Hidenari and Mariko
Terasaki Miller, *Showa Tenno Dokuhakuroku: Terasaki Hidenari Goyogakari Nikki*
(The Terasaki Hidenari Diaries: Showa Emperor's Monologue) (Tokyo: Bungei
Shunju, 1991), and Azumano Makoto, *Showa Tenno Futatsu no Dokuhakuroku*
(Showa Emperor's Two Monologues) (Tokyo: NHK Press, 1998). Also see Masumi
Junnosuke, Showa Tenno to Sono Jidai (The Showa Emperor and his Era) (Tokyo:
Yamakawa Shuppansha, 1998). The "Imperial Decision" of August 1945, accept-
ing the surrender terms of the Allies, brought an end to the war. His words made it
possible for peace to be restored, and a bloodless occupation to begin. The lives of
probably one million Japanese and tens of thousands of Allied forces were spared
by the avoidance of a final ground war on the Japanese main islands. If the
emperor had the ability to stop the war, critics ask, why did he permit it to start?
The above monologue, first published as a part of the diaries of the emperor's
goyogakari or advisor, Terasaki, shed light on this fundamental question. No
matter what his personal feelings, the emperor believed that if the government followed proper procedures when deciding a policy, then as a constitutional monarch
(as opposed to a despot), he had no choice but to recognize that decision. There

were only two times following the Manchurian Incident in 1931 when the emperor's own will was expressed at the time of a decision. One was when the cabinet collapsed at the time of the "2.26 (1936) Incident" and the second when Prime Minister Suzuki requested the emperor's opinion at the end of the war. The above views of the emperor on his role as a constitutional monarch were recorded and translated as the monologue, at the suggestion of Brigadier General Bonner F. Fellers, the military secretary to General MacArthur and a relative of Terasaki's American wife, Gwen. As the emperor did not appear in the end before the Tokyo Tribunal, the existence of the monologue was not known until its discovery in 1990 by Terasaki's daughter. For more on Terasaki, see Gwen Terasaki, *Bridge to the Sun* (Tokyo: Charles E. Tuttle Company, 1973).

16 "Statement Issued by Supreme Commander, Allied Forces in Japan (September 17, 1945)"; "Memorandum of Telephone Conversation, by the Acting Secretary of State (September 17, 1945)," both in *FRUS 1945*, vol. 6, pp. 715–17.

17 These reforms were the emancipation of women, the promotion of labor unions, and the democratization of economic, legal, and educational systems. See *GHQ Political Reorientation of Japan, vol. II.*

18 Ibid.; "The Shidehara–MacArthur Meeting," October 11, 1945, Eto, ed., *Senryo Shiroku, vol. 2*, pp. 111–17.

19 *Kido Koichi Nikki*, p. 1235. For more on the constitutional revision process, see Sato Tatsuo, *Nihonkoku Kenpo Seiritsushi* (The History of the Revision of the Japanese Constitution), 5 vols. (Tokyo: Yuhikaku, 1962).

20 Ashida Hitoshi, *Ashida Hitoshi Nikki* (The Ashida Hitoshi Diaries) (Tokyo: Iwanami Shoten, 1986); Tsuguta Daizaburo, *Tsuguta Daizaburo Nikki* (The Tsuguta Daizaburo Diaries) (Okayama: Sanyo Shimbunsha, 1991), p. 129; Matsumura Kenzo, *Sandai Kaikoroku* (Memoirs of Three Eras) (Tokyo: Toyo Keizai Shimposha, 1964), pp. 250–57.

21 *Ashida Hitoshi Nikki*, p. 1; Masuda Hiroshi, *Koshoku Tsuiho* (The Purge) (Tokyo: Tokyo University Press, 1996), p. 9.

22 See MacArthur, *Reminiscences*, pp. 346–48.

23 For a copy of the memo, see Otake Hideo, ed., *Sengo Nihon Boei Mondai Shiryoshu* (Documents on Postwar Japanese Defense Issues), (Tokyo: Sanichi Shobo, 1991), vol. 1, pp. 66–67.

24 Shiratori was one of 14 Class-A war criminals enshrined at Yasukuni in 1978.

25 Tanaka Hideo, *Kenpo Seitei Katei Oboegaki* (Notes on the Process of Making the Constitution) (Tokyo: Yuhikaku, 1979), pp. 91–99.

26 D. Clayton James, *The Years of MacArthur, vol. 3: Triumph and Disaster, 1945–1964* (Boston: Houghton Mifflin Co., 1985). Also see Richard B. Finn, *Winners in Peace: MacArthur, Yoshida, and Postwar Japan* (Berkeley: University of California Press, 1992).

27 "General of the Army Douglas MacArthur to the Chief of Staff, United States Army (Eisenhower), January 25, 1946," *FRUS 1946, vol. 8, The Far East* (Washington, D.C.: GPO, 1971), pp. 395–97.

28 The Milo E. Rowell Papers are most useful to understand in detail the progress of constitutional revision, which was published in book form in Japan as *Nihonkoku Kenpo Seitei no Katei* (The Process of Establishing the Japanese Constitution) (Tokyo: Yuhikaku, 1972). The microfiche publication, *Framing the Constitution of Japan*, compiled and published by the Congressional Information Service, Inc. is an excellent collection of primary sources in English including Rowell Papers.

29 Author's interview with Charles L. Kades at his home in Massachusetts, November 1982.

30 *Kenpo Chosakai*, Interview with Matsumoto Joji, cited in Saito Tatsuo, *Nihon Kokukenpo Seritsushi* (The History of the Japanese Constitution), vol. 3 (Tokyo: Yuhikaku, 1996), p. 59.

31 Diary entry for February 19, 1946, *Ashida Hitoshi Nikki*, vol. 1, p. 2.
32 Iokibe Makoto, "Japan's Democratic Experience," Larry Diamond and Marc F. Plattner eds., *Democracy in East Asia* (Baltimore and London: The Johns Hopkins University Press, 1998), pp. 87–89.
33 Hata Ikuhiko, *Amerika no Tainichi Senryo Seisaku* (U.S. Occupation Policy for Japan) (Tokyo: Ministry of Finance, 1976), pp. 58–59.
34 Iokibe Makoto, *Senryoki: Shushotachi no Shin Nihon* (The Occupation Period: The Prime Ministers and the New Japan) (Tokyo: Yomiuri Shimbunsha, 1997), pp. 301–4 and 391–99.
35 The Shoden Scandal was a bribery case caused by Hinohara Setsuzo, president of Showa-Denko Company, who illegally misused public funds devoted for postwar economic rehabilitation. Many politicians including Prime Minister Ashida Hitoshi were arrested and thus the Ashida cabinet resigned in 1948, although Ashida himself was later found not guilty.
36 Kosaka Masataka, *Saisho Yoshida Shigeru* (Prime Minister Yoshida Shigeru) (Tokyo: Chuko Sosho, 1968), pp. 58–59.
37 Borton, *Spanning Japan's Modern Century*, p. 259.
38 Sodei Rinjiro, *MacArthur no Nisen Nichi* (The 2000 Days of MacArthur) (Tokyo: Chuo Koron, 1974), pp. 237–39.
39 Nishimura Kumao, *San Furanshisuko Heiwa Joyaku, Nihon Gaikoshi 27* (The San Francisco Peace Treaty, Japanese Diplomatic History Series, Vol. 27) (Tokyo: Kajima Kenkyujo Shuppankai, 1971); Watanabe Akio and Miyazato Seigen, eds., *San Francisco Kowa* (The San Francisco Peace Treaty) (Tokyo: University of Tokyo Press, 1986); Toyoshita Narahiko, *Anpo Joyaku no Seiritsu: Yoshida Gaiko to Tenno Gaiko* (The Formation of the Security Treaty: Yoshida's Diplomacy and the Emperor's Diplomacy) (Tokyo: Iwanami Shoten, 1996); Kusunoki Ayako, "Senryoka Nihon no Anzen Hosho: Gaimusho ni Okeru Yoshida Doctrine no Keisei Katei, 1945–49 (Japanese Security Conceptions during the Occupation Period: The Foreign Ministry and the Formation of the 'Yoshida Doctrine',1945–49)," *Rokkodai Ronshu*, vol. 45, no. 3 (March 1999), pp. 1–55. Those studies are based on the diplomatic papers of Japanese Foreign Ministry, found in the collection of the late Yomiuri Shimbun reporter Doba Hajime, but which were declassified in 2002 by the Foreign Ministry and published in book form (see Chapter 2, endnote 2, for a more complete description).
40 Kojima, *Nihon Senryo*, pp. 25–29.
41 *Ashida Nikki*, vol. 7, p. 1.
42 For more on the Emperor's message, see Robert D. Eldridge, *The Origins of the Bilateral Okinawa Problem: Okinawa in Postwar U.S.–Japan Relations, 1945–1952* (New York: Garland, 2001), pp. 143–53. The Foreign Ministry had been thinking along these lines earlier that summer. Namely, Vice Minister Okazaki Katsuo, in a memo prepared on July 7, suggested an arrangement by which basing rights would be given to the Allies, but Japan would keep sovereignty and administration rights. See ibid., pp. 127–30.
43 Ibid., pp. 169–76.
44 Ibid., chap. 6.
45 Bureau of Policy, The Japanese Ministry of Foreign Affairs, "Rengokokugawa no Teian Subeki Heiwa Joyakuan no Naiyo no Sotei to Wagaho no Kibo Subeki Heiwajoyaku no Naiyo to no Hikaku Kento (Comparison of the Draft Peace Treaty assumed to be offered by the Allied Countries with the Desirable Peace Treaty for Japan)," January 26, 1946, Reel no. B'-0008, Flash no. 1, The Diplomatic Record Office of the Japanese Ministry of Foreign Affairs, Tokyo.

2   Conditions of an independent state
Japanese Diplomacy in the 1950s

Sakamoto Kazuya

The biggest issue in the negotiations over the peace settlement concerned what to do about Japan's security policy after the peace treaty. Prime Minister Yoshida Shigeru, who concluded both the Treaty of Peace with the Allies and the Security Treaty with the United States, avoided America's call for Japan to rearm and emphasized economic recovery instead. On the other hand, Hatoyama Ichiro, who succeeded Yoshida, established relations with the Soviet Union and sought an autonomous foreign policy. After Japan successfully joined the United Nations, Prime Minister Kishi Nobusuke proceeded to undertake negotiations with the United States to revise the Japan–U.S. Security Treaty and make both it and the relationship more mutual.

The road to the San Francisco Peace Treaty

The Korean War and Japan's Value

The Korean War had a major impact on the direction of postwar Japan. When war broke out in June 1950, MacArthur ordered the Japanese government to establish a 75,000-man National Police Reserve (*Keisatsu Yobitai*). This would subsequently become the National Safety Agency (*Hoantai*) in August 1952, and then the Self-Defense Forces (*Jieitai*) in 1954, forming the basis of Japan's postwar rearmament. Likewise, the mass production of war-related goods and the provision of services for American and United Nations forces acted as a major stimulus for Japan's economic recovery.

From the perspective of diplomatic history, however, the most important point of this drama was the way in which the Korean War elevated Japan's strategic value in America's eyes. With the start of the Cold War in the late 1940s, the U.S. government had already recognized the geopolitical importance of Japan in its overall grand strategy against the Soviet Union. If Japan's industrial might, educated population, and geographical location were to fall into enemy hands, America's own security would be endangered. Conversely, if the United States and its allies succeeded in making Japan into a loyal friend, Japan would serve as a strategic ally. This geopolitical concept remained somewhat shapeless until the Korean War, but the outbreak of fighting on the Korean Peninsula demonstrated Japan's strategic-military importance in East Asia. Had the U.S.-led United Nations force been unable to use Japan as a rear-area support base, it would have been almost impossible to maintain the front on the peninsula.

From the perspective of diplomatic history, it is also important that with the entrance of communist China into the Korean War, the political map of East Asia became divided along Cold War lines. Before the outbreak of the Korean War, the U.S. government had already begun to develop Japan as a friend of the Western camp. Meanwhile, even in early 1950, the American government did not yet view China, by this point under the control of the Communist Party led by Mao Tse-tung, as an explicit enemy. The United States held on to the hope that Mao would increasingly distance himself from the Soviet Union and pursue an independent foreign policy similar to the approach of Yugoslavia's Josip Tito. With the signing of a military alliance (the Soviet–Chinese Friendship Treaty) between China and the Soviet Union in February 1950, however, and the fighting between U.S. troops and Chinese "volunteer" forces which entered the Korean War in October of that year, Communist China became a sworn enemy of the United States in East Asia. It became even more important to develop policies that would strengthen Japan, America's new partner in the region.

This rise in Japan's strategic value created a favorable environment where Japan could realize a peace treaty and its independence, which had been unresolved issues for some time. In order to guarantee that Japan remained a member of the West, the United States, which was the most important of the Allies and the center of the peace treaty negotiations, came to recognize the need for an early and generous peace with Japan.

The peace treaty and the security treaty

Movement on the peace treaty began in the fall of 1949, when Great Britain and the United States agreed in bilateral talks the importance of a treaty with Japan.[1] Within the U.S. government, however, a division of opinion between the State Department and the military soon caused the discussions to bog down again. The State Department, seeing good political relations with Japan as a necessity and fearing the effect that a prolonged occupation would have on anti-American feelings, called for an early peace. The military in contrast saw no need for one. It stressed Japan's strategic value and sought to use bases in Japan as freely and for as long as possible.[2]

In April 1950 President Truman appointed John Foster Dulles, a former senator and an influential figure in Republican circles, as consultant to the secretary of state in order to handle the problems of the peace treaty with Japan within the U.S. government and in discussions between the Allies. Dulles was known as someone with rich international experience, having come from a family in which both his grandfather and an uncle had served as secretary of state and having himself served as an aide to President Woodrow Wilson at the Paris

Peace Conference in 1919 (as well as being a successful international lawyer in the prewar period). Truman's appointment of Dulles was an attempt to establish a bipartisan basis to solve important diplomatic issues. By this time, the Republicans had already begun to harshly criticize the Truman administration's China policy, and Truman wanted to prevent the peace treaty with Japan from becoming a political football amid the anticommunist hysteria over the "Who lost China?" debate.

Dulles first visited Japan as consultant to the secretary of state on the eve of the outbreak of the Korean War. His initial meeting with Prime Minister Yoshida on June 22 was disappointing. Yoshida avoided addressing the issue of Japan's post-treaty security situation and maintained a vague stance throughout the discussion, not committing to rearmament. Dulles let others in his delegation know of his unhappiness, likening himself to "Alice in Wonderland."[3]

With the outbreak of the Korean War, however, Dulles expected that the Japanese would awake to the threat that communism posed to Japan. Upon his return to Washington, he recommended to Secretary of State Dean G. Acheson that the Allies use this occasion and promptly proceed with a peace treaty for Japan. Acheson accepted Dulles's advice, but it was necessary to convince the military, now even more cautious in light of the outbreak of the war. In an attempt to reach a compromise with the Joint Chiefs of Staff, Dulles, after consultations with MacArthur and others, decided to seek a bilateral agreement with Japan that would give the United States "the right to maintain armed forces in Japan, wherever, for so long, and to such extent as it deems necessary."[4] Adopting this approach, the State Department and the Pentagon continued to coordinate their views, and on September 8, 1950, Truman approved the policy paper NSC 60/1, which detailed their agreement regarding the conditions for proceeding with a peace treaty vis-à-vis Japan.

Observing the movements on the U.S. side as reported in the press and elsewhere, Prime Minister Yoshida and the Foreign Ministry held discussions with experts and former Imperial military officers and began to finalize their views on a treaty.[5] An important concern in this process was the question of what to do about Japan's security after the peace treaty was signed. Yoshida, who highly valued Japan's postwar cooperation with the United States, believed that Japan would be able to handle internal security on its own but would have to rely on the United States to prevent direct invasion from outside. The stationing of U.S. forces in Japan following the peace treaty thus came to be seen as a matter of course. In essence, on the eve of negotiations, the views of the U.S. and Japanese governments with regard to basic security arrangements had begun to converge.

When negotiations began, however, two issues became problematic. The first was Japanese rearmament. For several reasons, Yoshida planned to resist attempts by the United States to pressure Japan to rearm, believing that for the time being rearmament was not desirable. The Japanese people, tired of war, were not likely to support rearmament. Nor would Japan be able to handle the burden that rearmament would place on its economy. It was feared that economic troubles would bring about social instability, resulting, ironically, in a less secure Japan. Moreover, there were voices both inside and outside of Japan expressing concern that rearmament would encourage the return of militarism.[6]

A second issue focused on how Japan would permit the stationing of U.S. forces on its territory following the peace treaty. The Foreign Ministry, in keeping with national sentiment calling for a clean break with the occupation, desired an agreement that permitted the stationing of U.S. forces on a limited and rational basis, to be signed separately from the peace treaty and closely linked with the objective of the United Nations.[7]

On January 25, 1951, Special Envoy Dulles and his delegation arrived in Japan for their second visit and began consultations with Yoshida and the Japanese government. The two sides clashed first over Japanese rearmament. For Dulles, rearmament was important in that it would show that Japan was contributing to the strengthening of the Western camp. At that very moment, American-led UN forces were fighting against numerically overwhelming Chinese forces and had been forced back below the 38th Parallel, losing Seoul for a second time at the beginning of January. It is likely that these events had an impact on America's demands, but in any case, Dulles could not hide his frustration with Yoshida's continued hesitance over rearmament.

Fearing that the problem would stall negotiations, the Japanese side decided that it had to suggest something which would be perceived as being the start of rearmament. A short proposal, submitted on February 3, stated that Japan would establish a 50,000-member land and sea "security force" (*hoantai*), which would be the start of a democratic military following the signing of peace treaty. Moreover, the Japanese government would also create a "Security Planning Headquarters" (*Jieikikaku Honbu*) established under a "Ministry of National Security" (*Kokka Chiansho*) that would develop into a Command Staff upon receiving the advice of its counterparts in the U.S. military.[8] Dulles and the U.S. side seemed to accept this for the time being as representing the Japanese government's true desires with regard to rearmament.

Two days before this document was submitted, the Japanese government proposed its own revised concept of the Japan–U.S. security relationship, based on the premise that U.S. forces would continue to be stationed in Japan following the peace treaty. (The earlier Ashida plan of 1947 was written on the premise of contingency use of bases by U.S. forces, not a fulltime garrison.) Discussions proceeded following the U.S. counterproposal, ultimately resulting in the Japan–U.S. Security Treaty. In these talks the U.S. side accepted several of Japan's requests, including one that the security treaty be signed separately from the peace treaty and that a separate agreement (Administrative Agreement) establishing the details of the stationing of U.S. forces be signed between the two governments later, in order to prevent the Japanese people from feeling overwhelmed by the contents of the treaty.

However, the United States did not accept the central premise of the Japanese side that the stationing of U.S. forces in post-treaty Japan should be established within the framework of the United Nations. Japan desired that the shape of the treaty take the following form:

> Because the preservation of Japan's peace and security is the same thing as the preservation of the peace and security of America and the Pacific region, if Japan should be attacked, America would defend Japan and Japan would cooperate to make this possible. Namely, both countries are charged with the relationship of collective self-defense [as per Article 51 of the Charter of the United Nations] and because of this relationship of both countries, Japan agrees to the stationing of U.S. forces in Japan.[9]

Officials in the Foreign Ministry believed that under this arrangement the problem of Article 9 of the constitution could be resolved and the appearance of equality with America would be maintained.

In response, the U.S. side argued that it could not enter into a collective self-defense arrangement with Japan, since Japan did not have a military or the means to defend itself nor could it help defend the United States. The American side refused the Japanese concept outright, citing the 1948 Vandenburg Resolution in Congress, which permitted U.S. association with the defense arrangements of foreign countries only if they were based on "continuous and effective self-help and mutual aid." The shape of the security treaty that the U.S. side desired (and which in fact came about) was essentially one in which "the U.S. would provide protection of Japan by stationing forces in its territory until a collective self-defense relationship based on the [UN] Charter, as desired by Japan, can be established."[10]

Moreover, because Article 1 stipulated that U.S. forces stationed in Japan "may" be utilized for the security of Japan, the treaty carried no clear guarantee by the U.S. government for the defense of Japan. Likewise, because the Administrative Agreement gave U.S. forces in Japan numerous special privileges, the security treaty as a whole left the strong impression that it was merely a stationing agreement, lacking any pretense of equality.

In the end, however, Japan did not undertake full-scale rearmament and was able to depend upon the United States for its external defense, because regardless of what the treaty stated, America would defend Japan out of its own interests in the event of an attack. Indeed, simply having U.S. bases in Japan was an important deterrent for any nation contemplating a violation of Japanese security. With agreement on the stationing of U.S. forces in post-treaty Japan secured, the U.S. side went on to delight Japanese negotiators with a generous draft of the treaty.

On September 4, 1951, representatives from fifty-two countries gathered in San Francisco for the start of the peace conference. On September 8, forty-nine countries, including Japan, signed the peace treaty, and later that same day, representatives from the United States and Japan moved to Sixth Army

Headquarters at the Presidio near the Golden Gate Bridge to sign the bilateral security treaty.

Evaluating the San Francisco Peace Treaty

On April 28, 1952, both the peace treaty and the security treaty went into effect, and Japan returned to the international community six years and eight months to the day that MacArthur first set foot in Japan as SCAP. The San Francisco Peace Treaty, concluded through America's leadership, was a treaty that showed few signs of being punitive in nature against Japan. For example, although Japan was made responsible for reparations, care was taken that reparations not harm Japan's economy or its potential for further recovery— quite in contrast to those forced on Germany in the Versailles Treaty.

The joining of hands with America in security affairs was extremely effective for Japanese security. The United States possessed both the desire and the ability to forward deploy its powerful naval, air, and ground might in East Asia, which was indispensable for the defense of Japan. Moreover, the United States maintained its military presence on the Korean Peninsula, which had the effect of removing a traditional element of instability for Japan as discussed in the Introduction.

Likewise, in the post-World War II era, the United States, with its over-whelming economic might, established and led an international liberal economic system, which helped Japan recover and grow economically. Not only did Japan profit from both direct and indirect aid immediately after the war, but it also benefited from: (1) the economic and political support it received when it joined the General Agreement on Tariffs and Trade (GATT) in 1955; (2) the financial assistance it received in order to participate in the free trading arrangements; (3) the technical support it received to develop its economy and to improve its production ability; and (4) the opportunity for Japanese to study at U.S. universities through the Fulbright and other programs. Most important, the fact that the United States opened its own domestic markets held great meaning for the economy of postwar Japan, which initially lost its access to Asian markets.

There was of course a price to pay for the San Francisco Peace Treaty, despite its many fruits. First of all, a peace treaty with the Soviet Union and other communist nations was not possible at this point. The Soviet Union participated in the peace conference but did not sign the treaty. Poland and Czechoslovakia followed suit. Because the United States and Great Britain disagreed over the question of the legitimate representative of the Chinese government—Beijing or Taipei—neither was invited. A peace treaty with these countries was left as an issue to be dealt with in the future.

In particular, relations with China became problematic following the peace conference. Yoshida had sent Dulles a letter stating that Japan would pursue relations with the government of the Republic of China (Taiwan).[11] In 1952, based on that statement, a peace treaty was signed with the Republic of

Taiwan. This agreement meant that the peace treaty with China—the country that experienced the most destruction in the war with Japan—was concluded only with Taipei, which Japan continued to recognize as the seat of the legitimate government of China until 1972.

The failure to see Okinawa returned was another price of the peace treaty. Through Article 3 of the peace treaty, Japan was forced to recognize the placement of Okinawa (and Ogasawara) under U.S. administration although it succeeded in being allowed to retain "residual sovereignty" over the islands. This became a major sticking point in bilateral relations later.[12]

One more price of the peace treaty was the division it caused in Japanese public opinion. The Socialist Party and many well-known intellectuals, who had come together to form the Peace Problems Discussion Circle (*Heiwa Mondai Danwakai*), strongly criticized Japan's signing of a peace treaty with countries centered around the United States, and demanded instead that Japan seek a treaty with all countries, including the Communist countries, such as the Soviet Union and China. This division over a "majority peace," or *tasu kowa* (also sometimes critically called a one-sided limited peace, or *tandoku kowa*) and "full peace" (*zenmen kowa*) would in turn develop into arguments over support for the Japan–U.S. Security Treaty and unarmed neutrality. Because of this, postwar Japanese diplomacy remained contentious, with the government exhausting much energy in constantly gauging the degree of its support among the public.

The Yoshida Doctrine and America

Following the signing of the peace treaty in San Francisco, Prime Minister Yoshida stayed in power in order to see the implementation of the treaty and Japan's return to the international community through to the end. For the time being, his biggest diplomatic problem was responding to America's calls for actual rearmament. In the discussions with Dulles on the peace treaty, he had promised that Japan would rearm to some extent following the conclusion of the peace treaty. The actual numbers of forces the U.S. government wished to see were made known in 1952. A force-level plan prepared by the Joint Chiefs of Staff suggested that Japan develop a 300,000-man ground force with ten divisions.[13]

Yoshida reacted negatively to these numbers. He believed it was more important to recover economic strength and provide stability in social-welfare areas first. When the United States demanded that Japan increase its police reserves from the current 75,000 to somewhere in between 150,000 to 180,000 during fiscal year 1952, Yoshida countered with a proposal for 110,000 but would not concede anything beyond that. He did, however, agree to the establishment of a National Safety Force and in that sense attempted to respond to America's desires.

The U.S. rearmament request for a ground force based on 10 divisions was reiterated in the basic policy papers for Japan (NSC 125 series) following the

transition in January 1953 from a Democratic to a new Republican administration under Dwight D. Eisenhower.[14] In the spring of that same year, when
bilateral negotiations began over accepting U. S. financial support using the
Mutual Security Act passed earlier that year, Japan was forced to produce a
long-term defense plan. With this, discussions began in earnest within the
Japanese government and among the public on plans for a defense buildup.

At Yoshida's request, Liberal Party Policy Research Council chairman and
former finance minister Ikeda Hayato visited Washington in October 1953 to
negotiate the arrangements with Assistant Secretary of State for Far Eastern
Affairs Walter S. Robertson and present the Japanese government's defense
buildup plan.[15] Although the plan called for the same number of divisions as
requested by the U.S. side, the total number of forces was limited to 180,000
ground troops, or about half the number requested. Ikeda explained the lower
number of forces as a reflection of domestic conditions: (1) the existence of
the peace constitution; (2) the strong pacifist feelings in Japan; (3) the poor
quality of life in Japan; and (4) the lack of a draft system. At the same time,
Ikeda argued that in light of America's naval, army, and air power in the
region, a ground force of that level would be enough for Japan to defend
itself.[16]

The Ikeda–Robertson talks, which continued in Washington for approximately one month, were in the end unsuccessful in reaching an agreement on
the scale and pace of Japan's defense buildup. Both sides made efforts to
compromise, but an actual understanding was beyond their reach. The U.S.
military did not budge on its target of a ten-division force of 325,000–350,000
men for Japanese rearmament. They were to become disappointed.

The focus on economic reconstruction

By the fall of 1954, however, the U.S. government ironically began to show
signs of supporting the Yoshida line focusing first on economic reconstruction
over or before rearmament. Within Japan that year, there had been a dramatic change in the domestic and international climate that made such a shift
necessary. A recession had hit the Japanese economy due to the drop in procurements related to the Korean War and the tight fiscal policies adopted at
the end of 1953. Domestic prices dropped for the first time in the postwar period,
with many businesses going under and unemployment rapidly rising.

Prime Minister Yoshida's political base rapidly weakened because of the
worsening economic situation, a shipbuilding scandal (involving a Yoshida
associate and later prime minister Sato Eisaku), and the controversy over
deliberations on a revised police bill in which the Socialist and Communist
parties sought to use force to prevent voting. The political situation became
fluid, with the conservatives maneuvering against Yoshida to come together
and form a unified party. Yoshida's political leadership essentially had been to
build cooperative relations with the occupation forces amid the unique circumstances of the occupation, and it was that special situation that supported

his ability to remain in power. When the occupation ended and GHQ disbanded, Yoshida had to look elsewhere for support of his policies. However, while Yoshida was a statesman, he was not a domestic politician skilled at functioning in the democratic free-for-all of postwar Japan. When the occupation ended, moreover, it was not only the Leftists who heavily criticized Yoshida but the prewar conservative politicians, such as Hatoyama Ichiro and Miki Bukichi, who had been purged and were returning at this point to political life.

In the middle of this political problem, the Bikini Incident occurred in March 1954, greatly damaging Japan–U.S. relations and further weakening the Yoshida government. A Japanese fishing ship, *Daigo Fukuryumaru* (Lucky Dragon No. 5), was covered in ash from a hydrogen bomb test in the Bikini Atoll; its plight caused outrage among the Japanese public, especially among antinuclear pacifists and those with anti-American sentiments. In addition to reporting to Washington that bilateral relations had reached their worst point in the ten years of the postwar era, the U.S. embassy in Tokyo emphasized that the psychological antipathy of the Japanese toward nuclear weapons was behind their increased calls for neutralism.[17]

The international situation also changed for Japan in 1954. Military tensions in the Far East decreased dramatically following the truce reached in the Korean War the year before and the peace agreement in the Indochina War in July. With this, the overt East–West clash appeared to have come to an end in Asia, with competition shifting to long-term economic development. Because of this, America was able to show more interest in the political and economic stability of its alliance partners, including Japan.

In light of these developments, a consensus was formed within the U.S. government that for the time being it was necessary to focus on Japan's political and economic stabilization, and to relax demands for rearmament.[18] In the summer of 1954, at the initiative of ambassador to Japan John M. Allison and his staff, a review of U.S. policy toward Japan was undertaken, which became the basis of a new basic policy on Japan (NSC 5516/1) in the spring of 1955.[19] This paper confirmed the principle that the U.S. government would not demand the rearmament of Japan at the expense of Japan's political and economic stability and should allow Japan to decide for itself the size and shape of its rearmament program. Moreover, it removed any reference to concrete numbers with regard to force levels.

At the time of the Yoshida's visit to the United States in November 1954, the U.S. government had already given up on the prime minister, who had increasingly lost the ability to govern effectively and showed no efforts at trying to help him. Upon his return to Japan, Yoshida faced strong domestic pressure to resign, ironically just as the U.S. government had come to recognize the validity of the Yoshida line with regard to light rearmament and a focus on the economy.

Yoshida's resistance to U.S. pressure to rearm was correct politically and economically from the perspective of Japan's domestic affairs at the time. The more rearmament demands were resisted, the more difficult it became for Japan to rid itself of its dependence on the United States for its security, however. Believing that the age of self-defense was over and that it was now the era of collective defense, Yoshida had likely come to believe that there was no particular need to break free from dependency on the United States in security matters, since the security of all nations was interconnected.[20]

The Hatoyama administration and the expansion of Japan's diplomatic horizons

The restoration of relations with the Soviet Union

Following the peace treaty, several issues needed to be resolved before Japan could more fully join the international community. One was the establishment of a peace treaty with the Soviet Union. Legally, Japan was still in a state of war with the Soviet Union, with borders undefined and many thousands of Japanese prisoners of war remaining in Soviet-controlled territories. Moreover, for Japan to be able to join the United Nations (where the Soviet Union held a veto in the Security Council), relations with the Soviet Union had to be improved.[21]

For Hatoyama, who took office as prime minister in December 1954, the restoration of relations with the Soviet Union was a politically attractive issue. In contrast to Yoshida, who resigned when he was already out of favor, the well-liked Hatoyama (who caused a boom in popularity among the people) viewed the establishment of relations with the Soviet Union—which even the diplomatically skilled Yoshida was unable to pull off—as a major foreign policy issue that was easy for the people to accept and welcome. Moreover, Hatoyama, who had been a politician in the prewar era, felt the necessity, stemming both from his political views and from the trend of public opinion, for a change in the "overly pro-U.S." foreign policy of his predecessor. Although cooperation with the United States was unquestionably necessary, there was also an inclination within the Hatoyama cabinet to keep a slight distance from the United States and pursue a more autonomous diplomacy.

In January 1955 the Soviet Union, through its former representative to Japan, Alexander I. Domnitsky (who had remained in Tokyo after the signing of San Francisco Peace Treaty), approached the Japanese government to open informal discussions on the normalization of relations. Following the death of Stalin in March 1953, the Soviet Union had announced a policy of peaceful coexistence with the West which called for a reduction in tensions and eventually led to the normalization of relations with former enemies Germany (West) and Austria. In light of this, Hatoyama responded to the Soviet's unofficial trial balloon by deciding to formally start discussions, overriding Foreign Minister Shigemitsu Mamoru's more cautious stance. Negotiations began on June 5, 1955, in London, with former ambassador to Britain Matsumoto Shunichi, then a Lower House member from the Democratic Party, designated as chief negotiator and minister plenipotentiary. Yakov A. Malik, the Soviet ambassador to Britain, represented the Soviet Union.

Discussions were held on diverse issues such as the repatriation of Japanese held by the Soviet Union, the fisheries dispute, the Japan–U.S. Security Treaty, and Japan's joining the United Nations. However, the most problematic issue was the disputed sovereignty of the Northern Territories which the Soviet Union had come to occupy on September 2, 1945, as the Instrument of Surrender was being signed in Tokyo Bay and still have not been returned as of the time of this writing. According to Matsumoto, there were three reasons why the negotiations did not go well for three reasons.[22] First, the Soviet Union took a tough stance with regard to territorial issues. With regard to the Kuriles, which Japan had administered since 1875 by the Treaty of Saint Petersburg, and Southern Sakhalin, which Japan administered from 1905 by the Treaty of Portsmouth, the Soviets essentially did not budge. The position of the Soviet government was that the possession of the Kuriles and Southern Sakhalin, despite the earlier treaties, had been resolved through the Yalta Agreement and the Potsdam Declaration, and that Japan had relinquished its rights at the time of the peace treaty (Article 2) and thus did not have the right to request a return of the islands.

The position of the Japanese government, on the other hand, was that changes in territory needed to be resolved by treaty, and the Yalta Agreement had no binding power on Japan as it was not a party to it. The Potsdam Declaration, it argued, must be read and interpreted together with the Cairo Declaration, which renounced territorial aggrandizement. The San Francisco Peace Treaty did not decide to which country the Kuriles and Southern Sakhalin, which Japan renounced, belonged. The Soviet position that the issue was already resolved and that Japan did not have a say in the matter was, in Japan's eyes, inappropriate.

Because of the differences in their positions, discussions between the two sides went nowhere. After about two months, however, Soviet representative Malik presented a compromise proposal, which while sticking to the principle that the issue was already resolved (and thus not open for discussion) suggested that the Habomais and Shikotan islands (which Japan considered a part of Hokkaido and the Soviets called the Lesser Kuriles) could be handed over. In response, the Japanese government instructed its negotiators to request that Kunashiri and Etorofu be returned as well. As a result, the negotiations hit a roadblock again, one that has yet to be resolved.

The Japanese government viewed Kunashiri and Etorofu as historically being Japanese territory and not a part of the Kurile Islands, whose sovereignty Japan had renounced in the San Francisco Peace Treaty. In the treaty of friendship that Japan, after opening up, first signed with imperial Russia in 1855, the two islands are recognized as Japanese territory. Thus the government's position that the islands historically were a part of Japan is, objectively speaking, correct. The second half of the official position, however, is subject to interpretation. At the San Francisco Peace Conference, Prime Minister

Yoshida had stated that the Habomais and Shikotan were a part of Hokkaido, and not a part of the Kuriles. Moreover, Yoshida explained that the historical circumstances regarding the ownership of Kunashiri and Etorofu differed from that of the North Kuriles (north of Uruppu). Nevertheless, Yoshida did not clarify that these islands were not a part of the Kuriles that Japan was ceding. Rather Yoshida called them "Southern Kuriles," in effect giving the impression that they were a part of the Kurile Islands as a whole. The Foreign Ministry in the beginning, as well in its Diet testimony, stated that the Southern Kuriles were included in the Kurile Islands referred to in the Peace Treaty. In fact, the Peace Treaty had not defined the geographical scope of the Kurile Islands. As a result, after further study, the Japanese government changed its interpretation.

Shigemitsu and the Foreign Ministry may have planned to use the call for the return of Kunashiri and Etorofu as a bargaining chip. But because of domestic circumstances, this position gradually hardened over time. The domestic situation, which was a second factor Matsumoto pointed to as making negotiations difficult, was a reflection of the division within the conservative camp over those wishing to see relations with the Soviet Union normalized and those who did not. With the exception of Foreign Minister Shigemitsu, the Democratic Party for the most part was in favor, while the Liberal Party in general was against normalization. In particular, Yoshida and his supporters, who were strongly critical of Hatoyama, did not recognize the benefits of establishing relations the Soviet Union and continued to take an antagonistic stance. This clash did not subside even following the establishment of the Liberal Democratic Party in November 1955, through the merger of the two large conservative parties. Rather, the influence of those opposing normalization actually increased with the enlargement of the ruling camp, which made it increasingly difficult for the government to compromise on the territorial issue.

Although discussions were resumed in the beginning of 1956 following an interruption in the negotiations in London, the talks deadlocked on the question of the territorial issue. Subsequently the Soviets introduced restrictions on fishing rights in the northern Pacific in an effort to put pressure on the Japanese side. To resolve this problem, agricultural minister Kono Ichiro flew to Moscow and reached a temporary solution, but the fishery agreement would not to go into effect until after the signing of a bilateral peace treaty or the restoration of diplomatic relations, whichever came first.

At the end of July, the Japanese government sent Shigemitsu to Moscow to resume negotiations with Soviet foreign minister Dimitri T. Shepilov. Shigemitsu himself was cautious with regard to the restoration of relations, and upon arriving in Moscow showed an uncompromising attitude. However, when he saw that the Soviet position with regard to the territorial issue was equally tough, he proposed several compromises. In the final proposal on territorial problems, Shigemitsu suggested that the Soviets withdraw their troops from the Habomais and Shikotan, without any territorial delineation taking place, and Japan would confirm its acceptance of the territorial clause of the San Francisco Peace Treaty (in which Japan renounced its rights to the Kuriles and Southern Sakhalin). This proposal, by not making a final settlement on borders, would have made it possible to shelve the question of Kunashiri and Etorofu. Shepilov, however, refused it, stating that a final settlement on borders was necessary and that the handing over of Shikotan and the Habomais was the largest concession the Soviets would make.[23]

At this point Shigemitsu decided that Japan would have to be satisfied with the return of only Shikotan and Habomais, with the recognition of Kunashiri and Etorofu as Soviet territory. But, when he asked for instructions to that effect, the cabinet unanimously rejected his request, and instead responded that public opinion was against such a compromise and thus Shigemitsu should not accept the Soviet proposal. Reluctantly, the foreign minister carried out his instructions.

Discussions temporarily ended here. At an international meeting on the Suez Canal problem in London in August, Shigemitsu met with Dulles, who was also attending the meeting, and explained the status of the talks. Dulles stated that if Japan were to make concessions to the Soviet Union, the United States, as per Article 26 of the Treaty of Peace with Japan, could obtain similar concessions and choose to annex the Ryukyu and other islands if it so desired.[24]

Matsumoto Shunichi, who had been placed in charge of the negotiations, points to America's attitude toward the normalization of Soviet–Japanese relations as seen in this "Dulles warning" as the third reason for the difficulty in negotiations.[25] Although the U.S. government did not oppose the talks, it did expect that Japan not easily give in to Soviet demands. In particular, it requested that Japan not make any compromises with the Soviet Union that would go against the U.S. position with regard to the San Francisco Peace Treaty. The compromise that Shigemitsu was prepared to swallow, however, was directly at variance with the American government's position in the treaty, namely, that the treaty did not hand over to the Soviet Union—which was not a signatory to the treaty—the Kuriles and Southern Sakhalin.

In this way, for both domestic and bilateral policy reasons, the Japanese government was unable to agree to clarify its border with the Soviet Union through the recognition of Soviet sovereignty over the islands of Kunashiri and Etorofu. Neither Japan nor the Soviet Union, however, desired to break off bilateral talks. The Japanese government sought a realistic option with regard to discussions, and, copying the so-called Adenauer Formula, as seen in the normalization process of relations between West Germany and the Soviet Union, decided to shelve the territorial problem and instead first announce the restoration of relations in a joint declaration and later deal with pending issues at the time of a peace treaty. Nevertheless, there was strong opposition within the LDP to shelving the territorial problem, and the Japanese government was forced to adopt a mixed negotiating approach in which it requested that there be continued discussion of the handing over of the Habomais and Shikotan, with other problems being shelved for the time being.

In October 1956, Hatoyama, suffering from illness, journeyed to Moscow to show his desire for a successful conclusion to the negotiations. After one week of talks in Moscow, Japan and the Soviet Union signed on October 19 a joint declaration that ended the state of war between Japan and Soviet Union, freed and returned Japanese POWs, supported Japanese efforts to join the United Nations, and promised the return of the Habomais and Shikotan after the signing of a peace treaty. However, despite strong requests by Hatoyama and the Japanese delegation, a clause saying that the territorial problem would continue to be discussed as a precondition for a peace treaty was not included in the joint declaration. In any case, upon his return to Japan, Hatoyama announced his decision to resign as prime minister, using the normalization of relations with the Soviet Union as his grand exit off the political stage to retirement.

Failure to revise the security treaty

The Hatoyama administration also attempted to seek the revision of the security treaty. In August 1955, during a trip to the United States, Foreign Minister Shigemitsu requested the revision of the security treaty to his counterpart, Secretary of State Dulles. He had prepared his own "personal proposal" for revising the treaty, which called for creating a mutual security treaty for the Western Pacific area.[26]

Shigemitsu explained his request in the following way. Domestically in Japan, the opposition parties and the Left were using the inequalities under the security treaty to propagate anti-Americanism, and in order to combat this, it was necessary to change the treaty into a mutual one similar to those with other alliance partners of the United States. If an equal treaty were signed, the public would be happy and the forces on the Left would likely fade away.

There is no doubt that Shigemitsu struggled with criticism of the security treaty by the Left. In early 1955, problems arose with regard to the expansion of the U.S.-operated Tachikawa Air Base outside of Tokyo and the introduction of Honest John missiles capable of carrying nuclear warheads, resulting in the rise in anti-treaty feeling. Moreover, the left wing of the Socialist Party made significant gains in the February 1955 general elections, no doubt in light of those feelings.

However, criticism of the security treaty was not limited to just the Left and opposition parties. Even among those who generally supported the Japan–U.S. alliance, there was a great deal of frustration with the treaty. Shigemitsu himself was among the critics; he suggested to Dulles that the security treaty had placed Japan in a state of only partial independence.

The decision of Yoshida to provide bases to the United States in exchange for protection was a necessary and rational choice if one takes into consideration the international situation at the time of the peace conference and

Japan's actual capabilities, coupled with the strong desire within Japan for as early a peace as possible. Relying on another country for one's security, however, was bound to cause a strong nationalist reaction among the people. Because the shape of the security treaty appeared to be no more than a base-leasing arrangement for which there were few limits on U.S. usage, the feeling was that much more intense. Following the end of the occupation in 1952, as the Japanese people's desire for true independence became stronger and stronger, as did the criticism of the security treaty.

The security treaty of 1951 in fact had numerous problems. For example, as part of Article 1 of the treaty, U.S. forces stationed in Japan could help put down domestic disturbances if expressly requested by the Japanese government (the so-called Internal Disturbances clause). Such a proviso injured the pride of the people of a sovereign country. Moreover, there were concerns that there were no limits, temporal or otherwise, on the use of bases by U.S. forces, that Japan could be drawn into a war without its knowledge, and that nuclear weapons—to which the people had a strong aversion—could be brought into Japan without its consent. The lack of a clear time limit on the treaty in particular was also pointed out as a problem. The biggest point of contention however was the apparent "one-sidedness" of the treaty, in that while Japan was obligated (in Article 1) to provide bases to American forces, the United States was not obligated to defend Japan.

Shigemitsu hoped to have these defects corrected and proposed a new mutual security treaty. But, after hearing Shigemitsu's proposal, Dulles was annoyed and took a tough attitude, saying that Japan was not only not prepared for it but did have the military strength to help defend the U.S., a precondition for a mutual treaty. Dulles pointed out that because of its constitutional restrictions, Japan was prevented from sending troops abroad and could not defend American soil, including, for example, Guam in the Western Pacific. Moreover, Dulles criticized Shigemitsu's proposal by stating that Japan did not even have enough military power to defend its own country, let alone America. Shigemitsu attempted to respond, but according to Democratic Party secretary general Kishi Nobusuke, who attended the meeting, Dulles's attitude was something like: "Shigemitsu, you talk big, but does Japan really have that kind of power?"[27]

Japan at the time did not in fact have the ability, nor was it prepared. The Hatoyama cabinet had sought constitutional revision and rearmament, but there was little hope of capturing a two-thirds majority necessary for revising the constitution in the Diet for the near future. (It was not until 2007 before the Japanese Diet had passed a national referendum bill which would facilitate constitutional revision.) Moreover, the defense buildup plan of Japan had not changed in the year following the end of the Yoshida administration. The Hatoyama cabinet had to deal with the problem of the consolidation of the conservatives, and Hatoyama himself was not in good health. Thus the forecast was that the cabinet would not last long. Moreover, Shigemitsu did not possess a strong base of support within the Democratic Party. From

Dulles's perspective, therefore, even if Japan made promises to the U.S., it was uncertain whether Shigemitsu could realize them, and there was every chance in the world that the issues would simply be deferred to the next cabinet.

Moreover, it seems that Shigemitsu's proposal itself hardened Dulles and made him cautious. Shigemitsu's "personal proposal" called for the signing of, in addition to a mutual security treaty, a supplementary arrangement by which U.S. ground forces would be withdrawn from Japan within six years, with naval and air forces being withdrawn within six years following that.[28] In other words, Shigemitsu was calling for the withdrawal of all U.S. forces from Japan within twelve years. What is more, he requested that during this time, the use of bases in Japan by U.S. forces would be limited to the purpose of mutual security. Shigemitsu's proposal was thus one that would dramatically change the essence of the existing security treaty.

Criticized by Dulles, Shigemitsu withdrew the proposal. Although it was simply a "personal proposal" by the foreign minister of Japan, the fact that a proposal calling for the complete withdrawal of U.S. forces after the signing of a mutual security treaty was put forward nevertheless showed the increasing unhappiness in Japan regarding the security treaty and the dangerous consequences that existed if it was left unattended. In that sense, Shigemitsu's proposal was an important stepping stone in the revision of the security treaty later that decade.

The Kishi administration and establishment of the postwar diplomatic order

The three principles of Japanese diplomacy

Kishi Nobusuke succeeded Ishibashi Tanzan, who resigned for health reasons after only two months in office, in February 1957. Kishi had served as minister of commerce and industry in the Tojo Hideki cabinet during the war and was held in Sugamo Prison as a "Class A" war criminal for much of the occupation period. Formerly a bureaucrat, Kishi turned into an extremely capable politician. Upon returning to the political world in 1953, he assumed an anti-Yoshida position and worked with Miki Bukichi and others to bring about a conservative merger. After becoming the first secretary general of the Liberal Democratic Party in 1955, he solidified alliances between the party and numerous interest groups, especially the business community, thus stabilizing conservative politics. As prime minister, Kishi sought to move away from the political arrangements of the occupation period by creating a domestic political system appropriate for a sovereign state and strengthening Japan's international position.

Japan was able to join the United Nations in December 1956, and in September 1957, the Kishi cabinet released its first Diplomatic Bluebook, in which the "Three Principles" of Japanese foreign policy were announced: (1) Assigning central importance to the United Nations, (2) cooperating with the free world, and (3) strengthening Japan's position as a "member of Asia."[29]

Harmonizing these principles was not always easy, and the Japanese government did not necessarily give equal emphasis to them. Nevertheless it can be said that postwar Japanese diplomacy has in fact sought to play a role in these three areas.

Regarding the centrality of the United Nations principle, in the same year that Japan released its Diplomatic Bluebook, it ran for a non-permanent seat on the Security Council and was elected. The opportunity to play a role as a member of the council came the next year. In July 1958, amid the rising political turmoil in the Middle East in the wake of the revolution in Iraq, the United States sent troops into Lebanon and Britain sent troops into Jordan at the request of the respective pro-Western governments of two Middle Eastern countries.

Japan disapproved of the dispatch of troops to Lebanon because the United States did not wait for a decision by the United Nations (which already had a monitoring group on the ground). Japan felt such a move would weaken the prestige of the United Nations and be detrimental to the international situation. Immediately thereafter, however, because Japan supported the U.S. proposal requesting the dispatch of a UN police force to Lebanon, Japan was seen as being torn between the principles of "UN-centered diplomacy" and "cooperating with the free world (the United States)."

Even then, after the U.S. proposal was rejected, Japan worked hard at playing an important role in the Security Council of which it was a non-permanent member at the time. In close coordination with UN secretary general Dag Hammarskjöld, Japan proposed a separate resolution that sought to expand and strengthen the UN monitoring group, protect Lebanon's territorial integrity, and permit a U.S. withdrawal. Japan's proposal was accepted by all of the Security Council members (with the exception of the Soviet Union), Lebanon, and the Arab League, but, due to the Soviet Union's veto, it did not pass. Nevertheless Japan's efforts were highly praised at the time.

The real problem emerged afterward. Secretary General Hammarskjold adopted Japan's proposal and expanded the number of the monitoring group, asking Japan to send ten officers. The Japanese government had to turn down the request, explaining that although there were no constitutional problems, the dispatch might go against the Self-Defense Forces Law and the Law on the Establishment of the Japan Defense Agency, both passed in 1954. According to newspaper reports, a feeling of dissatisfaction pervaded the United Nations at the time. Although it had called for "UN-centered diplomacy," Japan did not yet have the domestic support for cooperating with peacekeeping efforts of the United Nations.

Japan as a "member of Asia"

On the day that Japan's entry into the United Nations was accepted, Foreign Minister Shigemitsu gave a speech at the UN General Assembly in which he described Japanese politics, economics, and culture as having been born from a fusion of West and East, and stated that Japan could be "a bridge between East and West."[30] In this, the Japanese government made "strengthening Japan's position as a member of Asia" an important diplomatic resource for Japan. The Kishi administration put much effort into establishing Japan "as a member of Asia" in Southeast Asia, in particular, and sought to make much use of this diplomatic tool.

Improving relations with the countries of Southeast Asia had to begin with the payment of reparations as decided by the San Francisco Peace Treaty. Although the negotiations not always went smoothly, a conclusion was reached with some countries by the end of the 1950s, with compensation for Thailand, Malaysia, and Singapore being resolved later in the 1960s.[31]

Discussions went relatively smoothly with Burma, which did not participate in the San Francisco Peace Conference. The negotiations were completed in one month, and in November 1954, in addition to a peace treaty, an agreement on economic cooperation was signed obliging Japan to pay $200 million over a period of ten years. (In 1964, an additional economic cooperation agreement was added in which Japan provided another $140 million uncompensated.) In contrast, negotiations with the Philippines and Indonesia were long and drawn out. Although the Philippine government signed the San Francisco Peace Treaty, domestically there was strong opposition to ratifying it without a reparations arrangement. As a result, ratification could not take place until the reparations problem was resolved. Negotiations began in 1952, with the Philippines suggesting $8 billion. Discussions soon ran into difficulties. Finally in May 1956, after the Philippine side yielded, a bilateral reparations agreement, in which Japan agreed to pay $550 million over twenty years, was signed and the Philippines ratified the peace treaty.

Indonesia also signed the San Francisco Peace Treaty in 1951, but because of its dissatisfaction over the question of reparations, never ratified it. Indonesia's situation was thus different from that of the Philippines as it did not ratify the above treaty. Instead normalization of relations took place instead through a bilateral peace treaty. Negotiations over reparations began in 1951, but opinions between the two sides differed over the definition of war damage, the amount of reparations, and the method of payment. In January 1958, however, along with a bilateral peace treaty, a reparations agreement was signed by which Japan would pay $223 million over twelve years to Indonesia.

Of the three countries in the former French colony of Indochina, Laos and Cambodia did not request reparations. In 1958 and 1959, Japan signed 1 billion yen and 1.5 billion yen economic and technological cooperative agreements with each country respectively. Because of the actions of the Japanese Imperial Army and deaths, disease, and injury due to the lack of food during the war, Vietnam (South Vietnam) continued to request reparations. Negotiations went on for years, and an agreement was finally reached in May 1959 in which Japan agreed to pay $39 million over a five-year period.

All of Japan's reparations were in the form of the provision of products and services. The Japanese government placed orders with Japanese companies for goods and services amounting to the total cost of the reparations, and provided them to the receiving countries. Japan's reparations to the countries of Southeast Asia were thus an effective way to promote Japan's economic recovery in that they led to domestic production and exports through government support. In addition, reparations to Southeast Asia were in line with the expectations of both the U.S. and the Japanese governments, which sought to tie Japan's economy with that of Southeast Asia and help to stabilize the region. Both the Japanese government and the U.S. government viewed Southeast Asia as an important market and source of resources for the Japanese economy, which had lost the ability to trade with the Chinese mainland.

Prime Minister Kishi saw a diplomatic opportunity for Japan in the strengthening of economic ties with Southeast Asia. At the time of his visit to the United States in 1957, he announced his concept for a Southeast Asia Development Fund, premised on a large U.S. financial contribution, during the distribution of which Japan would provide its expertise.[32] Simply put, this proposal envisioned funds being provided by the United States with Japan providing technology and know-how in order to develop Southeast Asian labor and resources. Kishi believed that if Japan could assume a leadership role in Southeast Asian development, it would put Japan and the United States on more equal terms. He put much energy into realizing this vision and undertook two visits to Southeast Asia in the year he became prime minister. In fact his first trip abroad as prime minister was to Southeast Asia, even before he visited the United States.

Of course calling oneself "equal" while asking America for money to realize one's goal was unrealistic. Indeed the U.S. government was cool to Kishi's proposal, and the reaction of the countries of Southeast Asia was also not favorable. Yet it is not a mistake to say that Southeast Asia's economic development was a promising theme for developing a new frontier in Japanese diplomacy, enabling Japan to play a diplomatic role as a "member of Asia" while maintaining its policy of "cooperation with the free world."

The U.S. government finally became aware of the merits of Japan's policy of "strengthening its position as a member of Asia" while continuing as a part of the Free World. As seen in the success of the 1955 Bandung Conference, a meeting of representatives of twenty-nine African and Asian nations to promote economic and cultural cooperation and to oppose colonialism, it was becoming clear that the future movements of the countries of Asia and Africa could greatly influence the direction of the Cold War. In the middle of this, Japan's participation in the meeting as a member of the Free World was a good example for the countries of Asia and Africa showing the merits of cooperating with the free world. In the U.S.–Japan policy document NSC 6008/1, adopted in 1960 by the National Security Council, American policymakers came to recognize that Japan's contribution to the free world was through its economic might and through its "moderating influence" on the countries of Asia and Africa.[33]

In this way, Southeast Asia was a relatively easy place for Japan to promote its principle of "strengthening its position as a member of Asia." For Japan to truly become "a member of Asia," however, several difficult issues still had to be overcome, including in particular the improvement of relations with neighboring Korea (see Chapter 3) and China (see below, and Chapter 4).

Japan–China exchange at private levels

Following the San Francisco Peace Treaty, there were movements to improve relations between Japan and the People's Republic of China through expanding exchanges at private and popular levels in the economic and cultural spheres.[34] Often called a "building block" (*tsumiage*) style, these movements were the most realistic foreign policy for Sino-Japanese relations at the time given the constraints of the Japan–Taiwan Peace Treaty, signed in 1952. The Japanese government believed that if political and economic problems could be separated (the so-called *seikei bunri*, or "separation of politics and economics"), then trade relations with the mainland, which took in a large portion of Japan's exports in the prewar period, could be expanded. Likewise, the Chinese government was able to accept this approach by the Japanese government and in fact chose to cooperate, in light of the international thawing of relations following the Korean War and the need for domestic economic reconstruction. Between 1952 and 1958 private trade organizations from both countries signed four different trade agreements.

Private exchange between Japan and China proceeded during these years and trade expanded, but the amount of trade, even in a good year, remained under 3 percent of overall Japanese trade. One reason had to do with the U.S.-led COCOM (Co-ordinating Committee for Export Control to the Communist Bloc), which limited trade with China. Because there were secret understandings between the United States and Japan, the latter's trade with China was further restricted. Some in the U.S. government believed that in order to help Japan's economy as well as to accelerate domestic changes in China, increased trade between Japan and China was desirable. Until about the middle of 1957, however, Japan's trade with China was subject to controls tighter and more disadvantageous than those of other Western countries vis-à-vis East European countries and the Soviet Union because of the anti-China policies of the United States.

Nevertheless, even if there were no export restrictions due to strategic concerns, it is highly unlikely that Japan's trade with China would have expanded greatly. China, under its communist system, was undertaking heavy industrialization, and did not attempt to follow in the footsteps of prewar Japan, which bought resources cheaply and sold finished consumer products for a higher price. Within the Japanese government as well as the U.S. government, it was felt that even if China were to change and open itself to the West, Sino-Japanese trade would not have the same significance that it had in the prewar period.

Relations between Japan and China took a turn for the worse in 1958 under the Kishi administration. Initially, the Chinese government took a wait-and-see attitude with regard to Prime Minister Kishi, who had shown his mettle as the de facto minister of industry for Manchukuo in the 1930s. However, China criticized the Kishi government because of his expression of sympathy during a visit to Taiwan in June 1957 with Chiang Kai-shek's strong anticommunist views and efforts to recapture the mainland. Negotiations in November of that year for the Fourth Trade Agreement between Japan and China became extremely complicated over the question of establishing respective trade representation offices and the related diplomatic rights. On March 5, 1958, the trade agreement was finally signed, but events following the signing led to a rupture in the discussions.

What first poured fuel on the fire was the strong opposition of the government of the Republic of China (Taiwan) to the agreement. It strongly urged Japan not to approve an agreement that recognized the raising of the PRC's flag over the trade representative's office and other diplomatic rights. Taiwan, feeling that Japan's response was slow, ended commercial negotiations with Japan and prohibited Japanese imports. When the Japanese government stated that it would not recognize any special rights for private trade offices including the raising of the flag of the PRC, Taiwan acquiesced, but this time the Chinese government became embittered. Moreover, as China and Japan exchanged accusations, a young Japanese rightist tore down a PRC flag on display during a Chinese goods fair at a department store in Nagasaki on May 2, 1958, triggering the so-called Nagasaki (Chinese) flag incident. The Japanese government took the position that since it did not recognize the PRC, it could not recognize its flag, further angering the Chinese government. On May 11, the Chinese Foreign Office announced that all economic and cultural exchanges with Japan would be stopped.

For several years (until the signing of a new trade agreement in late 1962, as discussed in Chapter 3), relations between Japan and China were stalemated. Although some of the blame may rest with the Kishi cabinet's China policy, the fact that during this time, China, confident in both its domestic and its foreign affairs, was adopting a more aggressive line cannot be ignored. As seen in Mao Tse-tung's famous speech in the autumn of 1957 in which he stated that "the East is prevailing over the West," Chinese leaders were exhilarated by the Soviet Union's scientific successes (such as the successful launching of the Sputnik satellite in October) and believed that the global balance in the Cold War was turning in favor of the East. The economic recession that began in 1958 in the United States, moreover, was seen as a sign of a crisis in capitalism. Amid this, China began to adopt a more hard-line posture abroad, as demonstrated by its actions during the Taiwan Strait crisis of 1958, and domestically through its Great Leap Forward policies aimed at rapid communalization. These actions provided the groundwork for its tough stance vis-à-vis the Kishi cabinet.

Following the downturn in Sino-Japanese relations in 1958, the Chinese government began to take the position that politics and economics were indivisible and that economic exchange should be subordinated to politics. This became clear in the "three political principles" policy of August 1958, in which the Chinese government announced that in order for Sino-Japanese relations to be restored, three conditions would have to be met: (1) Japan had to stop viewing China as an enemy; (2) Japan could not be involved in attempts to create two Chinas; (3) Japan should not attempt to prevent the normalization of relations with China. The Chinese government's antagonism toward the Kishi government, which was seen as opposing those principles, grew, and China began to launch heavy criticism of the revision of the security treaty that the Kishi cabinet was then undertaking.

Security treaty revision

Relating to the three principles of Japanese diplomacy, the Kishi cabinet's most successful diplomatic effort was that of "cooperating with the free world (the United States)." It succeeded in firming up Japan–U.S. cooperation through the revision of the Japan–U.S. Security Treaty. That success was significant. Kishi, the politician, is often discussed in the context of the security treaty revision. But in fact the realization of the treaty revision was America's initiative.[35]

The U.S. government began preparing for the revision of the security treaty in 1958, three years after Dulles first turned down Shigemitsu's proposal. During this time, Japan had yet to increase its defense ability to any considerable degree and there was little enthusiasm for revising the constitution. Nevertheless, the American government took up treaty revisions.

One reason had to do with the existence of Kishi Nobusuke. The U.S. government, in addition to giving high praise for Kishi's political ability for arranging the merger of the conservatives in 1955 and strengthening the political base of the LDP, also appreciated his pro-U.S., anticommunist stance. The U.S. government welcomed Kishi as prime minister, who signaled the return of strong leadership to Japan after many years without it. When Kishi approached the United States to request the reexamination of the security treaty in order to make it more equal (as Shigemitsu had done), the U.S. government now had to respond in a more forthright way.

Kishi however had witnessed firsthand Dulles's rejection of Shigemitsu's request, and was cautious with regard to "revising" the security treaty. Kishi was a far more realistic politician than Shigemitsu and would not call without much preparation for a mutual security treaty in which Japan would be responsible for defending U.S. territory by sending troops abroad. What Kishi requested with regard to the security treaty, when he visited the United States in 1957 under the slogan of the "new era of Japan–U.S. relations," was partial "adjustments" through supplementary arrangements. Specifically, Kishi wanted the relationship between the security treaty and the United Nations made clearer as well as the inclusion of "prior consultation" and time-limit clauses in the treaty. (After Kishi's visit to the United States, an understanding was exchanged, clarifying the relationship between the United Nations and the Security Treaty.) Kishi, while responding in this way to domestic criticism of the security treaty, also attempted to lay the groundwork for making an equal and mutual security treaty between the United States and Japan by increasing Japan's military strength and attempting the revision of the postwar peace constitution.

The U.S. government, however, did not wait. By the time Kishi came into power, the American government was already concerned about the shape of the future of Japan, which had by this time recovered much of its strength. Japan was already well on the path to economic recovery, had restored relations with the Soviet Union, and had joined the United Nations. Japan's dependence on the United States, it was feared in some American quarters, would thus gradually weaken. If the Japan–U.S. security relationship continued to be seen as an unequal treaty by the Japanese public, then Japan might attempt to break with the United States and pursue neutralist policies.

Several incidents before and during 1958 caused this concern within the U.S. government to increase. The successful launching of the Sputnik satellite, boosting the self-confidence of the Soviet Union and the socialist camp, was one example. Within Japan, a great debate, provoked by fears of nuclear weapons and the missile age, emerged over the dangers of militarily aligning itself with either the United States or the Soviet Union. Moreover, U.S. base-related problems, such as seen in the Girard incident of 1957, greatly inflamed public opinion.[36]

The United States, on the other hand, became most concerned about the Okinawa problem. Beginning in 1956, the so-called island-wide protests, in which Okinawan anti-base and anti-American feelings rose, followed the forced expropriations of land for military use. The results of the January 12, 1958, Naha mayoral election held during this time were a shock to the U.S. authorities. The candidate who won, Kaneshi Saiichi of Minren (Liaison Council for the Protection of Democracy), was seen as being more anti-American than his rival, and was supported by the former mayor, Senaga Kamejiro, a politician with communist leanings who was removed by U.S. military authorities because of his political views.

The degree of the shock that the U.S. government received can be seen in the fact that immediately after the election, the American government began to reexamine its policies with regard to Okinawa and Japan. At the core of this review was the serious consideration given by Dulles to return partial administration over Okinawa to Japan. The proposal by Dulles and his staff was to consolidate U.S. bases throughout Okinawa into "enclaves" in which the U.S. would keep permanent or semi-permanent rights, with the administrative rights over the remainder of the island to be returned to Japan. President Eisenhower expressed his approval of this plan. He feared that the Okinawa problem could turn into a colonial problem like Cyprus for Great Britain or Algeria for France. The enclave proposal, however, was found to be difficult to implement early on for technical reasons. The bases in Okinawa were spread over too great an area and it would be difficult to consolidate them into one or two areas. Moreover, it was unclear where to install medium range ballistic missiles (MRBMs) were they to be introduced into Okinawa in the future.

In place of the partial return of administrative rights over Okinawa, the main focus of the review of Japan policy became the revision of the security treaty. It was Ambassador Douglas A. MacArthur II, the nephew of General MacArthur, who strongly recommended this approach. Ambassador MacArthur argued that in order for Japan to be linked to the United States, Japan had to be treated as an equal partner. However, the security treaty in its current form was acting to prevent this equality, thus making its revision necessary. MacArthur believed it was necessary for the United States to propose a new mutual treaty that would replace the old one, which was seen domestically in Japan as an unequal document and one that was signed during the occupation period. He argued that partial amendments would not truly resolve the problem, and that the longer a solution was put off, the weaker the U.S. position would become. Judging that it was best to move while Kishi, who was clearly pro-U.S., anticommunist, and a capable political leader, was in power, MacArthur in February 1958 prepared a draft revision and sent it off to Dulles.[37]

Interestingly, in preparing it, MacArthur referred to Shigemitsu's mutual security treaty draft. However, it was the position of the U.S. government, as seen at the time of the Dulles–Shigemitsu meetings, that in order for the treaty to become truly mutual, Japan would have to assume the responsibility of sending troops abroad—if the United States were attacked, Japan would be obliged to come to its assistance. As long as the U.S. government held to this position, it was impossible for a mutual security treaty to be signed, in light of the unfavorable domestic situation in Japan. MacArthur urged the U.S. government to drop that condition—the major point of his recommendations.[38] The ambassador argued that the U.S. government should make clear the fact that with regard to mutuality, Japan's obligation to America was simply the provision of bases. If this were made clear, then there would be no need for Japan to send troops abroad, and thus constitutional revision and the expansion of defense capabilities were not absolutely necessary. This recommendation was eventually accepted by Dulles, the State Department, Congress, and the military, and would eventually become the main position of the U.S. government with regard to treaty revision.

After suggestions from MacArthur, Prime Minister Kishi decided to embark on the complete revision of the security treaty in the summer of 1958. Having won the general elections in May, Kishi was full of confidence, and he prepared to introduce legislation revising the police duties bill, which would strengthen the power of police, and social welfare bill, which would deprive the Socialists of their own agenda, at the risk of a full clash with the Leftists and opposition parties. Believing that the security treaty would become a major point of contention with the opposition, Kishi, considering public opinion, sought a promise of "prior consultation" from the U.S. government with regard to base use and the introduction of nuclear weapons. Meanwhile, Ambassador MacArthur suggested that a new mutual treaty, in which America's guarantee for Japan's defense would be made clear as well as a promise of prior consultation, was possible. This suggestion was no doubt an attractive one for Kishi.

At the official start of the negotiations on the revision of the security treaty on October 4, it is highly unlikely that Kishi imagined that the negotiations would turn into a major incident that would effectively end his political life. Because the revised police bill was submitted to the Diet at almost the same time, the image of Kishi as a reactionary became stronger, which gradually cast a shadow over public discussions of the security treaty negotiations. No matter what the contents of the revised treaty, there was a strong sense among the opposition and, increasingly, the general public, that it would be dangerous for Japan because Kishi was involved. Because of clashes in the Diet over the submission of the police bill, Kishi's governing power weakened, and early discussions began within the LDP over choosing a successor, thus delaying the conclusion of negotiations. For example, the revision of the 1952 Administrative Agreement was not initially planned, but eventually had to be undertaken due to pressure from within the LDP.[39]

The new treaty was finally signed in Washington in January 1960. In Japan afterwards, however, deliberations over the treaty's contents and its forced passage (that is, without the participation of the leftist opposition parties) led to the rise of voices against the security treaty and mass strikes and demonstrations. The Hagerty incident, in which demonstrators at Haneda Airport surrounded the car of President Eisenhower's press spokesman, James C. Hagerty, on June 10 (shortly before the president's planned trip to Japan), with Hagerty and Ambassador MacArthur in it, symbolized the seriousness of the situation. Moreover, the Kishi cabinet was forced on June 16 to request the U.S. government to postpone President Eisenhower's trip to Japan celebrating one hundred years of Japan–U.S. friendship over security concerns following the death of a female Tokyo University student, Kaba Michiko, during demonstrations in front of the Diet building the day before. One week later, after seeing the treaty go into effect (thirty days after its ratification on May 20), Kishi announced his intention to resign.

Several days before this announcement, on the evening of June 18, Kishi, mentally prepared for an assassination attempt against him amid the surrounding chaos, returned to the prime minister's residence, where he waited along with his younger brother, Sato Eisaku, for the treaty to go into effect at midnight on June 19. This lonely scene not only demonstrated the resoluteness of Kishi in the establishment of the new security treaty, but also symbolized the essence of the security treaty crisis. This turmoil was more than anything an "anti-Kishi" movement, one that was against the prewar authoritarian nationalism that Kishi was thought to represent. Because of this, when the isolated Kishi resigned, the heat of the anti-treaty movement also rapidly cooled.

The new security treaty improved many of the defects of the old treaty by spelling out America's defense commitment to Japan (Article V), establishing a time limit (Article X), removing the clause of the old treaty which permitted the U.S. military to intervene to prevent disturbances in Japan, encouraging further economic cooperation between the two countries, clarifying the relationship between the treaty and the Charter of the United Nations (Article I), and recognizing the need for consultations, both prior and after, between the two governments over security matters (Articles IV, VI).[40] Moreover, the Administrative Agreement, which spelled out the details of base arrangements, was revised along the lines of the NATO Status of Forces Agreement (of 1951), as requested by Japan. There were defects, of course, including the facts that Okinawa was not included in the treaty area (ironically, as per primarily Japan's requests) and the promise of "prior consultation" was left somewhat vague. However, the new treaty removed items from the old treaty that inflamed Japanese nationalism and allowed it to take a more equitable shape appropriate for a relationship between two sovereign states.

Although it has been called a new treaty, in essence the basic structure of the earlier security treaty did not change. Japan continued to provide bases to the United States and the American troops on those bases continued to protect Japan. Japan was not obligated to send troops abroad. Moreover, the new treaty was not a mutual security treaty between equals, in which America would come to Japan's aid if the latter were attacked and Japan would come to America's aid if the United States were attacked. On this point, through the establishment in a very limited way of a joint defense area ("territories under the administration of Japan"), the appearance of the United States and Japan "act[ing] to meet the common danger" was created, but even in this narrow joint defense area, it would be many years before it began to take on any actual meaning. Moreover, because the Japanese government did not explain Japan's actions for joint defense in the context of the right to collective self-defense, the responsibility of joint defense remains not entirely clear theoretically.

Nevertheless, the United States' agreement to work out a new mutual security treaty, which was superficially among equals in that America accepted the need to publicly guarantee Japan's defense and to agree to new conditions of base use in Japan, meant that the U.S. government had come to accept the views of the Foreign Ministry at the time of concluding the original treaty. In that sense, through the revision of the security treaty, Japan was able to revise the bilateral security arrangement (which formed the basis of postwar Japan's diplomatic structure) in a way satisfactory to itself.

The meaning of the security treaty revision

Although the revisions to the security treaty were mostly cosmetic in nature, they did have a major impact politically. Through these changes, the security treaty became more acceptable to the Japanese people. Moreover, because the security treaty became a mutual one without having to revise the constitution, the security treaty and the constitution could now coexist more easily, and this revision likely helped to establish the acceptance of both the security treaty and the constitution by the Japanese public. Through the revision of the security treaty, the Yoshida line, which saw Japan focusing on economic growth and leaving security affairs to the United States, became even more firmly established. In fact, Japan in the 1960s, led by the cabinets of Ikeda Hayato and Sato Eisaku, two of Yoshida's disciples, was able to concentrate on high economic growth while keeping a distance from the unstable political developments in Asia, thanks to its being under the security umbrella of the Japan–U.S. bilateral security treaty, as will be discussed in Chapter 3.

Notes

1 For discussions on the conclusion of the San Francisco Peace Treaty and the Japan–U.S. Security Treaty, see Nishimura Kumao, *San Furanshisuko Heiwa Joyaku*; Hosoya Chihiro, *San Furanshisuko Kowa e no Michi* (The Road to the San Francisco Peace Treaty) (Tokyo: Chuo Koronsha, 1984); Michael M. Yoshitsu, *Japan and the San Francisco Peace Settlement* (New York: Columbia University Press, 1983); Igarashi Takeshi, *Sengo Nichibei Kankei no Keisei: Kowa, Anpo to Reisengo no Shiten ni Tatte* (The Formation of the Postwar Japan–U.S. relationship: From the Perspective of the Peace treaty, Security Treaty, and After the Cold War) (Tokyo: Kodansha Gakujutsu Bunko, 1995); Sakamoto Kazuya, *Nichibei Domei no Kizuna: Anpo Joyaku to Sogosei no Mosaku* (The Bonds of the Japan–U.S. Alliance: The Japan–U.S. Security Treaty and the Search for Mutuality) (Tokyo: Yuhikaku, 2000), chap. 1. In addition, the Japanese Foreign Ministry has opened its diplomatic records of documents more than thirty years old seventeen times since 1976. These documents can be viewed at the Diplomatic Records Office in Tokyo (www.mofa.go.jp/mofaj/annai/honsho/shiryo/). Many of the records relating to the San Francisco Peace Treaty were made available in the 7th Opening in 1982. After that, thanks to the establishment of the Joho Kokaiho (Freedom of Information Act) in 2001, some 3,000 additional documents are now available. These new documents have been compiled in a five-volume series edited by the Foreign Ministry entitled *Heiwa Joyaku no Teiketsu ni Kansuru Choso* (Records on the Conclusion of the Peace Treaty) and published in 2002. As a result of this recent declassification, it is now possible to more fully understand the Japanese government's thinking and actions with regard to the peace treaty, and to compare the documents with those on the U.S. side. In addition, the Foreign Ministry is reportedly currently preparing to declassify further documents relating to the peace treaty. Overall, although there has been a great deal of criticism, almost all correct, with regard to the Foreign Ministry's declassification process over the years, with regard to the San Francisco Peace Treaty, the documents are both voluminous and of high interest.

2 For the differences in perspectives of the Joint Chiefs of Staff/Defense Department and the State Department, compare the National Security Council documents NSC 49 and NSC 49/1. Both documents are in *Foreign Relations of the United States* (Hereafter, *FRUS*), *1949*, vol. 7 (Washington, D.C.: Government Printing Office, 1976), pp. 773–77, 1138–49.

3 William J. Sebald, *With MacArthur in Japan: A Personal History of the Occupation* (New York: W. W. Norton and Co., 1965), p 257.

4 NSC 60/1 can be found in "Memorandum for the President, Enclosure to Letter from Secretary of State to the Secretary of Defense (September 7, 1950)," *FRUS*, 1950, vol. 6 (Washington, D.C.: Government Printing Office, 1976), pp. 1293–96.

5 Details of the discussions can be found in the Foreign Ministry-edited *Heiwa Joyaku no Teiketsu ni Kansuru Choso*, vol. 1, ed. Foreign Ministry (Tokyo: Foreign Ministry, 2002), pp. 572–608.

6 "Wagaho Kenkai" (Suggested agenda), *Heiwa Joyaku no Teiketsu ni Kansuru Choso*, vol. 3, pp. 145–49. The Japanese title literally means "our views," but the Foreign Ministry gave the document at the time the English title "suggested agenda."

7 "Anzen Hosho ni Kansuru Nichibei Joyaku Setsumeisho" (An Explanation of the Japan–U.S. Treaty on Security), *Heiwa Joyaku no Teiketsu ni Kansuru Chosho*, vol. 1, pp. 684–88.

8 "Initial Steps for Rearmament Program (February 3, 1950)," *Heiwa Joyaku no Teiketsu ni Kansuru Chosho*, vol. 2, p. 192.

9 Nishimura Kumao, *Anzen Hosho Joyakuron* (Treatise on the Security Treaty), (Tokyo: Jiji Tsushinsha, 1959), pp. 16–17. This book was republished as Nishimura Kumao, *San Furanshisuko Heiwa Joyaku Nichibei Anpo Joyaku* (The San Francisco Peace Treaty and Japan–U.S. Security Treaty) (Tokyo: Chuko Bunko, 1999), pp. 21–22.

10 Nishimura, *San Furanshisuko Heiwa Joyaku Nichibei Anpo Joyaku*, p. 37.

11 "The Prime Minister of Japan (Yoshida) to the Consultant to the Secretary (December 24, 1951)," *FRUS*, 1951, vol. 6 (Washington, D.C.: Government Printing Office, 1977), pp. 1466–67.

12 For more on this, see Eldridge, *The Origins of the Bilateral Okinawa Problem*, particularly chaps 7 and 8.

13 For the JCS plans, see "Memorandum by the Joint Chiefs of Staff to the Secretary of Defense (December 12, 1951)," *FRUS*, 1951, vol. 6, pp. 1432–36. For Japanese documents on rearmament, see Otaka Hideo, ed., *Sengo Nihon Boei Mondai Shiryoshu* (Documents relating to Postwar Japan's Defense) (Tokyo: Sanichi Shobo, 1992), and for the political dynamics at the time, see Uemura Hideki, *Saigunbi to 55 Nen Taisei* (Rearmament and the 1955 System) (Tokyo: Bokutakusha, 1995) and Tanaka Akihiko, *Anzen Hosho: Sengo 50 Nen no Mosaku* (Security: Japan's Postwar Search for Security) (Tokyo: Yomiuri Shimbunsha, 1997).

14 "NSC 125/2, United States Objectives and Courses of Action with Respect to Japan (August 7, 1952)," *FRUS*, 1952–54, vol. 14 (Washington, D.C.: Government Printing Office, 1985), pp. 1300–1308.

15 For more on the Ikeda–Robertson talks, the memoirs of Ikeda's confidante Miyazawa Kiichi (himself later prime minister) are insightful. See Miyazawa Kiichi (translated and annotated by Robert D. Eldridge), *Secret Talks between Tokyo and Washington: The Memoirs of Miyazawa Kiichi, 1949–1954* (Lanham, MD: Lexington Books, 2007). Also see Sakamoto, *Nichibei Domei no Kizuna*, chap. 2.

16 Ikeda's comments can be found in Otake, ed., *Sengo Nihon Boei Mondai Shiryoshu*, vol. 3, p. 372.

17 For a more detailed description of the Lucky Dragon incident and its implications for Japan–U.S. relations, see Sakamoto Kazuya, "Kakuheiki to Nichibei Kankei: Bikini Jiken no Gaiko Shori (Nuclear Weapons and Japan–U.S. Relations: The Bikini incident and its Diplomatic Resolution)," in *Nenpo Kindai Nihon Kenkyu 16: Sengo Gaiko no Keisei* (Research on Modern Japan, vol. 16: The Formation of Postwar Diplomacy) (Tokyo: Yamakawa Shuppansha, 1994), pp. 243–71.

18 For more on this point, see Ishii Osamu, *Reisen to Nichibei Kankei: Paatonaashippu no Keisei* (The Cold War and Japan–U.S. Relations: The Formation of a Partnership) (Tokyo: Japan Times, 1989), chap. 6 and Sakamoto, *Nichibei Domei no Kizuna*, chap. 2.

19 "NSC 5516/1, U.S. Policy toward Japan (April 9, 1955)," *FRUS, 1955–1957*, vol. 23 (Washington, D.C.: Government Printing Office, 1991), Pt. 1, pp. 52–62.

20 For more on Yoshida, see the classic study of him by Kosaka Masataka, *Saisho Yoshida Shigeru* (Prime Minister Yoshida Shigeru) (Tokyo: Chuko Sosho, 1968). For more on Yoshida's thinking and actions, his memoirs *Kaiso Junen* (published by Shinchosha in 1957 and in English posthumously by Greenwood Press in 1973 as *The Yoshida Memoirs: The Story of Japan in Crisis*).

21 For an examination of the Hatoyama administration's negotiations with the Soviet Union, see Tanaka Takahiko, *Nisso Kokko Kaifuku no Shiteki Kenkyu: Sengo Nisso Kankei no Kiten, 1945–1956* (Historical Research on the Restoration of Relations between Japan and the Soviet Union: The Starting Point of Postwar Japanese–Soviet Relations, 1945–56) (Tokyo: Yuhikaku, 1993).

22 Matsumoto Shunichi, *Mosukawa ni Kakeru Niji: Nisso Kokko Kaifuku Hiroku* (The Rainbow to Moscow: A Secret History of the Restoration of Relations between Japan and the Soviet Union) (Tokyo: Asahi Shimbunsha, 1966), p. 157.

23 For Shigemitsu's negotiations, see Kubota Masaaki, *Kuremurin e no Tokusetsu: Hoppo Ryodo Kosho, 1955–1983* (Special Emissary to the Kremlin: Negotiations over the Northern Territories, 1955–83) (Tokyo: Bungei Shunjusha, 1983). The Foreign Ministry unfortunately has not yet declassified documents on the process of the negotiations.

24 Article 26 reads:

> Japan will be prepared to conclude with any State which signed or adhered to the United Nations Declaration of 1 January 1942, and which is at war with Japan, or with any State which previously formed a part of the territory of a State named in Article 23, which is not a signatory of the present Treaty, a bilateral Treaty of Peace on the same or substantially the same terms as are provided for in the present Treaty, but this obligation on the part of Japan will expire three years after the first coming into force of the present Treaty. Should Japan make a peace settlement or war claims settlement with any State granting that State greater advantages than those provided by the present Treaty, those same advantages shall be extended to the parties to the present Treaty.

In addition to exercising administrative control over the Ryukyu Islands, the United States also controlled the Ogasawara (Bonin) Islands.

25 For the background to Dulles's comments, see Sakamoto Kazuya, "Nisso Kokko Kaifuku Kosho to Amerika: Daresu wa Naze Kainyu Shita ka (The Japanese–Soviet talks on Restoration of Relations and America: Why did Dulles Intervene?)," *Kokusai Seiji* (International Relations), 105 (1994), pp. 144–62.

26 For more on Shigemitsu's proposal and its failure, see Sakamoto, *Nichibei Domei no Kizuna*, chap. 3. His proposal was declassified in 2002 in Japan based on a Freedom of Information Act request.

27 Kishi Nobusuke, *Kishi Nobusuke no Kaiso* (The Memoirs of Kishi Nobusuke) (Tokyo: Bungei Shunjusha, 1981), p. 130. For the heated exchange between Shigemitsu and Dulles, see "Memorandum of Conversation on Second Meeting with Shigemitsu on Defense Matters (August 30, 1955)," *FRUS*, 1955–57, vol. 23, pp. 96–104. The Japanese side's memorandum of conversation was also declassified in 2002 as part of the Japanese Freedom of Information Act.

28 "Summary of Japanese Proposal for a Mutual Defense Treaty with the United States to Replace Present Security Treaty," *FRUS*, 1955–57: 23, pp. 78–80.

29 See Japanese Foreign Ministry, *Diplomatic Bluebook* 1957.

30 Iguchi Sadao, ed., *Kowago no Gaiko, vol. 3 Kokusai Rengo* (Post-peace Treaty Diplomacy, vol. 3: The United Nations) (Tokyo: Kajima Kenkyusho Shuppankai, 1972), p. 15.

31 For the background of reparations talks with the countries of Southeast Asia, see Watanabe Akio, ed., *Sengo Nihon no Taigai Seisaku* (Japan's Postwar Foreign Policy) (Tokyo: Yuhikaku, 1985), chap. 6; Yoshizawa Seijiro, ed., *Kowago no Gaiko I Tai Rekkyo Kankei* (Post-peace Treaty Diplomacy, I: Relations with the Great Powers) (Tokyo: Kajima Kenkyusho Shuppankai, 1973), chap. 6; and Hagiwara Toru, ed., *Kowago no Gaiko II Keizai, 1* (Post-peace Treaty Diplomacy, II: Economy, part 1) (Tokyo: Kajima Kenkyusho Shuppankai, 1972), chap. 5.

32 For Kishi's Southeast Asia diplomacy, see Hiwatori Yumi, "Kishi Gaiko ni Okeru Tonan Ajia to Amerika" (Southeast Asia and America in Kishi's Diplomacy), *Nenpo Kindai Nihon Kenkyu 11 Kyocho Seisaku no Genkai: Nichibei Kankeishi, 1905–1960 Nen* (Research on Modern Japan, vol. 11: The Limits of Cooperative Policies: Japan–U.S. Relations, 1905–60) (Tokyo: Yamakawa Shuppansha, 1989), pp. 212–42.

33 "NSC 6008/1, United States Policy toward Japan (June 11, 1960)," *FRUS, 1958–60*, vol. 18 (Washington, D.C.: Government Printing Office, 1994), pp. 335–49.

34 For more on postwar Sino-Japanese relations, see Tanaka Akihiko, *Nicchu Kankei, 1945–1990* (Japanese–Chinese Relations, 1945–90) (Tokyo: Yomiuri Shimbunsha, 1997) and Soeya Yoshihide, *Nihon Gaiko to Chugoku, 1945–1972* (Japanese Foreign Policy and China, 1945–72) (Tokyo: Keio Tsushin, 1995).

35 For Kishi's views on treaty revision, see Sakamoto, *Nichibei Domei no Kizuna*, chap. 4.

36 The Girard incident occurred when a U.S. Army soldier, William S. Girard, shot and killed a woman collecting brass shell casings for extra money at Somagahara, a firing range in Gunma Prefecture in January 1957. For more on this, see George R. Packard, *Protest in Tokyo: The Security Treaty Crisis of 1960* (Westport: Greenwood Publishers, 1966), pp. 35–37.

37 "Treaty of Mutual Cooperation and Security between Japan and the United States," Central Decimal Files, 794.5/2–1858, RG 59, NA.

38 "Letter from the Ambassador to Japan (MacArthur) to Secretary of State Dulles (February 18, 1958)," *FRUS, 1958–1960*: 18, p. 8.

39 On party and domestic politics concerning the revision of security treaty, see Packard, *Protest in Tokyo*, and Hara Yoshihisa, *Sengo Nihon to Kokusai Seiji— Anpokaitei no Seiji Rikigaku* (Postwar Japan and International Politics: The Political Dynamics of the Revision of the Security Treaty) (Tokyo: Chuo Koronsha, 1988).

40 The establishment of the prior consultation system relating to the use of U.S. bases in Japan was a strong request made by the Japanese government to overcome domestic criticism of the security treaty. The U.S. government understood the Japanese position and accommodated this request by making the introduction (*mochikomi*) and deployment of troops from Japan in the event of a contingency in the Far East subjects of prior consultation. However, because of the strong desire of the U.S. military to protect the strategic value of the bases in Japan, the negotiations did not proceed smoothly, and it appears that a number of secret understandings were reached to resolve the issue. As many public statements to date have suggested, vessels carrying nuclear weapons that entered Japanese ports were not covered by the prior consultation clause due to a secret understanding between the U.S. and Japanese governments. In addition to this issue, recently declassified U.S. documents show that an understanding was reached to the effect that U.S. military operations based in Japan at the time of a contingency on the Korean peninsula, if done as a part of United Nations forces, would not necessarily be subject to prior consultation. Publicly, however, the Japanese government in testimony to the Diet stated that even such a situation *would* be a matter of prior consultation. For more, see Sakamoto Kazuya, "Nichibei Anpo Jizen Kyogisei no Seiritsu o Meguru Gimon: Chosen Hanto Yuji no Baai (A Question on the Establishment of the Prior

Consultation System in the Japan–U.S. Security Treaty)," *Handai Hogaku*, 46, no. 4 (October 1996), pp. 121–49, and Sakamoto, *Nichibei Domei no Kizuna*, chap. 5. According to documents obtained by the National Security Archives in Washington, D.C., and reported in the *Asahi Shimbun* (August 30, 2000), the explanation of these secret arrangements is made clear in briefing materials prepared for Secretary of State Christian A. Herter for his testimony in the Senate. (See "Description of Consultation Arrangements under the Treaty of Mutual Cooperation and Security," U.S.–Japan Treaty of Security and Mutual Cooperation (Conference Briefing Book), Office of East Asian Affairs Central Files, 1947–64, Box 24, Bureau of Far Eastern Affairs, RG 59, NA.) For the chapter contributor's appeal for a similar declassification on the Japanese side, see Sakamoto Kazuya, "Anpo Mitsuyaku o Kokai Suru Junbi o (Prepare the Declassification of the Secret Agreements on the Security Treaty)," *Ronza*, 66 (November 2000), pp. 52–61. For a helpful explanation of Japanese foreign policy and diplomatic secret arrangements, see Chuma Kiyofuku, *Mitsuyaku Gaiko* (Secret Diplomacy) (Tokyo: Bunshun Shinsho, 2002).

3 The model of an economic power
Japanese diplomacy in the 1960s

Tadokoro Masayuki

Two prime ministers, Ikeda Hayato and Sato Eisaku, each with long administrations, led Japan during the 1960s. The secure political situation, and the benevolent hegemonic power of the United Sates, provided the ideal environment for Japan's unusual high economic growth. Through this high growth, Japan's international standing increased dramatically and would further lead to the reduction in the domestic political tensions. On the other hand, some of Japan's fundamental problems remained unresolved and would become a major hindrance in Japan's diplomacy afterwards.

The establishment of the postwar constitutional system

The politics of low posture

In 1960, while the chaotic situation surrounding the ratification of the revised security treaty and the mass demonstrations in Tokyo and other major Japanese cities continued, a violent labor dispute dragged on at the Mitsui Miike Mines in Kyushu, which witnessed occasional clashes between the labor unions and police. The rhetoric of these disputes seemed to indicate that Japan was facing a fundamental decision regarding "Americanism" versus "neutralism" or "capitalism" versus "Socialism."

Kishi Nobusuke tendered his resignation in the middle of the unprecedented mass demonstrations involving tens of thousands of people in front of the National Diet building. Ikeda Hayato, a protégé of Yoshida Shigeru, became prime minister on July 19 on the eve of what appeared to be a revolution. When he succeeded Kishi, Ikeda first attempted to overcome the deep division in public opinion by adopting a more conciliatory style of politics known as "Tolerance and Forbearance" (*Kanyo to nintai*) and placing economic growth at the top of his agenda, as represented by his *Shotoku baizo keikaku*, or "Income Doubling Plan." In addition, regarding the issue of constitutional revision that Kishi had advocated, Ikeda announced in his first policy speech on October 21 before the Diet after assuming the premiership that "this sort of debate was one in which a conclusion should be reached only after the essential problems have been adequately discussed at all levels and when it appears that public opinion has matured in a natural direction," in effect putting off the question.[1]

Ikeda was a former bureaucrat in the Finance Ministry and had also served as finance minister during the Yoshida cabinet. In his younger days Ikeda had suffered from a serious case of pemphigus for several years, which nearly killed him. Because of this, he rose slowly in the ministry but won back his position in the chaos after the war. Because of these unique experiences Ikeda was unlike many elite bureaucrats in Japan. He was far from a smooth and risk-averse man sticking to the rules and procedures of his organization; he was an independent-minded patriot of sorts, pursuing ambitious dreams. Ikeda was known as sometimes being too candid in his remarks, saying that "the poor can eat barley if they cannot afford rice" and "it can not be helped if one or two companies go under" which, while perhaps truthful, was politically incorrect. The tolerance and forbearance slogan he adopted, encouraging a "low posture" for politics, was not so much a reflection of his personal style or beliefs but rather simply two concepts that had emerged from the needs of the day.

The consensus to be an economic state

Although the path that Ikeda chose was in many ways a continuation of that of his mentor, Yoshida Shigeru, its success was something that no policy-maker at the time, including Ikeda and Yoshida themselves, ever predicted. Unlike the 1950s, the 1960s were a period in which it was relatively easy to settle the conflict over the direction of Japan's basic political and diplomatic path and come to a new understanding through economic growth and consensus politics. On the one hand, the approach of the ultra-conservative traditional nationalists who sought to revise the constitution, making Japan a "truly independent country" or "Japanese Japan," free from the influence of the United States and free to pursue its own power and policies, was in effect discredited. Prewar politicians such as Kishi began to gradually fade from the public scene. On the other hand, the overly leftist pro-Soviet, pro-Chinese Socialist line, symbolized by Socialist Party chairman Asanuma Inejiro's statement in China that "American imperialism is the common enemy of Japan and China,"[2] also rapidly lost its appeal. In the 1960s, the repressive nature of the Socialist authoritarian regimes, as demonstrated by the harsh accusations traded between Soviet Russia and China and the Soviet military intervention in Czechoslovakia in 1968, became evident and further eroded support for a Leftist agenda. In the meantime, the living standard of Japanese became increasingly improved through high economic growth and those identifying themselves in the middle class continued to expand.

Reflecting these changes, a new and positive evaluation of the achievements of Yoshida developed among academic commentators of politics, such as Kosaka Masataka or Nagai Yonosuke, and this view rapidly gained wide approval.[3] The public's view of the constitution also indicated the special nature of the decade. In the 1950s public opinion had been roughly divided between those favoring constitutional revision and those against it, with those in favor slightly in the majority. In the 1960s, however, those opposing constitutional revision dramatically grew in number. Support for the postwar constitution stabilized at a relatively high number (see Figure 3.1). Public support for Self-Defense Forces (SDF) also began to increase from the first half of 1960s (see Figure 3.2).

The people's choice was to maintain a limited defense capability within the restrictions of the postwar constitution. Essentially, the general priority established at this time was first and foremost economic growth, with Japan neither adopting unarmed neutrality and socialism nor returning to the dark days of the prewar by adopting large-scale rearmament through a divisive constitutional revision process. In this sense, Japanese diplomacy during the 1960s was conducted in accordance with the established postwar constitutional framework and spirit. Where political and security matters were concerned, Japan presented a cautious posture in responding to U.S. demands while at the same time actively pursuing its national economic interests. In essence, it was during this time that the model of postwar Japanese diplomacy was formed. At the same time, as Japan's economic might grew, movements for improving Japan's position in international society through the use of economics as a tool of foreign policy became stronger.

The international environment of the 1960s

What made this style of diplomacy possible for Japan was the fact that the international conditions at the time were suited to its economy-first approach. Overall, the tense touch-and-go situation of the Cold War became relaxed, and although regional conflicts appeared occasionally, Soviet–American relations gradually stabilized, and the institutionalization of a bipolar system proceeded.

The summit meeting between President Eisenhower and Soviet leader Nikita Krushchev scheduled for May 1960 was canceled because of the downing of the American U-2 spy plane over the Soviet Union. Later, the October 1962 Cuban missile crisis brought tensions between the United States and the Soviet Union to the brink of nuclear war. This latter crisis, however, was resolved when the Soviet Union made some open concessions (with the U.S. responding in kind later, through the withdrawal of Jupiter missiles from Turkey). The U.S.–Soviet relationship then evolved into one that became a sort of partnership, albeit limited, that shared the common interest of avoiding an all-out war. It was around this time that people regularly began speaking of a "thaw" in relations. The overall reduction in East–West tensions was one condition that made Japan's light rearmament possible.

At the beginning of the 1960s, moreover, Japan was still a small economy, whose need to be involved in the military and strategic side of international politics was still very limited. True, Japan, as an alliance partner of the

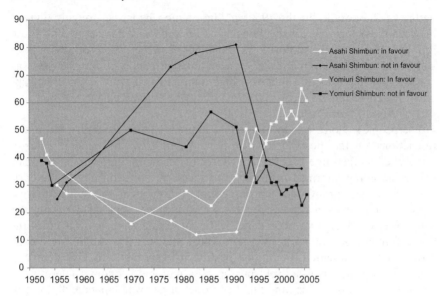

Figure 3.1 Changes in views of the constitution, 1950–2005

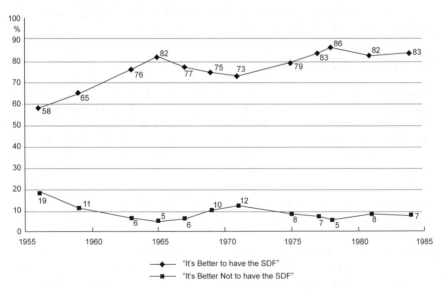

Figure 3.2 Changes in public support for the SDF, 1956–1984

United States, did, objectively speaking, play a role in the Cold War order, and through the provision of bases for the American military, was a part of U.S. global strategy. Were the Cold War to turn hot and the Soviet Union and the United States clash militarily, then the destruction not only of Japan but of the entire world could necessarily follow. At this time, however, Japan's own military might did not have a decisive effect on the world military balance. For example, the Cuban missile crisis caused great fear among the Japanese people, but Japan could in no way influence the outcome. For better or worse, Japan's responsibility in international politics was limited.

In any case, the most important issue for Japanese diplomacy was the maintenance of friendly relations with the United States. America's huge influence and its continued positive interaction with international society made possible Japan's policies of light armament and focus on the economy. The United States did in fact request that Japan play a more positive role in security affairs as a strong and loyal ally, but Washington was not dependent on Japan's military might. Instead, as had been recognized in the middle of the 1950s, the bigger danger for the alliance was a politically destabilized Japan. It was unimaginable at the start of the 1960s that some twenty years later, after Japan had become an economic power, the United States would call for "burden sharing" in the alliance and view Japan as an economic "threat." The youthful, sturdy America of the Kennedy years was in everyone's eyes a strong "empire."

Of course, the conditions facing Japan were not easy by any means. In retrospect, the high economic growth Japan experienced, called "miraculous" by many, was filled with uncertainty for many. In particular, in the first half of the 1960s, Japan saw several downturns in the economy, which caused Ikeda's standing in the party to become weak at times. In addition, while the Cold War was moving toward a relaxation of tensions as a whole, the Cuba Missile Crisis reminded Japanese of the dangers still present. Moreover, whereas relations between the United States and the Soviet Union were stabilized, Japan's immediate neighbors were more revolutionary in their ideology than were the Soviets. In particular China, with its strong influence in Southeast Asia, still did not have diplomatic relations with the United States, which supported the Nationalist Party on Taiwan as the government of China. As Communist China was not a member of the United Nations, it was not really even recognized as a legitimate member of international society. Its testing of a nuclear weapon in 1964 presented a serious problem for Japan's security. China, a new nuclear power about to enter yet another period of great domestic turmoil during the Great Cultural Revolution, was, in today's terms, a "rogue state" then.

The 1960s were also a period when many of the countries of Asia and Africa were gaining their independence and started to show their presence on the international scene. Their not joining either the U.S. or Soviet camps and instead choosing the third way as "non-aligned nations" was seen as an attractive option, and their futures were said to be bright. However, for Japan, which placed the relationship with the U.S. at its core, while trying to be "a member of Asia," the period was pregnant with tension in its diplomacy, particularly when the Vietnam War worsened and the friction between Japan's relationship with the U.S. and its relationship with Asia unavoidably came to the surface. The legitimacy of America's intervention was questionable, and this not only weakened domestic political support for traditional pro-U.S.

policy within Japan, but also made it difficult for Japan's diplomacy of trying to bring stability to the Asia region divorced from Cold War logic.

The Vietnam War damaged the United States politically and economically in an unprecedented way, and made Japan's relative economic standing larger than ever before as it benefited industrially and service-wise, while the U.S. found itself having a greater balance of payments problem. However, it was not until the 1970s before these changes in the balance of power internationally became apparent.

The road to becoming an economic power

The removal of discriminatory practices toward Japan

If the biggest goal of the Ikeda cabinet was high economic growth, then it is quite natural that economic matters would be emphasized in Japan's diplomacy as well. For Japan's economic growth, the role of trade is big. Because Japan is a heavily populated country with limited natural resources and space, it can not survive without imports of food and energy. It was critical for Japan, whose industrial competitiveness tended to be weak and ran deficits in balance of payments, to have access to export markets to accumulate foreign reserves to pay for its imports.

From this perspective, the biggest problem for Japan was Article 35 of the General Agreement on Tariffs and Trade, which allowed the member countries not to apply the agreement to particular contracting parties and enabled them to discriminate against imports from Japan.[4] Through its own diplomatic efforts and the strong support of the United States, Japan was able to realize its long-held desire and join the GATT in 1955. However, while the United States saw Japan's economic development as an important political goal in its strategy against the Soviet Union, the main fourteen countries of Europe invoked Article 35. While Japan was a member of the international trading system, it alone was the target of discrimination, calling to mind the unequal treaties in the Meiji period. This problem was serious and one that went beyond mere economic interests for Japan, a country attempting to establish its international position as a member of the free world.

These countries decided to invoke Article 35 in part because of the pressure exerted by their own textile-related industries, who demanded protection from Japanese competition. They decried the "unfairly" strong competition of Japanese goods as "social dumping" due to the low wages and long working hours in Japanese manufacturing. The memory of "unfair trade," such as the illegal use of trademarks by Japan in the prewar period, also influenced the debate. In addition, there was still hostility against Japan as a former enemy in these countries, the soothing of which required great diplomatic effort by Japan both before and after its accession to GATT.

In the 1960s, however, Japan's growth rate was high, and if Europe continued to subject Japanese goods to discriminatory practices, it would become difficult to export to Japan. In addition, Japan was assisted by the United States, which exercised great influence during the Kennedy Round of GATT negotiations in 1964 (leading to an antidumping agreement in 1967). The United States was critical of the anti-Japanese discriminatory practices of the European states as going against the principles of GATT, whose creation the U.S. had been central to, and called upon them to open their markets. Moreover, the environment at the time was conducive to promoting liberalization because the worldwide economy of the 1960s was steadily growing. Likewise, the continuation of discriminatory practices clearly against the principles of GATT became difficult to sustain over the long term because institutions and norms are very much relevant between states in international relations as well.

In order to bring an early end to these practices and to be treated equally, Japan made some concessions, including recognizing the implementation of a safeguard clause for limited measures against a sudden increase in imports from Japan and exercising voluntary restraints on its exports. In November 1962 the largest remaining hurdle, the signing of a trade and commerce agreement with Great Britain, was completed. On this occasion, Prime Minister Ikeda traveled to Europe to press for a resolution of the Article 35 problem. In particular, in meetings with officials in France, which continued to invoke Article 35, Ikeda requested its abolition. Eventually France and Japan concluded a commerce treaty in 1963, and the problem of discriminatory trade practices toward Japan, which had continued for almost twenty years in the postwar period, came to an end.

It was at this time that an article in *L'Express* reported President Charles de Gaulle had called Prime Minister Ikeda a "transistor radio salesman."[5] There is no proof that de Gaulle actually said this, and in fact at their meeting, Ikeda actively and articulately elaborated on his views of world affairs and the China problem.[6] What Ikeda really desired was not only economic benefits but, more important, the improvement of Japan's international position as a member of the free world and the securing of its participation in the management of international society using economics as a lever, within the framework of its light armament policies and alignment with the United States.

Japan as a member of the Free World

Although the Japanese economy was somewhat volatile in the 1960s, national income was expected to double, with the growth rate of the economy estimated at 7.2 percent. Indeed, during the years from 1961 to 1970, the actual growth rate was a surprising 10.9 percent (see Figure 3.3). On the basis of this unusually high rate of growth, Japan was able not only to remove the discriminatory practices against Japanese trade, but also to participate in the decisions of the global economy as a member of the developed world.

In 1963, Japan became an Article 11 country of GATT, promising not to introduce limitations on imports as a response to trade deficits, and the following year, it became an Article 8 member country of the International Monetary Fund, committing itself to removing controls on currency exchanges for trade and advancing the liberalization of its commerce and finance. With such steps Japan made the transition from a developing country to a developed one. As this liberalization was proceeding, the importance of Japan's presence at international economic forums quickly came to be recognized. For example, the Bank of Japan began to be involved in regular discussions at the Bank of International Settlements (BIS). Japan, which had been a founding member of the BIS when it was created in 1930, lost its membership as a result of the war. As Japan's economy grew, however, its absence from this important forum of central bankers of major economies, became unrealistic. Thus Japan's involvement meant that Japan was again recognized as an important member in international monetary affairs, although it had to wait until 1970 in the formal membership of the BIS.

Opposition to Japan's participation also existed within the Organization for Economic Cooperation and Development (OECD), as well as its predecessor, the Organization for European Economic Cooperation, which had started as a forum for European countries. However, Japan was eventually able to join the OECD in 1964 with America's support. Its inclusion in meetings in meetings of the finance ministers of the ten major countries further demonstrated that Japan had for the most part established its position as an important member of the free world.

In the background to these movements was both the fact that the economies of the countries of the West could no longer ignore Japan's existence and

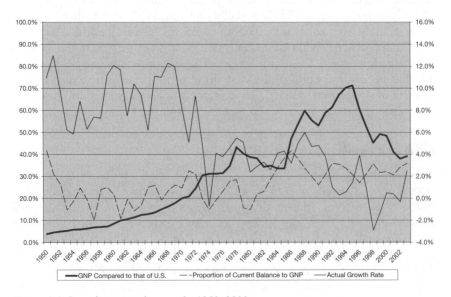

Figure 3.3 Japan's economic growth, 1950–2003

economic performance, and the concern that the United States had that the European Economic Community, which was developing fast, was moving from an open international trading system as established by the GATT–IMF framework to a closed regional one. It was America's intention to strengthen the Western alliance by making Japan a member of the advanced Western nation's club. On the other hand, within Japan, there was the desire to strengthen Japan's diplomatic position by becoming one of the three pillars of the Free World and reduce its over-dependence on the U.S. by deepening ties with the other Western countries (which the U.S. had made possible by acting as a bridge between Japan and Europe). In order to do so, it was necessary to strengthen its ties with Europe and join the club led by the United States and Western Europe.

The symbolic event that gave many people confidence Japan was no longer a defeated country but was in fact a member of the developed world was the Tokyo Olympics in the fall of 1964. Tokyo had originally been expected to host the 1940 Olympics, but the games were put off because of the turmoil of the war in China. The people of Japan were both nervous and excited about hosting the 1964 Olympics—the first time the summer games had been held in an Asian country—and saw this as an opportunity to show that postwar Japan had rebuilt itself. Many Japanese were afraid that preparations would not be completed on schedule, but ultimately the Shinkansen bullet trains and Meishin expressway were finished in time. The Olympics were Japan's happiest moment.

The challenges of high growth

As Japan's high economic growth continued, however, other new economic issues arose. The weakness of Japan's economy at the time tended to cause a shortage of foreign exchange reserves; as soon as the economy boomed, imports would increase, and a trade deficit would emerge. In order to control the country's foreign exchange reserves, the Japanese government adopted various protective measures such as limiting imports and restricting licenses for purchasing foreign exchanges so that it would be able to retain the necessary dollars and pounds with which to purchase imports from abroad.

As the Japanese economy became stronger, however, calls on Japan to liberalize its trade and currency were heard from other countries. Japan's economic policies gradually began to respond to these voices. But the efforts to increase country's openness received little international praise. Throughout the 1960s, Japan steadily reduced the number of the items with residual import barriers, but even in the early 1970s the level of trade liberalization did not reach that of other advanced countries. Likewise, relaxation of the restrictions on flows of capital only began in 1967.

In this way, while Japan's economy exhibited phenomenal growth during these years, the country was slow in liberalizing its trade and monetary policies. This slowness was due in part to the demands of some industries, fearing international competition, for protection of their individual interests, and to the fact that Japan just simply did not fully realize the impact that its own economy had worldwide. The balance-of-payment problem continued, and some in Japan feared that if Japan undertook trade liberalization too quickly, the deficit would grow. There were also concerns that if capital control was lifted a strong America would buy up all of Japan's companies. Liberalization was seen as a "second Black Ship," recalling Commodore Perry's 1853–54 forced opening of Japan's trade with the West, or at best a necessary price to pay for being a member of international society. Japan, despite being dependent on an open international economic system, completely lacked the realization that liberalization at this point was an important chance and opportunity for it to succeed in the long run.

As Japan's economy grew fast and its position as an advanced country was firmed up, Japan was asked by developing countries, whose influence was growing on the international scene, to increase its overseas aid, in such venues as the UN Conference on Trade and Development (UNCTAD). Many of Japan's neighbors in Asia were developing countries. Even if Japan tried to distance itself from the Cold War and identify itself as a member of Asia, or emphasized its being a member of the Free World, Japan would still be asked to assume some of the economic burden. Japan's cautious stance to contributing funds until the mid-1960s was due partly to its feeling that it could not freely give away aid in the face of unlimited demand, as well as being obsessed by "poor country" mentality, where Japanese perceptions of its own wealth lagged far behind its remarkable economic dynamism in the 1960s. At the same time, Japan, an emerging economic power, was faced with the dilemma of desiring to be both a member of the Free World as well as a member of Asia but was unable to fully assimilate into either group.

The Development of the Japan–U.S. Partnership

The drama of a new Japan–U.S. era

Japan–U.S. relations, which appeared to be on the brink of crisis at the time of the security treaty demonstrations, dramatically improved thereafter, eclipsing earlier troubled times. The main reason for this improvement was that the demonstrations against the treaty were not necessarily anti-American in nature, but rather were due primarily to the shadowy, undemocratic image of prewar Japan that people saw in the likes of Prime Minister Kishi. Therefore, if the "high growth" line being pursued by Ikeda succeeded, and his "low posture" political style put people at ease, then popular interest in the divisive political issues of the security treaty and rearmament would decrease sharply.

One more important factor contributing to improved relations had to do with the fact that the American side, reflecting on the treaty crisis, sought to create a new partnership. The fresh image of John F. Kennedy, who had recently become president in 1961, was widely welcomed in Japan. It is debatable whether Kennedy was a greater president than his predecessor, Eisenhower, but the image of the youthful Kennedy in the new television era as someone appropriate for mass democracy made a strong impression on many Japanese. Kennedy employed a large number of intellectuals in his administration, and one of them—America's top expert on Japan, the Harvard University professor Edwin Reischauer—became his ambassador to Japan.

Born in Tokyo, completely fluent in Japanese, and having a Japanese wife, Reischauer was most suited to repairing the "broken dialogue."[7] Moreover, Reischauer best represented the advocates of the "modernization theory" with regard to Japan, which stated that Japan had succeeded in rapidly modernizing ever since Meiji period, and as democracy took root in a new generation as a result of postwar reforms, Japan would likely come to possess values similar to those of other Western advanced countries. Reischauer emphasized Japan's significance in world history to Japanese audiences too:

> In the early years of this century, Japan achieved the status of a world power in a limited military sense. This position she lost as the result of World War II, but today once again, she has emerged as a major world power—not in a narrow military sense, but more broadly, as a leader in economic, political, and cultural activities. Japan is a nation to which others are looking for new trends in artistic and cultural pursuits and for new designs in economic and social enterprise. It is one of the nations of the world having the capacity to alter the course of world history.[8]

Reischauer used his rich contacts with the Japanese, visiting numerous places around the country and actively seeking to interact with a wide range of people from all walks of life and viewpoints. In addition, with Soviet–U.S. relations relatively stable, the United States began to move from its rigidly anticommunist policy. It no longer needed to rely solely on its connections with the prewar conservative governing elite like Kishi, but also sought to build connections with a wide stratum of Japanese society, including labor unions and the Socialist Party.

The catchphrase often used to describe Japan–U.S. relations at the time was "Equal Partnership." For Japan to call the much more powerful United States an "equal partner" was not a true reflection of reality, of course. It was, however, an expression of American interest in changing the bilateral relationship from one of "victor" and "vanquished" or "occupier" and "occupied" to a healthier diplomatic relationship between two independent countries. In fact, Japan by this time no longer sought economic support from America, which was demonstrated by Prime Minister Ikeda when he addressed the U.S. Congress during his visit to Washington in 1961, stating "I have not come here to ask for aid."[9]

The Kennedy–Reischauer approach was symbolic of Washington's efforts to create a position in international politics to constructively accommodate Japan, whose economy was rapidly growing. The attempt to develop its former enemy into a wealthy, peaceful, democratic partner was a reflection of

American liberal idealism. At the same time, the effort to make Japan a strong supporter of the Pax Americana was also representative of America's larger national interests.

The development of a limited defense capability

Although security issues were not highlighted in relations following the security treaty crisis, it did not mean that these issues no longer existed. In fact, important steps in security affairs were taken during this time. First, Japanese defense strength began to increase, if only slightly. In the middle of the still harsh public opinion toward the Self-Defense Forces, the Second and Third Defense Programs (1962–66 and 1967–71 respectively) both had as their objective defense against invasion by conventional means. Although the SDF was still a compact military in terms of size, the modernization of its weaponry had progressed. Defense spending increased from 157 billion yen in 1960 to 569 billion yen in 1970 and showed steady growth, even adjusting for inflation.

Nevertheless, with the rapid growth of the Japanese economy, the percentage of the defense budget as compared with the gross national product during this same period dropped from 1.23 percent to 0.79 percent. Moreover, the SDF continued to be in a delicate position politically. The SDF was not only excluded from matters of foreign policy, but it was questionable whether it could even function as a military organization. In February 1961, for example, Japan's ambassador to the UN Matsudaira Koto explained that he had been "placed in a very difficult situation" when UN secretary general Dag Hammarskjold had asked for Japan's participation in the Lebanon

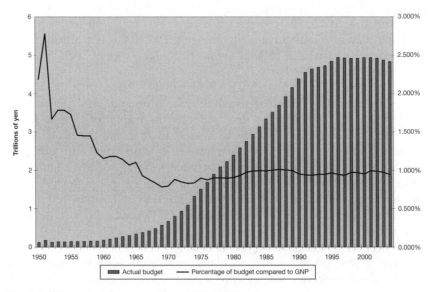

Figure 3.4 Japan's defense spending, 1950–2004

peacekeeping operations in 1958 (after Japan had made a proposal for a ceasefire) and stated that in the future Japan should participate in peace keeping (see Chapter 2). The opposition parties immediately expressed their outrage and Matsudaira was forced to retract his comment.[10]

Moreover, in 1965 the *Mitsuya Kenkyu* incident occurred. This involved a study conducted within the Defense Agency that simulated a conflict erupting on the Korean Peninsula and affecting Japan. Self-Defense Force officers explored what response they should take and what sort of legislation would be needed at the time of a regional contingency. Such studies are of course necessary, but within the Diet this one caused great consternation. Following this, it became politically impossible for the Defense Agency to be directly involved in preparing emergency legislation for many years.[11]

As long as Japan was an ally of the United States, of course, the likelihood of this sort of small-scale invasion of Japan was quite low. Nevertheless, if a clash between the United States and the Soviet Union did take place, Japan would have become involved. Similarly, a conflict on the Korean Peninsula could have spilled over and affected Japan. In this context the defense efforts of Japan were not without meaning. However, the threat perceptions of government officials led them to conclude, correctly in retrospect, that resources should be devoted to maintaining the deterrent effect of the Japan–U.S. alliance rather than focusing on minor improvements in the SDF's defense capabilities. Indeed, improvements in the SDF were, in addition to increasing the national defense strength, primarily geared to impressing the United States.

The Vietnam War and Japanese diplomacy

In the second half of the 1960s, however, Japanese relations with the United States were shaken by the escalation of the Vietnam War. The United States intervened on a large scale in the civil war between the antigovernment Viet Cong, which sought a united Vietnam to pursue a socialist path, and the anticommunist government of South Vietnam. Fearing that if South Vietnam were to fall, a chain reaction would set in whereby one country in Asia after another would turn communist—the so-called domino theory—the United States, over-confident in its own might, under the administration of President Lyndon B. Johnson, began to dramatically increase its involvement in Vietnam from the mid-1960s on.

From the American perspective, the United States was fighting to protect Japan and the free world from the threat of communism and believed it should be thanked for its efforts. But from the perspective of most Japanese, it was a war lacking legitimacy where the world's most powerful country was punishing Asia's poorest which was longing for independence. As a result Japanese public opinion toward the United States spiraled downward, and the efforts of Reischauer to forge a new relationship came largely to naught. Japan's "peace at any cost" type of pacifism and a traditional diplomatic inclination toward Asia and Africa came together in the movement against the Vietnam

War, and this was joined by the innate anti-Americanism of the Left. The anti-Vietnam War movement, which was beginning to grow around the country, became an important part of the student movement. In particular, with B-52s and U.S. naval vessels leaving for Vietnam from American bases in Japan, it became apparent to the Japanese that their country was in effect a participant in the war, leading to a new antibase movement throughout the country.

But even though the antibase and antiwar movements grew, this did not translate into a large number of seats in the Diet for the opposition forces such as the Socialist Party and the Communist Party. Rather, the electorate continued to support the Liberal Democratic Party, despite there being reasons to criticize the ruling party, such as corruption in the political world. The peace movement at that time, on the other hand, comprising the Socialist and Communist parties and labor organizations, had strong ideological and organizational overtones, and gave the impression of being out of touch with the middle class, who lived in cities and had prospered during the period of high growth. In response to the decline of the old Left, the new Left became active in protesting the pro-American policies of the LDP. Like their counterparts in other Western countries, many universities in Japan in the late 1960s were essentially taken over by student activists and classes were for the most part canceled. In addition, the active political participation of regular citizens gained more attention. One of the most salient movements of this kind was a new movement called the *Betonamu ni Heiwa o Shimin Rengo* (Beheiren), or Citizen's Federation for Peace in Vietnam. Beheiren sought to become a pure peace movement, divorced of ideology, and symbolized the coming of a new era for citizen participation in politics.[12]

The Japanese government found itself caught between the antiwar movement of its citizens and its relationship with the United States. It was faced with pressure by the pro-North Vietnam Japanese media to show a pacifist attitude by not contributing to the war on the one hand, and pressure to cooperate with the United States, which wanted to be able to use the bases in Japan freely, on the other. Involvement in the Vietnam War brought about a dilemma for Japanese diplomacy between the two principles of "pacifism" and "cooperation with the United States." Moreover, as discussed below, in order to realize the reversion of administrative rights over Okinawa, the Japanese government had to prove that it was a reliable partner in America's global strategy. The government was concerned that the return of Okinawa would become even more difficult if it placed further restrictions on the use of U.S. bases in Japan, which were extremely important to America.

The prime minister's response to this dilemma was, on the one hand, to seek the realization of actual national interests like the return of Okinawa through cooperation with the United States as an alliance partner, while, on the other hand, attempting to limit Japan's contribution in security affairs and emphasizing its peaceful, non-nuclear policies as necessary due to the domestic pacifist demands of the time. Although it probably was a prudent stance, it was not always a clear one.

Unresolved postwar issues

The normalization of relations with South Korea

Sato Eisaku, who replaced Ikeda as premier in November 1964 following the latter's successful holding of the Tokyo Olympics, was a loyal follower of the Yoshida line—cooperation with the United States, light armament, economy first. He was a politician who possessed a "wait-and-see" (*machi no seiji*) style of politics, cautiously waiting for the right time to make a decision. Nevertheless, in his own careful way, Sato began to address the political issues that Ikeda had not tackled due to his "tolerance and forbearance" approach that avoided high politics. One of these issues was the normalization of Japanese–Korean relations.

South Korea is a neighbor of Japan and, as a member of "the West," a country that shared strategic interests with Japan in the Cold War. Following Korea's independence from Japanese colonial rule in 1945, however, the two countries did not have official relations with one another for some twenty years. The strong anti-Japanese feelings among the Korean people brought on by Japan's long and harsh colonial rule invited this situation. In particular, Syngman Rhee, who became South Korea's first president in 1948, continued to adopt anti-Japan policies, including the unilateral declaration of the so-called Rhee Line in January 1952, in which Japanese fishing vessels were captured if they went beyond a certain point into South Korea's self-declared territorial waters. At the same time, Japan was for the most part insensitive to the strong antipathy of the Korean people toward colonialism, and rather than expressing understanding of the South Korean people's feelings of hatred of prewar Japan, the leftist parties in Japan instead supported North Korea, rejecting the government of South Korea as no more than a puppet of the United States. The Japanese people in general, moreover, were incensed by the anti-Japanese policies of Rhee and thus little support existed in Japan for improving relations with hardline South Korea. As a result, the normalization of bilateral relations was a complicated domestic political issue for both countries. When Japan signed the peace treaty with the allies in September 1951, it immediately began preparatory talks for normalization with South Korea, and although numerous official talks were held, negotiations were stopped on several occasions.[13]

For the United States, the failure of its two alliance partners to normalize relations between themselves was an impediment to implementing its strategy against the Soviet Union and China, and it continued to work at helping to restore relations between the two. In 1960 the Rhee government fell, and the political situation remained unstable into the next year under his acting successor, Chang Myon, who was eventually toppled by a coup d'etat led by Major General Park Chung-hee. Park realistically viewed an improvement in relations with Japan as necessary for South Korean national interests, in particular economic development. Thus on the Korean side a change was seen in its policies toward improving relations with Japan.

In the background of these developments was the attempt to resolve the biggest issue facing the two countries—that of Korean claims against Japan. In 1962 Foreign Minister Ohira Masayoshi and Kim Chong Pil of the Republic of Korea Central Intelligence Agency successfully came to an agreement in which Japan would provide $300 million in economic aid and loans of $200 million. Numerous impediments remained, however, regarding the legality of the 1910 annexation, fishery issues, and whether the government of South Korea represented the only legitimate government on the Korean peninsula. With the exception of the fishery problem, the others were all symbolic—but major—obstacles that required political adroitness.

In order to reach a conclusion to these negotiations, Sato chose as his foreign minister someone who actually did not have much background diplomacy, Shiina Etsusaburo. The negotiations did not go smoothly, but ultimately the fishery problem was separated from the main negotiations, and in February 1965, Shiina became the first postwar foreign minister to visit Korea. Upon arriving in Seoul, Shiina stated that the Japanese people "have felt remorse and deeply reflected upon the fact there was an unfortunate time in the past in our long history," and succeeded in calming the feelings of his Korean hosts. This attempt at improving relations and the psychological mindset in Korea allowed both countries the room to create a relatively loose document that permitted free interpretations on the difficult questions of jurisdiction and the legality of the annexation that the fundamentalists had been clashing over. The draft treaty was ready to be signed.

This basic agreement was seen by some in Korea as "humiliating" and invited strong opposition. In Japan as well, opposition to the treaty emerged from the Socialist and Communist parties and other leftist groups with strong ties to North Korea, who said the treaty was an anticommunist military alliance and would lead to the permanent division of Korea. There is no doubt, however, that for Korea, the economic boom under the leadership of Park acted as a strong tailwind in the successful improvement of bilateral relations. For the United States, which had helped to maintain the balance of power on the Korean Peninsula, the improvement in relations between Korea and Japan was an important step in the fight of the global Cold War. Despite some problems, Korean–Japan relations, particularly economic exchanges, progressed even more in the years following.

Chinese–Japan relations: without much improvement

In contrast to the successful resolution of postwar issues between Japan and Korea, relations between China and Japan improved little during the 1960s. With close historical connections to its neighbor, Japan desired to stabilize relations between the two countries. But because the United States did not recognize the Communist government in Peking and continued to support the Nationalist government in Taipei as the legitimate representative of China, Japan could not open formal relations with mainland China in the postwar period, despite the fact that Britain, France, and other European countries—all allies of the United States—gradually did so.

For its part, China launched its own criticism of the Kishi cabinet for undertaking the revision of the security treaty, describing "the signing of the Japan–U.S. military alliance treaty" as "proof that Japanese militarism had already returned and is evidence that Japan has already publicly joined America's aggressive military block."[14] Similarly Japan, out of deference to the United States and the obligation it felt to Chiang Kai-shek for his government's magnanimous treatment of Japanese soldiers immediately after the war, did not change its basic policy of recognizing Taipei as the official representative of China. Indeed, Japan went out of its way to help preserve Taiwan's seat in the United Nations.

At the same time, however, Ikeda believed that it was unnatural for Japan not to have diplomatic relations with its neighbor, which had a population then of 650 million, and thought that sooner or later, Peking would be granted China's seat at the United Nations. Considering its relations with the United States, Japan could not immediately recognize China politically, but assisting China's return to international society, while maintaining some sort of independent status for Taiwan, was seen as a realistic policy.[15] On the basis of this view, Japan sought to improve relations and expanded its trade with China through the *seikei bunri* approach, separating politics and economics. Although it continued to insist that the separation of politics from economics was impossible, China effectively moved toward accommodating Japan's approach. In September 1962, LDP advisor Matsumura Kenzo visited China, and in November of that year, a memorandum on trade was signed between the two countries that included an agreement on the manner of trade over the next five years and the establishment of liaison offices in each other's capitals. Taking the name of the two negotiators, Liao Chengzhi and Takasaki Tatsunosuke, who signed the memorandum, this agreement became known as "LT Trade."[16]

Behind this development were the relative stability of Chinese politics in the early 1960s and the fact that Sino-Soviet tensions were gradually increasing. China, led by Liu Shaoqi and Deng Xiaoping who began economic adjustment policies, recognized a certain economic value to trade relations with Japan following the disastrous failure of the Great Leap Forward, and some political value in improvement of relations with the West as a counterbalance with the Soviet.

During the Sato years, however, the improvement of relations between Japan and China slowed. This was related first to the nuclear tests conducted by China in October 1964 and Japan's reactions to them, as well as to Sato's support for increased American involvement in the Vietnam War. In 1966, moreover, the Cultural Revolution began in which China fell into a state of absolute chaos and it became impossible for a moderate foreign policy to emerge. Although an accurate picture of the Cultural Revolution is complicated, it was in essence a power clash in which Mao Tsetung, in order to remove the influential Liu from the leadership of the party, mobilized the students and mass public. As a result of the beatings and executions of party and government leaders in public over a four-year span by Mao and those in the movement known as the Red Guard and the concomitant state of paralysis that gripped government organizations, the safety of foreign embassies became impossible to guarantee, and China's isolation in international society became that much more severe. Ironically, the Cultural Revolution, which proclaimed the importance of continued revolution, was positively portrayed in the media in Japan.

Because of the uproar in China due to the Cultural Revolution, Japanese diplomacy toward China, which had continued seeking to gradually improve bilateral relations through the division of politics and economics, became stalled. When the "LT Trade" agreement expired in 1967, a "Memorandum Formula," by which a new understanding was signed every year, was used. In contrast to LT Trade, which had been a window for dialogue for both governments, agencies of both China and Japan responsible for managing the "Memorandum Trade" became a group that also worked at lobbying the Japanese government to improve its policies toward China.[17]

The stalemate, however, in Sino-Japan relations was due not only to the Cultural Revolution, but also concerned with the restraints on Japanese diplomacy centered on Japan's alignment with the United States and its support of America's involvement in the Vietnam War. The question of the reversion of Okinawa made it necessary for the Sato cabinet to place particular importance on its relations with the United States at this time.

Japan's diplomacy toward Southeast Asia

As we saw in Chapter 2, regarding postwar issues between Japan and the countries of Southeast Asia, there were countries like the Philippines and Indonesia that made their ratification of a peace treaty with Japan conditional on the resolution of the reparations issue. Because of this requirement, Japan focused on the issue of reparations in its discussions on restoring relations with these countries. Although talks were sometimes problematic, as in the Philippine case, most of the negotiations went well and were resolved for the most part in the 1960s. In that sense, compared with the talks with Korea and China, "normalization" with Southeast Asia was realized relatively smoothly.

As a result, Japanese reparations during the period from 1955 to 1977 totaled some $1.5 billion, a sum not insignificant for Japan at the time. There was more to this, however, than the simple payment of damages caused by the war. For one thing, compensation became a way in which export markets could be developed for Japanese goods. The lack of foreign currency reserves was severe for Japan in the 1960s, and in order to save foreign currency, reparations were paid out not in money but in goods, for which the Japanese government paid domestic producers in yen. Moreover, reparations had the effect of stimulating the economy because of the increased sales by Japanese companies.

Similarly, in the beginning, Japanese economic aid was meant to supplement reparations, and often was in actuality identical to reparations. In this sense, Japan's economic support in the first half of the 1960s should be called "quasi-reparation" (*junbaisho*). In the latter half of the 1960s, however, Japan's rapid economic successes began to bring results, and the use of economic assistance as a diplomatic tool grew in relevance as a motivating factor. In assisting Southeast Asia, Japan focused on the provision of capital and developing infrastructure, and sought to make contributions that furthered local economic interests. But Japan also intended to develop export markets, and in a sense such actions were a part of larger industrial policy. Southeast Asia, however, was not only an export market, but a provider of natural resources. Thus the region was seen as an important economic partner, and Japan thought that by contributing to the development of the local economy, it would be able to secure natural resources.[18]

At the same time, for Japanese diplomacy, Southeast Asia was not limited to being a place to pursue economic interests. As long as Japan made alignment with the United States in the Cold War its main approach to foreign policy, it was not able to maneuver too much in its relations with China or the Soviet Union. Nor did relations with South Korea quickly become an asset for Japanese diplomacy because of the "history problem." In Southeast Asia, by contrast, Japan could take the initiative using the Japan's explosively growing economic means. Japan's diplomatic effort to bring about a ceasefire in the conflict between Indonesia and Malaysia in the early 1960s was one of the first examples of this new trend. And foreign aid was one of the few areas in which Japan could demonstrate its autonomous foreign policy.

For Japan, which used the fact that it would not participate in power politics utilizing military means as a source of national pride, the prevention of the communization of the region through stabilizing the livelihoods of the people was a positive security policy that became part of the country's comprehensive security concept of later years. While on a trip to Asia in 1962, Ikeda, brimming with confidence as a successful example of economic reconstruction, explained to the leaders he visited that investment in infrastructure and improvement in the quality of its export goods were behind Japan's own economic power.[19]

In the Sato years, Japan's policies toward Southeast Asia became even more active.[20] After the army in Indonesia in 1965 launched a coup d'etat against President Achmed Sukarno, who had shown strong signs of favoring China and the local Communist Party, Japan, in an attempt to stabilize non-communist countries in the region through betterment of the living standards of the population, played a leading role in establishing the Asia Development Bank in 1966. It also hosted a Ministers' Meeting for Southeast Asia Development, demonstrating Japan's desire to actively participate in regional economic development. While similar attempts in the 1950s had been based upon the convenient assumption that American money would finance the projects, Japan, as a rapidly growing economy, was now in a position to pay its own way and consequently to play a more prominent role. In the early 1960s, Japan's Official Development Assistance amounted to approximately $100 million, but by 1965, that figure had increased dramatically to $244 million, and by 1970, it reached $458 million (see Figure 5.2). In the mid-1960s Japan also launched the Overseas Volunteer Corps (*Seinen Kaigai Kyōryokutai*), modeled on the U.S. Peace Corps.

In this way, Japan's foreign aid diplomacy toward Southeast Asia was quite significant in the Cold War context. The containment of communism was the primary goal of the United States in Asia, and stabilization of local economies and political situations of noncommunist states through Japan's economic assistance was very much welcomed and blessed by the United States. When Congress drastically cut America's own foreign aid as the Vietnam War worsened and the country's balance of payments problem grew more serious, there was a strong expectation that Japan would extend aid to the region to further U.S. goals.

For example, in seeking to obtain a promise from the United States for the return of Okinawa in 1967 during his trip to Washington, Sato carefully charted a diplomatic course in which he made the first of two visits to Southeast Asia to show his support of American policies there. The United States, however, wanted not only political support but concrete economic involvement as well. After drafting the joint Japan–U.S. declaration on the timing of the return of Okinawa to specify that the return would occur "within a few years," Sato visited Johnson to confirm the wording, believing that the meeting would be short. Instead he found "the president really hammering the point about economic cooperation."[21] According to declassified U.S. documents, President Johnson at this time strongly argued that because Japan, unlike Australia and Korea, could not send troops to Vietnam for the defense of the Free World, it was that much more obligated to exercise "leadership" in the economic sphere. Tying concrete and particular demands to the question of Okinawa, Johnson asked Japan to buy $500 million in U.S. bonds, provide a special fund of $100 million for the Asia Development Bank, donate televisions to South Vietnam for educational purposes, and build hospitals there.[22]

Japan's policy toward Southeast Asia did not go as smoothly as Japan had hoped. Among the countries of the region were important nonaligned nations such as Indonesia, who, remembering their colonial experiences, now harbored strong suspicions regarding the intervention of outside powers. Toward Japan, there was even more antipathy and concern because of the actions of the Japanese Imperial Army during the war. Indeed, although all nine Southeast Asian countries (with the exception of North Vietnam) were invited to the Ministers' Meeting for Southeast Asia Development in 1966, Burma, which had adopted a neutralist policy, decided not to participate citing the meeting's image of strengthening the "Western camp," and nonaligned countries, such as Indonesia and Cambodia, opted to limit their participation to observer status.

In the election to decide the location of the headquarters of the Asian Development Bank, Tokyo's loss to Manila symbolized the feelings of caution toward Japan's taking the initiative and the concern of Southeast Asian countries who did not want to get entangled in the Cold War policies of the United States.[23] With its international balance of payments still weak, Japan, in order to promote its diplomatic objective of stabilizing the region by raising the living standards of the people there, had to maintain a delicate balance between a development strategy that was no more than an extension of U.S. Cold War strategy to use an economic lever in favor of anti-communist regimes on the one hand, and the abrupt requests from Asian and African countries on the other.

The reversion of Okinawa

Near the end of World War II, 550,000 Allied (mainly U.S.) troops had gathered off of the main island of Okinawa. The ensuing battle saw enormous casualties, particularly of civilians caught in the fighting, including young female students who were a part of the Himeyuri (Red Lily) Corps and who killed themselves rather than face capture and humiliation. The battle of Okinawa was a major land battle fought on Japanese territory, and in the aftermath Okinawa was placed under a direct U.S. military occupation. The island played an important role in America's strategy in the East–West Cold War, and continued this role in the Vietnam War as well.

In many ways, America's administration of Okinawa was that of an occupying army that suppressed of local autonomy and displayed a lack of regard for the concerns of the civilians. As a result, the desire of the Okinawan people, who had felt they were mistreated by Japan both before and during the war, to return to Japan grew. For both the Japanese people and the Okinawans, the continued occupation of Okinawa years after the war was a symbol of the victor lording it over the vanquished rather than being a healthy relationship between two alliance partners. America began to be viewed among Japanese as an arrogant imperial power, no better than the Soviet Union, which continued to occupy the Northern Islands.

The return of administrative rights over Okinawa was the biggest issue on the agenda of the Sato cabinet. In January 1965, Sato visited the United States for the first time as prime minister, and requested the return of Okinawa. In August that year, Sato became the first postwar prime minister to visit Okinawa, showing his strong desire to deal with the question of reversion by stating that "as long as Okinawa's return to the homeland remains unrealized, the 'postwar' for Japan is not over." On the U.S. side as well, there were those like Ambassador Reischauer and other specialists who recognized early on that if the U.S. occupation of Okinawa continued, normal relations with Japan could not be maintained. In addition, as early as 1962 President Kennedy had stated that he "would recognize the Ryukyus to be a part of the Japanese homeland and look forward to the day when the security interests of the Free World will permit their restoration to full Japanese sovereignty," thus suggesting America's agreement for reversion in principle.[24]

The actual reversion, however, did not proceed smoothly. On the U.S. side there was a strong desire to avoid the loss of the rights of the American bases in Okinawa that would occur through reversion. Moreover, with the Vietnam War was becoming hotter, Okinawa's strategic importance had been reconfirmed for many. In addition, Japan's antinuclear policies presented a problem for the United States, which maintained a large stockpile of nuclear weapons in Okinawa at the time. The Japanese government had on numerous occasions made clear that it would not make or deploy nuclear weapons, and Prime Minister Sato, in his January 27, 1968, policy address to the Diet, officially announced Japan's "Three Non-Nuclear Policies" in which Japan would "Not manufacture, possess, or allow the introduction of nuclear weapons." Three days later, Sato set forth a more comprehensive set of "Four Nuclear Policies," including the "Three Non-Nuclear Policies" as well as promotion of peaceful use of nuclear energy, thus forming the basis of Japan's long-standing nuclear policies.

The problem lay in the policy which said that Japan would "not allow the introduction of" nuclear weapons. Initially, Sato's speech was to include only two principles, "Not to manufacture or possess," but for some reason, "no introduction" was included without much serious study. It was at this point that a difference emerged between the two countries over interpreting this policy. The U.S. interpretation was that "non-introduction" meant that such weapons could not be introduced on a standing basis but that the transit of such weapons aboard ships in Japanese ports and military planes landing in Japan was permitted. The Japanese government explained the three principles to its public that the weapons would not be placed or transited through Japan. In this way, both governments probably agreed to proceed using their own interpretations. As long as these three principles existed, Japan would not be able to accept the presence of U.S. nuclear weapons on Okinawa were it to be returned. Because of this issue, the discussions between the United States and Japan on how to reach an agreement in which reversion "without nuclear weapons, on a par with the mainland" (*kakunuki, hondonami*)—the formula Japan desired in order to remove nuclear weapons from Okinawa and place U.S. bases on the same status as those in the rest of Japan—could only be undertaken under the policy of neither confirming nor denying (NCND) the existence of nuclear weapons.

While making efforts to maintain good relations with the United States as the Vietnam War intensified, Prime Minister Sato was able to obtain a promise from President Johnson clarifying the timing of the reversion of Okinawa, which was announced in a joint declaration that also reaffirmed the importance of the bases. Sato, apparently quite satisfied with his accomplishments, wrote "If only Yoshida and Dulles could see us now. What would they be saying?" on November 15, 1967, the day of the declaration, as he visited Arlington Cemetery where Dulles is buried.[25] This somewhat emotional expression reflects his strong attachment to the Okinawa issue as well as his sense of accomplishment at solving the Okinawa problem, which his mentor Yoshida Shigeru left to be done later when he concluded the peace treaty with the allies. The situation in Okinawa, however, worsened. In 1968, Yara Chobyo, who called for the immediate and unconditional return of Okinawa, was elected chief executive in the first public election for a chief executive (governor) in Okinawa, and protestors surrounded a U.S. base.

There was great concern that if the political situation in Okinawa were left unresolved, not only would the use of the bases there become impossible for the United States, but the Japan–U.S. Security Treaty itself might be endangered since either country could announce its intention in 1970 to withdraw from it as its ten-year initial time limit approached. For this reason, President Richard M. Nixon, who succeeded Johnson following the latter's decision not to seek reelection amid the worsening situation in Vietnam, told Prime Minister Sato in their November 1969 meeting that the United States would return Okinawa by 1972.

The "non-nuclear, on par with the mainland" formula was agreed upon with regard to U.S. bases, which become the focal point. Mace-B missiles, the nuclear weapons that had been stored in Okinawa, were removed prior to reversion. The U.S. decision was based on the fact that the Mace-Bs had become obsolete with advances in technology, as well as the change in the strategic environment in which the need to locate nuclear weapons forward had decreased. However, out of caution, an agreement was reached to reintroduce nuclear weapons in the event of a contingency in the Far East. At the same time, Prime Minister Sato also stated that the security of Korea was "essential" for Japan and that of Taiwan was "an important factor," thus linking the Japan–U.S. alliance with the security of the Far East and showing a cooperative stance with regard to U.S. strategy. These statements are referred to as the "Korea Clause" and the "Taiwan Clause" of the Japan–U.S. alliance. Thus the trade-off for Japan to secure the reversion of Okinawa "on par with the mainland" was a guarantee that the military functions of U.S. bases necessary for American Far Eastern strategy, including the war in Vietnam, would not be impaired, and was the expression of political support for America's overall diplomatic position with regard to relations with China. These were generous terms by which to recover territory lost in war. However, from a larger perspective, the return of Okinawa served America's purposes as well. The "military occupation" of Okinawa by the United States had the potential to greatly damage Japanese domestic support for the Japan–U.S. relationship since opposition to the administration of the islands strengthened groups critical of America's strategy. Thus from a long-term strategic perspective, the return of administrative rights of Okinawa to Japan was useful for the United States.

At the same time, the strategic environment surrounding Okinawa was changing as well. Although Okinawa remained an important U.S. military facility in the Far East, Nixon, who had ordered the steady withdrawal of U.S. forces from Vietnam and was seeking to adjust relations with China, was attempting to release the United States from the burden of fighting Communism on every front around the world. In the Guam Doctrine of 1969, subsequently known as the Nixon Doctrine, America would step back to a certain degree from Asia. In addition, Nixon was also quietly proceeding with improving relations with the communist countries. Japan did not become aware of these large movements in the international environment until first of the two Nixon shocks of 1971, discussed in the next chapter.

It is an interesting paradox that the same Nixon administration that was making these grand-scale strategic calculations also linked the reversion of Okinawa with petty political interests in the textile industry. Nixon desired some sort of restriction on the export of textiles from Japan, which he had promised southern textile makers in order to get their support at the time of the 1968 presidential election.[26] Textiles had at one point been Japan's main industry, but by 1970 Japan was no longer competitive and Japanese textiles no longer represented a major threat to the U.S. market. The textile industry in Japan, however, was still a powerful lobby in Japanese politics. Prime Minister Sato, with his characteristic "wait-and-see" style of politics, did not actively exercise leadership to resolve this problem, and as a result the problem dragged on. It eventually had a far more harmful effect on bilateral relations than its actual importance warranted.

The successes and liabilities of the 1960s

It was in 1956 that Japan's Economic White Paper declared that the "postwar was over." By the late 1950s, Japan had recovered from the material and institutional destruction of the war, and prewar elite leaders like Kishi Nobusuke were active again in politics. Ten years later, however, Japan had become the number three economic power in the world, and had moved from being a recipient of financial support from the World Bank and the United States to becoming one of the world's leading donors. By 1970, Japan had become one of the most important actors in international affairs. It was just a matter of time, many observers inside and outside of Japan predicted, before Japan turned its economic power into military power. It was an era in which the Yoshida line—alignment with the United States and light rearmament with a focus on economic recovery—had succeeded, almost too well, in allowing Japan to return to international society and occupy an important place in world affairs.

Japan's rapid economic growth not only increased its international standing but also improved the standard of living of the Japanese people. Through this economic leap, the political divisions in the country were lessened. One result of this was a national consensus with regard to acceptance of the postwar constitution. Japan would not participate in power politics using military power on the international stage, nor would it adopt a line of unarmed neutrality, but instead would base its foreign policy on close relations with the United States. Thus, while depending upon the alliance with the United States for strategic deterrence, the Self-Defense Forces with limited military capabilities became increasingly accepted by a large number of Japanese citizens, although voices questioning the constitutionality of the Self-Defense Forces were always heard. Japan, with its non-Western tradition and having faced a major defeat in World War II, became an important member of the international society without a large military power. This is a success story, which served as a precedent that gave hope to the developing countries of Asia and Africa.

But problems existed with this success story. First, although Japan became an important member in international society through its economic might, it did not succeed in satisfying its newly recovering national pride. Japan became rich, yet this did not mean that international society would pay it respect. Although Japan had succeeded in its goal of catching up with the West economically, the Japanese people of the second half of the 1960s, rather than enjoying their success, began to strongly question the country's focus on "GNP-ism" with the inherent problems it caused, such as the severe pollution gripping Tokyo and elsewhere and a lack of a satisfying lifestyle outside of work.

Because of Japan's dependency on the United States for its security needs, there was a certain feeling of frustration. In one sense, the alliance with the United States allowed Japan to pursue light armament and helped Japan's economic development, and thus the benefits were great. However, with those on the right calling for "autonomous defense" and those on the left decrying "American imperialism," there was a strange similarity in the sense that both sides were frustrated with the inability of Japan to act as an independent state.

The fact that Japanese citizens, despite increasing affluence, did not face the national problems of a modern citizenry, such as the exercise of military power and sacrifice they might have to make for the sake of the public good, would become a major liability for Japanese diplomacy afterwards. Although the Japanese have been fortunate in not having to give serious thought to their responsibilities as citizens and the actions to be taken by the government in times of emergency, and instead have been able to focus their energies on daily comforts and needs, this situation is not necessarily healthy for a nation-state. Japan, under the protection of the United States, has not developed the ability to make decisions and take action on its own and share the resulting burdens and risks. Japan's successes and liabilities of the 1960s would have a major impact on its diplomacy in the very turbulent 1970s.

Notes

1 For Ikeda's speech at the thirty-sixth Session of the Diet on October 21, 1960, see the data base created by Professor Tanaka Akihito at http://www.ioc.u-tokyo.ac.jp/~worldjpn/ (accessed March 2003). With regard to the status of the declassification of documents from the 1960s, the Foreign Ministry's fourteenth declassification of its documents dealing with the Ikeda administration (1960–64) in 1998 have made it possible to examine the first half of the 1960s in great detail. Importantly, the conversations between Ikeda and heads of state during his trips to North America, Europe, and Southeast Asia are now available. With regard to the Sato years

(1964–72), unfortunately, the systematic declassification of documents has not proceeded as quickly. The government's hesitation over the numerous security issues surrounding the reversion of Okinawa is likely the reason. In any case, the diaries of Sato Eisaku have already been published (in 1997) as have those of Sato's official secretary, Kusuda Minoru, in 2001. Moreover, the memoirs of Sato's secret emissary during the Okinawa reversion talks, Wakaizumi Kei, were published in 1994 (Wakaizumi Kei, *Tasaku Nakarashi wo Shinzemu to Hossu*, Tokyo: Bungei Shunjusha, 1994, an English translation was published in 2002 by University of Hawaii Press with the title *The Best Course Available: A Personal Account of the Secret U.S.-Japan Okinawa Reversion Negotiations*). Kusuda's and Wakaizumi's books included documents of Sato's dealings with the Johnson and Nixon administrations. On the U.S. side, relations with Japan during the Kennedy years (1961–63) have been covered with the publication of the *Foreign Relations of the United States, 1961–1963*, but at the time of this writing, the *FRUS* volume for the Johnson years has yet to be published. (Translator's note: The *FRUS* volume for 1964–1968 was published in 2006.) The National Security Archive, founded in 1985 and located within the George Washington University, has aggressively used the Freedom of Information Act in the United States to make documents accessible, and as Sakamoto noted in Chapter 2, the introduction of a related act in Japan in 2001 has allowed a similar process to begin.

2 Nihon Shakaito Ketto 40 Shunen Kinen Shuppan Kanko Iinkai, ed., *Nihon Shakaito 40 Nenshi* (40 Years of the Socialist Party) (Tokyo: Nihon Shakaito, 1985), p. 392.

3 For representative examples of their views, see Kosaka Masataka, "Genjitsu Shugisha no Heiwaron (A Realist's View on Peace)," *Chuo Koron* no. 903 (January 1963) pp. 38–49, and Nagai Yonosuke, "Nihon Gaiko ni Okeru Kosoku to Sentaku (Limits and Choices in Japan's Foreign Policy)," *Chuo Koron* no.941 (March 1963), pp. 46–85.

4 Article 35, dealing with the non-application of the agreement between particular contracting parties, stated:

(1) This Agreement, or alternatively Article II of this Agreement, shall not apply as between any contracting party and any other contracting party if:

(a) the two contracting parties have not entered into tariff negotiations with each other, and

(b) Either of the contracting parties, at the time either becomes a contracting party, does not consent to such application.

(2) The contracting parties may review the operation of this Article in particular cases at the request of any contracting party and make appropriate recommendations.

5 *L'Express*, August 8, 1963, p. 4.

6 "Ikeda Sori Hoo no Sai no Kaidan Yoshi (Summary of Conversations during Prime Minister Ikeda's Visit to Europe)," Ikeda Sori Oshu Homon Dainikan (Reel 2, Visit of Prime Minister Ikeda to Europe), A' 1534, Foreign Ministry Diplomatic Records Office, Tokyo.

7 For Reischauer's background, see Edwin O. Reischauer, *My Life between Japan and America* (New York: Harper & Row, 1986). For his views on Japan, see his *Japan: The Story of a Nation* (New York: A. Knopf, 1970).

8 "Speech by Reischauer at U.S.–Japan Society Meeting, May 23, 1961," in Kajima Heiwa Kenkyujo, ed., *Nihon Gaiko Shuyo Bunsho-Nenpyo 2* (Important Documents and chronology of Japanese diplomacy, vol. 2) (Tokyo: Hara Shobo, 1984), pp. 339–40.

9 Speech at the US Congress on June 22, 1961 (see http://www.ioc.u-tokyo.ac.jp/~worldjpn/ (accessed March 2003)).

10 Tanaka, *Anzen Hosho* (National Security) (Tokyo: Yomiuri Shimbun, 1997), pp. 207–11.

11 Ibid., pp. 215–16.

12 For more on Beheiren, see the advertisement it took out in the *New York Times*, November 16, 1965.
13 For more on the normalization of relations between Japan and Korea, see Yoshizawa Seijiro ed., *Kowago no Gaiko* (Japan's Diplomacy after the Peace Treaty) *vol. 1* (Tokyo: Kajima Hiewa Kenkyusho, 1972) and Chong-sik Lee, *Japan and Korea: Political Dimension* (Stanford: Stanford University Press, 1985). For a discussion of the role of Shiina, see Tong Won Lee, *Kannichi Joyaku Teiketsu Hiwa* (The Secret Story of the Conclusion of the Korean–Japanese Treaty) (Kyoto: PHP Kenkyujo, 1997).
14 Kazankai, *Nicchu Kankei Kihon Shiryo, 1949–97* (Basic Documents of Sino-Japanese Relations) (Tokyo: Kazankai, 1998), pp. 174–75.
15 For Ikeda's view on China, see the record of his conversations with European leaders relating to China issues, November 1962. "Ikeda Sori Hoo no Sai no Chugoku Mondai ni Kansuru Kaidan Yoshi, Oshu Kyoku, Showa 37 Nen 11 Gatsu (Summary of discussions on China problem during Prime Minister Ikeda's Visit to Europe as Prepared by the European Division, November 1962)," Ikeda Sori Oshu Homon Dainikan (Reel 2, Visit of Prime Minister Ikeda to Europe), A' 1534, Foreign Ministry Diplomatic Records Office, Tokyo.
16 For more on the so-called "LT Trade," see Soeya Yoshihide, *Japan's Economic Diplomacy with China, 1945–78* (New York: Oxford University Press, 1998), pp. 79–105.
17 Nicchu Keizai Kyokai, ed., *Nicchu Oboegaki no 11 Nen* (11 Years of the Japan–China Memorandum) (Tokyo: Nicchu Keizai Kyokai, 1975), p. 130.
18 Regarding the historical development of Japan's foreign aid policy, see Ozawa Katsuhiko, "Nihon no Taigai Enjo (The Historical Evolution of Japan's Overseas Assistance)," in Hashiimoto Kohei, ed., *Senryaku Enjo Chuto Wahei Shien to ODA no Shoraizo* (Strategic Aid: Supporting the Middle East Peace [Process] and the Future of ODA) (Kyoto: PHP Kenkyujo, 1995). See also Atsushi Kusano, *ODA no Tadashii Mikata* (Correct Ways to View ODA) (Tokyo: Chikuma Shobo, 1997).
19 "Ikeda Sori Ajia Yonka Koku Homon no Sai no Kakkoku Shuno to no Kaidan Yoshi, Ajia Kyoku (Summary of Conversations with Heads of State during Prime Minister Ikeda's Visit to Four Countries in Asia as Prepared by Asia Division of Foreign Ministry)," Ikeda Sori Ajia Shokoku Homon Kankei Ikken, Showa 37 Nen 4 Gatsu (Reel 1, Visit of Prime Minister Ikeda to countries in Asia, April 1962), A'0357, Foreign Ministry Diplomatic Records Office, Tokyo.
20 Regarding the domestic political context of Japan's aid to Southeast Asia, see Tanaka Yoshiaki, *Enjo to Iu Gaiko Senryaku* (Economic Assistance as a Diplomatic Strategy) (Tokyo: Asahi Shimbun, 1995), pp. 126–32.
21 Sato Eisaku, *Sato Eisaku Nikki* (Sato Diaries) (Tokyo: Asahi Shimbunsha, 1997–99), Vol. 3, p. 176.
22 "Memorandum of Conversation, November 15, 1967," Record Number 83866, National Security Archives, Washington, D.C.
23 However, Japan would retain the post of president of the Asian Development Bank.
24 "Statement by the President upon Signing Order Relating to the Administration on the Ryukyu Islands. March 19, 1962," *Public Papers of the Presidents of the United States: John F. Kennedy, January 1 to December 31, 1962* (Washington, D.C.: Government Printing Office, 1963), pp. 247–48.
25 *Sato Eisaku Nikki*, vol. 3, pp. 175–76.
26 On the textile conflicts, see I.M. Destler, Haruhiro Fukui, and Hideo Sato, *The Textile Wrangle: Conflict in Japanese-American Relations, 1969–1971* (Ithaca NY: Cornell University Press, 1979).

4 Overcoming the crises

Japanese diplomacy in the 1970s

Nakanishi Hiroshi

In contrast to the 1960s, a time of prosperity, the 1970s were the "Crisis Years." It looked as if the Nixon Shocks and the Oil Crisis would rob Japan of the conditions for its prosperity. However, Japan overcame these crises and further strengthened its foundations to become an economic power. In addition, as détente gave way to a rise in tensions in the Cold War, Japan would cooperate with the west as an important player. Yet, despite being well off domestically, Japan's political situation was unstable and no answer to how Japan should undertake its diplomacy as an economic power was found before the conclusion of the decade.

The end of the Sato administration

1970: a quiet watershed

The year 1970, though not seen as significant at the time, was in many ways a major turning point in postwar Japanese history. Following Sato Eisaku's resounding diplomatic success in reaching an agreement with the United States for the reversion of Okinawa, the Liberal Democratic Party scored a landslide victory in the general elections in late 1969, crushing the rival Socialist Party.[1] A few months later in March 1970, the Osaka International Expo opened to much fanfare. Japan was flush with excitement at holding its first major international event since the 1964 Tokyo Olympics. In contrast, when the ten-year term of the 1960 Japan–U.S. Security Treaty came to an end in June, there were hardly any political ripples. Kosaka Zentaro, chair of the Foreign Affairs Committee of the LDP, stated at the Executive Council (Somukai) that "effective June 22, the established time limit of the Japan–U.S. Security Treaty has passed. However, based on Article 10 of the same treaty, the Government of Japan wishes to continue with the treaty arrangements," and no one even raised a fuss.[2] The much-anticipated "crisis of 1970" turned out to be an illusion.

The *seppuku*-style suicide of the well-known author Mishima Yukio following his occupation of the Ground Self-Defense Forces Eastern Army Head-quarters in Ichigaya, Tokyo, in November that year shocked intellectuals, but his actions had virtually no political repercussions. This incident, as well as the hijacking of the Japan Airlines plane, *Yodo*, by the members of Japan Red Army, showed just how far removed the radicalism of the extreme Right and Left was from mainstream political sentiments.[3] Mishima's death on the far Right and the escape from Japan of the *Yodo* hijackers on the far Left symbolized the changes in Japanese society and the marginalization of the "intelligentsia" class who had at one point played a significant role in place of those who were less ideological and more objective in outlook.

As Japanese society and politics began to stabilize, Sato was elected LDP president for a fourth time, becoming the longest serving prime minister in Japanese history. Sato's running a fourth time would have the effect of changing Japanese political history afterwards. He apparently was uncertain whether he should run again thinking that it was probably better to transfer the party president's position to his designated successor (Fukuda Takeo) when he was still powerful. The reasons are not wholly clear, but one factor in his decision to run again may have been his fear that his rival Miki Takeo could win the LDP presidential contest. During the Okinawa reversion negotiations, Sato had been concerned about Miki's statements, which he found to be anti-American in content and an attempt to play up to public opinion. On the day of Sato's victory in the LDP elections in 1970, he recorded in his diary that "the problem for the next two years is how to develop a successor other than Miki."[4] Sato's victory may thus have been symbolic of the limits of his power rather than of its strength.

At the same time, being that vain animal called a politician, Sato had his share of natural ambition to use the return of Okinawa scheduled for 1972— arguably Japan's biggest diplomatic success in postwar history—as his *hanamichi*, or grand departure. Tanaka Kakuei, then a rising star within the LDP and a master of reading others' ambitions and desires, may have manipulated Sato's vanity to avoid tapping Fukuda as successor at this stage. Tanaka knew full well that though he could not win yet, he would have a fair chance in the next party elections scheduled for 1972. Sato in contrast may have decided to stay in power thinking that more time was needed for Fukuda to develop political power. To Sato's great disappointment, this in the end worked to Tanaka's advantage. If Sato had turned power over to Fukuda in 1970, it is likely that Japanese politics would have subsequently developed very differently, much as if Yoshida had resigned in mid-1952 after the Peace Treaty came into effect rather than waiting until his influence hit rock-bottom in late 1954.

Once 1970 was over, the last two years of the Sato administration proved tumultuous. Sato saw repeated surprises in international affairs, not least from the United States, Japan's key ally. Sato lost his political credibility as a result, thereby assisting Tanaka's political rise in domestic and international affairs. Indeed, Tanaka defeated Fukuda in the LDP presidential election of 1972 in a semi-revolt within the party. This election left a deep scar within the LDP and would result in intense personal and factional power struggles for decades afterward. The year 1970, with its relative serenity, marked the calm before the storm and the coming of an era when Japan was challenged continuously by a combination of domestic turbulence and international shocks.

The Nixon administration and bilateral friction

After securing America's agreement to return Okinawa, the largest remaining diplomatic issue for the Sato administration was the problem of restricting exports of Japanese textiles to the United States, as mentioned in Chapter 3.[5] As noted, the Nixon administration placed high emphasis on this issue in part due to the promise candidate Nixon had made to southern textile makers during the 1968 presidential election; the controversy was in effect the result of business lobbying and games politicians play. Underneath this, however, lay changes in the structure of the international political economy. The conflict over textiles reflected the fact that the U.S. economy had lost its absolute predominance and that Japan's weight in the international economy had increased so much that its economic conduct could not help having international political implications. In retrospect, this issue was not simply the first real example of economic friction between the United States and Japan but also represented a case that would become more common in the future of a two-faceted problem: a dispute caused by structural changes in the bilateral relationship, on the one hand, and complex interdependence where domestic interests cross over national boundaries on the other.

Sato tried to resolve this problem by first appointing Ohira Masayoshi and then Miyazawa Kiichi as minister for international trade and industry, but neither man was given clear instructions by Sato, who apparently was not convinced that political intervention could resolve the issue, nor were they able to persuade the domestic textile industry to restrain its exports to the United States. Although industry cooperation was finally gained through a draft voluntary export restraint proposal prepared by the U.S. Congress, Nixon was unhappy with this approach because he could not gain from it politically. He expressed his dissatisfaction with the deal and demanded a bilateral accord on a governmental basis.[6] In the end, Sato appointed Tanaka, who was secretary general of the LDP, as MITI minister in order to resolve the textile issue. For Sato, this move may have meant a political setback, because he let Tanaka escape his close surveillance, giving him an opportunity to muster political resources within the party. For Tanaka, accepting this post was a high-stakes gamble, a chance to employ his tact while risking humiliation if he failed. Tanaka won the gamble through his usual tactic: providing economic handouts to gain support. He convinced the textile industry to cooperate with export restraints by promising government compensation. After a supplementary budget of 200 billion yen for compensation to the Japanese domestic textile industry was prepared, a bilateral accord with the United States was agreed to in October 1971 that limited exports to the United States over a period of three years. Ironically, Japan's U.S. textile exports then stagnated well below the agreed quota. Not only the American but the Japanese textile industry as well began to decline losing out to cheaper imports from Southeast Asia, indicating that the quota on Japanese textiles may not have been necessary in the first place. The textile wrangle did not make much economic sense, but left deep scars of disillusionment and distrust in the minds of officials on both sides of the Pacific, not least in the mind of the American president.

Meanwhile, the Nixon administration pursued policies that had a major impact on the world. On July 15 President Nixon announced that he planned to visit Beijing personally the following year and that his special assistant for national security affairs, Henry A. Kissinger, was at that moment in China making the necessary arrangements. One month later, on August 15, Nixon announced the "New Economic Policy" that his administration was adopting: namely, the freezing of wages and prices, adding a 10 percent surcharge on imports, and suspending the gold-dollar exchange. These two announcements not only represented a fundamental shift in American foreign policy, but because they were abrupt and undertaken without prior international consultation, they took other nations by surprise. Particularly for Japan, the psychological fallout was enormous, and these events became known as the "Nixon Shocks." In both cases, the Sato administration took a hard beating from the media and the public for being slapped in the face twice by its key ally and not being able to respond properly.

For Japanese at that time, the "Nixon shocks" seemed to indicate that the American administration was shifting from its pro-Japanese policy as seen in the return of Okinawa, to an anti-Japanese policy of harming Japanese economic interests and getting close with China. The sudden change in America's China policy, on which it had been understood that Japan and the United States would consult closely with one another, and the fact that Japan was not informed of the change until the very last minute, greatly injured the Japanese government, which had long prided itself as being America's number one partner in Asia. A veteran diplomat and former ambassador to the United States, Asakai Koichiro, had once said that his worst nightmare was "waking up at one point to discover that the United States and China had restored relations without telling Japan."[7] This was in fact what happened to Sato, in that he only heard of the statement a few minutes before it was released. As became known later, the announcement was treated with great secrecy even within the Nixon administration.[8] Nixon's decision nevertheless reflected a lack of consideration of Japan.

It was not that the Sato administration did not have a China policy of its own. However, Sato and his brother Kishi, as well as their underlings including Fukuda, had close relations with the government of the Republic of China in Taipei, and they were exploring ways to open relations with China without ending these ties to Taiwan. At the General Assembly session of the United Nations in the fall of 1971, Japan backed the United States in co-sponsoring a resolution that sought to preserve Taiwan's seat in the General Assembly via dual representation. While this was in part a gesture of support for the United States as the Senate was then debating ratification of the Oki-nawa reversion agreement, it was also a reflection of the Sato administration's attempt to maintain relations with both Taiwan and China.

However, at the UN General assembly, the Japan–U.S. proposal was not passed.[9] It was a particularly strong blow to Sato since the measure had been introduced despite the opposition of some members in the LDP. At the same time, the Sato administration was quietly exploring ways to open relations with China, including using private citizens to sound out the possibility of nego-tiations and having LDP secretary general Hori Shigeru pass a letter to Tokyo governor Minobe Ryokichi, who was to visit China, to hand to Chinese lea-ders to that effect. But China, as seen in Zhou Enlai's meetings with Kissinger in which the former expressed concerns with Japan's militarization and its strong ties with Taiwan, viewed Sato's policy toward Taiwan with suspicion and its response to Sato's overtures accordingly was not receptive. In contrast to Kissinger's visit to Beijing a second time in late 1971 and the negotiation of a Sino-U.S. communiqué with Zhou, Sato's China policy was still stalled.

With regard to the New Economic Policy of the Nixon administration, the Japanese government was not unaware of the need for a major revaluation of international currency, caused by the rise in inflation in America and the drop in its gold reserves. Within the Finance Ministry, there had been an ongoing secret study on the impact of a higher revaluation of the yen. In this sense, the revaluation that took place was not a complete surprise to some Japanese officials. However, to most Japanese, who believed that the Japanese economy was still weak and that Japan could not maintain exports if the exchange rate—set at 360 yen to the dollar—was eliminated, the subject of a revaluation was taboo.[10]

With the announcement of Nixon's New Economic Policy, countries around the world closed their foreign exchange markets. Japan, in contrast, left its open, buying dollars to support the yen rate. It believed that the gov-ernment's control over currency exchanges was strong enough to avoid spec-ulation and assumed that, since America's true target was Europe, adjustment between the United States and Europe would return the yen rate to its pre-vious rate. These predictions both turned out wrong. Japanese trading com-panies successfully abused exchange controls through fictitious trade contracts to sell dollars. In addition, after the transatlantic adjustment was over and Germany began to float the deutschmark, the appreciation of the yen became the focal point of the international exchange system. Japanese officials kept the exchange market open until August 28, when they finally grasped the situation and agreed to float the yen.

Although the countries of Europe were in conflict with the United States, they called upon Japan to raise the value of the yen, and as a result, Japan was isolated on the question of currency diplomacy. In response, Japan attempted to lower to the greatest extent possible the value of the yen to the dollar. Later in December 1971, a finance ministers gathering was held in Washing-ton, D.C. At this time, the United States asked Japan to raise the value of the yen by 17 percent. Japanese Finance Minister Mizuta Mikio revalued the yen by 16.88 percent to 308 yen to the dollar, reminding some back in Japan of the Great Depression, when Japan took the yen off the gold standard and the yen appreciated by the same percentage. With this rate for the yen seen as the standard, the other countries revalued their currencies and the so-called Smithsonian Accord was reached (see Figure 4.1).

This sort of Japan–U.S. friction was a reflection of the contradictions found in the diplomacy of the Nixon administration. America was readjusting its diplomatic policies to match its strength and was seeking to reduce its commitments abroad. Its approach was twofold. In addition to asking its allies to do more, it also sought a kind of détente, in which it would improve relations with its potential enemies to the greatest extent possible. The reversion of Okinawa was a reflection of the expectation that Japan should play a larger international role. However, the demand for allies to assume a larger share of the burden and the movements toward détente, as seen in the rapprochement between the United States and China, caused Japan to be confused. The friction seen in the Japan–U.S. relationship at this time was symbolic of the relationship evolving from a bilateral one to a more international one.

Defense policy and the "Okinawa Diet"

The Sato administration thus began to lose momentum amid the changes in the international environment brought about by the policies of the Nixon administration. This situation was true in defense policy as well. Sato attempted to respond to the Nixon Doctrine, in which there were greater expectations for alliance partners to play a larger role in security affairs (see Chapter 3).

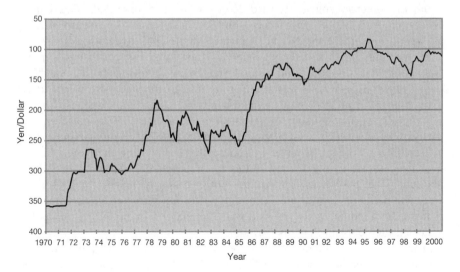

Figure 4.1 Yen–Dollar exchange rate, 1970–1991

For instance, Sato's appointment of Nakasone Yasuhiro, a LDP faction leader who was exceptionally hawkish among postwar politicians with regard to security matters, as Defense Agency director general in 1970 was seen as an attempt to give the impression both domestically and internationally of a more active role in defense.

In fact, Nakasone was the first director general to release a White Paper for defense, which is important to improve transparency both domestically and abroad, and to undertake other actions to gain the support of public opinion, which the Defense Agency and Self-Defense Forces had avoided doing in the past.[11] However, his emphasis on autonomous defense and his demonstration of a strong interest in revising the basic defense policy of Japan brought Chinese criticism of Japanese "militarism." Sato too began to be increasingly concerned with Nakasone's proactive stance, recording in his diary that he had to warn Nakasone that "it is important to be careful in revising the basic defense outline."[12] In the cabinet reshuffle of 1971, Nakasone was not reappointed to head the Defense Agency, and publication of the Defense White Paper's stopped after only one edition (the White Paper was started again in 1976).

The confusion in Japan's defense policy also seems to have been caused by the uncertainties in Nixon's security policies. The Nixon administration had called on Japan to actively take a more responsible role, but it did not clarify what exactly it sought from Japan. For example, Japan signed the Non-Proliferation Treaty in 1970, but in July 1971, during his visit to Japan, Defense Secretary Melvin Laird suggested in statements that he would accept Japan's possession of nuclear weapons. Yet, at the almost the same time, Kissinger was visiting China and telling Zhou Enlai that America did not welcome Japan's expansion of its military role.

Japan's defense policies toward Korea were also unsettled. The United States removed 20,000 of its forces from South Korea in 1970, demonstrating its will to implement the Nixon Doctrine. At the 1968 Korea–Japan cabinet-level meeting, Japan stated that "Korea's safety and prosperity has a major impact on that of Japan," and a similar statement, known as the Korea clause (see Chapter 3, Section 4) was made at the time of the Sato–Nixon meeting in November 1969 and subsequently confirmed by Korean and Japanese leaders. At the Korea–Japan cabinet-level meeting in August 1971, however, this clause was removed, and at a September meeting of U.S. and Japanese cabinet members, Foreign Minister Fukuda called for revising the Korea Clause. During his visit to the United States in January 1972, Sato stated that he thought "the phrase used then did not necessarily reflect things today," implying a change in attitude. Although Sato soon retracted this comment as a misunderstanding, it can be said that the shaking of Japan's Korea policy reflected the confusion of this period.[13]

The reversion of administrative rights over Okinawa also fell into some confusion at the last stage. The Okinawa Reversion Agreement, which outlined the detailed arrangements regarding Okinawa's return, was signed on

June 6, 1971, by representatives of both countries. However, during discussions on its ratification in the fall session of the Diet, the opposition Socialist, Democratic Socialist, and Komeito parties expressed their dissatisfaction with the agreement, charging that the promise of "without nuclear weapons, on a par with the mainland" had not been fulfilled. Demonstrations were held throughout the country. In order to avoid a forced passage of the ratification in the Diet, the LDP agreed to a Komeito demand for passing a Diet resolution on the three non-nuclear principles and further base reductions in Okinawa as a condition for its acceptance. Through this arrangement, bundled with the unanimous approval of resolutions on strict adherence to the three non-nuclear principles for Japan, including Okinawa, and the rapid reduction of U.S. bases in Okinawa, the Lower House finally ratified the reversion agreement. The controversies in this Diet session reinforced the impression that the Sato administration was losing its ability to rule.

On June 17, 1972, following the Okinawa reversion ceremony on May 15, Sato announced his resignation. But it was not the grand *hanamichi* that he had previously imagined. In his final press conference as prime minister, Sato, angered at the press, had them leave the room, leading to a strange TV broadcast where the press section was empty. It was a sad and solitary exit for Japan's longest-ruling prime minister who had overseen remarkable economic growth and the return of the land occupied after the nation's complete defeat a quarter of a century earlier. Sato's exit was a telling indication of the need for a new approach in both domestic politics and diplomacy. Tanaka, who had amassed political clout over the previous two years, dealt an upset victory against Fukuda in the presidential election in the LDP. The agenda of the new administration was to develop a new approach for Japanese diplomacy that could respond to the new international environment.

Japanese diplomacy in the period of détente

Changes in Sino-Japanese and Soviet–Japanese relations

Politics has a tendency to place the actors at the mercy of events. For example, it is not unusual for a politician to fail in the field in which he or she is believed to be strong, and to succeed in their weaker areas. In Tanaka's case, this was certainly true. Tanaka, as he himself recognized, was a domestically oriented politician and used the fact that he was not sophisticated and was from a backward province (*ura-nihon*) as a political weapon to muster support from the countryside. As premier, however, Tanaka's biggest accomplishment was in the field of diplomacy: notably, his success in restoring relations with China.

Tanaka's victory over Fukuda Takeo in the LDP presidential election was not unrelated to his proactive stance with regard to Sino-Japanese relations. The support of Miki Takeo and Nakasone Yasuhiro was key to Tanaka's victory, and his acceptance of their desire for a more pro-Chinese policy was important in his rise to power. Also of crucial importance was the backing of the LDP faction Kochikai, led by his close friend Ohira Masayoshi, who was strongly in favor of improving relations with China himself and whom Tanaka appointed foreign minister.

At his first press conference as LDP president, Tanaka announced that his "Plan for Remodeling the Japanese Archipelago (*Retto Kaizo Keikaku*)"[14] and "Restoring Relations with China" were to be key agendas for his cabinet, and at the first cabinet meeting, Tanaka declared that he was going to speed up the normalization of relations with the People's Republic of China. By this time the Chinese side had also expressed to Japan its desire to improve relations. In June 1971, the Chinese informed a visiting Komeito Party delegation of their conditions for normalizing relations: (1) that Japan recognize the PRC as the only legitimate representative of China and that Taiwan was an inalienable part of China; (2) that the question of Taiwan was to be regarded as an internal Chinese matter; and (3) that the peace treaty between Japan and Taiwan was illegal and thus must be terminated. These conditions became known as the "three principles of restoring Sino-Japanese relations."

In a further step, at the time of Nixon's visit to China in February 1972, China positively spoke of the role of the Japan–U.S. Security Treaty in restraining Japanese militarism. In addition, later that year in July, Zhou Enlai called on Komeito chairman Takeiri Yoshikatsu to visit China and proposed a draft joint declaration toward the normalization of bilateral relations. In this draft Zhou prepared a statement that included the above three principles, the termination of the state of war between the two countries, and a clause stating that neither country would recognize hegemony in the Asia-Pacific region. In addition, China renounced war reparations from Japan. The stance of the Chinese government had clearly become more positive toward improving relations with Japan, unlike during the situation during the Sato administration.[15]

Takeiri immediately relayed this information as well as a memo of his conversation with Zhou to Tanaka. Likely encouraged by this development, Tanaka had the LDP formally approve his plans for a "visit to China" and "normalization of relations with China" on August 22. Tanaka then set off for Hawaii to meet with Nixon and explain Japan's position at their meeting. On September 9, Tanaka sent Furui Yoshimi and Tagawa Seiichi from the LDP and former diplomat Matsumoto Toshikazu to China to relay Japan's views, and then sent LDP vice president Shiina Etsusaburo to Taiwan to explain Japan's position a week later on September 18.[16] Thus when Tanaka set out for Beijing on September 25, he had done his homework.

But negotiations in Beijing were far from easy.[17] The difference in attitudes between the two countries was striking. The Japanese side, while prepared to break ties with Taiwan if necessary, did not wish to see the Japan–Republic China peace treaty of 1952 portrayed as illegal and chose to stick to the legality of it. For example, the Chinese proposal to insert a phrase regarding the renunciation of claims against Japan in the joint communiqué troubled Japanese officials, for the phrase could be interpreted wrongly as recognizing the right of the People's Republic of China to claim reparations against Japan, which Japan understood as having already been forfeited at the time of the signing of the peace treaty between Japan and the Republic of China in 1952. Likewise, Japan did not wish to include the "anti-hegemony clause" in the joint communiqué, as it was vague and might harm Japanese relations with other countries, especially the Soviet Union. The Chinese side, despite its interests in the strategic opportunities of improving relations with the capitalist countries, became increasingly annoyed with Japan's requests. Zhou went as far as calling Takashima Masuo, the director of the Foreign Ministry's Treaty Bureau, a "legal swindler." To make matters worse, in Tanaka's speech, his apology for the war to the Chinese people was translated as "nuisances caused," provoking great anger among the Chinese side as being an insufficient apology.

In the end, the "right" (*ken*, as in *kenri*) in "right to claims against Japan" was removed in the joint communiqué and China agreed to renounce its demand for war reparations from Japan. With regard to the anti-hegemony clause, an agreement was reached on the insertion of the phrase "the normalization of Sino-Japanese relations is not directed at any third country." Japan also insisted that the Tanaka speech was inadequately translated and that the sincerity of the apology was genuine. The preface of the joint communiqué included the following wording: "The Japanese side is keenly conscious of the responsibility for the serious damage that Japan caused in the past to the Chinese people through war, and deeply reproaches itself." Normalization of relations was agreed at this summit meeting. The harmony of interests of both countries at this moment overcame relatively minor differences. Nevertheless, a pattern that would continue to plague the bilateral relationship was already seen at this point—the Chinese side would demand an apology for the war based on the feelings of the Chinese people, and Japan would respond from a legalistic perspective that the issue was already resolved.

The joint declaration called for negotiations for the arrangement of economic exchanges as well as a peace treaty.[18] Agreements on trade, commercial flights, shipping, and fishing were signed in 1974 and 1975, and in September 1974 the Chinese side proposed starting negotiations on a peace treaty. By that time, however, the question of whether to include the anti-hegemony clause in the treaty or not had become a major problem. China strongly called for its inclusion, but Japan opposed it.

The reason for Japan's opposition was likely due to consideration of the Soviet Union. Since the 1968 crackdown in Czechoslovakia, China had begun to state its opposition to Soviet–U.S. hegemony, and after the inclusion of anti-hegemony wording in the 1972 Shanghai Declaration, use of the clause became increasingly directed at the Soviet Union. When it became clear at the beginning of 1975 that China had demanded the inclusion of the clause in the Sino-Japanese peace treaty, the Soviet Union began to express its displeasure at the anti-Soviet nature of the pact.

The overall international environment at the time provided the background to Japan's concern over the Soviet opposition. The diplomacy of the Nixon administration was based on rapprochement with China as well as on developing cooperative relations with the Soviet Union, which led to the period of détente. Japan's diplomacy at this time was an attempt to break free of the Cold War and search for a type of diplomacy appropriate for the détente period. The Tanaka administration was resolved to improve relations with the Soviet Union while it attempted to normalize relations with China.

The Soviet Union as well, watching the improvement in Sino-Japanese relations, began to take diplomacy with Japan seriously, and in October 1972, Secretary Leonid Brezhnev sent Prime Minister Tanaka a letter. Later that month, Foreign Minister Ohira visited the Soviet Union and agreed to begin talks on a peace treaty. Subsequently Tanaka visited the Soviet Union in October 1973 and in a joint declaration, both countries announced "the resolution of unresolved problems and the signing of a peace treaty will contribute to the establishment of true friendship between both countries." The Japanese side interpreted "unresolved problems" to include the problem of the Northern Islands.

Because of the improvement in Soviet-Japan relations, Japan sought to maintain a balance between China and the Soviet Union. Although Tanaka was forced to resign because of the failure of his economic policies and personal financial scandals in December 1974, this policy was essentially continued during the Miki Takeo cabinet, which succeeded him.[19] Miki himself strongly desired the signing of a peace and friendship treaty with China, and sought, despite the misgivings of the more cautious Foreign Ministry, a compromise on the anti-hegemony clause by attenuating its anti-Soviet nature. But because this was just before the deaths of Mao and Zhou and a great deal of political confusion existed at the time, China was not forthcoming in its response.

In contrast, Foreign Minister Miyazawa Kiichi visited the Soviet Union in January 1975, and Soviet foreign minister Andrei Gromyko reciprocated by visiting Japan a year later, in January 1976. In the joint declarations following these meetings, the phrase "unresolved issues" continued to be used, but there were no actual developments toward a peace treaty. The Soviet Union proposed a friendship and good neighbor treaty with Japan in an effort to dissuade it from signing a peace treaty with China. The Soviet offer, however, ignored the territorial question, included wording against the Japan–U.S. Security Treaty, and simply was not of enough value for the Japanese side to seriously consider it. In September 1976 the pilot of a MIG-25, the Soviet Union's most advanced fighter at the time, landed his plane in Hokkaido with the hope of defecting to the United States. Tension grew between the Soviet Union and Japan over what to do with the plane. Not only vis-à-vis Japan, but in all areas, the Soviet Union in the late 1970s began to show an increasingly hardline stance in its policies. In the end, détente diplomacy toward China and the Soviet Union was not consolidated during the Tanaka–Miki years.

Japan–U.S. relations and security policy

The years following the two Nixon shocks of 1971 were a time to restore confidence between the U.S. and Japan. The rapprochement between China and the United States was initially a blow to Japan, but essentially it was a policy Japan could welcome. Moreover, Japanese public opinion welcomed the U.S. withdrawal of troops from Vietnam and the peace with the North arranged at the Paris Peace Conference in January 1973. As discussed in the next section, although there was some difference in the responses of Japan and the United States to the first oil crisis, both countries were able to maintain cooperative policies. According to Japanese public opinion polls, while those answering that they "like" America plummeted to 18 percent in 1973 and 1974, from 1975 on the percentage increased dramatically (see Figure 4.2), thanks in no small part to the efforts of President Gerald R. Ford, who succeeded Nixon following the latter's decision to resign as a result of Watergate.

But because of Nixon's resignation in the wake of the Watergate scandal and infighting within the LDP as a result of Prime Minister Tanaka's financial scandals, solid relations between the two countries' political leaders were not established. Although Ford visited Japan in November 1974, becoming the first sitting president to visit there, discussions with Tanaka, whose administration was almost over, did not bear any immediate fruit. Moreover, when Prime Minister Miki asked the United States for its cooperation in uncovering the Lockheed scandal, Japanese domestic political rivalries became tied to relations with the United States, making it even more difficult for Miki to take any political initiatives.

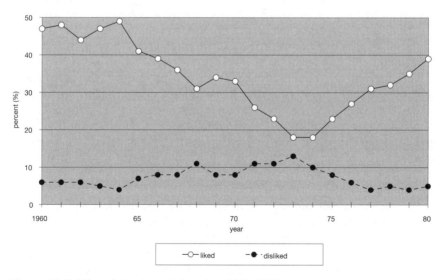

Figure 4.2 Public opinion toward America, 1960–1980

Despite the political turmoil on both sides of the Pacific, an important review of Japanese security policy was quietly taking place. Partly it was a search for a new national identity commensurate with the Japan's new international status. As Zbigniew Brzezinski suggested in his book, *The Fragile Blossom*, Japan was searching for an identity.[20] What role could and should Japan play as an economic power? Would Japan follow a realist path of transforming its economic base into a political or military power, thereby throwing away its postwar pacifism? If not, what was the alternative? These are the questions that would always beset Japan.

At this point in history, Japan defined its security role in the context of its relationship with the United States. In 1972, from the end of the Sato cabinet to the early part of the Tanaka cabinet, the Japanese government formally announced its legal interpretation that the exercise of the right of the collective defense was constitutionally prohibited. Previously, the principle of no-dispatch of the SDF beyond its territory was widely accepted, but there were many uncertainties over what Japan could and could not do in terms of international security. Through the debate on the right of collective defense, the Japanese government defined itself as a uniquely economic power, contributing to world peace via mutual economic prosperity.

The Japan–U.S. Security Treaty was also redefined in this perspective. On the one hand, the series of changes in the international environment, such as U.S.–Soviet détente, Sino-U.S. rapprochement, and the end of the Vietnam War, greatly reduced the fear that Japan would be drawn into a conflict as a result of the security treaty. On the other hand, this situation brought about the need to reexamine the meaning of the security relationship. From the outset, the Japan–U.S. alliance was established to cope with the threat from the Soviet Union and the PRC. Since the drastic changes to the international system in the early 1970s greatly reduced the threat to Japan, the *raison d'être* for the alliance was being questioned. The answer that emerged was the view of the alliance as one that contributes to the stability of the region and helps to maintain the status quo. In other words, the treaty was increasingly seen as serving the purpose of reassurance. From this perspective, the person who took the lead in security policy was Kubo Takuya of the Defense Agency. He viewed the Japan–U.S. security alliance as one that would "shed its initial role of containing communism to one that would seek to deter war in the region and maintain the status quo (not recognize the use of force to change the status quo)" and concluded that "until peace and security were demonstrated in the East Asia region, it was desirable to maintain the security treaty with the United States."[21]

The designation of the security treaty as one that was less about fighting threats and instead to preserve the status quo and promote a reduction in tensions required a reevaluation of defense policy. That opportunity came up in the drafting of the Fourth Defense Program, directed by Prime Minister Tanaka, which bore the title "The Limit of Defense Capabilities in the Time of Peace." This was announced as "Defense Capabilities in Time of Peace" in

February 1973, but the document was subsequently withdrawn after causing a controversy in the Diet over its content.[22] The Fourth Defense Program itself was not realized due to the effects of inflation and other problems.

The issue of the revision of defense policy was continued during the Miki cabinet under Defense Agency Director General Sakata Michita who believed Japan's defense policy needed to gain wide support from the people. He created a "Thinking about Defense Study Group" (Boei o Kangaeru Kai) comprising intellectuals from the private sector and resumed the publication of the Annual Defense White Paper. At the same time, he developed a "National Defense Program Outline" (*Boei Keikaku no Taiko*) that would form the basic document of defense policy to replace the defense plans then in effect. His administrative assistant, Kubo, became the center of this drafting. Kubo saw the meaning of defense capability as not preparing for any particular threat, but rather as reducing uncertainty by having a certain, limited amount of defense. This idea was called "basic defense capability" (kibanteki boeiryoku) and would form the basis of the Defense Outline, taking the shape of Japan's capability to "resist on its own a limited and small-scale attack on Japan."[23]

The cabinet approved the outline on October 29, 1976, but some believed a cap should be placed on defense spending. As a result, the Miki cabinet also decided that "for the time being, the total annual defense-related expenditures should try not to go beyond one-hundredth of the gross national product for that year." Despite the caveats "for the time being" and "should try," this decision was the basis of the "within 1 percent of GNP limit" debates during the 1980s over Japan's defense spending (see Chapter 5).

The change in the meaning of the Japan–U.S. Security Treaty also led to a review of Japan's regional role. The handling of the Taiwan Clause and Korea Clause included in the Sato–Nixon communiqué in 1969 became a problem. Regarding the Taiwan Clause, the Japanese government expressed the view that its meaning had changed with the Sino-U.S. rapprochement. In November 1972 Foreign Minister Ohira stated in the Diet that the clause was predicated on an understanding of the Taiwan situation in 1969, and "because the government viewed the possibility of an armed conflict realistically breaking out in the area as having disappeared, the understanding of the Taiwan clause had also changed."[24]

The situation was more laden with tension relating to Korea. Although the Tanaka administration did not adopt an explicit change in policy, there was a shift in emphasis from efforts to strengthen security ties with South Korea to statements that the peace and security of the entire Korean Peninsula were important to Japan. In this shift could be seen a desire to avoid strengthening the strong-arm tactics of the Pak government at that time. The kidnapping of an opposition politician, Kim Dae Jung (later president), from a Tokyo hotel in August 1973 by members of the Korean Central Intelligence Agency and the discovery in August 1974 of plans for the assassination of President Pak by a Korean–Japanese man, Moon Seg An, made bilateral relations very tense in this period.

Ultimately, at the suggestion of the United States, an understanding was reached between Korea and Japan over these two incidents, and the Miki administration worked on improving relations with Korea. Reflecting this, the statement "the security of the Republic of Korea is essential to the maintenance of peace on the Korean Peninsula, which in turn is necessary for the peace and security in East Asia, including Japan" was included in the joint announcement to the press released during Miki's visit to the United States in August 1975.[25] The wording reflects the Miki administration's attempt to maintain cooperative relations with the United States and Korea while at the same time bringing about a reduction of tensions on the Korean peninsula. Although security relations between the two governments could not be discussed publicly, Miki did announce Japan's intention to provide loans to Korea to assist in its five-year economic development plans, showing support for the Pak government and also contributing to stability on the peninsula.

In addition, the Miki administration realized the ratification of the Non-Proliferation Treaty. At this point, for Japan, two of its three non-nuclear principles—not to possess or manufacture nuclear weapons—were no longer just part of a unilateral domestic stance but in fact became an international pledge.

The first oil shock and the structure of cooperative policies

The first oil shock, in October 1973, was for Japan a blow of major international proportions, arguably the largest one since the end of the World War II. First, the fact that war in the Middle East, a region in which Japanese had showed little interest, had a major impact on their daily lives surprised the public. Second, just as the rapid growth of their country was allowing the Japanese to forget the poverty of earlier years, this incident shook people's complacency and demonstrated the vulnerability of the Japanese economy to the outer world. Third, in spite of Japan's neutrality in the Middle East conflict and friendly economic relations with the oil-producing countries in the region, Japan initially did not enjoy a "friendly state" status due to its close relationship with the United States. The oil shock was thus a striking reminder to the Japanese that they lived in an interdependent world, where peaceful prosperity had to be based on a stable international order.

The oil crisis had two elements. First, Arab oil-producing countries attempted to use oil as a political weapon. Second, oil-producing developing countries used the price cartel to raise oil prices through the Organization of Petroleum Exporting Countries, OPEC (for example, the price of a barrel of oil in January 1974 was four times what it was in January 1973).

First on November 18, 1973, oil ministers from the Organization of Arab Petroleum Exporting Countries (OAPEC) decided that they would end limitations on oil exports to the European Community countries with the exception of the Netherlands. The non-inclusion of Japan came as a great surprise, and without clarifying the Arab position, Japan hurriedly began to show a "pro-Arab" attitude. The Japanese government told Secretary of State

Henry Kissinger, who was visiting Japan in mid-November to call for solidarity against the Arabs, that without a guarantee from the United States of oil to Japan, it could not support the U.S. position. Chief Cabinet Secretary Nikaido Susumu, on November 22, stated it would be necessary for Israel to withdraw from the areas occupied since the Third Middle East War of 1967 and that it would likely be necessary for Japan to reexamine its position with regard to Israel in light of events in the future, going one step away from traditional policy statements and moving toward the Arabs. In addition, Tanaka sent Vice Premier Miki to the Middle East to ask for continued supplies of oil in exchange for economic assistance. In fact, it was at this point that Japan's overseas assistance, which had mostly been intended to promote trade and economic development in Asia, became global in nature with an eye on securing natural resources, and Japan began to steadily increase the amount it provided for aid. The Arab states responded favorably to Japan's stance and at the December 25 OAPEC meeting decided to recognize Japan as a friendly country, announcing that it would supply Japan with the oil it needed.

The hasty Japanese move was partly a result of pressure from the public. Japan was the world's largest importer of oil, with about 70 percent coming from the Middle East. Thus the impact of the OAPEC decisions was particularly dramatic. Japanese found their daily lives affected as near riots broke out in stores across the country over the purchase of toilet paper and other goods. It was more a psychological panic than an actual shortage, but the Japanese government felt a strong need to show the public that it was responding appropriately.

To what extent the Japanese move was effective is unclear. It is also difficult to assess how this stance should be viewed. On the one hand, Japan's response may be justified as a rational act to defend its vital interests. But on the other hand, the Japanese stance may have been a shortsighted, even unprincipled, "whatever-it-takes-to-get-oil" approach to diplomacy. In any case, it was clear that Japanese diplomacy was not ready to respond to this kind of crisis, where politics and the economy were mixed.

As for the second element of the oil price hike, Japanese policy was more stable. The rapid rise in the price of oil quickly brought to the surface the changes in the international economy. The increase demonstrated the limits of mass production and mass consumption and pointed to the unavoidable decline of the international political and economic order known as the Pax Americana.

Indeed, the possibility of a future lack of natural resources in the future had been noted shortly before the oil crisis. Commentary such as the Rome Club's report "The Limits to Growth" became the focus of great discussion.[26] The Tanaka cabinet also viewed the securing of natural resources as important from a mid- to long-term perspective. In the spring of 1973 Minister of International Trade and Industry Nakasone Yasuhiro visited the Middle East, and in the fall of that year discussions on the problem of the development of the Tyumen oil fields in Siberia was an important issue during Tanaka's visit to the Soviet Union. What the oil crisis did do was to make the long-term possibility of resource scarcity an immediate crisis.

In the middle of these changes in the postwar international economic order, countries were to some extent restricted and guided not only by the reality of interdependence but by the memory of the collapse of the world economy between the two wars. As a result, each country, amid increasing friction, took measures to reduce demand and placed importance on coordinating its economic policies with the others. For example, in order to put pressure on the oil producers, the oil consumer countries, at Kissinger's suggestion, met in February 1974. Even France, which placed importance on cooperating with the oil producers, was critical of the meeting. In the end, through a compromise between France and the United States, an agreement was reached establishing the International Energy Association.

Another example of the new form of cooperation caused by the fundamental changes in the world economy was the change in the international currency system. The Smithsonian Accord, agreed to by the developed countries in December 1971, had become difficult to sustain by early 1973. In February Japan shifted to a floating currency system, followed by the countries of Europe in March. This signaled a farewell to the fixed exchange rate and a shift to a floating mechanism. The changes meant risks in the exchange rates for international transactions, but when the economies of the developed countries fell into stagflation, which coincided with the inflation and the recession that were occurring as a result of the oil crisis, each country was free to implement its economic policies flexibly without worrying about exchange rates.

In November 1975, at the urging of French president Giscard d'Estaing, the leaders of the five major developed countries met at Rambouillet in France in order to discuss economic policies. Prime Minister Miki represented Japan. This meeting, known as the G-5 Summit, became a regular annual gathering that would provide an opportunity for the developed countries to come together to coordinate their economic policies. Despite the numerous challenges, the 1970s fortunately did not witness a repeat of the tragic history of the 1930s. Japan's participation in these summit meetings demonstrated that it was an important player in the management of the international economy, and symbolized Japan's presence as one of the three pillars of the world along with North America and Western Europe.[27]

The Asia-Pacific region under détente

Developments in international affairs in the early 1970s also led to changes in Japan's relations with the countries of East Asia and the Asia-Pacific region. Although the direction of these changes was still not clear in the middle of the decade, the period can be described as one in which a new regional framework was emerging.

One key component for Japan's regional diplomacy was an adjustment in its relations with Southeast Asia. This was the combined result of numerous factors, which included important political changes such as the fact that China had stopped being a revolutionary force seeking to overturn the status quo and the fact that the Vietnam War was drawing to a close with the U.S. withdrawal. Economic factors were also significant, such as Japan's economic growth and the high yen, which had an immense economic impact in Southeast Asia.

The peace in Vietnam brought about the normalization of relations with North Vietnam. Japan moved were very quickly this time, and indeed informal contacts had been explored between both governments near the end of the Sato administration. In the summer of 1973 discussions were held for the normalization of relations at both countries' embassies in Paris, with the establishment of diplomatic relations agreed to on September 21 of that year. Ambassadors were not sent, however, because of problems that emerged in the discussions over the question of economic assistance to North Vietnam and the recognition of the revolutionary government in South Vietnam. In the end Japan agreed to provide 13.5 billion yen in economic assistance, and with the unification of Vietnam in 1975, the latter problem disappeared. In early 1976 ambassadors were exchanged with unified Vietnam for the first time.

Japan's relations with the members of the ASEAN (Association of the Southeast Asian Nations) were also altered. The catalyst was a trip to Southeast Asia by Prime Minister Tanaka in January 1974 when, during visits to Thailand and Indonesia, anti-Japanese riots broke out, shocking Japanese who thought that friendly relations with these countries, centered on economics, had been well established. One of the reasons for the anti-Japanese backlash in the region was that Japan to some extent became a scapegoat. Despite a certain level of economic development, many of these countries still retained undemocratic regimes, and political frustration exploded at the time of Tanaka's visit, as Japan was seen as financially supportive of these governments. But the underlying reality was that Japan's economic presence had become large enough to have political ramifications. Because of the liberalization of foreign investment, many Japanese companies had set up operations in these countries, giving the impression that Japanese goods were inundating Southeast Asia. The episode during Tanaka's visit demonstrated that for the people of Southeast Asia, Japan's presence was, thirty years after the war, again becoming psychologically overwhelming.

Following this incident, Japan sought to rebuild its relations with Southeast Asia, but this rebuilding had to wait until the effects of the ongoing changes in the international environment became clearer. The Southeast Asia Development Ministerial Meeting and the Asia Pacific Association Conference, which had begun during the 1960s, began to lose their meaning with the end of the Vietnam War, and their functions ceased. ASEAN also looked for a post-Vietnam role, and despite the desire of Prime Minister Miki, Japan's participation in the first meeting of the heads of state of the ASEAN countries, held in February 1976, was not approved. Japan simply sent a message of greetings to the gathering.

Britain's joining the European Community in the early 1970s also had an impact on the Asia-Pacific region. The Commonwealth countries in Southeast Asia had to pay more attention to the region to which they belonged. In particular, Australia actively sought to strengthen ties with Japan as a regional partner. In 1971 the Sato government and the administration of Australia's Labour Party, led by E. G. Whitlam, agreed to establish regular cabinet-level meetings between the two countries. In October 1972 the first meeting was held, with Foreign Minister Ohira participating, and a joint research project was initiated on the future of Australian–Japanese economic relations, keeping in mind the future development of the Asia-Pacific economy. Some disputes emerged with Australia's export of natural resources and agricultural products to Japan around the time of the oil crisis, but in June 1976 the Basic Treaty of Friendship and Cooperation was signed between the Miki administration and the Conservative government of Malcolm Fraser. The treaty's preamble stated that the "co-operation between the two countries should have in view not only their own mutual benefit but also their common interest in the prosperity and welfare of other countries, including those in the Asian and Pacific region, of which they are part," demonstrating that the development of a regional international relations in the Asia-Pacific area was one of the objectives in strengthening relations between Japan and Australia.[28]

Japan's foreign policies gradually took shape. They were based on Japan's identity as a unique economic power that would aid in bringing world peace through economic prosperity, furthering harmony between the Western and non-Western worlds, and closing the gap between the advanced and developing economies. This newly emerging identity was expressed in the image of "Imperial Diplomacy." Emperor Hirohito and his family became visible in the international arena during this period. Hirohito visited seven countries in Europe in 1971 and the United States in 1975. In 1974 the State Guest House (originally built in 1909 as a residence of the crown prince) was renovated and opened for heads of state, and President Ford was received there.[29] Even though there was the lingering question of the emperor's war record, Hirohito took on a new role as symbol of a peaceful postwar Japan.

The reigniting of tensions and cooperative policies

The ending of détente

Détente did not proceed directly toward ending the Cold War. International tensions actually grew at the end of the 1970s and at the end of the 1980s. The Cold War came to a sudden end defying all expectations (see Chapter 5). Japanese diplomacy, which had been in the process of creating a new framework after surviving the upheavals of the early 1970s, once again began to shudder with the reigniting of tensions at the end of the decade.

Tensions increased in the second half of the 1970s principally owing to the behavior of the Soviet Union. The Soviets tried to capitalize on America's weakened interest in foreign affairs because of the effects of the Vietnam War and the Watergate scandal by intervening in conflicts in the Middle East and Africa and later in Latin America, as well as by increasing its naval might and modernizing its military, including its nuclear weaponry. Caution was increasingly necessary with regard to the Soviet Union and eventually debate was heard on the need to take actions to confront it.

This situation alone, however, is not enough to explain the reigniting of tensions during this period. As Cold War tensions waned during the détente years, a sort of nostalgia for the Cold War structure seems also to have been at work. Although the Cold War was filled with danger, it was also a fact that the East–West tension stabilized international politics. When this tension was relaxed due to détente, the order that had been stabilized began to shake and a new and strong feeling of uncertainty emerged.

The Fukuda Takeo cabinet, which replaced the Miki cabinet in December 1976, was charged with handling Japanese diplomacy during the last stages of détente. At the start of his government, Prime Minister Fukuda announced his "Omni-directional Peaceful Diplomacy (Zenhoi Heiwa Gaiko)," which could be understood to mean the continuation of détente diplomacy through the maintenance of the Japan–U.S. alliance while improving relations with both China and the Soviet Union. But the situation did not develop in the way that Fukuda had desired.[30]

A major obstacle was the Soviet Union's intransigence. Although Japan did not view the Soviet Union as a serious military threat, the uncooperative stance of the Soviets not only had the effect of stalemating relations with Japan but also helped to push China and Japan closer together. A classic example is the negotiation of fishing rights between the Soviet Union and Japan. Although the Law of the Sea was then under deliberation and the world was moving in the direction of establishing a 200-mile economic zone, Japan found the Soviet Union's unilateral declaration of the establishment of exclusive fishing rights in the Okhotsk Sea insensitive to its needs. Because this issue could be linked to the two countries' territorial problem, talks became contentious. An agreement was finally reached but only after separating the territorial problem from the question of fishing rights.

In 1976, however, the Soviet Union placed greater restrictions on visiting graves in the Northern Islands which it first began to permit in 1964, and in 1977 it became clear that it was building military bases on the islands. Also in 1977, as Sino-Japanese relations were improving, the Soviet Union invited Foreign Minister Sonoda Sunao to Moscow and proposed a new treaty of friendship and cooperation. When the Japanese side responded that a resolution of the Northern Territory problem and a peace treaty had to come first, the Soviet Union in a tit-for-tat refused to include the phrase acknowledging "unresolved problems" in the joint declaration and began to state that the territorial question was already resolved. Japanese anger toward the Soviet Union mounted steadily.

As a result, the foreign policy of the Fukuda administration shifted to one that was similar to the structure of the Cold War in which Japan strengthened its bilateral relationship with America and cooled relations with the Soviet Union, though this time with China being on the Western side. With the United States, the strengthening of bilateral defense cooperation became the focus. Of course, it was natural to improve the operational utility of the Japan–U.S. Security Treaty as it was a stabilizing factor in the region. A meeting that took place between Secretary of Defense James Schlesinger and Director General Sakata in August 1975 became the impetus for defense cooperation.

Because the Soviet Union was increasing its military might, the Japan–U.S. alliance had to adjust to this new threat and to move in the direction of role-sharing. During the meeting with Sakata, Schlesinger requested that Japan increase its defense capability with regard to defense of the sea lines, its anti-submarine warfare, and its role in air defense. This thinking was based on the changes in the international environment in the mid-1970s, as well as the desire to see Japan increase its role in responsibility-sharing for the defense of the neighboring seas.

Regarding bilateral defense cooperation, both governments decided to distinguish between the security situations in their security treaty's Article 5 ("an armed attack against either Party in the territories under the administration of Japan") and Article 6 ("for the maintenance of international peace and security in the Far East") and study them separately. This was due in part to the legal interpretation that Japan could not constitutionally exercise its right to engage in collective self-defense. In the subsequent official-level studies, only the "Article 5 case" was studied because of Japanese legal restraints. In the atmosphere of increasing tension in the region, Japan sought to reduce both the risk of "abandonment" of its own security and the risk of "entrapment" in the military conflict away from its own territory.

Related to this was the question of the withdrawal of U.S. troops from Korea. The U.S. Democratic Party candidate for the 1976 presidential elections, Jimmy Carter, called for the withdrawal of U.S. troops from Korea and eventually went on to defeat incumbent Gerald Ford. The Fukuda Cabinet immediately voiced its concern that the withdrawal of U.S. troops would have a major impact on the military balance in Northeast Asia. While Japan would not directly be involved in the defense of Korea, it expressed a deep interest in the latter's security, defining Japan's regional security role.

One more type of Japan–U.S. defense cooperation was seen in Japan's establishment of Host-Nation Support (HNS), widely known as the "Sympathy Budget."[31] HNS began in the fiscal year 1978 as an additional financial outlay to help pay for the stationing of U.S. troops in Japan. As part of the 1960 Status of Forces Agreement, the United States is obligated to pay the costs of maintaining American troops in Japan, with the Japanese government paying for the provision of facilities and areas to U.S. forces. In the mid-1970s, due to the rise in the yen, the U.S. government began requesting an increase in the amount Japan shouldered. In 1978, Defense Agency Director General Kanemaru Shin agreed to pay some of the labor costs of the

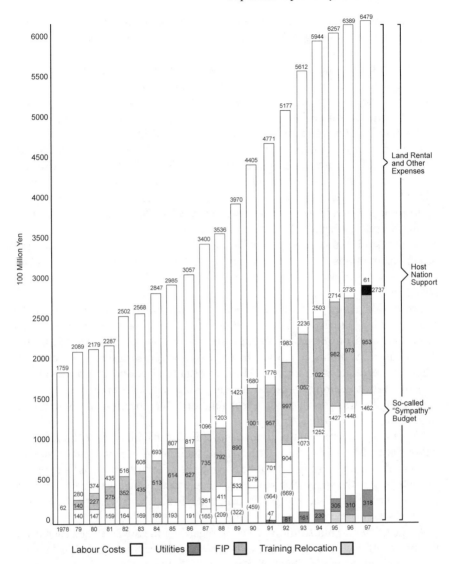

Figure 4.3 Host nation support for U.S. forces in Japan, 1978–1997

Japanese workers on the bases. Kanemaru himself seemed to think that this sort of expense was necessary to secure the commitment of the United States to Japan, but in order to convince the less enthusiastic bureaucracy and skeptical public, Kanemaru employed the phrase "sympathy budget," which has become the expenditure's more popular name. The United States, of course, does not consider this outlay as one of "sympathy" and instead has looked at it as a normal fiscal increase stemming from the change in the economic situation and Japan's high economic growth. Later, the two governments agreed to increase the level of Japanese fiscal support for the construction of housing and barracks, as well as for the severance pay of Japanese workers.

Between China and Japan in this period, the signing of a bilateral treaty of peace and friendship remained the biggest hurdle. In the fall of 1977, Deng Xiaoping, vice-chairman of the Communist Party of China, told a visiting delegation of Japanese Diet members that if Prime Minister Fukuda made up his mind, the treaty problem could be "resolved in one second," in effect calling for the speeding up of the signing. However, several problems remained. Within the LDP were those politicians, led primarily by the pro-Taiwan faction, who were cautious about signing a peace treaty with mainland China. Fukuda, as mentioned above, had deep ties to Taiwan. Moreover, opposition to a peace treaty grew when, in April 1978, 100 mainland Chinese fishing vessels gathered off the Senkaku Islands in a show of sovereignty. Nevertheless, Fukuda took the initiative to persuade the party in May and began negotiations on a peace treaty. Soviet leader Brezhnev sent a letter to Fukuda in an attempt to stop the talks with China, but Japan ignored his efforts.

The anti-hegemony clause continued to be the major sticking point of the bilateral talks. Japan finally decided to stop opposing it in principle, and instead focused on including a clause stating that it was not directed at any third country as discussed earlier. In August, Foreign Minister Sonoda visited China to negotiate with Foreign Minister Huang Hua and succeeded in getting the anti-hegemony clause to appear as Article 2 together with a statement that the treaty would not affect relations that the signatories had with other countries in Article 4.[32]

Negotiations succeeded this time for several reasons. First, since the Japanese public favored a peace treaty with China, the Fukuda cabinet made signing one a goal in order to rally the public around the administration and strengthen its base within the party. Second, it was likely that China was ready to compromise because of the danger it perceived from the Soviet threat. Third, there was U.S. support to move ahead.

As the Carter administration's concern regarding the Soviet Union increased, the power of the anti-Soviet hard-liner National Security Advisor Zbigniew Brzezinski grew while that of Secretary of State Cyrus Vance waned. According to his memoirs, Brzezinski viewed the improvement of relations between China and Japan as important from the perspective of putting pressure on the Soviet Union. At the time of Fukuda's visit to Washington in May 1978, Carter promoted the signing of a peace treaty between China and Japan, and Brzezinski himself visited Japan later that same month and requested the early signing of a treaty.[33]

Despite the existence of the "third-country clause" in Article 4, the Soviet Union did not hide its displeasure with the Sino-Japan treaty. However, hopes for a positive response from the Soviet Union had long since been abandoned. To Japan, it was clear that détente had ended.

The Fukuda Doctrine and the Pacific Basin Cooperation Concept

Needless to say, the reigniting of Cold War tensions at the end of the 1970s did not necessarily mean a complete return to the situation prior to détente, as evidenced in the development of international relations in the Asia-Pacific region. While feeling the effects of the changes in the international environment, Japan furthered its détente-period diplomacy toward the region. This was seen in concrete form particularly with the Fukuda Doctrine, announced in August 1977, and the Pacific Basin Cooperation Concept (*Kantaiheiyo Rentai Koso*) undertaken by the Ohira cabinet.

The Fukuda Doctrine can be seen as the fruition of Japan's attempts at rebuilding its Southeast Asia diplomacy during the détente period. It stated that: (1) Japan would not become a military power; (2) Japan would work to build a relationship of mutual confidence based on "heart-to-heart understanding" not only in politics and economic matters but in social and cultural ones as well; (3) Japan would be an equal partner, strengthening ties with the ASEAN countries, attempting to develop relations with the countries of Indochina on the basis of mutual trust, and contributing to the prosperity and peace of the entire area of Southeast Asia.[34] In other words, in addition to revising its economics-focused Southeast Asia diplomacy, Japan was seeking to build a new post-Vietnam War international order in Southeast Asia based on cooperative relations.

This sort of policy was being studied within the Foreign Ministry prior to the start of the Fukuda cabinet. After officials undertook consultations with the ASEAN countries throughout 1976, a Japan–ASEAN Forum was held in Tokyo in March 1977. The ASEAN side had gradually developed a certain level of self-confidence and began to view the strengthening of relations with Japan more positively, not simply as an act of implying subordination of their countries to Japan. In August of that year, Fukuda was invited to the second meeting of the heads of state of ASEAN. In 1978, a Japan–ASEAN foreign ministers' meeting was launched, and in 1979 this format expanded to include the foreign ministers of the United States, Canada, Australia, and the European Community.

However, cooperation between ASEAN and the countries of Indochina, one of the most important points of the Fukuda Doctrine, was not realized due to Vietnam's deepening ties with the Soviet Union, its invasion of Cambodia, and the Sino-Vietnam War. ASEAN, whose stance was slightly different from that of the United States, continued to demand the withdrawal of Vietnamese forces from Cambodia, and coordination between Japan and ASEAN allowed them to present a framework for the resolution of the Cambodian conflict upon the ending of the Cold War.

The Pacific Basin Cooperation Concept promoted by Ohira, who had succeeded Fukuda in December 1978, was in one sense a continuation of the Fukuda Doctrine, and in another sense, a different approach. Because it emphasized interdependent relations in the Asia-Pacific region and was not a simple concept calling for the creation of a Cold War bloc focusing on power politics, it was a part of the détente policy. However, it was different in its approach as compared with the Fukuda Doctrine because the formation of the concept and its implementation were not government-led and instead placed emphasis on private exchanges, and because it included Australia as a partner and took into consideration America's view of emphasizing relations with advanced nations.

Ohira did not share Fukuda's style of policymaking, which was led by the bureaucracy. Shortly after the start of Ohira's cabinet, he established several study groups comprising people from the private sector to examine issues in politics, economics, society, and culture. Among these was the Pacific Basin Cooperation study group, headed by Okita Saburo, who had been involved from the 1960s in examining questions of cooperation in the Pacific. After the submission of the interim report in November 1979, Ohira appointed Okita foreign minister, suggesting just how much importance Ohira placed on the Pacific Basin concept.[35] There were strong concerns, however, mostly in the Foreign Ministry, about the response of the United States and the countries of Southeast Asia, and when Ohira visited Australia in January 1980, he was uncertain to what extent the Pacific Basin concept should be promoted as government policy. In the end, Ohira and Prime Minister Malcolm Fraser agreed to hold a seminar to examine the issue.

This conference was eventually held in Canberra in September, following Ohira's sudden death in June, under the title "Pacific Community Seminar." In addition to the governments of the developed countries—Australia, Japan, Canada, America, New Zealand—and those from ASEAN, South Korea, and the South Pacific, representatives from private cooperative organizations that had been active in the Pacific region also participated. This meeting later developed into the Pacific Economic Cooperation Conference (PECC), becoming an organization made up of government officials, scholars, and those from the worlds of finance and business. This informal style of international consultations became the start of the increasingly important "track two" diplomacy in the Asia-Pacific region.

The development of international cooperation through interdependence was seen in Ohira's policies of economic cooperation with China as well. Visiting China in December 1979, Ohira announced that Japan would provide 50 billion yen for six infrastructure construction projects in fiscal year 1979. Subsequently, further yen loans were provided. This decision was, in part, based on realistic thinking as an attempt to bring China over to the West, and at the same time was intended to expedite China's active participation in the international relations of the Pacific Basin through economic cooperation. The three principles that Ohira had announced when providing this economic assistance to China—(1) cooperation with the West; (2) consideration of existing relations with ASEAN; and (3) non-cooperation in military matters—were based on the model of international relations that the Ohira cabinet was trying to create in the Asia-Pacific region. The concept of the Asia-Pacific region, shelved in 1970, had begun to take actual form in 1980. Japan played a significant role in this process.

Cooperation and friction in economic policies

The reigniting of international tensions was a factor in strengthening the international political and economic cooperation that had been developing from the middle of the 1970s, particularly among the advanced Western states. The increased political need to maintain this unity in the West, however, also delayed serious efforts to create a system to stabilize the international economy. A cycle was evident in which economic problems repeatedly became political in nature, causing friction, but eventually bringing about a temporary compromise. In the economic summits that had become annual events, cooperation between each country's macroeconomic policies was discussed with some success. In the Tokyo Round of negotiations under the GATT that started in 1973, agreements were finally reached in 1979 on trade in services and in agriculture, as well as the procedures for resolving disputes—problems that had all been pending for some time.

In particular, Japan's trade surplus became an important issue for the developed countries. In 1976, as Japan's commodity prices stabilized and economic growth recovered after the oil crisis of 1973, the trade surplus began to grow enormously. Japan's rate of growth was 6.3 percent in fiscal year 1976 and its balance of payments stood at over $4.6 billion. Europe and the United States criticized Japan's "flood" of exports, with an American steel company eventually charging a Japanese steel company with dumping activity in violation of the GATT agreement.

In response to this criticism, Prime Minister Fukuda, a former Finance Ministry official, certainly was not passive at the London Summit of the G6 in May 1977. At seventy-two, Fukuda was the oldest of the participants and a living witness to the collapse of the world economy following the world depression in the 1930s. He argued persuasively for the importance of international cooperation, earning high praise and the respect of his counterparts. For cooperation to succeed, the growth of the international economy was vital, and in particular, it was necessary for countries in the black—Japan, the United States, and Germany—to act as "engines of growth." Fukuda announced at this time that Japan's growth rate for the fiscal year 1977 would be 6.7 percent and Japan would run a $700 million deficit in its balance of payments.

Japan's surplus continued to grow, however, and trade friction with the United States was becoming more serious. As an emergency measure, the Fukuda cabinet sought to expand imports by increasing its oil reserves and to increase its growth rate to 7 percent by issuing public bonds during the compilation of the fiscal year 1978 budget. In addition, the former diplomat and ambassador to the United States Ushiba Nobuhiko was appointed state minister for external economic affairs, a newly created post, and asked to undertake negotiations with U.S. Trade Representative Robert Strauss. In January 1978, an agreement was reached that Japan's economic growth rate should be 7 percent, its balance of payments be reduced dramatically, and imports of meat and oranges from the United States be increased and custom duties lowered. At the Bonn Summit of the G6 that July, Japan promised to take additional financial measures to ensure a 7 percent growth rate and to speed up the pace of its increases in Overseas Development Assistance (ODA).

At this summit, the United States stated that it would reach 4 percent growth while preventing inflation, and West Germany announced that it would take additional economic stimulus measures representing 0.5 to 1.0 percent of its GNP, suggesting that cooperation in macroeconomic policies among the developed countries was being realized. In reality, however, inflation rose in America, prompting the need to put the brakes on the economy, and in Germany, which questioned the engine theory from the beginning, adequate stimulus measures were not taken. Japan issued public bonds in order to stimulate the economy, but its growth rate did not even reach 5 percent in 1978. While its trade surplus continued to grow, the issuance of bonds become common (reaching 39.6 percent of its budget) and the amount of bonds issued at 25 percent of GNP.

Ohira Masayoshi, Fukuda's rival within the LDP, had supported the Fukuda government as secretary general of the LDP (having formed an alliance with Fukuda), but he became increasingly frustrated with Fukuda's running of the government, including the 7 percent growth promise that ended up increasing deficit spending. After gaining the support of the Tanaka Kakuei faction, Ohira defeated Fukuda in the LDP presidential elections and became prime minister in December 1978. He quickly withdrew the 7 percent growth goal and fired Minister Ushiba. The Carter administration was said to be very unhappy with Ohira's initial moves, however. In order to improve relations, Ohira visited the United States in May 1979, reaching an agreement on the unresolved problem of the government procurements for the NTT public telephone corporation, about which the United States criticized Japan as discriminating against foreign companies. Moreover, Ohira, who was a Christian, was able to deepen his personal relationship with the strongly Baptist Carter and, seeking to earn America's understanding, actively discussed the importance of the bilateral alliance.

The focus of policy coordination among the advanced economies also began to shift. In addition to the collapse of the engine of growth theory, the rapid rise of oil prices was again becoming a common concern among the developed countries. As a result of the complete stoppage of oil production in Iran at the end of 1978 because of the mass riots and violence of those opposing the strong-armed modernization policies of King Muhammad Reda Shah Pahlevi, OPEC decided to gradually raise the price of oil. Moreover, in February 1979 an Islamic revolution occurred in Iran, and its ability to procure oil became unclear. Indeed, the price of a barrel of oil that had been $15 in January had jumped to \$37 by June. In the rush to buy and secure oil, the second oil crisis occurred.

At the same time that an OPEC meeting was being held in Geneva in June, the Tokyo Summit of the G6 meeting—the first time Japan acted as host—was also under way, visibly showing that international politics was divided between oil producers and oil consumers. As a result, the Tokyo Summit was called the "Energy Summit." As stated at the time by French president Giscard d'Estaing, agreement was reached on "the reduction of imports and the development of alternative sources of energy [which] will prevent high prices on the oil market."

Serious bargaining, however, was going on behind the scenes. Although there was an attempt to announce the limitation of imports by establishing an overall goal for oil imports, each country was in fact trying to get the most advantageous import limit for itself. The leaders of the United States, Britain, France, and Germany began to undertake informal negotiations among themselves, and after reaching an agreement on their own with regard to import limits, they attempted to obtain Japan's acceptance. This limit was difficult for Japan to accept, for the import limit allotted to Japan was far lower than the one the MITI estimated as Japan's minimum requirement. Ohira, as chair, was forced to decide between working for the overall success of the summit or protecting his country's national interests. In the end, Ohira was saved when the United States presented a compromise proposal that took Japan's concerns into consideration to some degree.

The Tokyo Summit vividly demonstrated the existence of both cooperation and friction in policy coordination. Moreover, ironically, the import limits that had been agreed to after much hard work lost their meaning with the changes in oil procurement during the 1980s. This situation demonstrated that the market is often volatile enough to make the work of policy coordination among governments futile.

Nor did the developed countries respond to the Iranian Revolution in unison. The hatred of the Iran's revolutionary government toward the United States for its longtime support of the Pahlevi reign was deep, and the Iranian government took no action when radicals seized the U.S. embassy in Teheran and held the diplomatic staff hostage. The United States introduced sanctions. Japan, which was dependent on Iran for 15 percent of its oil, had been attempting to improve relations with the revolutionary government and had recently decided to restart an oil project that the Iranian government had requested. Secretary of State Vance took the unusual step of criticizing Japan as "insensitive" for its continued purchase of oil from Iran.

The Ohira cabinet, caught between the United States and Iran, struggled to find an appropriate response. Iran saved Japan from this dilemma when it demanded in March 1980 that the price of oil be raised. The Japanese government advised companies to refuse to sign the contract, and in May, Japan joined the European countries in the embargo against Iran. The Carter administration, under fire both for his domestic policies and in foreign affairs, greatly welcomed this move, even taking out a newspaper advertisement to highlight Japan–U.S. cooperation.[36]

The rapid rise in energy prices due to the second oil crisis ultimately brought about an ironic result in relations between Japan and the United States. Bilateral trade friction, a result of the dramatic rise in the importation of fuel-efficient Japanese automobiles, became serious and this problem would continue to be a major issue throughout the 1980s.

Comprehensive security

The Soviet Union's foreign policy became increasingly intransigent by the end of the 1970s. The Soviet Union signed a treaty of friendship and cooperation with Vietnam which ended up encouraging the latter to invade Cambodia in December 1978. Subsequently China sent troops to punish Vietnam. The Soviet Union also acquired rights at Cam Ran Bay and Danang airfield, expanding its military presence in the Pacific area. In addition, the Soviet Union invaded Afghanistan in December 1979; the East–West conflict became even more hardened and dangerous than it had been for years.

The Carter administration instituted a hard-line policy toward the Soviet Union. In addition to increasing the United States' own military strength, Carter called on America's allies to show unity against the Soviets. In response, Prime Minister Ohira demonstrated even greater support for the United States, and at a reception during his visit to Washington in May 1979, described America as an "irreplaceable friend and ally."

The most explicit expression of the alliance relationship was the strengthening of defense cooperation. In November 1978, at the end of the Fukuda administration, the cabinet approved the "Guidelines for Japan–U.S. Defense Cooperation."[37] Its contents examined: (1) "Posture for Deterring Aggression," in which America's "nuclear deterrent capability and forward deployments of combat-ready forces and other forces capable of reinforcing them" would be maintained; (2) "Actions in Response to an Armed Attack against Japan" (a situation as envisioned in Article 5 of the security treaty), in which U.S. forces would support SDF operations and do anything "to supplement functional areas which exceed the capacity of the SDF" in the event that Japan was forced to "repel limited, small-scale aggression"; and (3) "Japan–U.S. Cooperation in Situations in the Far East outside of Japan which will have an important influence on the security of Japan," or those that fall under Article 6 of the security treaty.

With the Guidelines in place, the Self-Defense Forces and the U.S. military expanded their joint exercises. But because Japan's defense policy was based on the principle of the "exclusive defense" of Japan, it could not undertake military roles outside of the archipelago and the study of situations relating to Article 6 of the security treaty was shelved. By this time the Carter administration had already reexamined its decision to remove its forces from South Korea, which meant that the United States would continue to play the leading role for some time. As a result, the Japan–Korea security dialogue ended without significant movement.

What the United States desired of Japan was a visible show of the unity with the West against the Soviet Union. In response, Japan implemented sanctions against the Soviet Union for its invasion of Afghanistan, and boycotted the 1980 Moscow Olympics (see Chapter 5). It was also important for Japan to show that it was contributing materially. The focus was on speeding up the development of greater defense capability. As 1980 began, Secretary of Defense Harold Brown repeatedly referred to the need for Japan to increase its defense capability, and Carter too, in meetings with Ohira during the latter's visit to Washington in May that year, called for the early realization of Japan's defense buildup plans, still being drafted within the Defense Agency. Prime Minister Ohira responded that Japan would "seriously consider what sort of ally it should be, and do what it can."

Japan's economic scale was huge, however, and the strategic situation around Japan was different from that which faced the United States and Europe. It was thus nearly impossible for Japan to spend the same amount on defense relative to GNP that the other countries in the West were allocating. What emerged was the concept of "strategic aid," by which foreign economic assistance would be used as a way to strengthen the overall position of the West. Through combining defense spending with foreign assistance, the overall expenditure on this "comprehensive security" was thought to be a way to demonstrate that Japan was making a real contribution to the West.[38] The Fukuda cabinet had already announced in May 1977 that in order to lower the trade deficit, it would double ODA over a period of five years, and Ohira had begun to promote his policy of not only accelerating this assistance but of strengthening support for countries near conflict areas. In 1980 Japan extended aid to Pakistan, Turkey, and Thailand, explaining in the 1979 *Diplomatic Bluebook* that this aid was to "guarantee security in a broad sense."

Although not seen in the framework of strategic aid, the yen loans to China begun by the Ohira cabinet also had a similar political connotation. At this time China was in the process of implementing a plan for rapid modernization, but its infrastructure base was weak and joint ventures were failing. In this situation, aid in the form of loans to China would likely help stabilize Sino-Japanese relations and strengthen China's alignment with the West through supporting the reform and liberalization policies of Deng Xiaoping.

The result was a dramatic increase in Japan's assistance during this period. Japan's ODA went from $458 million in 1970, of which most went to Asia, to more than $3.3 billion in 1980 and became global in nature (see Figure 5.2).

This "Comprehensive Security (*Sogo Anzen Hosho*)" policy no doubt had some merit. If one thinks about the international situation that Japan faced and the fact that conflicts involving developing nations and their failures at modernization are often the reasons behind worldwide tensions, then Japan's use of its economic resources to contribute to the stabilization of international society was quite appropriate. This approach is vulnerable to criticism, however, as a weak attempt to resolve problems with money to avoid outside censure and difficult political debates. The problem was whether leaders could put proper weight on economic might within an overall strategy, but the 1970s, which saw continued crises and dramatic changes, did not really leave leaders the time to think and plan for the future. The sudden death of Ohira during a heated election campaign in June 1980 perhaps best symbolized the struggling Japan of the 1970s.

Evaluating Japanese diplomacy in the 1970s

The 1970s was a period when the fundamental structure of the postwar world changed tremendously. During this decade, Japan's position as Asia's only developed country and a major economic power supporting the world economy was solidified. Japanese diplomacy as well was able to move beyond the simplistic debate over dependence on America or independence, toward the question of playing a larger and deeper role both globally as well as regionally. With the exception of perhaps the Soviet Union, which was adopting hard-line policies at the end of the Brezhnev period, it can be said that there was no country with which Japan's relations had clearly worsened during the 1970s. In that sense, Japan developed into a major country which played an important part in international cooperation. When Ezra Vogel designated Japan "as number one" in 1979, the translation of his book by that name became a bestseller in Japan, no doubt satisfying the sense of accomplishment among the Japanese.[39] Japanese diplomacy during the 1970s may be described as a success.

At the same time, the "success" of Japanese diplomacy during the period was more an accidental result than the fruit of attentive policymaking. The cases of the revaluation of the yen and the limitations on textile exports, as well as oil imports, in retrospect, need not have been so important, and within the government there were some who were quietly saying that it was necessary for Japan to make concessions. In the real political process, however, domestic consensus was often reached because of *gaiatsu*, or "foreign pressure." The political process in Japan was domestically oriented, and rather than taking international initiatives, emphasis was placed on avoiding friction within Japan.

Of course, the developments in cooperative international relations in the Asia-Pacific region can be viewed as important successes of Japanese diplomatic initiatives in the 1970s. Even in this case, however, the stage was already set as a result of the Sino-U.S. rapprochement and the end of the Vietnam War, which greatly helped to reduce political tensions in the region. Japan certainly worked toward creating a basis for cooperation in the region, but that does not mean that those efforts alone caused cooperation.

Japanese diplomacy during this period was for the most part focused domestically and failed to take initiatives in part because the domestic political situation itself was unstable. The five prime ministers during the 1970s each had a diplomatic vision and showed ambition with regard to foreign policy. But with each of their administrations lasting only two years and their domestic (and intra-party) base of support for the most part largely unstable, there was a tendency to put off problems that could touch off great opposition.

Because policy was made on the basis of domestic considerations, several problems remained. First, there was the problem of Japanese identity. Within this lay the structural problems Japan faced as the only non-Western, developed country in Asia and as a country that had a strong economy but small military power. Yet in addition to those problems was the experience of the 1970s, in which Japan on the one hand continued to hold an image of itself as a weak, small country at the mercy of the changes in the international environment, and on the other hand, sought to leave its postwar position as a defeated country and instead be treated as a major power. The self-styled identity formed in the period was that Japan was a unique country in history, economically prosperous, willing to cooperate with others, seeking world peace and prosperity via economic means. This self-identity to a large extent reflected the Japanese consensus at the time, but the question lingered whether Japan could take such a unique path in an interdependent world.

Hence even in the 1970s, the question of an identity beyond its strong economy, the question of diplomacy beyond friendship, and the dilemma of peace and power were never resolved. Although it was an undeniable fact that Japan's strength lay primarily in its economy, there was the belief that this alone was insufficient. The Sato administration had already begun to recognize this problem, and the search for autonomous defense during the Tanaka and Miki administrations, the "heart-to-heart" approach of the Fukuda Doctrine, and the "cultural era" slogan of Ohira all showed interest in the need for something beyond simple economic might in Japanese diplomacy. In the end, however, military and cultural aspects did not play a prominent role in Japanese diplomacy, and while Japan was called an economic power, it could not avoid being called at the same time an economic "only" power.

Japan's emphasis on domestic priorities in diplomatic affairs, a lack of self-image of itself, and a tendency to throw money around when other solutions were troublesome, in the end prevented Japanese diplomacy from becoming truly autonomous in the 1970s. If one takes a slightly harsh view of Japan's diplomacy in this period, it can be said that Japan was tactically able to develop a more autonomous form of international cooperation, but failed in the strategic sense.[40] In any case, while there were many crises and changes, the fact that the structure of the Cold War continued and provided the basic framework of Japan's diplomacy meant that Japan was not forced to fundamentally reevaluate its policies. The issues that remained in the 1970s reappeared as a legacy and possibly a debt following the end of the Cold War.

Notes

1 The LDP gained 288 seats, an increase of 11 seats from the previous election of 1967. By aligning 14 independent candidate winners with the LDP, the party's total number of seats rose to 302. In contrast, the JSP lost 50 seats in the election, dropping its total to 90, the lowest number of JSP seats up until that time.

2 "Nichibei Anpo Joyaku no Keizoku ni Kansuru Jiminto Seimei (Statement by the LDP on the Continuation of the Japan–U.S. Security Treaty)," in Yoshihara Koichiro and Kubo Ayazo, eds., *Nihon Gendaishi Shiryo: Nichibei Anpo Joyaku Taiseishi,4* (Documents on Modern Japanese History: The Structural History of the Japan–U.S. Security Treaty, vol. 4) (Tokyo: Sanseido, 1971), p. 444.

3 The *Yodo* incident was the first hijacking incident in Japan. The radical left-wing student hijackers escaped from Japan to North Korea. The DPRK welcomed them as revolutionary colleagues, but their status was closer to confinement. Nearly thirty years later, the surviving members and their families drew media attention regarding their return to Japan and possible involvement in the abduction cases of the Japanese citizens conducted by a secret agency of the DPRK.

4 Sato Eisaku, *Sato Eisaku Nikki* (The Sato Eisaku Diaries) (Asahi Shimbunsha, 1998), vol. 4, p. 194.

5 The classic study on the textile trade dispute is I.M. Destler, Haruhiro Fukui, and Hideo Sato, *The Textile Wrangle: Conflict in Japanese-American Relations, 1969–1971* (Ithaca, NY: Cornell University Press, 1979).

6 Nixon, for example, sent an unusually strongly worded letter to Sato on March 11, 1971, expressing his "disappointment and concern at the course the textile matter has taken." The letter is reprinted in Iokibe Makoto and Wada Jun, eds., *Kusuda Minoru Nikki* (The Diary of Kusuda Minoru) (Tokyo: Chuo Koron Shinsha, 2001), pp. 797–801. Kusuda was a journalist for the *Sankei Shimbun* who served as an adviser for Sato at the start of his administration and later became his personal secretary.

7 This remark by Asakai became well known as "Asakai's nightmare." Hara Eikichi, *Tekio no Susume: Nihon Gaiko Shicho to Sono Sentaku* (Recommending Adaptability: The Historical Currents and Choices of Japanese Diplomacy) (Tokyo: Keio Tsushin, 1990), p. 295.

8 In his memoirs, Kissinger was apologetic regarding this conduct. He explained that he was afraid of a leak by the Japanese government, but he admitted that a more considerate approach to Japan might have been possible. Henry Kissinger, *White House Years* (Boston: Little, Brown, and Co., 1979), pp. 761–62. In order to repair the psychological damage, Nixon traveled to Anchorage in order to meet with Emperor Hirohito, who was stopping over on his trip to Europe in 1971.

9 The Albanian proposal to replace for the Republic of China with the PRC was approved by a vote of 76 yes', 35 no's, and 17 abstaining. The important reverse important question resolution was denied by the count of 55 yes', 59 no's, and 15 abstaining.

10 On the Japanese response to Nixon's "New Economic Policy," see Tadokoro Masayuki, *Amerika Koeta Doru* (Tokyo: Chuokoron Shinsha, 2001), pp. 146–54.

11 The first White Paper on defense, *Boei Hakusho*, was published in October 1970. Publishing this sort of document was planned before Nakasone took the office, but the actual outcome was influenced by Nakasone's own ideas. The English version began to appear in 1977 under the title *Defense of Japan*.

12 *Sato Nikki*, vol. 4, pp. 312–13.

13 Chong-sik Lee, *Japan and Korea: The Political Dimension* (Stanford: Hoover Institution Press, 1985).

14 Tanaka Kakuei (translated by Simul International), *Building a New Japan: A Plan for Remodeling the Japanese Archipelago* (Tokyo: Simul Press, 1973).

15 On February 24, 1972, Zhou Enlai informed Nixon of China's intention to normalize relations with Japan in the near future, not with the Sato administration but with the next cabinet. National Security Archives, Washington D.C. The record is published in Japanese translation. *Nikuson Hochu Kimitsu Kaidanroku* (Secret Conversations of Nixon's China Visit), trans. by Mori Kazuko and Mori Kozaburo, (Nagoya: Nagoya Daigaku Shuppankai, 2001), pp. 166–67.

16 To be precise, it was Taiwan and not Japan who formally severed diplomatic relations after Japan's normalization with the PRC. Following the Tanaka visit to China, Foreign Minister Ohira read an announcement in Beijing that the ROC-Japanese Peace Treaty had lost its validity and hence was discontinued. Immediately after this announcement, Taiwan announced the discontinuation of diplomatic relations with Japan. On the talks at this time, see Masaharu Takahashi and Juichiro Wakayama, "Nicchu-ka Nittai-Kade Yureta Nihon Gaiko (Japanese Vicissitudes between China and Taiwan)," *Chuo Koron*, vol. 118, no. 4 (April 2003), pp. 60–78, which reprints the letter from Tanaka to Chang Kai-shek on September 13, 1972.

17 The excerpts of the discussions between Tanaka and Zhou in September 1972 as well as the related conversations between Takeiri and Zhou were published in the *Yomiuri Shimbun*, June 23, 2001.

18 The English translation of the Joint Communiqué is at http://www.mofa.go.jp/region/asia-paci/china/joint72.html (accessed March 2003).

19 The fate of Tanaka deserves special mention. In 1976 foreign bribery by the Lockheed Company was disclosed in the U.S. Senate. That same year Tanaka was arrested for receiving part of this Lockheed bribe. Tanaka was later found guilty but appealed over the course of several years. During this time, he continued to wield strong influence over Japanese politics as a "Shadow Shogun" until he was incapacitated in 1985 by cerebral infarction. He died in 1993. The "Lockheed Scandal" was no doubt the largest political scandal in modern Japanese history, and made such struggles part of the regular landscape of Japanese politics.

20 Zbigniew Brzezinski, *The Fragile Blossom: Crisis and Change in Japan* (New York: Harper & Row, 1972).

21 "Nichibei Anzen Hosho Joyaku o Minaosu (Reexamining the Japan–U.S. Security Treaty)," in Kubo Takuya Iko Tsuitoshu Kankokai, *Iko Tsuitoshu Kubo Takuya* (Essays in Remembrance of Kubo Takuya) (Tokyo: Kubo Takuya Iko Tuitoshu Kankokai, 1981), p. 55.

22 Otake Hideo, *Nihon-no Boei-to Kokunai Seiji* (Japanese Defense and Domestic Politics) (Tokyo: Sanichi Shobo, 1983), p. 119.

23 The English translation of the 1976 Defense Program Outline is at http://www.ioc.u-tokyo.ac.jp/~worldjpn/documents/texts/docs/19761029.O1E.html (accessed March 2003).

24 Nagano Nobutoshi, ed., *Nihon Gaiko Handobukku* (Handbook to Japanese Diplomacy) (Tokyo: Simul Press, 1981), pp. 87–88.

25 http://www.ioc.u-tokyo.ac.jp/~worldjpn/documents/texts/JPUS/19750806.O1E.html (accessed March 2003).

26 Donella H. Meadows, et al., *The Limits to Growth: A Report for the Club of Rome's Project on the Predicament of Mankind* (New York: Universe Books, 1972).

27 Recently the records of the conversations between Sato and Nixon at San Clemente in January 1972 have been opened, revealing that it was actually Sato who proposed to have regular meetings among the leaders of the major powers in the free world. The records are reprinted in Iokibe and Wada, eds., *Kusuda Minoru Nikki*, pp. 810–27.

28 The treaty is in the Australian Department of Foreign Affairs and Trade website at: http://www.dfat.gov.au/geo/japan/japan_treaty.html (accessed March 2003).

29 Takahashi Hiroshi, ed., *Showa Tenno Hatsugenroku: Taisho 9 Nen kara Showa 64 Nen no Shinjitsu* (Comments by the Showa Emperor: The Truth from 1920 to 1989) (Tokyo: Shogakukan, 1989), pp. 186–89.

30 Fukuda himself later explained what he meant by "omni-directional peaceful diplomacy" in his memoirs. See Fukuda Takeo, *Kaiko Kyujunen* (Memoir of 90 Years) (Tokyo: Iwanami Shoten, 1995), pp. 271–72.

31 Although little known, under Article 25 of the old Administrative Agreement of 1952, Japan was obligated to bear a significant amount of the local costs (land rental, transportation, and services, and so on) of stationing American troops in Japan. The payments were to be reduced as Japan increased its own defense capabilities, but the amount of those reductions was often a subject of heated negotiations between the two countries. With the revision of the Security Treaty in 1960, these costs were eliminated.

32 The English translation is at http://www.mofa.go.jp/region/asia-paci/china/treaty78.html (accessed March 2003).

33 Zbigniew Brzezinski, *Power and Principle: Memoirs of the National Security Adviser, 1977–1981* (New York: Farrar, Straus Giroux, 1983), pp. 216–18.

34 The speech is reprinted in Sueo Sudo, *The Fukuda Doctrine and ASEAN* (Singapore: Institute of Southeast Asian Studies, 1992), pp. 241–47.

35 The English translation of the final report is Pacific Basin Cooperation Study Group, *Report on the Pacific Basin Cooperation Concept: Translation of the Report to Prime Minister Masayoshi Ohira* (1980).

36 Okita Saburo, *Ekonomisuto Gaisho no 252 Nichi* (252 Days of an Economist Foreign Minister) (Tokyo: Toyokeizai Shimposha, 1980), pp. 89–90.

37 See http://www.ioc.u-tokyo.ac.jp/~worldjpn/documents/texts/docs/19781127.O1E.html (accessed March 2003). On the formation of the 1978 Guidelines, see Koji Murata, "Boei Seisaku no Tenkai: Gaidorainu no Sakutei o Chushin ni (Development of Defense Policy with Special Reference to the Guidelines)," *Nenpo Seijigaku: Kiki no Nihon Gaiko 70 Nendai* (The Annals of the Japanese Political Science Association, Japanese Foreign Policy during the Crises of the 1970s) (Tokyo: Iwanami Shoten, 1997), pp. 79–96.

38 The phrase "comprehensive security" is the translation of "Sogo Anzen Hosho," a concept invented in Japan in the late 1970s. It was popularized in the 1980 report of The Comprehensive National Security Study Group (a brain trust under Ohira) entitled *The Report on Comprehensive National Security*. On the rise of the concept itself, see Nakanishi Hiroshi, "Sogo Anzen Hoshoron no Bunmyaku (The Development of the Comprehensive Security Concept in the 1970s), *Nenpo Seijigaku: Kiki no Nihon Gaiko 70 Nendai*, pp. 97–115.

39 Ezra F. Vogel, *Japan as Number One: Lessons for America* (Cambridge: Harvard University Press, 1979).

40 Masataka Kosaka, one of the leading scholars of international relations at this time and an extensive writer on diplomatic affairs, characterized the 1970s as the period as an "ordeal of affluence." Kosaka Masataka, *Yutakasa no Shiren* (The Ordeal of Affluence), (Tokyo: Shinchosha, 1979).

5 The mission and trials of an emerging international state

Japanese diplomacy in the 1980s

Murata Koji

This chapter explores Japan's attempts through the 1980s to strengthen the U.S.–Japan relationship and to expand the diplomatic horizons of Japan to the global level, in the process moving from being just an economic power to an "international one." However, this was accompanied by increased trade friction with the United States, a restart of the so-called "history problem" with the countries of Asia, and problems with Europe. Moreover, with the end of the Cold War, the path of Japan as an "international state" was once again questioned.

The 1980s began before the reverberations of the Soviet invasion of Afghanistan had a chance to settle, and ended when George H.W. Bush and Mikhail Gorbachev concluded their historic meeting on the island of Malta. The 1980s started off as tension-filled, but completely changed by the end of the decade. They represented the decade of the "New Cold War" but also corresponded with the end of the Cold War itself.

For Japan the 1980s were symbolically a time between the deaths of two major figures. On June 12, 1980, during the middle of the campaign for both the Lower House and Upper House elections (the first time that the elections for both houses were held on the same day), Prime Minister Ohira Masayoshi died of a massive heart attack, the first time a prime minister had died in office in the postwar period.[1] As a result, the election turned out to be one in which many "sympathy votes" went to the LDP. With a high voter turnout of 74.6 percent, the LDP captured a stable majority of 284 seats in the Lower House and 69 in the Upper House, which when added to the 66 who were not up for reelection, brought their total to 135. (In Japan, the term for a House of Councillors member is six years, and half the seats are up for election every three years. In the 1980 election, 126 Upper House seats were being contested.) Following his death and the subsequent Suzuki Zenko cabinet (1980–82), Nakasone Yasuhiro formed his cabinet, domestically spelling the end of LDP factional power politics, known as "Sankaku Daifukuchu (which gets its name from the names of the following individuals: Miki [Takeo], [Tanaka] Kakuei, Ohira [Masayoshi], Fukuda [Takeo], Nakasone [Yasuhiro])," and internationally inaugurating a period in which the Japan–U.S. relationship became even closer and the alliance stronger. It was also a decade in which

Japanese diplomacy became more active. As Nakasone has said, it was a time when Japan was turning into an "international state."

On January 7, 1989, Emperor Hirohito died. The death of the Showa Emperor, as he is posthumously known, symbolized not only the end of the 1980s but in many ways the conclusion of the postwar era, and indeed the finality of the Showa period, when Japan showed itself to be an economic power. Representatives from 164 countries, including 55 heads of state and delegations from 28 international organizations, attended the state funeral held on February 24. In addition, there were 2,000 accredited journalists there, 1,500 of whom were foreign journalists. The numbers of attendees, greater than those for former prime minister Yoshida Shigeru in October 1967 (the first state funeral in the postwar period) or for Ohira nine years earlier, recognized not only Japan's achievements as an economic state after recovering from the defeat of World War II but also Japan's position as "international state" with a broad global horizon and larger role in the political and security fields. Japan's position in international society grew increased bigger during this decade.

The political situation in Japan afterwards became quite unstable with the resignation of Prime Minister Takeshita Noburu in the wake of the Recruit scandal, the swift rise and fall of the Uno Sosuke cabinet, and the establishment of the Kaifu Toshiki cabinet without a strong political base. The one-and-a-half-party system, in which the LDP was the predominant party for decades in the absence of a strong opposition party and which had supported much of the country's postwar stability and prosperity, was showing its institutional fatigue. In the area of international politics as well, the end of the Cold War was a great shock to the simple, stable, and basic foundation of postwar Japanese diplomacy, namely the firm maintenance of the Japan–U.S. bilateral relationship amid East–West confrontation. In this sense, as is discussed in Chapter 6, the confusion seen in Japanese diplomacy during the Gulf crisis and war from August 1990 to February 1991 was truly symbolic. Having recovered from the crisis-filled 1970s, Japan during the 1980s gradually moved from simply being an economic power to functioning as an international state seeking to exert leadership in global political and diplomatic affairs. At the same time, Japan began to lose the basic domestic and international framework that had served it so effectively up until to that time.

The road to the Japan–U.S. alliance

The end of the Ohira administration

At the end of 1979 the United States faced one foreign threat after another. First, following a revolution led by Islamic fundamentalists in Iran, a key American ally in the region, the U.S. embassy in Teheran was occupied on November 4 and sixty-two of its diplomatic staff were held hostage. Then on December 27, the Soviet Army invaded Afghanistan. In the end Afghanistan became the Soviet Union's "Vietnam," where much of its economic, military, and political resources were wasted, and helped to speed up the end of the Cold War. In this way, not only was America's Middle and Near East strategy shaken, but the era of U.S.–Soviet détente ended a mere half year after the signing in June 1979 of the second Strategic Arms Limitation Treaty (SALT II). Facing both of these crises, President Jimmy Carter announced the Carter Doctrine in January 1980, defining the Persian Gulf as a region in which America's "vital interests" were concerned and stating that "an assault on that area would be repelled by any means necessary, including military force." In the aftermath of the Soviet invasion of Afghanistan, U.S.–Soviet relations became tense, détente failed, and what was described as the "New Cold War" began. Moreover, the Carter administration created the Rapid Deployment Force (RDF), with the Middle East in mind as the U.S. did not have a standing force capable of dealing directly with the Middle East at this time. The RDF developed into Central Command, which was later heavily involved in the Gulf War and Iraq War of later years.

Friendships are truly demonstrated in times of crisis. This is as true in international relations as it is in human relations. The confrontation between Iran and the United States presented a difficult choice for Japan, dependent as it was on Iran for 15 percent of its oil imports. Because Japanese companies broke the U.S.-led embargo and continued to purchase oil from Iran, public opinion in the United States quickly turned against Japan. Japanese diplomacy learned from this mistake, and did not repeat it following the Soviet invasion of Afghanistan. Immediately after the announcement of the Carter Doctrine, Prime Minister Ohira stated in his policy speech to the 91st Ordinary Session of the Diet on January 25, 1980, his country's strong support of the United States "even if our country has to make sacrifices."

However, the concept of "shared existence, shared sacrifice" (*kyozon kyoku*) with the United States had to be backed up by action. On April 25, the Japanese government announced that Japan would not participate in the twenty-second Summer Olympics, to be held in Moscow. (On the same day, Special Forces of the U.S. military unsuccessfully attempted to rescue American hostages from the embassy in Teheran.) The Ohira Cabinet found political meaning in deciding not to participate in the Olympics.

Immediately after this decision, Prime Minister Ohira left for a trip to the United States, Mexico, and Canada. It was the year of the U.S. presidential election. At their meeting on May 1, Ohira expressed to Carter his willingness to see the 1978 Mid-term Defense Review (for the years 1980–84) implemented ahead of schedule, which had long been a desire of the U.S. side. Earlier that spring, the destroyers *Hiei* and *Amatsukaze*, the latter being Japan's first guided missile destroyer, and other vessels participated for the first time in the multilateral Rim of Pacific (RIMPAC) exercises with the navies of the United States, Canada, Australia, and New Zealand. With the increase in tensions in the New Cold War, Japan was demonstrating a greater interest in defense cooperation with the United States, as seen by the rapid buildup of its defense strength and further implementation of the 1978 Guidelines for Japan–U.S. Defense Cooperation, such as joint exercises.

Without returning from his three-nation visit, Ohira extended his trip to Europe to attend the state funeral for President Josip Tito of Yugoslavia, who died that May. Ohira exchanged greetings with the Soviet general secretary, but according to one version of events, Leonid Brezhnev did not even know who Ohira was. (Brezhnev was at this point in a weakened physical and mental condition, according to some observers of Soviet affairs at the time.) Following the conclusion of the Treaty of Peace and Friendship between Japan and China in August 1978, Japan's relations with the Soviet Union cooled dramatically, as discussed in Chapter 4. A vote of no confidence submitted by the Socialist Party awaited Ohira when he returned to Japan and was passed when non-mainstream faction members of the LDP absented themselves from the vote. Ohira decided to dissolve the Lower House and called for elections to be held in conjunction with the Upper House elections. The prime minister's death during the campaign came at a time when Japan was beginning to clarify its position as a "member of the West," and just when Japan–U.S. cooperation was becoming more active.

The Suzuki cabinet adrift

After a brief time when Chief Cabinet Secretary Ito Masayoshi served as acting prime minister, the next cabinet began on July 17, headed by Suzuki Zenko, an LDP veteran weak in foreign affairs. Suzuki had been second-in-command in Ohira's faction (Kochikai) and thus he assumed the premiership without having been the actual head of a faction. Had the LDP not won the election so decisively, it was unlikely that a leader this weak and lacking in charisma would have been chosen. Meanwhile, in August in South Korea, the administration of Chun Doo Hwan was formed following a coup against acting president Choi Kyu Ha, and in the November presidential election in the United States, Carter lost to Ronald Reagan. Facing numerous international crises, the Carter administration, in its remaining days, somewhat unsympathetically requested that Japan increase its defense spending after the death of Ohira, Carter's close friend. At the end of December, when the Japanese government decided on a 7.6 percent increase in its 1981 defense budget, the U.S. government, which had strongly hoped for a 9.7 percent increase, publicly stated that it "could not but be disappointed." For the Suzuki cabinet, however, it was a difficult decision, particularly because the defense budget that passed was higher than that for social security (7.60 percent).

The Reagan administration, which came into office in January 1981, displayed a foreign policy that was very different from that of Carter. The same was true of Reagan's Japan policy. In March, when Foreign Minister Ito visited Washington, Secretary of Defense Caspar Weinberger called for an increase in Japan's air and antisubmarine defense capabilities. Quality, not quantity, was the new approach. As Japan–U.S. defense cooperation progressed, the American side learned more about the actual state of the Self-Defense Forces and was able to make more specific requests. As a result, Defense Agency Director General Omura Joji stated in Diet testimony that "it was now possible for Japan to divide responsibilities in functional areas with the United States for defense of the seas in the North Western Pacific."[2]

In the economic arena, in contrast, the issues of the closed nature of Japan's markets and the rapid increase in its car exports to the United States became more serious. U.S. Trade Representative William E. Brock III explained during Senate testimony on February 24, 1981, that "Japan was a very attractive market for U.S. industry, but because it possessed unique characteristics, the U.S. government would request that it further open up." In conversations with Deputy Vice Minister of International Trade and Industry Amaya Naohiro, Brock warned that the "automobile problem was a 'political time-bomb,' and even if there were great efforts to resolve the issue there was no guarantee that it would not explode."[3] In fact, following the second oil shock in 1979, the sale of Japanese-made economy automobiles jumped dramatically, with 1.77 million being sold in the United States in 1979. This figure represented 76.3 percent of the United States' imported car market. The consequent layoff of 300,000 U.S. autoworkers became a considerable political problem. Automobiles were one of America's key industries, and the impact of Japanese imports on that market was far larger than textiles had been a decade earlier.

In the end, just before the 1981 Japan–U.S. summit meeting, MITI minister Tanaka Rokusuke visited the United States and reached a four-point agreement: (1) Japanese automakers would voluntarily limit their exports to the United States to 1.68 million vehicles; (2) for 1982, makers would limit their exports to 1.68 million and 16.5 percent of the expansion in the interim of the U.S. car market; (3) a decision as to whether or not to continue the voluntary export restraints a third year would be made at the end of the second year; and (4) in any case, voluntary export restraints would end at the end of March 1984 at the latest. With this agreement, the problem cooled down somewhat.

In May 1981 Prime Minister Suzuki and President Reagan met for their first summit in Washington. During these meetings, Suzuki reportedly told Reagan that "if the defense budget were suddenly increased, there would be strong criticism in the LDP, which would pave the way for a Socialist-led government. If that were to happen, Japan–U.S. relations would lose out."[4] The "threat of the weak" was an often-used tactic in postwar Japan–U.S. relations. Although it was already hard to say that Japan was "weak," Suzuki, as leader of the LDP faction Kochikai, faithfully followed in the footsteps of his predecessors in adhering to Japan's basic diplomatic policy of light armament using political and economic constraints as an excuse of sorts.

In the joint communiqué released afterward, however, the word "alliance" was employed for the first time, as seen by the statement in which both countries "recogniz[ed] that the alliance between [them] is built upon their shared values of democracy and liberty, [and] reaffirmed their solidarity, friendship and mutual trust." The communiqué continued by stating that "in insuring peace and stability in the region and the defense of Japan, [the two leaders] acknowledged the desirability of an appropriate division of roles between Japan and the United States," with Japan "to seek to make even greater efforts for improving its defense capabilities in Japanese territories and in its surrounding sea and air space, and for further alleviating the financial burden of U.S. forces in Japan." At a session of the National Press Club gathering after the summit, Suzuki, speaking without much preparation, stated that an "appropriate division of roles" was the defense of "sea areas around Japan up to several hundred nautical miles and the sea lanes up to 1,000 nautical miles." America took this statement by the prime minister as a concrete promise. Newspapers back in Japan all reported a "strengthening of the image of a military alliance."

After returning to Tokyo, Prime Minister Suzuki repeatedly expressed his unhappiness that the joint communiqué did not properly reflect the content of their discussions and that "a military implication was not intended" with regard to the Japan–U.S. alliance relationship. Vice Foreign Minister Takashima Matsuo's reported comment that "an alliance without any military or security matters is just nonsense" infuriated the prime minister. Foreign Minister Ito, who resigned after assuming responsibility for causing the confusion in Washington, pointed out critically that "of course the Japan–U.S. Security Treaty encompasses military matters." His resignation was meant as a sign of protest against the prime minister.

Suzuki was not the first prime minister to use the word "alliance"; former premier Ohira had used it at the summit meeting with Carter in May 1979. Yet many Japanese politicians and citizens were not prepared to openly accept the military dimension of the alliance even after entering the 1980s.

In any case, a "promise" is indeed a promise. At security meetings in Hawaii that June, the U.S. side requested that Japan defend the air and sea areas surrounding Japan, as well as the sea lines of communication up to 1,000 nautical miles. This security role was much more than the National Defense Program Outline had anticipated, and was, in the words of Foreign Minister Sonoda Sunao, as if plans for a small house were suddenly expected to be expanded into a "10-story building." Forced to make tough decisions, the Suzuki cabinet, facing a 5 percent reduction across the board in the budget for 1983 (the first-ever minus-ceiling), decided to spare ODA and defense from cuts in the budget. Although the Reagan administration desired an improvement in the quality of Japan's defense capability, Japan continued with increases in quantity. Nevertheless, the American government praised Japan's defense efforts. When it became clear, however, that the U.S. trade deficit with Japan had grown to more than $13.6 billion, the largest in history, the U.S. Congress exploded in anger, calling for greater efforts in defense by Japan to stop its "free riding." In Japan the phrase *boei masatsu*, or "defense friction," began to be heard alongside *boeki masatsu*, or "trade friction."

In addition, there was pressure from South Korea. The Reagan administration believed it was necessary to repair U.S.–South Korean relations, damaged during the Carter–Park years, and chose President Chun Doo Hwan to be its first official state visitor. Feeling confident in having improved relations with the United States, South Korea began to emphasize the "special relationship" between South Korea and Japan and, using the concept of "role sharing" as it appeared in the Japan–U.S. joint communiqué, began to call strongly for loans from Japan from the perspective of security. By standing up to North Korea on the 38th Parallel, South Korea was taking on a large share of Japan's defense and thus Japan, in its view, had an obligation to financially assist South Korea. At talks between the two countries' foreign ministers in August 1981, the South Korean side requested $6 billion in loans. In Foreign Minister Sonoda's words, Japanese–Korean economic support tied to security issues was for Japan "not just difficult but impossible."

Before this problem could be resolved, the textbook issue shook relations with both South Korea and China. A newspaper in Japan had reported domestically that during the textbook review process led by the Ministry of Education in June 1982, Japan's "invasion" (*shinryaku*) of Asia was changed to an "advance" (*shinshutsu*). (Subsequently, among the major papers, the *Sankei Shimbun* alone noted that they had incorrectly reported the story, but the damage was already done.) In succession, the governments of China and South Korea strongly protested to the Japanese government. The problem worsened when National Land Agency Director General Matsuno Yukiyasu described these protests as "interference in domestic affairs." Although the Foreign Ministry worked hard to calm the situation, China withdrew its invitation for a visit by Education Minister Ogawa Heiji in August. Because this happened just before the Twelfth Conference of the Chinese Communist Party, there may have been a desire by Chinese leaders to demonstrate an "independent and autonomous foreign policy" vis-à-vis Japan.

Bargaining continued between the LDP, Foreign Ministry, and Education Ministry. At the end of August, Prime Minister Suzuki observed that

> while he believed that a proper evaluation of the prewar acts of our country should a wait the judgments of future historians, it is a fact that in China and around the world there is strong criticism and belief that Japan was an invader and it is necessary for our government to recognize that.

This was followed by an official statement by Chief Cabinet Secretary Miyazawa Kiichi, a nephew of Education Minister Ogawa,[5] that the government "deeply recognizes the great pain and damages caused by Japan to the countries of Asia, including South Korea and China." In this way, the government assumed the responsibility for correcting the process of textbook review and the problem was temporarily resolved (although the textbooks that had already cleared the review were not amended). This vague solution to the problem, however, left the seed of discontent in both China and South Korea and among domestic conservatives. The former group found the government's response to the use of the "history card" by Japan's neighbors pathetic, and the latter group saw in the episode an inability on the part of Japan to reflect on the past and an example of Japan's effrontery. This cycle would repeat itself again and again in the future. The incident demonstrated the burden of historical legacies on Japan's Asia diplomacy.

Returning from a trip to China just after this, Prime Minister Suzuki abruptly announced on October 12 that he would not run in the next LDP presidential election. Employing a phrase that the Ministry of International Trade and Industry used to describe Japan, Suzuki called Japan the "10 percent country" (*Ichiwari Kokka*) for its reaching 10 percent of the world's GNP. The Suzuki cabinet, however, was not able to make the international role of Japan as a 10 percent country clear.

The strengthening of the Japan–U.S. alliance and bilateral rivalry

Enhancing the Japan–U.S. alliance

At the time of his inauguration as prime minister on November 27, Nakasone Yasuhiro, as the leader of a minor faction of the LDP, needed the support of the largest faction, the Tanaka group, when forming his cabinet. Usually the prime minister appoints someone from his faction as chief cabinet secretary, who would serve as a chief of staff and press secretary, but in Nakasone's case he went so far as to appoint Gotoda Masaharu from the Tanaka faction. As a result, the Nakasone cabinet was initially ridiculed as the "Tanaka-sone cabinet" and the "Kaku-ei cabinet," the latter term using the character for "shadow" (*ei*) in place of the similar sounding *ei* (but with a different meaning) in Tanaka's given name, implying that Tanaka Kakuei exercised great influence on the cabinet from behind the scenes. But in actual policy, particularly in the area of foreign affairs where the constraints of factional politics are more limited than in domestic policy, Nakasone placed great emphasis on security issues and displayed independence in thinking. The Japan–U.S. relationship, which had gone forward because of Ohira's strong showing of Japan as a "member of the West" and which had taken a half step backward with Suzuki, was greatly advanced by Nakasone.[6]

On January 11, 1983, Nakasone traveled to South Korea for his first foreign visit as prime minister. It was also the first time in the postwar period that a Japanese prime minister had made an official visit to South Korea. Nakasone had already sent a close associate, Sejima Ryuzo, a former president of and then advisor to the trading company Nissho Iwai, which had strong ties to South Korea, to Seoul to lay the groundwork.[7] In South Korea, Nakasone stated that "it was necessary to solemnly reflect on the unfortunate history between the two countries," and, showing his admiration for Korean culture, sang a Korean song. (Nakasone studied Korean intensively in order to deliver part of his speech as well as sing in Korean, another example of his flair for personal diplomacy.) Nakasone's diplomacy was, in this way, often about performance, which can be an important aspect in diplomacy. In the case of Japanese–South Korean relations, which had experienced great psychological damage, this approach was particularly important. (Reagan, the former actor and radio announcer, was equally skilled at performance, as seen by his speeches referring to a "strong America" and description of the Soviet Union as an "Evil Empire.") With regard to the problem of economic cooperation, South Korea de-linked the issue from security affairs, and an agreement was reached by which Japan would provide loans of $4 billion over seven years. In their joint declaration, Nakasone and President Chun stated that Japanese–Korean relations had entered a new era. Postwar Japanese diplomacy had been involved in the security affairs of the Korean Peninsula in the context of Japan–U.S. relations (see Chapters 3 and 4). In fact, in visiting South Korea, Nakasone was hoping to indirectly respond to America's increasing desire for Japan to expand its defense capability and to bring to Washington such a gift immediately thereafter. As Chief Cabinet Secretary Gotoda recalled in his memoirs,

In order to break the impasse with the United States, it was necessary to repair relations with South Korea, which the United States was worried about. In this sense, relations with South Korea could be said to be related to problems of peace and security.[8]

On January 17, Nakasone visited Washington for his first meeting with President Reagan. Before leaving for the United States, Nakasone overcame domestic criticism in his decision to exclude the transfer of weapons technology to the United States from the general list of Japan's 1967 "Three Principles on Arms Exports" and also decided to increase Japan's defense spending by 1 percent more than the previous fiscal year in the Ministry of Finance draft.[9] Moreover, Nakasone told Reagan that "Japan and the United States have a shared destiny," and in the joint communiqué, the phrase "alliance relationship" was reaffirmed. Subsequently, "alliance" came to be commonly used. In the past, as director general of the Defense Agency, Nakasone had sought to pursue an autonomous defense policy with the Japan–U.S. alliance taking a second tier, but was unsuccessful. Upon becoming prime minister, Nakasone became a strong advocate of the alliance. In the détente years, the former approach may have been possible, but in the New Cold War period, it was very clear that there were limits to autonomous defense for a non-nuclear state. In an interview with the *Washington Post* during his visit to Washington, Nakasone went so far as to observe that Japan was "an unsinkable aircraft carrier [and Japan in case of emergency would help to] completely control the four straits around it." (The expression "unsinkable aircraft carrier" was used by the interpreter. Rather than being upset, Nakasone was delighted by the impact the statement had.)

Needless to say, Nakasone's performance made President Reagan, who had adopted a strong stance vis-à-vis the Soviet Union, very happy. The two established a personal relationship of mutual confidence and trust, symbolized by the use of first names, and bilateral relations entered the "Ron–Yasu period." Both of them had to break the image of weakness of their respective predecessors. Moreover, Nakasone, attempting fiscal reconstruction and administrative reforms domestically, hoped to implement the neo-conservative agenda of "small government" and deregulation shared by Reagan and British prime minister Margaret Thatcher. The 1980s was perhaps the last decade where a clear shared ideology served as an absolute policy coordinate in both foreign and domestic affairs. In this way Nakasone, who had been more of a nationalist, adjusted to the trend of the times and showed his great political skills. It was also important that within the Reagan administration, George P. Shultz, who highly valued the relationship with Japan, replaced Alexander M. Haig, Jr., who stressed China's strategic importance over that of Japan. As Shultz noted in his memoirs, "For me, the centerpiece has always been Japan. By far the largest economy in Asia, Japan is a key strategic partner and a dramatic example of successful democratic governance in an area where that is scarce."[10]

However, Nakasone's statements and behavior in America caused great concern in Japan among the opposition parties and in public opinion, and in February, his cabinet approval rating dropped 5.1 percent. The need to pay close attention to the bilateral relationship and at the same time secure domestic support was the historical dilemma of the Japanese government. Nevertheless, the positive posture of the Nakasone cabinet in security affairs did not change. "It was a good opportunity," Nakasone records in his memoirs, "to push the debate on security issues in the Diet."[11]

At the ninth G7 summit, held May 28–30, 1983, in Williamsburg, in addition to bringing about greater economic cooperation through coordination on policies to support "continued non-inflationary growth" and a multilateral system for currency stability, the unity of the West on security matters was made clear. At this time discussions had not been going well between the Soviet Union and the United States over the Soviets' removing Intermediate Nuclear Forces/SS-20 missiles from Europe. In the Williamsburg Summit declaration, however, the G7 countries made clear they were "united in efforts for arms reductions and will continue to carry out thorough and intensive consultations. The security of our countries is indivisible and must be approached on a global basis." At the summit, it was Nakasone who most strongly supported the U.S. position in the negotiations, and who had the phrase, "the security of our countries is indivisible," included in the declaration on security released on May 29. Nakasone's view of "security as indivisible" and his call for a global response was due to his belief that simply withdrawing the SS-20s from Europe and redeploying them to Asia would not solve the security problem, and he worked to get the summit participants' agreement that Japan's defense would not be endangered. It was a rare show of multilateral diplomacy by a Japanese prime minister. His cutting into the line to stand next to Reagan, the host of the summit, was another example of this "performance diplomacy."

In this way, the Williamsburg Summit became the stage on which Japan played a global security role. While his predecessor, Suzuki, had described Japan as a "10 percent country," Nakasone professed to make Japan an "international state." This was an attempt to define Japan's position not in terms of quantity but instead in quality, and to politically reflect Japan's economic power. Within the U.S., Secretary of State Shultz also emphasized the significance of economics in international politics, and highly praised Japan's importance in Asia, over China.

An action that underscored the Nakasone cabinet's positive posture in security affairs was its response to the September 1 downing of the Korean Air Lines passenger jet. On that day, the Seoul-bound KAL flight from New York was shot down by a Soviet fighter on the excuse that the plane, assumed to be a U.S. reconnaissance flight, had violated Soviet territorial air space. The crew and all 269 passengers on board were killed, including 28 Japanese, a U.S. congressman, and 60 other Americans. Initially there were reports that the plane might have made an unscheduled landing in Sakhalin, but U.S. intelligence sources, based on American and Japanese reports, came to the conclusion early on that it had been downed by the Soviets. The Soviet government, however, remained quiet and there was no evidence to prove the allegations. After consulting with Gotoda, Prime Minister Nakasone decided to make public the transcripts of the messages from the Soviet fighter plane that had been picked up by SDF radar facilities. The Defense Agency had wanted to avoid letting the degree of its radar capabilities be known, but as a result of the disclosure, the Soviet Union admitted that it was responsible for the downing.[12]

In addition to damaging the image of the Soviet Union further, this incident had the effect of strengthening the solidarity of the West. The U.S. Senate went so far as to pass a resolution unanimously thanking Japan. Moreover, this incident widened the understanding of the unseen role that Japan was playing on a daily basis in supporting America's strategy in East Asia.

In November President Reagan visited Japan and became the first American president to address the Japanese Diet. Noting the military expansion of the Soviet Union, Reagan declared that "Japanese–American friendship is forever." His speech was so popular that it was interrupted twenty-five times for applause. Responding to Reagan, Nakasone stated that Japan "would overcome any challenge in paying the price to defend freedom and peace." It was an expression that went even further than Ohira's earlier statement that Japan would respond "even if our country had to make sacrifices." Nakasone and Reagan went to Nakasone's weekend villa, Hinode Sanso, outside of Tokyo, with their wives for a visit, showing off the bilateral friendship and the Ron–Yasu relationship. For Nakasone, the stabilization and strengthening of the U.S.–Japan relationship was a valuable political asset because the LDP lost the elections held at the end of 1983 following former Prime Minister Tanaka's court ruling finding him guilty.

According to a July 1985 public opinion poll in Japan, 71.4 percent of those responding felt that the Japan–U.S. Security Treaty was beneficial to Japan.

After that, Nakasone moved to increase the 1 percent of GNP limit on defense spending decided by the Miki cabinet some ten years before. On September 1, the Nakasone cabinet raised the prominence of the Defense Agency's 1984 "Mid-Term Defense Estimates" to a government plan "Mid-Term Defense Program" (for the years 1986–90). Nevertheless defense spending for 1986 was still kept under the 1 percent GNP limit. At the end of 1986, however, questions arose as to whether defense spending for 1987 could be kept within the limit. In a cabinet decision on January 24, 1987, the 1 percent GNP limit was officially lifted. Behind this decision were the victory of the LDP in the general elections (joint elections of the Upper and Lower Houses) in July 1986 and the recognition of the need to increase Japan's financial support for the stationing of U.S. forces in Japan. Although spending for defense remained at 1.004 percent of GNP (see Figure 3.4), the decision was significant as a political expression of the desire of the Nakasone cabinet to "break political taboos" and to see "a complete modification of postwar politics." Many on the U.S. side welcomed this move. With the victory in the elections, Nakasone's term as LDP president was extended another year. The fact that his term as prime minister was five years long (the longest serving prime minister since Sato Eisaku) and his defense policy was consistent was very important for the strengthening of the bilateral alliance.

Around this time, in April 1985, the U.S. Air Force sent two F-16 Air Wings (forty-eight fighters) to Misawa Air Base, and in September 1986 the cabinet decided to participate in studies on the Strategic Defense Initiative (SDI) being actively pursued by the Reagan administration. The dispatch to Misawa of the F-16s, which were capable of carrying nuclear weapons, was in response to the Soviet buildup in the Far East, raising the deterrent effect toward the Soviet Union. As seen in Chapter 3, Japan had adopted the "three Non-Nuclear policies" in the 1960s, and it would have been politically impossible to permit the stationing of F-16s actually carrying nuclear weapons. Nevertheless, U.S. officials estimated that the Soviet Union did not believe that Japan would honor its non-nuclear policies, and thus the bluff of having fighters capable of carrying nuclear weapons stationed in Japan worked. The SDI project, otherwise known as "Star Wars," was a big plan, envisioning the downing and destruction of enemy nuclear missiles before they reached U.S. shores—essentially making nuclear missiles ineffective. If this were realized, the basis of mutual nuclear deterrence would have been overturned. Moreover, the Nakasone cabinet agreed to go ahead with joint Japan–U.S. development of the next generation fighter plane (FSX), which the Japanese Defense Agency had thought to undertake domestically only. In this way, the Japan–U.S. alliance during the Ron–Yasu years gradually took real shape and form.[13]

The making of the bilateral rivalry

On the other hand, bilateral trade friction grew during this same period. First came the question of Japan's liberalization of imports of farm products, such as meat and citrus products. In April 1984 an agreement was finally reached to permit the increase over the following four years of U.S. exports of high-quality meat to an annual average of 6,900 tons and oranges to 11,000 tons. Automobile exports from Japan were another issue. In October 1983 Japan agreed to limit its exports to the United States to 1.85 million beginning in fiscal year 1984. Seeking to limit Japanese car imports, the U.S. House of Representatives passed a "Local Contents Law" the following year, requiring a certain percentage of locally made parts to be used in car production. With this, Japanese automakers began intensively to shift to local production facilities in the United States. The revision of the foreign exchange law and foreign trade management laws in Japan at the end of 1979 made it possible for large-scale direct investment in the United States.

The next issue to emerge was the steel problem. At the end of 1984 Japan agreed to limit its share of the U.S. steel market to 5.8 percent for a period of five years. In 1985 the United States requested the start of a Market Oriented, Sector Specific (MOSS) dialogue on four areas—electronic communications, electronics, forestry and agricultural products, and medicine and medical equipment—as proof of the openness of the Japanese market. At the same time, the U.S. Congress passed one protective bill after another. It was this same year that the famous journalist Theodore H. White published a widely read article, "The Danger from Japan," describing the large export of Japanese goods to the United States as "adversarial trade."[14] The following year, the Japanese government quickly implemented an action program, lowering duties on 1,849 imported goods.

The problem of semiconductors emerged next. In June 1985 the Semiconductor Industry Association of America brought an action suit against the Japanese semiconductor industry under Article 301 of the Commerce Law, and the U.S. Trade Representative's office began its investigation. Semiconductors were vital for much of America's increasingly technical and modern economy, symbolizing that for America the issue was not simply trade friction, but national security as well. Both countries reached an understanding with the signing of the June 1986 U.S.–Japan Semiconductor Agreement, in which Japan would initiate policies to expand access of U.S. products to the Japanese market. At this time, the United States requested that after five years, the share of the market for foreign-produced semiconductors should be raised to above 20 percent, and although a secret side-letter was exchanged with the Ministry of International Trade and Industry expressing Japanese support for this request, the U.S. government took the side-letter as a "promise," and this became the seed for future friction.[15]

According to a statement by the U.S. Commerce Department, the U.S. trade deficit in 1985 had risen to more than $122 billion, with the deficit with Japan at $43.5 billion. Moreover, the U.S. external debt stood at $107 billion, making the United States a debtor nation for the first time in seventy-one years (since 1914, the year World War I began). In 1986 the U.S. trade deficit jumped again to more than $144 billion, of which the deficit with Japan rose to more than $54 billion. Likewise, the U.S. debt doubled to more than $263 billion, becoming the largest in the world. Moreover, with regard to Japan–U.S. relations, Japanese exports to America were for the most part manufactured goods, while U.S. exports to Japan were largely food products and primary goods, the trade pattern between developed and developing nations. In the middle of this, at the end of the same year, the Dutch journalist Karel van Wolferen published his article entitled "The Japan Problem," and the phrase "Japan bashing" became common.[16] According to an opinion poll taken in May 1987, 69 percent of Americans saw Japanese trade practices as unfair.

If bilateral economic problems in the first half of the 1980s were centered on individual goods, with Japan agreeing to exercise self-restraint, then the second half can be said to have shifted to macroeconomic policies, such as the exchange rate and economic structures. The focus of trade friction moved from the torrent of Japanese goods to the closed nature of the Japanese market.

Behind the round of trade frictions in the first half of the 1980s were problems on the U.S. side resulting from "Reaganomics," the policies aimed at supporting high interest rates and a strong dollar, as well as the extreme consumerism seen at the time. The new secretary of the treasury, James A. Baker III, keeping in mind the 1986 mid-term elections, which would be the last elections held during the Reagan years, paid particular attention to the problem of the high dollar. In September 1985, a meeting of the finance ministers and central bankers of the five developed nations (G5) was held in New York at the Plaza Hotel. In an effort to deter protectionism by the U.S. Congress, the ministers decided to adjust the high dollar, which was contributing to the unequal trade balance by cooperative intervention. This agreement became known as the Plaza Accords. In this way, the United States abandoned its longtime policy of noninterference with the exchange rate. The dollar-yen rate, which was 240 yen to the dollar at the time, jumped to 200 yen, and then to 150 yen to the dollar in February 1987. Because of the substantial dollar-buying policy implemented by the Japanese government, the level of foreign currency held by Japan jumped from $26.5 billion in 1985 to $81.5 billion in 1987. As the historian Watanabe Akio noted, "The Plaza Accords gained attention as well because it was the first time that the G-5, which had been a bit like a veneer, began to play an active role out front. The shifting of the battle front over the economy between the State and the Market to the exchange rate symbolized this."[17]

On the one hand, in dollar terms, the personal income of individual Japanese increased and the value of the Japanese market as a whole grew. Of course, American pressures to enter the Japanese market increased as well. Unfortunately, the Plaza Accord was intended to coordinate policies with regard to intervening in the currency exchange market, as well as in macroeconomic areas, but financial coordination did not go well on both sides. Nor was a solution found with regard to the problematic U.S. budget deficit.

Shortly after the Plaza Accord, Prime Minister Nakasone launched a committee called the Advisory Group on Economic Structural Adjustment for International Harmony (Kokusai Kyocho no Tame no Keizai Kozo

Chosei Kenkyukai) and appointed Maekawa Haruo, a former president of the Bank of Japan, as its chair. In April 1986, the committee released what became known as the Maekawa Report, which called for the reduction of the current account surplus through increasing domestic demand, the shifting of Japan's economy from an export-oriented structure, improvement of market access, and the liberalization and internationalization of finance. As an example of his performance style, Nakasone went on TV to call on all Japanese to buy 100 dollars of imported goods. However, in actuality Japan did little more than grudgingly make minor efforts at opening the market after pressure from the United States. Measures at structural reform were completely ignored. Moreover, through the management efforts of Japanese companies which feared the possibility of recession caused by the rise of the yen, a dramatic change in the trade balance with the United States did not occur. Thus the frustration on the American side became chronic. In light of this, the strengthening of the Japan–U.S. alliance during the Ron–Yasu era can be seen as an effort to counterbalance the increased rivalry between the two countries in the economic arena.

The limits of Nakasone diplomacy

The strengthening of the Japan–U.S. alliance also had its limits. First of all, in April 1987, it became known that Toshiba Electronics had gone against COCOM restrictions and exported sensitive technology to the Soviet Union. As a result, Soviet submarines could operate more quietly, making them harder to detect. The image of Japan as insensitive and reckless, seeking economic profit at the expense of the security of the entire Western bloc, was strengthened by this incident. Even more than when it had continued to buy oil from Iran despite the hostage crisis, Japan's behavior in this incident deserved censure. Anti-Japanese opinion grew in the United States, with scenes of members of Congress smashing a Toshiba-made radio cassette player on the steps of the Capitol building being widely shown in the news. Moreover, Japan was in the middle of its bubble economy. In March that year, a Japanese company had paid more than 5.8 billion yen for Van Gogh's *Sunflower*, further increasing the arrogant and out-of-touch image of Japan.

In the middle of this, Nakasone attended what would be his final summit meeting with President Reagan in September. Because Iraq had mined the Persian Gulf as the Iran–Iraq War worsened, Nakasone promised Reagan that Japan would come up with a concrete plan to secure the safe passage of shipping in the Gulf. It was an opportunity to make up for lost ground due to the Toshiba COCOM incident. However if SDF minesweepers were sent, it was likely that the decision would be met with domestic criticism by the public and opposition parties as an unconstitutional dispatching of forces abroad. Once again, the dilemma between domestic public opinion and assuming international responsibility was evident. Moreover, Gotoda himself was also cautious, and in the end the Nakasone cabinet elected to deal with the problem through nonmilitary means, such as economic cooperation. It continued to be impossible to extend the scope of Japan–U.S. alliance cooperation to the Middle East.[18]

Regarding East Asian diplomacy, Nakasone welcomed China's Deng Xiaoping to Japan in November 1984, with the latter giving a speech at the Diet. It was the first time a Chinese politician had spoken before the Japanese parliament. Earlier that year in March, Nakasone had visited China, meeting with Communist Party secretary general Hu Yaobang and senior politicians such as Deng and others. At that time, he promised 470 billion yen as the second stage of loans. Shortly after that, Nakasone visited India, expanding his Asia diplomacy. In addition, in September of that year, President Chun became the first president of South Korea to visit Japan. With this visit by Chun, as well as that of Nakasone to South Korea earlier and Reagan's visits to Japan and South Korea, all three countries had exchanged state visits with one another, effectively demonstrating the level of trilateral cooperation between the United States, Japan, and South Korea. During a reception at the Imperial Palace, the emperor stated that he "regretted the unfortunate history between their two countries." In response, Chun stated "it was important to turn this unfortunate history into the basis for a brighter, closer relationship in the future between South Korea and Japan." Although in South Korea there was some criticism that the emperor's words were insufficient, the joint communiqué stated, "a new chapter in relations between Japan and South Korea is opening." The Nakasone administration's diplomacy toward East Asia was seen to be going well at this point.

However, when Nakasone visited the Yasukuni Shrine on August 15, 1985, for the fortieth anniversary of the end of the Pacific War—the first time a postwar prime minister had done so in an official capacity—China expressed its displeasure with Japan at a meeting between their foreign ministers in October. Although Prime Minister Nakasone, the foreign minister, and two others from the cabinet put off visiting the Yasukuni Shrine in an official capacity out of respect for the concerns of Japan's neighbors the following year, sixteen members of the cabinet did go.[19] Immediately after this, Minister of Education Fujio Masayuki stated with regard to the textbook controversy, "the critics act as if they have never committed an invasion of this sort in history," resulting in outbursts from China and South Korea. In a magazine, it was further reported that Fujio had stated that with regard to the annexation of 1910, "Korea was responsible as well and also has some things to reflect on itself." Despite protests from South Korea, Fujio would not retract his statements, leading to his dismissal from the cabinet.

Moreover, when the Nakasone cabinet approved a defense budget that broke the GNP 1 percent barrier, China publicly voiced its objections. In the past China had expressed its understanding toward the strengthening of the Japan–U.S. alliance in order to prevent Soviet hegemony, but when Japan, the United States, and South Korea were working together to strengthen their anti-Soviet stance, China feared being unnecessarily entrapped by this quasi-alliance, and gradually began to change its diplomatic stance. In addition Hu, who was in favor of strengthening Sino-Japanese ties, was removed in January 1987 by some in China who felt that liberalization was moving too quickly.

Likewise, when the Osaka Supreme Court announced its decision in February that the ownership rights to the Chinese student dorms at Kyoto University belonged to the government of Taiwan, China protested strongly. China's top leader, Deng, criticized the decision by stating that "Japan, more than any other country in the world, owes China." A senior official from the Foreign Ministry caused a stir when he commented that Deng "was acting like a god" and said further that "all people become stubborn when they get old." In Japan, which has adopted the separation of power among the three branches of government, the executive branch cannot intervene in a decision of the judiciary. Still, in light of the politicized atmosphere of the dormitory issue, as well as the Yasukuni Shrine visit, the breaking of 1 percent GNP barrier, and the Fujio comments, it was a sensitive time in Sino-Japanese relations.

Postwar Japanese diplomacy toward East Asia has often been called "apology diplomacy." Yet although the government has offered sincere apologies, a politician will often make an unnecessary statement that reduces the value of the apology and creates the need for another one, thus creating a vicious circle. In particular, the 1980s were a delicate period in that although those who had gone through the war were at this point in the minority, they were still quite numerous. Nor were the irresponsible and offensive remarks of politicians limited to East Asian diplomacy. At a national study meeting of the LDP, Prime Minister Nakasone emphasized Japan's high level of education and stated that "there were many blacks, Puerto Ricans, and Mexicans in the United States and on average their [intellectual] level was very low." There was understandably great outrage in the United States, and Nakasone sent a message of apology. While Japan was attempting to strengthen its relations with the United States and East Asia, such statements suggested that the international understanding possessed by Japanese politicians (and probably ordinary Japanese) was far from adequate. In this sense, the motto adopted by Nakasone, "International State," was at best a concept centered solely on the nation-state, lacking consideration for the ethnic groups and pluralistic cultures that make up society. The limits of Nakasone's internationalism, driven as it was by nationalism, can be found here.

Untoward comments by politicians did not stop after the end of the Nakasone administration.[20] During April and May 1988, National Land Agency Director General Okuno Seisuke stated that "the real invaders were the Caucasian race, and only Japan is being made to look bad," and was forced to tender his recognition. Later that same year in July, LDP Policy Research Council chairman Watanabe Michio stated, "In America where credit cards prevail there are those people, such as blacks, who think just because 'they are broke' they don't have to pay for anything," to which the United States strongly protested.

Having been in office five years, Nakasone resigned on November 6, 1987, after designating Takeshita Noboru his successor. At the end of the month, the United States and the Soviet Union came to an agreement on the complete removal of their intermediate-range nuclear force stockpiles, while discussions between Japan and the United States over the liberalizing of Japan's agricultural market ended without an agreement. These two events symbolized both the melting of the international environment upon which the Japan–U.S. alliance had been predicated and the increasing rivalry in the Japan–U.S. relationship.

The globalization of Japanese diplomacy

The Asia-Pacific economy and Japan

Japanese diplomacy during the 1980s centered on the Ron–Yasu years and was characterized by both the strengthening of the alliance and the increasing of bilateral rivalry. At the same time, however, Japanese diplomacy during this time showed signs of evolution into a "global state."

With regard to the Asia-Pacific region, as seen in Chapter 4, Prime Minister Ohira visited Beijing in December 1979, promising the first yen-based loan of 50 billion yen and cooperation in China's modernization policies. At that time, Ohira announced the "Three Ohira Principles," namely that Japan would (1) not undertake military cooperation (with China); (2) not undertake these loans at the expense of aid to ASEAN; and (3) not control China's market at the expense of the United States and Europe (even if they were not part of providing the loan package). Japan explained that it began yen-based loans at this time in order to: (1) show its support of China's reform policies; (2) express its appreciation for China's renunciation of reparations for the war; and (3) attempt to bring China over to the West in the wake of the very tense international environment following the Sino-Vietnam War of February 1979.[21]

Subsequently, as noted earlier, the Nakasone cabinet in 1984 agreed to a second loan of 470 billion yen, and in August 1988, the Takeshita Noburu cabinet announced its intent to grant a third loan of 810 billion yen for a six-year period (1990–95). China was developing as a world economic power for the twenty-first century, and Japan's economic assistance was helping to create an important foundation for this. As a result of the help it received from the United States after the war, Japan grew to become America's economic rival. This was not a failure of America's Japan policy, but rather an example of its success. In the same way Japan has helped China succeed in modernizing. China, too, is likely to become an economic rival of Japan, and this should be looked upon not as a failure but as an example of success.

It is not only China. South Korea, Taiwan, Hong Kong, Singapore, and other newly industrializing economies (NIEs) have adopted an active, export-oriented industrialization strategy and have seen dramatic growth in their economies for which the Japanese role was large. The share of NIEs in total world exports was 1.9 percent in 1965 and jumped to 8.3 percent in 1988. Compared with the near collapse under debt of other NIEs such as Brazil, Mexico, and other Latin American countries, the economic activities of the Asian NIEs stand out. The rapid economic growth has gradually led to the spread of democracy within the countries of this region. Japan's own economic rebirth was the model for these countries, and the ASEAN countries are imitating the NIEs. The high value of the yen following the Plaza Accord permitted the Japanese economy to support China's modernization policies and the economic activities of the NIEs and ASEAN countries. In addition to receiving, along with the United States, a large amount of the exports of these countries in East Asia, Japan, through its direct investment and capital flow into East Asia, has contributed to the region's development. Likewise, by importing many products made in Asia, Japan has caused an unprecedented "Asian boom" to take place. Recognizing this, the Takeshita cabinet, formed in November 1987, actively sought to permit foreign students from developing countries, particularly Asian countries, to study in Japan. (In 1983 the planning began for the acceptance of about 100,000 foreign students studying in Japan by 2000. At the time the number of foreign students was only 8,000, but by 1995—the year it peaked—the number had jumped to 54,000. Since then, there has been a decline.)

Throughout the 1980s, the Asia-Pacific region, including Australia and New Zealand, has been the world's most dynamic economic zone. The "Pacific Basin Cooperation Concept" announced by Prime Minister Ohira took shape in 1980 with the creation of the Pacific Economic Cooperation Conference (PECC), and led to the development of the Asia Pacific Economic Conference (APEC) in November 1989. One of its principal objectives early on was to deter any tendency to close the European Community and North American markets. "Asia Pacific" was used out of concern that "Asia" alone would conjure up images of the prewar sort of exclusive regionalism. In fact, APEC's founding countries were the six ASEAN countries and Australia, New Zealand, South Korea, Japan, the United States, and Canada. In co-founding APEC, Japan and Australia played important leadership roles.

Japan also gave a great deal of foreign economic assistance to the Asia-Pacific region. This was done to some degree out of consideration for the United States. As an American ally, Japan gave "strategic aid" to "countries bordering areas of conflict," such as Thailand, Pakistan, and Turkey (see Chapter 4, section 3). In its economic aid given to the third world, moreover, Japan hoped to reduce the degree of its criticism in America for the trade deficit and lack of forthcoming defense cooperation. In fact, Japan's growing trade surplus made the rapid increase in ODA possible (see Figures 5.1 and 5.2). Some countries criticized Japan's assistance policies as lacking in principles and too restricted, the quality of the assistance as poor, and the assistance as mostly tied loans instead of outright donations. This led to Japan being called an "Irresponsible ODA Power." However, it cannot be denied that Japan's

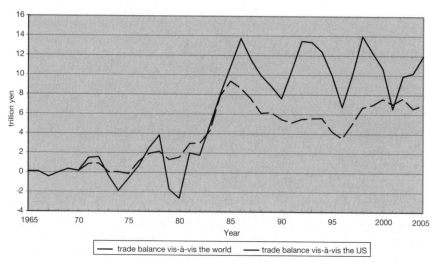

Figure 5.1 Changes in Japan's trade balance, 1965–2005

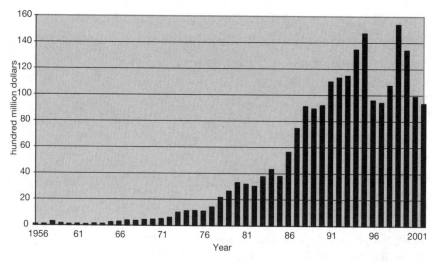

Figure 5.2 Changes in Japan's ODA, 1965–2001

ODA advanced the rapid economic development of the Asia-Pacific region. Moreover, in the case of middle-income countries in a rapidly growing Asia, the paying back of loans had a further stimulating effect on development.

The first mid-term goal of the ODA policy drafted in July 1978 saw the $2.2 billion in aid in 1978 rising to $2.8 billion in 1980 (in fact the actual rate grew 116 percent to $3.3 billion). The second mid-term goal for ODA, drafted in January 1981, planned to see ODA in the first half of the 1980s double that of the second half of the 1970s (in fact, due to the second oil shock crisis, only 84.6 percent of the goal was reached, or $19 billion). Because of this, Japan's ODA budget for the 1981 to 1985 period rose to almost 2.5 trillion yen. In the third mid-term goal, drafted in September 1985, it was decided to give $40 billion in assistance, but because of the high yen, that goal was already reached by May of 1987—less than two years later. In the fourth plan, drafted in June 1988, a total of a minimum of $50 billion was set, and in 1989, Japan passed the United States as the largest donor of ODA. However, ODA began to decline in 1996, and after a one-time spike in 2000, has been on the decline ever since.

Japan thus provided a model of development for the countries of the Asia-Pacific, became an immense market for their goods, invested capital, contributed to the development of regional economic cooperation, and funneled a large amount of ODA into the region. Japan's "bubble economy" came to an end, but it is likely that Asia's will continue for some time.

Friction and cooperation with Europe

Compared with its relations with the United States and Asia, Japan's postwar dealings with Europe are much weaker. Prewar Japan modeled its modernization on that of Germany, England, and France, which makes the postwar period an interesting contrast.

Nevertheless, Japan and the countries of Western Europe are joined in one sense as common allies of the United States. For example, at the time of the Soviet invasion of Afghanistan, Prime Minister Ohira stated that it was necessary to find a solution based on "cooperation with the countries of Europe and other friendly states centered on the United States." Ohira had close personal relations with Helmut Schmidt of West Germany. Prime Minister Nakasone had taken the position that the "the security of [the West] is indivisible," emphasizing the importance of the solidarity of Europe and East Asia. Since the start of the G5/G7 summits in 1975 (see Chapter 4), trilateral cooperation between Japan, Europe, and the United States has been important to Japan. A private group, the Trilateral Commission, launched in 1973, has also served as a significant forum for former officials, politicians, businesspersons, scholars, and opinion leaders to informally exchange opinions. It was the globalization of Japan's economy, however, that brought about friction with Europe and the need for cooperative policies.

Because of the succession of bilateral agreements between Japan and the United States, countries in Europe began to fear that Japanese producers would change their sights and take over the European markets. In fact, Japan's trade surplus with the EC jumped from $10 billion in 1981 to more than $200 billion in 1987. In April 1982, France charged one customs office in an isolated part of the country with handling customs transactions on all Japanese-made video recorders, in effect stopping all shipments into France.

Moreover, Italy and France raised a furor when they tried to apply voluntary restraints on automobiles made by Japanese companies within Europe. Prejudice and a lack of mutual understanding stood in the way. Earlier, as discussed in Chapter 3, President de Gaulle reportedly called Prime Minister Ikeda a "transistor radio salesman," and in the 1980s, a report in Europe described the Japanese as "living in rabbit huts and poisoned by working too hard." European views of Japan were still fairly harsh.

There was great change in 1985. First, movements in Europe toward integration at all levels were seen. In January Jacques Delors assumed the position of president of the European Community, and in a speech before the European Parliament, he proposed the elimination of national borders by 1992. In June, the EC Commission issued a White Paper on the regional market, pointing out in detail the existing difficulties on the movement of goods, people, services, and capital, recommending that these restrictions be eliminated by the end of 1992. Moreover, the "Protocol on a Single Europe," prepared at the end of the same year (and going into effect in July 1987), changed the decision-making procedures in the EC Ministers Meeting from unanimity, which had been the tradition, to a weighted majority. With this, the decision-making process toward European integration moved one step closer. In January 1981, Greece had joined the EC, followed by Spain and Portugal in January 1986. The share of world GNP held by the EC reached 18.6 percent. Now confident, the EC began to demand the opening of the Japanese market. Moreover, being stimulated by the EC market integration, Japan and Australia began to exercise more leadership in economic cooperation in the Asia-Pacific region.

In September 1985 the Plaza Accord was announced. This agreement symbolized the relative decline of America, struggling with deficits in both finance and trade, and the increase in the global economic power of Japan and Europe. At the summit in Tokyo in May 1986, the need for surveillance (of economic growth rates, balance of payments, interest rates, and other economic indicators at a multilateral level) for macro-policy coordination was discussed. However, even after this agreement, America's large trade deficits did not disappear, and instead, because inflation was feared, the G7 (Italy and Canada had joined the G5 in February 1987) announced the Louvre Accord, which sought to "stabilize the currency markets for the time being." In October, "Black Monday" occurred. The drop in world stock prices was the result of the market's lack of confidence in the discord between Japan, the United States, and West Germany over reductions in the U.S. budget deficit. (At the Venice Summit in June 1987, the Japanese prime minister requested the United States make efforts to reduce its own budget deficit.) With the advance of the internationalization of the financial and capital markets, the economic policies of each individual country have a chain-reaction effect, and overall policy coordination between Japan, the United States, and Europe is necessary. (Yet there is a tendency for this need for overall policy coordination to happen immediately after the rapid expansion of the international financial markets.) Meanwhile, in order to prevent the collapse of stock prices, in the wake of Black Monday, Japan adopted a long-term low interest policy, which raised the value of stock and land, triggering the "bubble economy." In the middle of this growth, the seeds of a future disappointment were already being laid.

In the trilateral relationship, Japan's position has been an important one. In addition to being one of the founding members of the G7, Japan stands at the center of economic cooperation in the Asia-Pacific region. At the time of the 1988 Toronto Summit, Prime Minister Takeshita, who had visited the ASEAN countries and spoken with South Korean president Roh Tae Woo by telephone, called for greater dialogue with ASEAN and the NIE countries and more aid for the Philippines, in effect taking on the role of Asia's representative. Takeshita's style of diplomacy was somewhat quiet and subtle, and while he continued the tenets of Nakasone's diplomacy, he also began laying the groundwork for a type of post-Cold War diplomacy for Japan, emphasizing the expansion of ODA.

Throughout the 1980s Japan, as a "global state," was able to act as a bridge between the Asia-Pacific region and America and Europe. The 1980s were a period that saw the New Cold War on the political and military fronts, and the remarkable deepening and expanding of mutual international interdependence on the economic side. Until then, Japan had pursued "free riding" (actually, "cheap riding" is probably a more accurate phrase) in the military sphere. Economically, Japan had done very well, with its behavior almost being "mercantilist." In the 1980s, however, Japan began to make important contributions in both security and the economy. Although the deepening of interdependence would continue into the 1990s era of globalization, the New Cold War would end before anyone predicted.

The end of the Cold War

Changes in the Japan–U.S. Relationship

The year 1985, besides the Plaza Accord and greater movement in the EC toward the unification of its markets, saw the birth of the administration of Mikhail Gorbachev in the Soviet Union in March. With this, the dialogue between the Soviet Union and the United States resumed. When we reflect that in all of the Soviet Union there existed only 50,000 personal computers to America's 30 million, or that the percentage of telephones in Soviet households in the cities was just 23 percent and in the rural areas only 7 percent, it is a wonder that the New Cold War was still going on.

Nakasone, who could also think strategically at a global level, attended the funeral of Secretary General Konstantin Chernenko, meeting early with Gorbachev and expressing a desire to improve relations with the Soviet Union. (The Foreign Ministry initially disapproved of Nakasone's plans to go to the Soviet Union due to the slight to former Prime Minister Suzuki, who despite traveling to the Soviet Union for the funeral of former secretary general Yuri Andropov in February 1984, was not granted a meeting with Chernenko.) At the end of 1987, the United States and the Soviet Union signed the Intermediate-Range Nuclear Force (INF) Treaty, beginning nuclear arsenal reductions for the first time. With this, the New Cold War, which had begun with the Soviet invasion of Afghanistan, ended and the situation began to move toward the end of the cold war itself.

In the middle of this, clear changes were occurring in the Japan–U.S. relationship as well. President George H.W. Bush, whose administration began in January 1989, chose Japan as the site of his first foreign trip. He was to participate in the funeral for the Showa Emperor. At this time, however, serious problems had been emerging between the two countries. In November the year before, both countries had exchanged a memorandum of understanding on the joint development of the FSX fighter, but during the shift from the Reagan to the Bush presidency, the U.S. Congress began to express its opposition.

In the memorandum of understanding, Japan would pay for all of the development costs and the United States would provide Japan with the technology for building an F-16 fighter. However, within the U.S. Congress, voices of concern were raised that the FSX joint development project was essentially giving Japan state-of-the-art technology for free, which would endanger the future of America's superiority in the aircraft industry. Within the U.S. government, a difference of opinion existed between the State Department and the Defense Department, both of which valued the country's political and security relationship with Japan, and the Commerce Department, which was looking out for America's economic interests. The Bush administration decided to request a "clarification" of the already worked-out memorandum of understanding from the Japanese government. The result of this review was the decision that America would place restrictions on the transfer of some important technologies to Japan, Japan would provide to America technologies that it desired, and the U.S. side would be guaranteed a 40 percent share of the work in the production and development stages. This agreement meant many concessions by the Japanese side, and one participant at the time described them as a "Humiliation at Canossa." Originally, the Defense Agency had wanted to produce the FSX domestically, and only agreed to joint production because of America's desire.

This FSX problem was special in that the Commerce Department came to exercise influence over an issue of technical cooperation in a security matter. The Japan–U.S. relationship had entered a new stage in which it was no longer possible to separate security and economic issues. The promise of technical cooperation by the Nakasone cabinet was to haunt the government in a boomerang effect that no one expected.[22]

As if a second wave of attack, at a June 1989 high-level meeting of Japanese and U.S. officials, the promotion of the Structural Impediments Initiative (SII) was agreed upon. The year before had seen the drafting of the Omnibus Trade and Competitiveness Act. This law sought to protect U.S. industries through the strengthening of measures against foreign countries in commerce and finance, while at the same time increasing exports and strengthening America's competitive strength. In particular, the Super 301 Clause, the focus of the law, required that the USTR office identify and report unfair trading practices abroad to Congress and, if a solution was not found within one year's time, to implement retaliatory measures.

America wielded Super 301 like a sword, calling for improvements in Japan's land policies and distribution system, and reforms in its antimonopoly laws and domestic structures. The United States was no longer going to wait for Japan to implement measures on its own, as called for in the Maekawa Report. Such threats came close to interfering in the internal affairs of another state, and Japan said that it would not negotiate under the threat of sanctions. If there were problems, however, Japan was willing to discuss them at any point. Japan requested America, likewise, to reduce its budget deficit, improve the investment activities and production of its companies, deregulate, and promote exports. This incident indicated that America, in taking strong actions such as Super 301, had by this point lost room to spare, and that bilateral trade friction had gone beyond issues in specific areas to become a problem in the economic structure of each country.

The August 1988 Omnibus Trade and Competitiveness Act was premised on the ability of the United States to unilaterally judge the trading practices of other countries as "unfair," an approach related to the view of the so-called revisionists. The conventional view of the relationship was that both countries possessed common values such as democracy and free trade. Revisionism, in contrast, argued that Japan and the United States were different, and because of this, instead of negotiations, a new bold approach was necessary to address the alien Japan. While "Japan bashing" had been seen from about the middle of the 1980s, arguments appearing in Clyde V. Prestowitz Jr.'s *Trading Places*, Van Wolferen's *The Enigma of Japanese Power*, and James Fallows' "Containing Japan" began to take on new momentum in 1989. At the same time, a generational shift occurred among America's Japan specialists, who had traditionally taken a positive view of bilateral relations. It was in this period that Japanese direct investment in the United States, such as in Columbia Pictures and Rockefeller Center, became more conspicuous and started to make some Americans uncomfortable.

The criticism of Japan by the revisionists, lacking in objectivity and in some cases courtesy, was of course not welcome among the Japanese. These critics seemed to apply a zero-sum model, viewing the relative decline in America's economic standing as absolute ruin, and Japan's relative increases in the trade relationship as inherently bad.

However, Japan's attempts to close its ears to these "unfair" criticisms were probably also "unfair" as well. For too long Japan had taken for granted the liberal policies of the United States, which needed Japan as an ally during the Cold War. With the end of the Cold War and the spectacle of Japan's inflated economy, some sort of reexamination of this stance was needed.[23] In the United States, serious attempts were underway to examine the state of America's industries and education, and to learn from Japan, as seen by the Massachusetts Institute of Technology's report "The Mind in America" and Alan Bloom's work, *The Closing of the American Mind*.[24] (Incidentally, Bloom's work, which viewed cultural relativism, which became prevalent in the 1960s, as the reason for the worsening for America's higher education, would have an enormous impact on the "neo-con" movement in the 1990s and during the administration of George W. Bush, the son of President George H.W. Bush.)

However, in almost a mirror image of the "Japan bashing" seen in the United States, discussions on America's decline were quite common in Japan. The continuous pressure by America on Japan was dismissed as simply "Japan bashing," and despite the fact that Japan was singularly winning the game of trade, a curious "victim mentality" began to emerge. In 1989 Morita Akio and Ishihara Shintaro published *The Japan That Can Say "No."*[25] With the fiftieth anniversary of the Japanese attack on Pearl Harbor approaching, there were voices in the Japanese media that a "1991 crisis" in bilateral relations would develop if anti-Japanese feeling intensified any further in America.

When the United States and Japan were about to undertake discussions on the Structural Impediment Initiative, the Tiananmen Square incident occurred in Beijing in June 1989. The Chinese government used force to suppress groups of students calling for democratization in the heart of the capital. Because the reformer Gorbachev was then in China for his historic visit, the world's media covered the demonstrations. The United States and other countries immediately criticized the strong-arm tactics of the Chinese government. The Japanese government as well recommended the return of its nationals in China and issued a warning against undertaking trips to China. It also froze not only contacts with high officials, but also the disbursement of loans. Although Japan kept in step with the West in its response, it was also, as China's neighbor, the most cautious of the countries of the West. Afterward, human rights would become a major issue between the United States and China, and Japanese diplomacy would have to deal with the added task of coordinating its relations with both countries.

President Bush and Secretary General Gorbachev announced the end of the Cold War at their meeting in Malta on December 3, 1989, and agreed to work toward creating a "New World Order" and promoting discussions on arms reductions. The international relations of the United States, China, and the Soviet Union, the major powers surrounding Japan, differed greatly at the end of 1980s from what they had been at the beginning of the decade.

While seeking to improve the Japan–U.S. alliance throughout the 1980s, Japanese diplomacy, which placed relations with the United States at its center, was also beginning to face new difficulties with the end of the Cold War. The spreading of economic friction into defense areas, the increasing problem of economic structures themselves, the rise of revisionism, and the changes in Sino-U.S.–Soviet relations all posed significant challenges.

The meaning of Japanese diplomacy in the 1980s

A distinguished scholar of international politics, Kosaka Masataka, once wrote that much of the second half of the 1970s through the 1980s was a period of "excessive conflict" (*yobun no tairitsu*).[26] Indeed, with the international environment of the New Cold War and the personalities of leaders like Nakasone and Reagan, the 1980s were a period of strong ideological division. In 1980 the United States and the West boycotted the Moscow Olympics, because of the Soviet invasion of Afghanistan, and in retaliation, the Soviet Union and the Eastern bloc boycotted the Los Angeles Olympics in 1984. However, the 1988 Seoul Olympics, held at one of the frontlines of the Cold War—South Korea—were a great success, with Roh's *Nordpolitik* (seeking to deal positively with neighbor North Korea) being introduced to the world. This perspective embodied the structural changes that had occurred in less than ten years in international affairs.

Japanese diplomacy of the 1980s did not lose its meaning with the end of the Cold War. First, the efforts of Japan to strengthen the Japan–U.S. alliance throughout the 1980s were not in vain. The strengthening of the alliance during the New Cold War contributed to the end of the Cold War itself by dividing and then exhausting the resources of the Soviet Union, which was confronting the United States in both Europe and Asia. In one sense, the historical meaning of the Japan–U.S. alliance as an anti-Soviet military one ended with the end of the Cold War. However, East Asia possessed many other potential sources of regional conflict, such as the Korean Peninsula and the Taiwan Strait. Even when U.S.–Soviet confrontation was most evident during the Cold War, the Japan–U.S. alliance acted as a deterrent. Moreover, in neighboring countries, and within the United States and Japan as well, some viewed U.S. forces in Japan as a "cap in the bottle" with regard to a resurgence of Japanese militarism. As a measure of stability in the region, the Japan–U.S. alliance continues to function well after the end of the Cold War. There do not appear to be any significant reasons why the alliance will rapidly disappear or weaken in the immediate future.

If we consider the dramatic and historic changes of the end of the Cold War, however, it should not come as a surprise that questions have emerged from people in both countries with regard to the continued significance of the Japan–U.S. alliance. An alliance is not a part or piece of a treaty. It is instead an institution. Because the Japan–U.S. alliance was institutionalized during the 1980s, it could withstand even the shock of the end of the Cold War and avoid calls for its dissolution. This was the result of what G. John Ikenberry has called the "mutually binding" effect. No matter what direction the alliance takes in the future, much time and discussion will be required to make the necessary decisions. Moreover, if Japan's economic position were to decline relatively, it would be increasingly necessary to think more positively about the means other than economic (this does not necessarily signify military) by which Japan can contribute internationally. National power includes the ability to gather and analyze information, as well as the ability to introduce one's culture abroad. It is multidimensional, and because it is multidimensional it forms the basis of comprehensive security, mentioned earlier.

Second, economic cooperation in the Asia-Pacific region was one of the big successes of Japanese diplomacy during the 1980s. Indeed, the overly ambitious economic growth strategies adopted by the countries of Asia had the effect of bringing about an economic crisis in the summer of 1997. However, an extremely pessimistic view of the future of Asia's economy is as bad as an extremely optimistic one. The basic posture of Japanese diplomacy—seeking coexistence with prosperous neighbors—should be maintained in the future. While the United States and Japan continue to possess areas of confrontation and friction, without their cooperation and the stability of their relationship, it is quite clear that the Asia-Pacific region cannot develop further.

Likewise, Japan's cooperation with Europe, which is increasingly moving toward integration, will become even more important in the future. International cooperative policies were institutionalized in 1985 with the Plaza Accord. Japan's road to becoming a "global state"—actively contributing in the political and military fields, expanding its diplomatic horizons with Europe and Asia, and so on—was unavoidable.

On the other hand, following the collapse of the "bubble economy," trade friction between the two countries dwindled. Indeed, it can be said that Japan's long recession has now become a new seed of friction with the United States. Just like the Cold War, whose end no one was able to predict, it seemed that the "bubble economy" of Japan would go on forever, but looking back, it ended surprisingly abruptly. During Japan's period of high prosperity, America's decline was much talked about. Yet there is no need to consider Japan's decline as inevitable. As Kosaka predicted early on,

> Many Americans believe that Japan has overtaken the United States economically, but this may just become a brief historical episode. A Japan that returns to a state appropriate to its actual size, and not its overly inflated one, might in fact end up being healthy for Japan and the world.[27]

And yet Japan lacked the ability to reflect on and reform itself during the 1980s, the period when the slogan "Japan as Number One" was often heard. It is clear that the political and economic framework that supported postwar Japan is no longer functioning effectively. Keeping in mind that history does not move in linear fashion, those studying history must attempt to examine and be ready for the next era.

Notes

1 More recently Prime Minister Obuchi Keizo collapsed from a stroke in early April 2000 and died on May 14. His cabinet in the meantime had resigned en masse on April 5 following his collapse.

2 *Asahi Shimbun*, July 14, 1981.

3 *Asahi Shimbun*, February 11, 1981.

4 Uji Toshihiko, *Suzuki Seiken 863 Nichi* (863 Days of the Suzuki Administration) (Tokyo: Gyosei Mondai Kenkyujo, 1983), pp. 186–87.

5 For more on Miyazawa, see Eldridge, *Secret Talks between Tokyo and Washington*, p. 5.

6 For essential readings on the Nakasone years, see Nakasone Yasuhiro, *Seiji to Jinsei: Nakasone Yasuhiro Kaikoroku* (Politics and Life: The Memoirs of Nakasone Yasuhiro) (Tokyo: Kodansha, 1992); Nakasone Yasuhiro, *Tenchi Yujo: 50 Nen no Sengo Seiji o Kataru* (World of Friendship: On 50 Years of Postwar Politics) (Tokyo: Bungei Shunju, 1996); Maki Taro, *Nakasone Seiken 1806 Nichi* (1,806 Days of the Nakasone Administration) (Tokyo: Gyosei Shuppankyoku, 1988); Gotoda Masaharu, *Naikaku Kanbo Chokan* (Chief Cabinet Secretary) (Tokyo: Kodansha, 1989); Gotoda Masaharu, *Sei to Kan* (Politicians and the Bureaucrats) (Tokyo: Kodansha, 1994); Kusano Atsushi, "Nakasone Yasuhiro: Daitoryoteki Shusho no Menmoku (Nakasone Yashuhiro: The Appearance of a Presidential Prime Minister)," in Watanabe Akio, ed., *Sengo Nihon no Saishotachi* (The Prime Ministers of Postwar Japan) (Tokyo: Chuo Koronsha, 1995), pp. 337–73. Nakasone's memoirs, *Seiji to Jinsei*, were translated into English and appear as *The Making of the New Japan: Reclaiming the Political Mainstream* (Surrey: Curzon Press, 1999).

7 Nakasone, *Tenchi Yujo*, pp. 445–46. See also Nakasone, *The Making of New Japan*, p. 210.

8 Gotoda, *Naikaku Kanbo Chokan*, p. 89.

9 For more on the "Three Principles," see http://www.mofa.go.jp/policy/un/disarmament/policy/ (accessed May 2003).

10 George P. Shultz, *Turmoil and Triumph: My Years as Secretary of State* (New York: Scribner, 1993), p. 173. Shultz devotes a whole chapter to Japan. In contrast, there are only a handful of references to Japan in both of Haig's memoirs, *Caveat* (1984) and *Inner Circles* (1992).

11 Nakasone, *Tenchi Yujo*, p. 439.

12 It is not entirely clear who had the information first, but according to some reliable reports, the signals communication intelligence gathered went through Misawa Airbase in Aomori Prefecture to the United States before it reached the Defense Agency and rest of the Japanese government.

13 For an excellent study of postwar Japan's security policies, including those of the Nakasone administration, see Tanaka, *Anzen Hosho*. Also see Joseph P. Keddell, Jr., *The Politics of Defense in Japan: Managing Internal and External Pressures* (New York: M.E. Sharpe, 1993), which covers the Nakasone years in great detail.

14 Theodore White, "The Danger from Japan," *New York Times Magazine*, July 28, 1985.

15 For a recent, detailed study of trade friction over semiconductors, see Oyane Satoshi, *Nichibeikan Handotai Masatsu: Tsusho Kosho no Seiji Keizaigaku* (Japan–U.S.–Korean Friction over Semiconductors: The Political Economy of Trade Negotiations) (Tokyo: Yushindo, 2003).

16 Karel van Wolferen, "The Japan Problem," *Foreign Affairs*, Spring 1987.

17 Watanabe Akio, *Taikoku Nihon no Yuragi, 1972* (The Shaking of the Great Power Japan, 1972) (Tokyo: Chuo Koron Shinsha, 2000), p. 348.

18 Gotoda, *Naikaku Kanbo Chokan*, pp. 104–8.

19 One of the reasons that Nakasone did not go apparently had to do with his concern that it would lead to the downfall of secretary general Hu Yaobang.

20 Wakamiya Yoshibumi, *Sengo Hoshu no Ajiakan* (The Postwar Conservative View of Asia) (Tokyo: Asahi Sensho, 1995), translated and published under the same name by the Long-Term Credit Bank of Japan, Ltd., in 1998 as part of its International Library Selection series (no. 8).

21 Hattori Kenji, "Nicchu Keizai Koryu no Kinmitsuka: Chokiteki Antei o Moto-
    mete (Closer Economic Relations between Japan and China: Toward Long-term
    stability)," in Kojima Tomoyuki, ed., *Ajia Jidai no Nicchu Kankei* (Sino-Japanese
    Relations in the Asian Era) (Tokyo: Simul Shuppankai, 1995), pp. 161–63.

22 Teshima Ryuichi, *Nippon FSX o Ute* (Shooting Down the Japanese FSX) (Tokyo:
    Shinchosha, 1991), provides a detailed study of the problem.

23 For a reasoned but critical examination by a Japanese scholar of the "Japan-bash-
    ing" phenomenon and descriptions of Japan as "different," see "Anitsu na Fucho
    ga Umu 'Nihon Tataki' (The Life of Ease that Gives Rise to 'Japan Bashing'),"
    and "Kokusai Kankei ni Okeru Ishitsuron (The Debate about Japan as Different
    from the Perspective of International Relations)," both of which appear in Kosaka
    Masataka, *Kosaka Masataka Gaiko Hyoronshu: Nihon no Shinro to Rekishi no
    Kyokun* (Collection of Essays on Diplomacy by Kosaka Masataka: Japan's Path
    and the Lessons of History) (Tokyo: Chuo Koronsha, 1996).

24 Allan Bloom, *The Closing of the American Mind* (New York: Simon and Schuster,
    1987).

25 Shintaro Ishihara, *The Japan that Can Say No: Why Japan Will be First among
    Equals* (New York: Simon and Schuster, 1991). Morita's name did not appear on the
    English version published in English two years after the original Japanese version.

26 Kosaka Masataka, *Gendai no Kokusai Seiji* (Contemporary International Politics)
    (Tokyo: Kodansha Gakujutsu Bunko, 1989), p. 220.

27 Ibid., p. 247.

6   Japanese diplomacy after the Cold War

Iokibe Makoto

For Japan, the end of the Cold War was sort of a "double defeat." First, its bubble economy burst and it found itself in a long recession. Second, it badly mishandled its response to the Gulf Crisis and War. However, it successfully managed the Cambodian peace process and peacekeeping operations there. Moreover, it was able to redefine the Japan–U.S. alliance having overcome the Okinawa incident of 1995 and the crisis in the Taiwan Strait in 1996. The 1997 Asia financial crisis also struck, but Japan contributed a great deal of funds to help the region overcome it. After the 9/11 terrorist attacks, Japan greatly expanded its international security role by dispatching the SDF to the Indian Ocean and Iraq. At the same time, Japan has had to deal with a dangerous neighbor, North Korea, seeking to develop nuclear weapons and advanced missile technology and is facing the challenge of a rising China.

The decade after the end of the Cold War saw on the one hand the ending of the bipolar system of the Cold War period that historian John Gaddis paradoxically called the "Long Peace," and on the other the coming of a period of rapid change filled with crises and challenges. This international fluidity has not changed even after the start of the twenty-first century, nor is its direction clear. When evaluating current events, there are of course no declassified official documents on which to base one's judgment. Moreover, the facts behind events are not even known with certainty. Similarly, when writing about current affairs, there is the problem of simply compiling a chronology of events, seeking to avoid misinterpretations by steering clear of analysis. But a danger also exists in making premature evaluations, rushing to interpret events whose outcomes are still uncertain. Aware of both challenges, this chapter discusses Japanese diplomacy and the international changes following the end of the Cold War, offering where possible tentative interpretations.

The decade after the Cold War was also the last decade of the century. For Japan, it was not a particularly good time. Indeed, it has been called the "Lost Decade" due to the inability of Japan to get out of the quagmire of the recession in which its economy, which Japan had in the 1980s boasted to be the strongest in the world, found itself after the bursting of the bubble.

The political morass matched that of the economy. The year the Cold War ended, 1989, corresponded to the year in which the Showa Emperor died, ushering in the Heisei Era. It was also the year in which the foundations of LDP's long hold on the reins of government began to weaken, leading to the eventual end of the 1955 system. The Takeshita Noboru cabinet, which took office in November 1987 and had looked like it would be a stable administration following the long Nakasone cabinet, fell due to the Recruit stocks-for-favor scandal. The Uno Sosuke cabinet also fell quickly after that, this time due to a personal scandal of the prime minister concerning a former lover. Following these scandal-related political upheavals, the Kaifu Toshiki cabinet was formed in August 1989 and political reformers within the LDP would push their agenda until the LDP itself broke apart in June 1993.

Calling for further reforms, Ozawa Ichiro left the LDP and established another party. His and other political groupings, including the Socialist Party, cooperated in having Hosokawa Morihiro installed as the first non-LDP prime minister in thirty-eight years. With this, the 1955 system ended, as did the LDP's predominance. The voters had strong hopes that political reform was going to occur, but in the end, a new sustainable political system or structure to replace the LDP and Socialist Party did not emerge. Instead, the 1990s saw nothing more than confusion and political realignments surrounding rebuilding an LDP-led system or one centered on other parties.

After the Cold War, Japan faced international criticism for its inability to respond appropriately to the Gulf crisis and war. This does not necessarily mean that Japanese diplomacy after the Cold War was also a "Lost Decade." While it is true that the poorly performing economy cast a large shadow on the decade, it is necessary to examine the successes and failures of Japanese diplomacy more objectively during this time.

From victor in the Cold War to loser in the 1990s

In 1989, the year the Cold War ended, Japan's economic power in the post-war period was at its height. The Japanese economy, which had recovered from the recession following the oil crisis of the 1970s, demonstrated its strength in industrial goods in the next decade, with the United States and Europe unable to catch up. As the 1980s began, Japan was called the *ichiwari kokka*, or a "country that has 10% of the world's GNP" (see Chapter 5), but by the end of the decade, Japan's economic share had risen to an astonishing 15 percent

It is therefore no surprise that in the United States in the immediate wake of the Cold War, public opinion polls showing that Japan had replaced the Soviet Union as the number one threat began to appear, as did suggestions that "the victor in the Cold War was not the United States but Japan and Germany." With the disappearance of the East–West Cold War structure in which two powers—the United States and the Soviet Union—were in conflict, economic power began to be seen as more important than ever. Would the economic superpower Japan be able to shine in such a world? This was the question posed around the time of the G7's Houston Summit of July 1990.

On the diplomatic front, on the eve of the G-7 summit, Japan argued to North American and European members that the sanctions imposed against China following the Tiananmen Square incident of 1989 should be ended, believing it unwise to continue to isolate the world's largest country. President George H. W. Bush agreed. Because human rights were such an important issue to the countries of the West, they were cautious but in principle went along with Japan's initiative. Japanese diplomacy was leading the "return to normalcy" in East Asian international relations following Tiananmen. Could an economic power also exercise political influence in Asia?

The Gulf crisis and war

The description of Japan as the victor in the Cold War is not entirely accurate. Japan did not play a key role in the Cold War, but instead sought to avoid fighting while benefiting from the Cold War structure. The difference between a key player and one that simply benefits indirectly is significant, as can be seen in Japan's failure to respond adequately at the time of the Gulf War.

It was not so much Japan's diplomatic skills and ability that were questioned at the time of the Gulf War, as the understanding of the international situation that existed among ordinary Japanese. Through Article 9 of the constitution, postwar Japan strongly believed the achievement of peace to be the greatest good. Postwar Japan was the only country in the world that seriously debated the legitimacy of war in self-defense, a given in most countries. Although an absolute majority of Japanese had come to approve of the Self-Defense Forces (see Figure 3.2), progressive forces led by the Socialists, then the largest opposition party in Japan, continued to oppose both wars in self-defense and the existence of the SDF. Moreover, the type of resistance practiced by the Socialists led to paralysis in the Diet as they boycotted or delayed deliberations on other pending items by linking them to security fears. At the same time the ruling parties, who believed Japan's highest priority was trade and focused on the economy under the security umbrella of the United States, avoided proposing more realistic security policies for fear of upsetting the opposition parties. As a result, the understanding of security issues among the general public was limited to the concepts of the divisive debates of the 1950s—war or peace, return of militarism or democracy, invasion or self-defense. In the minds of the people in postwar Japan, war had only two meanings—self-defense or aggression by Japan.[1] The Gulf crisis and war that began on August 2, 1990, with Iraq's invasion of Kuwait was, for Japan, a war of neither self-defense nor aggression committed by Japan, and thus was something that did not appear in the vocabulary of most Japanese. Instead, postwar Japanese had long believed that not fighting other countries or being involved in wars between other countries was the legitimate way of pacifism and thus would automomatically earn the applause of international society. This understanding was appropriate during the years when Japan was being socially rehabilitated (due to its actions during World War II) and was economically devastated. Since 1975, however, Japan has been a G5/G7 summit participant with other advanced democracies and an important member in the Western alliance of Europe, the United States and Japan as the world's second-largest economy (see Chapter 4).

As one of the three pillars of the international economy and itself occupying some 15 percent of the world's GNP, Japan, which was dependent on the Middle East for more than 70 percent of its oil, should have been more willing to share the management burdens for world peace and security. When an outlaw resorts to violence, leading countries interested in preserving the world order take the initiative to jointly stop such aggression. The use of force on the ground is a question of appropriateness and ability, and Japan did not have to participate in that, but it certainly could contribute in the economic and civilian sectors. Recognizing the crisis as a serious challenge to international security, Japan should have made proactive proposals to respond to it, taking whatever actions were permissible under the Japanese peace constitution. Under the extreme pacifism of postwar Japan, however, even participation in rear area support, transport, and medical services was not supported or even contemplated by the Japanese people.

Unable to play any positive role in the Gulf crisis and war, Japan became the focus of international criticism and eventually offered $13 billion in support, but remained the subject of ridicule for its "checkbook diplomacy." In this sense the war was Japan's "defeat." After the end of the conflict it sent four minesweepers to the Persian Gulf. Only then did its contribution begin to be recognized but it was a case of too little, too late.[2]

The Korean Peninsula after the Cold War

There was one more small defeat for Japanese diplomacy. The sudden changes following the end of the Cold War began to sweep the Korean Peninsula. South Korea's President, Roh Tae Woo, began to focus on "Nord Politique." In September 1990 South Korea was successful in establishing relations with the Soviet Union and offered the Russians economic assistance. In parallel, South Korea also quietly began to take the necessary steps to establish relations with China. By linking the international changes resulting from the end of the Cold War with its own national interests, South Korea completely outmaneuvered North Korea.[3]

Surprised by these movements, North Korea launched a diplomatic offensive and abruptly approached Japan. In September 1990, Kim Il Sung invited a delegation from the LDP and Socialist parties, led by LDP kingpin Kanemaru Shin, to Pyongyang, expressed anger at the Soviet Union, and proposed the immediate normalization of relations between North Korea and Japan. Hands were shaken and promises made but Kanemarv's inexperience in foreign affairs was apparent. Excluding those who could offer diplomatic advice from his delegation, Kanemaru promised North Korea an apology and compensation from Japan, not only for the thirty-six years of colonial rule, but also for the forty-five years of the postwar period in which relations had not been restored. The last pledge raised eyes and caused consternation in both Japan and South Korea.

If at this time Japan seriously wanted to restore relations with North Korea and bring that difficult country into the fold of international society, it would have been appropriate for Prime Minister Kaifu, as the one ultimately responsible for national policy, to stand at the forefront, concentrating all of his energy on the task and making use of both diplomatic and unofficial private channels after extensive preparations. Instead, as a result of leaving the matter to an unofficial visit by the Kanemaru delegation, the opportunity was lost. In contrast to South Korea, which showed the desire and ability to link its national interests with the dramatic international changes then taking place, the Japanese government lacked an international sense of direction and found itself adrift.

As Japan entered the 1990s, its economic bubble burst. The shock was all the more severe because postwar Japan had placed so much confidence in its economic activities. What was very curious was the fact that Japan's elite, made up of the political world, led by the LDP, the economic ministries and agencies, led by the Finance Ministry, and the business world, led by the financial community, did not take any effective measures to stop the damaging effects of the burst bubble on the economy. Not only that, but the elite did not possess the knowledge, spirit, or ability to deal with the twin root causes of the illness following the collapse of the bubble, namely non-performing loans and recession. In June 1992, Prime Minister Miyazawa Kiichi pointed out the importance of the problem of non-performing loans at a speech before an LDP audience, but there was nothing done at this point. The decade of the 1990s was basically "lost" due to this problem. Like the military defeat of the Japanese Empire in World War II, the collapse of the bubble economy and the failure of Japan to rebuild its economy in the 1990s can be termed a "defeat" for an economic power.

The search for a post-Cold War diplomacy

The birth of APEC

Even in the middle of the so-called lost decade, Japanese diplomacy was still able to take several meaningful initiatives.

In November 1989, at the same time that the Cold War was ending, APEC (Asia Pacific Economic Cooperation) was born, and at its birth, MITI took the lead. Since 1985, when Jacques Delors became commissioner of the European Community, the integration of Europe had been moving quickly. In response, in North America, there was some progress in creating a regional organization centered on the North American Free Trade Agreement. In the middle of this, fearing that regionalism in Europe and North America might turn protectionist, some at MITI thought a framework to support economic development and regional cooperation for the entire area of the Pacific was necessary, through which friction between Asia and the United States could be averted.[4]

The Sakamoto Report, compiled by Sakamoto Yoshihiro, International Economy Division chief at MITI, in June 1988 proposed such a concept for a regional organization. During the Cold War, the Pacific was divided between the West (led by the United States) and the East (Communist China). Moreover, for a long time, "Pacific" meant for Japan the developed countries of the North, and "Asia" referred to the developing countries of the South. To create a community in the "Asia-Pacific" region, divided as it was between North and South and East and West, was extremely important for Japan, which struggled with its identity. Since the 1960s, Okita Saburo had been active in proposing this sort of regional cooperation, and the advisory group under Prime Minister Ohira Masayoshi had furthered it with the "Pacific Basin Cooperation Concept" (See Chapter 4), and the PECC (Pacific Economic Cooperation Conference), in which governmental and private individuals had been active in the 1980s.

The birth of a framework for regional cooperation involving Japan like APEC, which replaced the Cold War structure, was psychologically significant. The creation of APEC, however, was not recorded as a bright achievement for Japan. Because the formal organ for foreign affairs was not MITI but the Foreign Ministry, and out of concern that Japan's leadership in the region evoked negative feelings based on historical memory, the honor of creating APEC was given to Australia. Japan had to be content with a backseat.

After APEC's establishment, its core became the middle and small powers of ASEAN. In this region, it is not the major political powers like America or China or the developed economic countries like Japan or Australia, but rather the medium-sized and small countries making rapid and steady progress that are the main actors. This structure reflects the diversity of the Asia-Pacific region as well as the fact that unlike the regional integration in Europe and North America, the countries of the region prefer not to hurry institutionalization, not to impose restrictions on other members, and instead to create regional economic cooperation based on an "Asian way." This was precisely what the "Sakamoto Report" emphasized.

Nevertheless, APEC is not a gathering of those who accept the Asian way of consensus. The United States and other Western countries like Australia, New Zealand, and Canada were not content with a simple exchange of opinions by cabinet ministers but instead called for the creation of an institution to develop actual free trade in the region. In September 1992, an advisory group was created to develop a future vision for APEC, and after recently elected U.S. president William J. Clinton proposed that heads of state attend, APEC meetings entered a new stage.

The success of the PKO Cambodia mission

Under the clouds of the "two defeats," the most successful undertaking of Japanese diplomacy was perhaps its efforts at peace-building in Cambodia.

On the one hand, Japan undertook this initiative to bring about peace in the war-ravaged country, and on the other hand, the passage of the International Peace Cooperation Bill (*Kokusai Rengo Heiwa Iji Katsudoto ni Taisuru Kyoryoku ni Kansuru Horitsu*) made it possible for Japan to participate in the United Nation's peacekeeping operations (PKO) in Cambodia. Japan played a significant role in bringing peace to Cambodia and helping it to rebuild.

In the 1980s, Prime Minister Nakasone Yasuhiro sought a political role for Japan commensurate with its economic strength. As mentioned in Chapter 5, along with strengthening the Japan–U.S. relationship with President Reagan, Nakasone actively spoke out at the Williamsburg Summit in May 1983 on issues of global security, raising Japan's presence to a level never before seen. In addition, in 1985 Nakasone released the Maekawa Report, calling for structural changes in the Japanese economy in conformity with the international development. In May 1986, when Tokyo hosted the G7 summit, postwar Japan displayed itself as a leading country in the international arena.

Takeshita Noboru, who replaced Prime Minister Nakasone in November 1987, was known as a domestic specialist. He was able to exercise his domestic ability in the area of diplomacy, however, and he too desired to increase Japan's international role. Approving the policy proposal of the Foreign Ministry led by Vice-Minister Murata Ryohei, Takeshita announced the "Plan for International Cooperation," with three prongs: (1) the expansion of ODA for developing countries; (2) the promotion of international cultural exchange, seeking to expand relations with the countries of Europe and elsewhere from simple economic ties to mutual understanding between peoples; and (3) contributions to peace-building in regions in conflict via diplomatic efforts, the dispatch of personnel, and aid for reconstruction. Compared with the DeGaullist style of Nakasone, Takeshita's approach followed the traditions of postwar Japan as an economic state and sought to augment Japan's international role as a civilian power (see Chapter 5).

At this time the Ministry of Foreign Affairs began to reexamine the possibility of participating in PKO activities, which had been the hope of many within MOFA since the late 1950s, when Japan joined the United Nations. In addition, the Asia Bureau within the ministry increased its involvement in the Cambodian peace. But as a result of the domestic impasse due to the Recruit Scandal, it became politically impossible for the Takeshita cabinet to propose participation in the PKO. Afterward, the Gulf crisis occurred, and in the middle of this hurricane of events, LDP secretary general Ozawa Ichiro hurriedly prepared a Bill to Allow Cooperation with UN Peacekeeping Forces, which would permit limited SDF participation in a multilateral force. Within the Diet and the government, however, agreement was not easily reached. In November 1990, the LDP, Komeito, and Democratic Socialists finally agreed that the above-mentioned Ozawa's bill would die but a new bill for purely PKO activities would eventually be proposed. That bill was later passed on June 15, 1992.

A primary issue for the government was whether the SDF could participate in PKO activities in light of the peace clause of the constitution. The three-party agreement and Prime Minister Kaifu himself had until a certain point considered creating an organization separated from the SDF to be solely responsible for PKO activities. However, UN Peacekeeping Operations are made up of the militaries of each country providing forces, and if a separate organization were created, the view was that it would result in confusion and problems at the local level when conducting PKO, and thus lawmakers agreed to the dispatch of the SDF. Although the SDF was to be included in PKO activities, a proposal by the Komeito effectively prevented the SDF from monitoring ceasefires and disarming warring parties – activities that could lead to the danger of being drawn into a military confrontation.[5]

The Cambodian peace process, in contrast, was a continuous endeavor led by the Foreign Ministry's Asia Bureau under Fujita Kimio, Hasegawa Kazutoshi, Tanino Sakutaro, Ikeda Tadashi, and others. Within the Foreign Ministry, the Asia Bureau had a particular tradition of independence. Until the 1970s, the North America Bureau and the Treaty Bureau were seen as the place for the traditional elites, while the Asia Bureau was considered a group of local specialists. The spirit of resistance vis-à-vis the mainstream North America hands by the China/Asia specialists could also be seen at the time of the restoration of relations with China. Later, with Asia's development, the positions of Asia Bureau chief and ambassador to the main capitals in Southeast Asia became important and were attractive posts where able diplomats could show off their skills. The rivalry between Americanists versus Asianists has receded somewhat, but the independent spirit of the Asia Bureau remains strong.

With regard to the Cambodian problem, Japanese diplomacy was initially limited to the role of supporting the policy of ASEAN and the permanent member of the UN Security Council that the Phnom Pen government, a puppet of Vietnam, should be abolished and a government by the three factions, including Pol Pot, should be restored. Japan began to take an active role, however, around 1989, when Kono Masaharu, chief of the Asia Bureau's Southeast Asian Section, took the initiative to seek peace in Cambodia in pursuit of Japan's own goal of reintegrating Cambodia centered around Prince Norodom Sihanouk combined with the administrative capability of Phnom Pen government. Area experts within the Foreign Ministry such as Minister Imagawa Yukio, who possessed a deep understanding of the local situation, were main source for this new policy. Japan also worked at getting the cooperation of China and Thailand, who had close relations with Pol Pot, to seek an end to the civil war, and helped at many levels in establishing the framework for the peace agreement reached in Paris in October 1991. In 1992, when the United Nations Transition Authority for Cambodia (UNTAC) was created with UN Undersecretary Akashi Yasushi as representative, Japan passed the PKO cooperation bill and was eventually able to dispatch 1,200 SDF and other personnel.[6]

UNTAC was an unprecedented PKO mission—bringing peace to a country long torn by civil war and in the process of rebuilding its government—and was full of problems until the very end, including Pol Pot's refusal to give up armed conflict. In the spring of 1993, when UN volunteer Nakata Atsushi and later civilian police officer Takada Haruyuki were killed, Japanese public opinion was shaken and debates about immediate withdrawal from UNTAC were heard. On May 11 Prime Minister Miyazawa, agreeing with the judgment of the Foreign Ministry that these incidents did not mean the complete end of the peace agreement, decided to continue Japan's support of and participation in UNTAC.

That this decision was the correct one was shown at the time of the Cambodian general elections held between May 23 and 28 for the Constitutional Drafting Congress that would give legitimacy to the rebuilding of the Cambodian government. Some 90 percent of voters in Cambodia turned out. For the first time Japan had actively participated in efforts to bring peace to a region, and these efforts were successful.

The experiences of the Japanese people between the time of the Gulf War through that of the participation in the Cambodian PKO process brought about great changes in the thinking of the Japanese people. In the middle of the Gulf crisis, when participation of the SDF in a multinational force became the topic of debate, a majority of the people opposed it. However, when Japan's unenthusiastic response earned international criticism, public opinion realized it was necessary to provide financial support and later the dispatch of minesweepers after the end of hostilities. When the efficient work of the minesweepers received international praise, public opinion came to regard the need for international contribution somewhat positively.

And yet at the time when the PKO cooperation bill became the subject of heated debate and confrontation in the Diet, the Socialist Party had demonstrated its strong opposition by threatening that its members would all resign their Diet seats. Public opinion was also divided. The SDF were eventually dispatched as a part of the PKO mission in Cambodia following passage of the bill in the Diet, which set out the "Five Principles" for Japan's participation in PKO activities; these included a freeze on primary activities such as disarming the warring parties and monitoring ceasefires. During this time public opinion was still mixed, but following the success of the mission in Cambodia, a majority of the public came to support SDF participation in PKO missions. Not only this, but the public came to favor *discussion* of the revision of Article 9 of the constitution to allow for meaningful Japanese international contributions (see Figure 3.1).

The success of the Uruguay Round and the birth of the WTO

President George H. W. Bush's call for a "New World Order," centered on the United States following the end of the Cold War and the victory of multinational forces in the Gulf War, was well received. But because of the worldwide recession that was then beginning, Bush lost in the subsequent presidential election to Bill Clinton, who claimed that Bush did not focus enough attention on domestic affairs and the economy.

As pointed out by historian Noda Nobuo, in a speech at a symposium celebrating Kyoto's 1200-year history, the post-Cold War era would be defined by "ethnicity, religion, and Asia." Outside of the United States, ethnic conflicts began to break out in the former Yugoslavia and Soviet Union, federations comprised of many ethnic groups, and in the unstable region of Africa. Following the Iranian revolution in 1979, Islamic fundamentalism has been on the rise, as has Christian fundamentalism in the United States. In Japan, there were even cases of a religious group, Aum *Shinrikyo*, using terrorism. Conflicts based on "geography and history," once suppressed by the Cold War, began to be seen in greater numbers. Europe, Japan, and the United States, instead of responding by cooperating to establish order, moved toward protectionism and rivalry, and it was feared that joint cooperation would be replaced by a situation in which all three former partners would establish competitive regional blocks. Harvard's Samuel P. Huntington even predicted a "clash of civilizations," suggesting the seriousness of the projected disorder. Moreover, national feelings over wartime issues, which had been suppressed during the Cold War, suddenly came to the surface in the form of the debate on the history problem, making it difficult for Japan to respond.

What brought a stop to this flow of events and demonstrated that an international cooperative system could exist in the post Cold War era was the success of GATT's Uruguay Round in December 1993. This round expanded and strengthened of the rules of GATT, which had previously focused on industrial goods, turning to the problematic area of agricultural products and the rapidly developing area of services. With the creation of a World Trade Organization, the post-Cold War world would possess an even better international institution for solving trade disputes.

In this process, the Tokyo G7 summit, in which Japan acted as chair for the third time, provided an opportunity for a new world economic order. At the Miyazawa–Clinton meeting in the April before that, the two sides had failed to agree on "numerical targets" for the program to decrease Japan's trade surplus. The LDP, the predominant party since 1955, split up over the issue of political reforms in June 1993, and it appeared that Prime Minister Miyazawa would be the last prime minister under the 1955 System. It was far from certain that the lame-duck government of Japan would be able to successfully host the summit. It was also feared that the 1993 summit would mark the end of not only the LDP but also the trilateral system of cooperation between Japan, the U.S., and Europe.

These fears turned out to be groundless, as Prime Minister Miyazawa showed his grace under pressure. Japan compromised on the issue of duties on malts, calling for the strengthening of cooperation between Japan, the United States, and Europe. With regard to Japan–U.S. relations as well, an agreement for a framework on comprehensive talks was reached, thus avoiding a breakdown in bilateral relations. These efforts paved the way for agreement in the Uruguay Round later in the same year during the Hosokawa administration.

Japan–U.S. automobile trade friction and its watershed

Since the second half of the 1970s, when the Japanese economy regained its competitive ability in exports by overcoming the oil shocks, trade friction with the United States, which was the largest importer of Japanese industrial products, had not stopped. Numerous trade agreements, often under the name of "voluntary export restraints," were signed. Japan increased its direct investment in the United States, thus increasing domestic employment and demand there, and worked to open and expand the Japanese market for imports. Despite this, Japan's trade surplus to the United States continued to rise. As mentioned in Chapter 5, arguments within the United States that Japan should be excluded from the world economy on the grounds that Japanese society was too unique to compete with other countries on an equal footing became louder.

When Clinton took office in January 1993, he announced that his administration would take effective measures against Japan and would seek to address the inequality of trade at a macro-level as well as seeking "numerical targets" on specific areas. As a result, bleak exchanges took place at the April 1993 Miyazawa–Clinton summit and the February 1994 Hosokawa–Clinton meeting, precipitating a break in the talks. Japan–U.S. trade friction reached a peak with the talks in June 1995 over cars and car parts.

The minister of international trade and industry in the Murayama Tomiichi cabinet, Hashimoto Ryutaro, and U.S. Trade Representative Mickey Kantor engaged in some tough negotiations. MITI investigated the international trading rules of the GATT and WTO compared with actual practices, and prepared reports covering recent years in English and Japanese on fair and unfair trade. In light of this research, the demands for bilateral numerical targets were considered to be unfair, a finding Hashimoto used in his responses. Unlike past times when the U.S. and Japan had disagreed, Japan gained the support or at least the sympathy of the EU and ASEAN countries. Clinton finally withdrew his call for numerical targets, and on June 28 the talks were concluded. The resolution reached in the summer of 1995 can be seen as the end of the long era of Japan–U.S. trade friction. The U.S. economy had already been performing well since 1993, and the Japanese economy, in contrast, was worsening since the burst of the bubble economy in 1992. The United States had lost the objective and fundamental conditions for forcing Japan to undertake voluntary restraint and concessions. With the changing economic fortunes of both countries, Japan's persistent resistance to making unnecessary concessions succeeded in the end.

The season of crisis and security

The collapse of the security myth

Through the visit to Pyongyang by former president Jimmy Carter, war was barely averted on the Korean Peninsula during the North Korea nuclear crisis of June–October 1994. The seriousness of the situation was not fully known at the time in Japan, in terms of the security of both Northeast Asia and the Japan–U.S. relationship. Moreover, the Hanshin-Awaji or Kobe earthquake of January 17, 1995, followed by the March 20 sarin gas attack by the Aum Supreme Truth (*Aum Shinrikyo*) cult, were great shocks that overturned the myths of safety that had existed in postwar Japanese society. In addition to the challenges presented by natural disasters and terrorist groups, equally shocking to the Japanese public was the inability of the Japanese government to manage foreign and domestic crises.

As we have seen, public opinion regarding security matters underwent changes due to the experience of the PKO mission in Cambodia. Fundamental changes were also seen at the political level in June 1994 with the birth of a coalition cabinet that included the Socialist Party, the LDP, and the Sakigake (Pioneer) Party, and was headed by Murayama Tomiichi, chairman of the Socialist Party. It was the first time in forty-seven years that the prime ministership was occupied by someone from the Socialist Party—a party that had continued its opposition to any involvement in security matters in the postwar in part because of Japan's aggression in the prewar period. Prime Minister Murayama, however, deemed the stability and continuity of the government to be of utmost importance, and, accepting responsibility as the head of government, recognized the SDF as constitutional and announced his support for the Japan–U.S. security treaty, in effect discarding the Socialist Party's platform.

Not only was this a dramatic departure from the Socialist's long-held views, but the confrontation or "domestic Cold War" under the 1955 system came to an end. Japanese politics were free from the yoke they had long been under. And yet the political debate was still only at the starting line for discussing security issues. Various "should not's" had been removed from the list, but the Japanese had made no preparations for what Japan "should do" for its own security and that of international society. When it first had to respond to a crisis, it found itself completely unprepared.

The Japanese thought postwar Japan possessed one of the world's safest and richest societies, in which people could live a long life without exerting much effort. Entering the 1990s, however, events showed how surprisingly fragile Japan really was, and just how shallow was its ability to respond to crises—in the area of international relations (Gulf Crisis); economics (after the bubble); natural disasters; and religious terrorism.

These failures of the decision-making apparatus demonstrated the limits of a once successful system. Japan's postwar system was an excellent one in the early years, allowing a defeated and starving people to concentrate on improving economic life in peacetime. Japan freed itself from international security matters by relying upon the alliance with the United States, and the Japanese people freed themselves from crucial decisions by concentrating on economic development under the institutionalized arrangements made by the LDP–bureaucracy coalition. Said another way, the voters entrusted policy and decision-making to the LDP and government and concentrated on their work and daily lives. At the larger level, Japan left the difficult international decisions to its partner, the United States.

It was wise at the time for Japan to leave security matters to the United States considering that the Soviet Union, Japan's next-door threat during the Cold War, was too huge a superpower for Japan alone to cope with. The United States was the only country in the world that had the capability and will to deter the Soviets. With the end of the Cold War, however, Japan, by then an economic superpower, had to confront various kinds of crisis for which its system and the mindset of the people were not prepared.

The Okinawa rape incident and the Taiwan Strait missile crisis

The passing of trade friction in the summer of 1995 brought about a quiet calm. What broke this tranquility was an earthquake of sorts in security matters. It was actually as if two earthquakes hit—one a direct hit caused by an active fault, the other one caused by the shifting of oceanic plates.

The brutal rape of an Okinawan schoolgirl in September 1995 by three American servicemen brought about cries of "no more" from the residents of Okinawa. It was a direct-hit earthquake of sorts that the U.S. bases in Japan, which form the foundation of the Japan–U.S. security relationship, were in danger of being blown away by the powerful winds of civil society.

China's missile practice near Taiwan took place earlier that year, in July and August, and turned into an international crisis during its peak in March 1996. The future security of the region would be called into question if China, slowly recovering its position as Asia's superpower, reverted to the use of force to make its opinion known. China's actions amounted to a South China Seas earthquake for the entire East Asia region.

These two shocking events brought about opposite responses. The Okinawa incident showed that the thinking among the general public in developed societies, focusing on amenities and the environment, was moving away from a tolerance of large infrastructures and heavy burdens common to traditional security. If the possibility of a military threat were to disappear in post-Cold War Asia, both the U.S. and the Japanese governments would not in principle object to a reduction of U.S. forces in Japan. However, the Taiwan Strait crisis demonstrated that the traditional power games were not in fact a thing of the past.

Following the end of the Cold War, there was a time when it was thought that as long as the common enemy (the Soviet Union) had collapsed, there was no longer any reason to maintain NATO and the Japan–U.S. Security Treaty, an extreme version of the so-called "peace dividend." However, Europe faced the tragic and dangerous situation in the former Yugoslavia, and Asia witnessed the alarming movements of North Korea and the problems in the Taiwan Strait. The U.S. military presence in both regions was reappraised as necessary, not for an actual strategic threat, but instead to prepare against various factors of instability in the region.

China was the country most concerned with this situation, viewing it as an attempt by the United States to reassert hegemony and "contain" it. Ironically, China's own behavior in the Taiwan Strait provided the proof of the need for such an international framework. China's premonitions were realized by its own actions.

The Chinese government itself was not necessarily trying to bring about the unification of China by force when it undertook missile tests on Taiwan Strait. Instead, China was nervous that Taiwanese President Lee Teng-hui sought to increase the legitimacy of Taiwan's democracy through a possible victory in the elections of March 1996 after being embened by his successful visit to the United States. The missile tests could be described as a political message to clearly demonstrate to the people of Taiwan and the world that China would never recognize Taiwan as an independent country.

In response, the Clinton administration, ever careful to avoid a military clash through miscalculation, sent two aircraft carrier task groups to the Taiwan area, bringing to an end the missile firings to demonstrate its interest in seeing a peaceful resolution to the conflict. Far from attempting a war against China, the United States sent China a political message that it would not permit unification with Taiwan by force.[7]

The result of the above maneuvering was the confirmation by both China and the United States that the United States continued to recognize a "One China" policy and that it demanded of China a "peaceful" solution.

Redefinition of the Japan–U.S. Security Treaty

In January 1996 the LDP had regained power with the creation of the Hashimoto Ryutaro cabinet, which undertook to confront these crises head-on. Relatively young and eager to learn, Prime Minister Hashimoto, with his equally strong desire to win, was an appropriate leader at this time. According to Funabashi Yoichi in *Alliance Adrift*, in 1993, when the LDP lost power after thirty-eight years and was in the opposition, Hashimoto, who had become head of the Policy Research Council within the party, began to concentrate his studies on security and crisis management.[8] This focus came to the fore as the Hashimoto cabinet began to struggle with matters of security.

In addition to the aftermath of the Okinawa incident and the challenge of the Taiwan Strait crisis, the Hashimoto cabinet was faced with a number of situations that sprang from the fluid world of the post-Cold War period, such as the hostage crisis at the Japanese embassy in Peru, the Cambodian crisis, and the Indonesian crisis. Except for the Peru incident, which was handled ineffectively and ended with bitter results, Hashimoto showed a quick and decisive responsiveness to crises unlike any that of other prime minister before him, as seen by the decision to fuel U.S. vessels at sea during the Taiwan Strait crisis, and the dispatch of SDF airplanes for the first time in postwar history to evacuate Japanese nationals in the crises of Cambodia and Indonesia (East Timor). These relief actions were defined as one of the government's duties in the new Japan–U.S. Guidelines for Defense Cooperation in 1997.

The development of the Japan–U.S. Security Treaty following the Taiwan Strait crisis held structural significance for the Asia-Pacific region. The two governments jointly advanced their security relationship. First came the "Redefinition of the Japan–U.S. Security Treaty." The joint declaration, "An Alliance for the Twenty-first Century," which sought to continue the treaty and make it more effective, was announced following the Japan–U.S. summit meeting in Tokyo in April 1996. Just before the meeting, Hashimoto and Clinton reached agreement on the return and relocation of Marine Corps Air Station Futenma on Okinawa, which had been viewed as impossible by those at the working level, conditioned on its functions being relocated within the prefecture. In the joint declaration, the two leaders recognized the need to consolidate and reduce U.S. bases in Okinawa, promised to deal jointly with the base problems as highlighted by the rape incident, supported the continued presence of approximately 100,000 U.S. forces in the region to contribute to the peace and security of the Asia-Pacific, and agreed to begin the drafting of the New Guidelines for Japan–U.S. Defense Cooperation. In the wake of the Taiwan Strait crisis, the United States and Japan confirmed that the use of force to resolve the Sino-Taiwanese problem would not be permitted. The United States and Japan explained that the New Guidelines were not meant to "contain" China, but instead represented a policy of "engagement" by which China would constructively participate in international society.

The new strategic policy was carefully prepared. On the U.S. side, two Harvard professors, Joseph S. Nye and Ezra F. Vogel, joined the administration and took the lead in crafting East Asia strategy after the Cold War under Secretary of Defense William J. Perry, which came to be known as the "Nye Initiative."

The Japanese side recognized the need for a new defense policy to respond to the post-Cold War situation, and in February 1994, the Hosokawa Morihiro cabinet established the Advisory Group on Defense Issues (*Boei Mondai Kondankai*) headed by Higuchi Hirotaro, chairperson of Asahi Breweries, and professor Watanabe Akio as the drafter. Their report was completed in August that year shortly after the start of the Murayama administration.[9] On the basis of its recommendations, which continued to emphasize the importance of the Japan–U.S. security relationship amid the growing multilateral framework of the post-Cold War world, the New Defense Outline was completed in November 1995. Close dialogue and discussions between Japan and the United States were undertaken at this point becoming the basis of the "Redefinition of the Japan–U.S. Security Treaty."

The redefinition of the security treaty, prepared at the working level, had been scheduled to be jointly announced at the time of APEC meeting in Osaka in November 1995, but was postponed because of the last-minute cancellation of President Clinton's trip to Japan due to a deadlock in

Washington over the budget. At the same time tensions were building in the Taiwan Strait. Those crises ironically had the effect of giving life to the redefinition of the security relationship. As a result, the Hashimoto–Clinton meeting of April 1996 was the first summit in a long time that was truly forward-looking in nature.

The era of competitive–cooperative diplomacy

From crisis to cooperation

While China continued to express its unhappiness with the redefinition of the Japan–U.S. alliance and the announcement of the New Guidelines, it also made efforts at developing cooperative relations, and became particularly eager to establish friendly relations with the United States. For China, confronting America's hegemony militarily would be unwise. Despite America's increasing hegemony, it was not only possible for China to coexist with the United States but was also in its interest to continue its policies of "reform and openness" and to seek economic development in the U.S.-led international system. China's strategy of developing "comprehensive national power" (including both economic might and military might), in which it plans to overtake Japan and stand on par with the United States through high growth over the next twenty to thirty years, might be a realistic long-term national goal. If China could develop absolute strength in East Asia, Taiwan would likely give up and seek to rejoin China even if the PRC did not employ force. This would be in keeping with the theory of Sun Tzu, who said, "Fighting and winning one hundred battles is not the best strategy. The best strategy is making the enemy give in without fighting at all." Seeming to follow this long-range strategy, China under Jiang Zemin and Zhu Rongji attempted to adopt the approach of realizing national interests for the time being primarily through economic and other non-military activities, a continuation of the Deng Xiaoping line.

After the crisis of the spring of 1996, it appeared that the major countries in the Asia-Pacific sought a diplomatic relationship, competition with cooperation. For example, President Clinton, who improved relations with Japan, next invited Chinese President Jiang to the United States in October 1997 and undertook a state visit himself to China in June 1998, thus showing that America knew how to handle both Japan and China. It was not a time of choice between East or West as it had been during the Cold War, but instead a kind of party in which each member had many partners across East and West, North and South. In this multilateral dance, it was disadvantageous for a country to have a bad relationship with a particular country. At the same time, it also could be a burden to keep an inflexible alliance relationship. The term "partnership" was used often when leaders met with one another, as if changing partners while dancing. The latter half of the 1990s was an age of "competitive-cooperative diplomacy" in East Asia.

Two characteristics should be pointed out about this situation. The first has to do with the fact that the structure of order in the Asia-Pacific is predicated to a large extent on the presence of U.S. forces. Unlike Britain in the nineteenth century and the United States in the 1920s, the United States since World War II has been actively engaging in substantial commitments, forming a network of alliances across the Pacific. The Japan–U.S. Security Treaty, expanded and enlarged in many ways under the "Redefinition," forms the backbone of the American presence in the entire region. The use of force to change the status quo by anyone would not be permitted, and through this stability would come shared prosperity. Following the end of World War II, the United States created an alliance system known by the metaphor "hub and spokes," with the United States at the center. Among them, the Japan–U.S. alliance is becoming the main part of this system and could serve as the nucleus of a regional security organization.

Second, the characteristic of the security system has changed. As seen in Chapter 4, the Kubo concept saw the Japan–U.S. Security Treaty as assuming responsibility for regional stability in the post-Vietnam years, and in the 1990s following the end of the Soviet threat with its collapse, this role for the security treaty became even quite clearer. With the end of the Soviet Union, the Japan–U.S. security relationship has lost the character of a military alliance focused against an imagined enemy and has come to perform as the twin functions of deterrence and defense against different types of disturbances in the Asia-Pacific order caused by various factors of instability.

Second, it should be emphasized again that various multilateral organizations exist in this region. APEC is the most comprehensive one across the Pacific, and ASEAN, born in 1967 during the Vietnam War, has made good progress as the pivotal regional organization in Southeast Asia and has sponsored the birth of several broader organizations, such as the ASEAN Regional Forum (ARF, 1994) and the ASEAN + 3 (Japan, China, Korea), a meeting of the heads of state of the countries of East Asia that began in 1997 and includes the same countries as in an earlier (1991) proposal by Malaysian president Mahathir Mohamad for an East Asian Economic Caucus. In addition, the Asia-Europe Meeting (ASEM), a joint summit meeting for the countries of APEC and the EU, was started in 1996, holding meetings every other year. Of course these meetings take place in addition to the already existing global activities of the WTO, IMF, G8 (G7 and Russia), and United Nations organizations.

In other words, in the Asia-Pacific, a three-layered structure exists: APEC and numerous other multilateral forums exist on one level, bilateral relations proceed at another, with the Japan–U.S. Security Treaty serving as the bedrock of security. These multiple layers are characteristic of the international relations as a whole after the Cold War. Although it is not a rigidly institutionalized system, it can be said to be a soft new order in the Asia-Pacific in the post-Cold War period addressing some of the hard and real challenges facing the region.

Hashimoto diplomacy

Prime Minister Hashimoto was one of the important actors in this multi-lateral diplomatic game. Not only did he dramatically improve relations with the United States, but he was also able to bring about closer relations with ASEAN. Even relations with far-off Europe and Russia were improved during his two and a half years in office.

Major changes were taking place in Europe at the time. A battleground for two world wars, Europe became a "valley" between the two superpowers—the United States and the Soviet Union. The integration of Europe was an attempt to strengthen itself. With the end of the Cold War on the one hand, and the continuing integration of Europe on the other, the postwar problem of the unification of Germany was resolved peacefully in October 1990. Following the collapse of the communist system in the Soviet Union and Eastern Europe, the European Union, born from the February 1992 Maastricht Treaty and the work of the forty-five years since the European Coal and Steel Community in 1951, has been trying to deepen institutions, as seen by the issuance of the Euro, and widen itself, to include all of Europe. Europe, centered on Western Europe, went from being the "valley" to a central actor along with the United States in international society. For Japanese diplomacy, relations with the major countries of Europe and the rapidly integrating EU have become very important not only in the context of bilateral relations, but also in its ability to deal with global issues, as seen in rapid expansion of consultation between Japan and the EU on a number of issues (as first laid out in July 1991 in the Joint Declaration on Relations between the European Community and its Members States and Japan).[10]

Japanese relations with Britain have been extremely good from the Thatcher period (1979–90), being described as the "Second Anglo-Japanese Alliance," an allusion to the first alliance of 1902–22. In contrast, relations with France have been for the most part difficult. However, with the election of Jacques Chirac, known as someone knowledgeable about Japan, as the president of France in May 1995, Franco-Japanese relations improved, ushering in the dawn of competition among countries in Europe which sought to further their relations with Japan. Ultimately Japan's relations with both the United States and Europe improved, and for Hashimoto at the G8 summit, it was not a bad place to be.[11]

Particularly worthy of note in Hashimoto's diplomacy is the change in relations with Russia. Japan has historically not had good relations with any of its neighbors—Korea, China, or Russia. There are many reasons for this state of affairs. In the late nineteenth century, tsarist Russia adopted a southern strategy in the Far East, thereby making a clash with the newly expanding nation of Japan virtually inevitable. In the postwar period, Japan, as part of the Western camp, was destined to confront the communist Soviet Union. Yet, there was no real reason to have bad relations with the Russia at that time, which had overturned its former system and was striving to democratically reform its domestic structure. The Russia of today, however, has since gone back on its democratization process and once again become an autocratic state.

The problem of Russia's joining the G7 summit was a delicate one. Russia, new to having a liberal democracy and a market economy, did not really possess a developed economy. The countries of Europe nevertheless wanted to include Russia. Rather than banishing their large neighbor, they wanted to bring Russia into the club of advanced nations and turn it into a country that could be worked with. (This is the same feeling that Japan has toward China, and perhaps even more so.) The United States, from a strategic point of view, agreed, for abandoning Russia, the second-largest holder of nuclear weapons in the world, was unwise. In the end, it was only Japan that opposed Russia's joining the G7 summit. Japan continued to be spiteful toward Russia, which persisted in holding on to the Northern Territories.

Hashimoto took the initiative to break with the past. At the Denver Summit in June 1997, Hashimoto told Russian president Boris Yeltsin that he would welcome Russia's participation in the G7 club, turning it into an opportunity to dramatically improve Russo-Japanese bilateral relations. After several meetings, including bilateral summits in Krasnoyarsk and Kawana, both leaders seemed to have developed a mutual friendship. Hashimoto stressed "a long-term perspective," pointing out that a resolution of the Northern Territories problem could be reached through the deepening of Russo-Japanese relations. He thus no longer adhered to the traditional approach of insisting on a resolution of the issue prior to improving relations. It was a fresh change, but in reality only limited progress has been made both in furthering the bilateral relationship and in resolving the territorial issue. A peace treaty between Japan and Russia remains to be signed, a dialogue, exchanges, and cooperation have been proceeding to a certain degree.

The East Asian financial crisis and Japan

The economic crisis and the Hashimoto cabinet

Even in the middle of the seemingly unending recession of the 1990s, there were moments that looked as if the worst phase was over and a new day was starting. In the beginning of 1997, there was a great rush to purchase things prior to the planned increase in the consumption tax from 3 to 5 percent, suggesting that the economy was improving. The Hashimoto cabinet made no efforts, however, to take measures to help lift the fragile economy to compensate for the increased taxes, and instead adopted a 9 trillion yen effective tax rise, thus taking the wind out of the economy. The failure to help the economy ended up truly hurting it, and as the economy spun further out of control, the increase in failed loans shook the core of the financial system.

As the saying goes, "misfortune comes in a group." In July 1997 the Thai baht rapidly lost value, and soon the financial issues involving all of East Asia, including Indonesia and Korea, developed into an economic crisis for the region, and turned into a political crisis in Indonesia.

The Hashimoto cabinet attempted to respond with a plan developed by Sakakibara Eisuke of the Finance Ministry that proposed the creation of an Asian Monetary Fund in addition to the existing IMF to assist the Asian financial crisis. It was an effort to respond to the crisis by strengthening regional multilateral frameworks. Japan demonstrated that it was prepared to assume the responsibility for it. It was a well-timed proposal, but the Finance Ministry pursued it as its own initiative and did not consult with the U.S.[12] The U.S. in turn rejected the plan, which lacked conditions for reform. America argued that giving financial assistance to the Asian countries without requiring them to reform would invite a moral hazard. There were many in the IMF and among U.S. specialists who assumed that Asia's crony capitalism had invited the crisis and that structural adjustments and essential reforms should be given. The U.S. not only rejected the proposal to establish the AMF, but did nothing to provide financial assistance to the region.

Because of this, the Japanese government then started to provide emergency assistance on a bilateral basis. First Japan extended $4 billion to Thailand, followed by $5 billion to Indonesia and $10 billion to South Korea. These special appropriations made available a total of $43 billion in April 1998. In the age of the interdependence of the Asian economies, one country's economic collapse spelled dangers for all. Assisting other countries in the region was thus on the one hand an act of enlightened self-interest, necessary for Japan's own economy. Japan extended a helping hand even though it was in the middle of a recession of its own.

The Hashimoto cabinet showed its strength in diplomacy, but in its own economic matters, there were a series of failures. The budget cuts following the passage of the Special Measures Bill for the Promotion of Structural Reform in Finances in November 1997 brought about unfortunate results. To undertake severe fiscal retrenchment policies in the middle of the depression made the situation critical. Of course reforms to improve the basic structure had to be undertaken, but they would be a fundamental mistake if carried out to the point where the very existence of the national economy became endangered. The reform fundamentalists in the IMF often call for surgery, but U.S. treasury secretary Robert Rubin and others came to recognize that error. During the economic crisis, they saw that the expansion of demand and imports was a priority and began to strongly call upon Japan to cut taxes and increase spending.

In this way, the United States proposed two contradictory ways for Japan to deal with its problems. Unfortunately, no one in Japan or Asia had heard of this type of strong medication before. What is even more unfortunate, of the two prescriptions, Japan ended up mistakenly taking the wrong one and sinking deeper into recession.

The birth of the Obuchi cabinet amid the depths of the recession

The first half of 1998 was one of the darkest periods facing postwar Japan. Domestically, the corrosion of the financial system and the economic recession were two major problems that defied help.

Internationally as well, Japan lost out in the game of "word politics." Within the United States, China was seen as being able to maintain both its financial standing as well as help sustain the Asian economy under Zhu Rongji, while Japan was viewed as hopeless. In addition, President Clinton, who visited China in June, reaffirmed the "three No's" with regard to Taiwan, and even criticized Japan with Jiang, pleasing his Chinese hosts. The game of national interests is not only based on military or economic powers, but requires skill in international "word politics."

The LDP lost in the Upper House elections that took place in July 1998 during the middle of this bad time. The Hashimoto government, taking responsibility for the loss, resigned *en masse* and was replaced by the Obuchi Keizo cabinet. The Obuchi cabinet started from a very low point, both with regard to the situation Japan faced at the time, and in popularity ratings, but before long Obuchi demonstrated an ability that defied most predictions. The prime minister changed the tradition of dividing cabinet posts among the various factions, and instead kept four posts for himself to allot. The exercise of this right to appoint cabinet members, which had not been used since the time of Yoshida Shigeru, made possible the appointment of the former prime minister Miyazawa Kiichi as finance minister and the writer Sakaiya Taiichi as economic planning minister. Moreover, though it amounted to almost a complete acceptance of a proposal by the opposition Democratic Party due to the LDP's poor showing in the Upper House, the Obuchi cabinet worked out a framework for reconstructing the financial system. Obuchi also attempted to improve the predicament of the ruling party, which had lost its majority in the Upper House, through a coalition with the Liberal Party. Under the leadership of Finance Minister Miyazawa, the Japanese government sought to improve the economy through several ways, including a 24 trillion yen stimulus package and more than 6 trillion yen in tax cuts.

Although there were some signs in Thailand and South Korea that the worst of the financial crisis was over, the Japanese government announced the $30 billion "New Miyazawa Plan" in the fall of 1998 with the intention of aiding those countries in Asia still struggling economically, in addition to the $43 billion already pledged. This time, the U.S. government praised the plan and Asian countries welcomed it. In addition, the Ministry of International Trade and Industry announced the granting of special yen-based loans in the amount of 6oo million yen.

International views by this point had changed. In the second half of 1998, Russia, which had been guided by the IMF, fell into a financial crisis. That in turn produced a crisis in American hedge funds. Financial crisis broke out in Brazil as well. It was no longer possible to view the situation from afar as in 1997. The United States itself proposed a $41.5 billion rescue package in conjunction with the IMF. With regard to the financial crisis in Asia, the U.S. government looked to Japan for help.

The autumn diplomatic rush

From the fall of 1998 until the end of the year, world leaders paid many visits to the Asia-Pacific region. In the first half of each year, the G8 summit meetings are held, while the latter half is the season for the leaders in the Asia-Pacific, as noted earlier. The APEC heads of state meeting is held in the fall, and in December the ASEAN gathering is convened. Around this time as well, the leaders of Japan, China, Russia, and the United States bilateral convened summits. In 1998, South Korean president Kim Dae Jung joined the stage as a prominent actor. From October onward, Obuchi held meetings with the leaders of South Korea, Russia, the United States, China, and in October attended the APEC heads of state meeting in Malaysia as well as the ASEAN +3 meeting in December in Hanoi.

Of note was the meeting with President Kim during his visit to Japan in October. Kim called for the creation of a fruitful future that would go beyond the history problems of the past, and said that the history problem was one that Japan had to face and answer on its own. Kim also stated that South Korea would no longer raise the issue. Prime Minister Obuchi apologized for Japan's colonization of Korea in the document of joint declaration "New Japan-Korea Partnership for the Twenty-first Century," responding in grand fashion to President Kim's call for cooperation. The time for reconciliation in the long-problematic Korean–Japanese relationship had surprisingly arrived.

When President Kim spoke in Tokyo of the need to move the relationship with Japan forward, he mentioned three things about postwar Japan that he believed deserved praise, namely, Japan's peaceful development, its democratization, and its aid to developing countries. It was probably difficult for Kim, as the representative of the Korean people whose national pride was damaged during the years of Japanese occupation, to speak so positively about Japan. The inability of the Korean people to praise the good things about today's Japan and their tendency to speak only of its bad actions in the prewar is a true reflection of the bitterness held by the people of that country. Despite this, their president spoke positively of Japan and in doing so opened up a new relationship between the two countries focused on the future.

Subsequently, both countries jointly sponsored the 2002 Soccer World Cup, which brought the people of both countries closer together. Moreover, both peoples began to better appreciate each other's culture and countries, as a result of regular travel and many forms of cultural exchange.

Opportunities and challenges in Sino-Japanese relations

In order to promote Sino-Japanese relations, the visit of Chinese President Jiang Zemin to Japan was planned. Jiang was continuing the line adopted by

Deng Xiaoping in the late 1970s to develop China's economy through the international market economy. Although there were setbacks at the time of the Tiananmen Square massacre in 1989 and the Taiwan Strait missile crisis in 1996, the policy of making the people of China richer could not be stopped. In order for industry to develop, a stable and peaceful international environment was necessary, particularly in China's relations with the United States and Japan. From 1997, through reciprocal visits by the heads of state, the Sino-U.S. relationship improved dramatically to a point where they were describing each other as a "strategic partner." Regarding Sino-Japanese relations as well, an advisory body known as the 21st Century Committee recommended that both countries pursue "mutual interests" rather than "emotions" in order to improve relations. Both countries adopted this approach and prepared an agenda of thirty-three items of mutual interest for signing at the time of Jiang's visit to Japan.

Unfortunately, however, Jiang's trip was put off by six months due to floods in China, and it was not until the month after Kim's visit to Japan that Jiang was able to come. The Chinese side demanded an official apology in writing, which Japan had given President Kim, but Prime Minister Obuchi did not agree to this and instead gave an apology orally. This was done because China did not show the same willingness as South Korea not to raise the history problem any more. Jiang was dissatisfied, and criticized Japan's actions in the war on several occasions, even at a dinner at the Imperial Palace. The impolite behavior of this guest in turn angered Japanese public opinion. The thirty-three items of mutual interest were in the end signed, but no one cared anymore.

The destructive results of the visit also shocked the Chinese side. If they had been paying attention, they would have been aware of the fact that with the exception of China, all the countries in Asia, including South Korea and those in Southeast Asia, had all come to positively evaluate Japan's postwar progress and its role today and no longer raked up the past. China's criticism of Japan exposed China's isolation and led people there to recognize that it was not in China's interest to pursue it any more. Afterwards, at summit meetings, China only gave a perfunctory mention of the history issue before moving on to other issues. For the People's Republic of China, which came into being as an extension of the war with Japan, patriotism and anti-Japanese sentiment are two sides of the same coin, and it has been impossible for appearance's sake to not raise the issue. Nevertheless, for all essential purposes it has been trying to not touch on the issue.

For Japan, moving beyond the history problem means that it can expand its role in the region as a "member of Asia." Prime Minister Obuchi did not miss this opportunity, and during his visit in 1999 to China, he helped China's drive for membership in the WTO. Sino-U.S. relations had unexpectedly and dangerously worsened with the mistaken bombing of the Chinese Embassy in Belgrade during the air strikes on Yugoslavia in April, and the issue affected China's accession to the WTO. While in China, Prime Minister Obuchi agreed to help China and acted as a bridge between the United States and

China. Under Obuchi, Japan's relations with the United States, China, and South Korea were all extremely good. It was a time when reconciliation with the countries of Asia on the history problem was seen and the possibility of Japan being welcomed by these countries to assume the position of the leader of Asia was sincerely felt. As explained later, this feeling, however, was only shortly lived.

Economies are cyclical in nature, and no matter how tough an economic situation may be, it does not necessarily spell the end of the country. In a time of economic troubles, however, people can become psychologically insecure and resort to violence out of despair and panic. Such action can destroy a country and civilization as a whole. The history of the world's sliding into war following the Great Depression in 1929 teaches us precisely this lesson. Following the Asian economic crisis, the cabinets of Hashimoto and Obuchi did not repeat the foolish cycles of history, but instead took the initiative to strengthen the frameworks for cooperation.

Twenty-first century shocks: Japanese diplomacy after 9/11

The Koizumi–Bush partnership

On the eve of the twenty-first century, Prime Minister Obuchi gathered a few dozen intellectuals and scholars and created the "Council on Japan in the 21st Century (*21 Seiki Nihon no Koso*)," headed by Dr. Kawai Hayao, a clinical psychologist and expert on the Japanese psyche, and instructed the group to study the issues facing Japan and the direction for it in the new century. The final report presented in the beginning of 2000 called for Japan to pursue its "enlightened national interests" in a globalizing world. It dismissed the argument that Japan had to chose between the U.S. and Asia, and instead put forward an agenda in which the Japan–U.S. relationship would be maintained and strengthened in the twenty-first century while deepening relations with Japan's neighbors in Asia and creating a new regional community. It also called for Japan to expand its role in security affairs, but at the same time to act as a "civilian power" in its foreign relations, emphasizing the economy, technology, and culture. It also argued the need for Japan to lead in the rebuilding of an international order and to possess the vision to develop such a concept and the language to articulate it.

After Prime Minister Obuchi's massive stroke in April 2000, party leaders in the LDP chose Mori Yoshiro to succeed Obuchi, who was in a coma, as prime minister. Because the nomination occurred behind closed doors, the Mori administration was viewed as being undemocratic and against the times from the very beginning. Mori was blamed for the continued recession, the lack of progress with reforms, and the failure at crisis management. His off-color comments, such as calling Japan a "Divine Nation," and actions, including continuing to play golf after he was informed that a Japanese fisheries high school training ship (the *Ehime Maru*) was sunk after an accident with a U.S. submarine (the U.S.S. *Greenville*) off Hawaii, were also the subject of criticism. Japanese society was angered that the problem of the "Lost Decade" was continuing into the new century without a resolution in sight.

It was Koizumi Junichiro, a reformer, who allied himself with the people in their frustration and uncertainty and succeeded in making their pain his gain politically. Unlike Mori, Koizumi was not designated by the party elite, but instead was elected by the strong support from local party members and the overwhelming momentum of public opinion as a whole. Koizumi's politics did not rely on the party structure or the bureaucracy, which is what previous LDP administrations had done as part of the "1955 System." The prime minister gained the support of the people, and his legitimacy, by attacking the vested interests and corruption that had developed under the four decades of LDP control. He was a populist in every sense of the word, even stating that he would "destroy" his own party, if necessary, in order to pursue his reforms.

The main issue facing the Koizumi administration when it started in April 2001 was clearly domestic structural reform, with diplomacy relatively non-important. If the prime minister himself was not skilled at diplomacy, one would have thought that he would have chosen someone who could be trusted to handle foreign affairs carefully. Instead, he chose Tanaka Makiko, the daughter of Tanaka Kakuei, who was extremely popular for her outspokenness but lacked the experience and judgment to handle foreign policy. Although her appointment was justified as necessary due to the public outrage over the many scandals caused by the Foreign Ministry, it was seen as problematic for treating foreign affairs as an extension of domestic politics.

However, ironically, Koizumi was able to produce huge successes in diplomacy by strengthening the Japan–U.S. relationship to a level previously never attained, following the 9/11 attacks. Fortunately, rebuilding a good Japan–U.S. relationship had been an agenda item of the George W. Bush administration when it started.

Bush, who had barely won in the presidential elections in the fall of 2000, criticized Clinton's East Asia policy for having focused on improving relations with Communist China and North Korea at the expense of Japan, and instead made the Japan–U.S. alliance the centerpiece of his strategy. Richard L. Armitage, a pro-Japan former official who had worked at drafting a policy paper on the alliance, was made Deputy Secretary of State in the new administration. His policy was to help Japan to expand its international role and bring the relationship up to the same level as the Anglo-American relationship, all the while respecting Japan's autonomy. Visiting the United States in June 2001, Prime Minister Koizumi was able to begin to build a personal relationship with President Bush.

The 9/11 terrorist attacks and the war in Afghanistan

Without major powers surrounding and threatening it, America's degree of security is high. Other than the British attack on Washington, D.C., during the War of 1812 and Japan's attack on Pearl Harbor in 1941, the U.S. has never seriously been threatened before. Due to this, the 9/11 attacks in New York and Washington were all the more of a shock. Nineteen terrorists hijacked four planes, crashing two into the World Trade Center Twin Towers and another into the Pentagon (with a fourth one crashing in a field in Pennsylvania after a struggle between the passengers and the hijackers), killing more than 3,000 people. Twenty-four Japanese were among those indiscriminately killed. President Bush had an appointment with destiny to become the representative of America at this time who needed to unite the country in its battle with terrorism.

Prime Minister Koizumi visited the site of the attacks two weeks later and expressed his support for the U.S.-led war on terrorism. This expression was done in recognition of Japan's slow response ten years before at the time of the Gulf War. Japan not only did not contribute militarily with the SDF at the time of the Gulf Crisis and War, but did not do anything that satisfied the U.S. and other coalition partners in non-military areas either. Amid this international criticism, Japan contributed 13 billion dollars, but this financial contribution did nothing more than smooth ruffled feathers. In contrast, by going to America and pledging his support for the war on terrorism, Koizumi from the beginning furthered his relationship of trust and mutual understanding with the United States.

Al Qaeda, the terrorist group responsible for the attacks, was headed by Usama Bin-ladin who had been hiding in the Taliban-controlled Afghanistan. The Bush administration began its war against the Taliban and Al Qaeda in October. Many observers thought the U.S. military would also have a tough fight, considering that the 1979 invasion of Afghanistan had not gone well for the Soviet Union either. However, the U.S. military proved superior. The Taliban were driven from Kabul, the capital, a little more than a month after the start of the bombing, but they were not completely destroyed.

During this time, the Koizumi cabinet saw the Anti-terrorism Special Measures Law passed in the Diet and began refueling and other rear area support by the Maritime Self-Defense Forces for the militaries of the U.S. and other coalition partners. Although it was still rear area support, the fact that the SDF had been sent a long distance from Japan's shores to assist in a war was simply revolutionary under the postwar constitution.

One other noteworthy thing was the role Japan actively played in contributing to Afghanistan's rebuilding. In January 2002, Ogata Sadako co-chaired the Afghanistan Reconstruction Conference in Tokyo, at which 4.5 billion dollars was raised. In contrast to the strong criticism in Washington that Japan did not shed blood alongside the United States at the time of the Gulf War, at the time of the Afghanistan War, praise was heard in both countries for the creation of the mutually supportive relationship that had formed—the United States primarily military and Japan working at economic reconstruction. This is probably an example of the way the Japan–U.S. alliance should operate, the combination of civilian- and military sides working together.

The Iraq War

International terrorist groups lost at least one place to operate from when the Taliban were removed from power in Afghanistan. Seeing the United States military in action, no country was willing to harbor terrorists. This sort of international containment approach was the most convincing for the United States to use and perhaps the best in the initial stages of the war on terrorism. However, Bush was not content with this direct and immediate approach alone. In January 2002, he described Iraq, Iran, and North Korea as belonging to an "Axis of Evil," and in March that year proclaimed that the war on terrorism had "entered the second stage," suggesting a global-scale campaign against terrorism. He also announced what has become known as the Bush Doctrine, the right of the U.S. to use preemptive strikes against rogue states attempting to possess weapons of mass destruction and terrorist groups for which deterrence had no effect.

When Prime Minister Koizumi met President Bush again in September 2002 at the time of the UN General Assembly, he urged him to seek international support when dealing militarily with Iraq. Within the administration, Secretary of State Colin L. Powell had urged the same thing to the President the month before. In November, the Security Council unanimously passed Resolution 1441 demanding that Iraq fully cooperate with weapons inspectors. Iraq initially agreed. However, in February 2003 the United States, which was dissatisfied with Iraq's degree of compliance, called for a new resolution to be passed to permit the use of force in making Iraq comply. In response, France, Germany, and Russia, who wanted to see inspections continue, opposed the U.S. motion and an agreement at the U.N. on the use of force against Iraq became impossible to reach.

The Bush administration, along with Britain and Spain in a coalition of the willing, agreed to go to war even without a UN resolution, and hostilities began on March 20. Amid the demonstrations against the war worldwide, Prime Minister Koizumi immediately and quite clearly announced his support for the war.

The public reason for the start of the war was that from the time of the Gulf War, Iraq had possessed weapons of mass destruction which went against the will of the international community as seen in numerous resolutions and agreements with Iraq. On the eve of the war, another reason was added—drive Saddam Hussein from power and build democracy in Iraq. Iraq's possible willingness to provide terrorist organizations with weapons of mass destruction was also mentioned as a reason to go to war. Others said the U.S. was doing it to gain control of Iraq's oil fields, as well as to protect Israel. Likewise, other reasons given were the bringing of democracy and order to the troubled Middle East. However, with the exception of bringing an end to Saddam's violent rule, the other reasons lacked real proof. The influence of neo-con thinking, which believed that the U.S. should use military force if necessary to promote democracy abroad, on the launching of the

Iraq War was later written about in detail by Bob Woodward (*Plan of Attack*) and Jim Mann (*Rise of the Vulcans*).

America's superior military might was proven during the Iraq War. Not only was it seen in the destructive ability of its weaponry, but also in the accuracy—which only the United States has attained—of its precision-guided missiles. Most targets could be hit just about any time and anywhere. The Iraqi military did not have a chance. The American military arrived in Iraq's capital of Baghdad in just three weeks, and on April 9, among cheering crowds, the statue of Saddam was pulled down. President Bush declared victory on May 1, aboard an aircraft carrier in front of a banner saying "Mission Accomplished."

However, the United States was unable to bring a new order to Iraq as quickly as it had won the war. The United States had not had time to fully develop an occupation policy for Iraq. While it often referred to the occupation of Japan as a successful model, Japan, which had experienced the People's Rights Movement in the 1880s and the period of Taisho Democracy in the 1910s and 1920s, and Iraq were not the same. Moreover, as discussed in detail in Chapter 1, the United States had made exhaustive plans for the occupation of Japan after World War II; for postwar Iraq, it had not. Nor did the U.S. government have a clear idea of who it wanted to involve in the rebuilding of Iraq, and who was to be excluded. With civil order and vital infrastructure not restored after more than a month, U.S. forces began to become the targets of terrorist attacks. These attacks increased over time and were said to be done as a struggle against occupation, with the U.S. and its coalition partners being viewed as foreign occupiers. In addition, members of international terrorist groups made their way into Iraq and the number of suicide bombers increased. From August, when the UN office in Baghdad was attacked, to November, all of Iraq became the site of a guerilla war. In December, Saddam Hussein was captured by U.S. forces, but the terrorist attacks did not stop.

In the middle of this, the Koizumi cabinet passed the Iraq Reconstruction Special Measures Law (*Iraku Fukko Shien Tokubetsu Sochiho*) in July. This permitted the SDF to participate in humanitarian reconstruction efforts in "non-combat zones" after a certain level of peace had been restored. However, shortly after the bill was passed, the terrorist attacks on the UN building and other soft targets increased. After the LDP-led ruling coalition won a stable majority in the Lower House election in October, Koizumi had planned to decide to dispatch the SDF based on the above special measures law in November. However, it was a precarious time to do so. U.S. forces were losing 100 personnel a month in the attacks, and 30 Italian troops were killed in another terrorist attack. In addition, two Japanese diplomats were killed in an attack on their car in late November.

Nevertheless, Koizumi announced on December 9 the dispatch of the SDF to Iraq. Koizumi explained to the nation that it was necessary to eliminate terrorism even if there were casualties involved. His leadership brought about a revolution in thinking to the Japanese postwar generation who had been brought up to believe that "one human life is worth more than the planet," and used that logic as a reason not to do anything.

The biggest reason for Koizumi's decision to dispatch troops was probably based on his desire to maintain and strengthen the good relationship he had developed with the United States. It was also a decision made out of larger considerations, before Japan (and South Korea) became a hostage to North Korea's game of brinkmanship.

However, this decision also meant that it treated the situation in Iraq as a dependent variable of the Japan–U.S. relationship. It was far from clear that the situation in Iraq would turn out alright in the end. As the situation worsened in November 2003, the Bush administration announced it would return sovereignty to Iraq the following year in June.

National elections were held in conflict-ridden Iraq in January 2005. Although many in the Sunni faction boycotted the elections, 60 percent of the electorate voted, including the Kurds and Shia faction. While there was strong opposition to U.S. military intervention, it would be difficult to deny the cleansing function that democracy and elections provided. Moreover, other areas, such as Lebanon, finally appeared to be headed toward stability, Libya gave up its nuclear weapon program, and elections were also held in Saudi Arabia, Egypt, and Palestine. In short, there were signs of democracy coming, albeit in a zigzag fashion, to the Middle East. (While the United States was involved in its protracted war in Vietnam, the countries in the area had come together and formed ASEAN to promote regional development. Perhaps the same sort of thing could develop in the Middle East.)

The SDF dispatched to Iraq conducted their humanitarian operations in the most peaceful part of Iraq, the Shia-controlled southern part in the community of Samawah. Avoiding danger and protected by Dutch and Australian troops, the forces were able to provide water, repair schools, and lend support to hospitals, building up a close relationship with the local population. While there were strong desires for more economic cooperation and business activity among the population, this frustration did not turn into feelings of hostility toward the SDF. The SDF were not there to keep order by pointing their weapons at civilians but instead were given the mission of restoring infrastructure, supporting the needs of the civilians, sponsoring festivals with them, and otherwise providing care to the people of the region, an unusual mission as compared to those of other militaries. The same was true for the humanitarian operations in East Timor. In the same way that the SDF provided relief to victims of the 1995 Hanshin-Awaji Great Earthquake, they are now doing so for post-conflict areas around the world.

Focused on the war on terrorism, the Bush administration began to realize that terrorists breed in the misery of failed states, and it began to reevaluate the importance of ODA and dramatically increase spending for it. It can be said that the United States and the countries of Europe have begun to realize that the rebuilding of economies provides the foundation for stability and peace, something Japan has argued for many years. Ironically, this understanding came around the time that a movement had already started in Japan to limit ODA spending due to Japan's fiscal difficulties. (The decision to reduce Japan's ODA was made in 1997. In 1998, it was increased temporarily to deal with the Asian financial crisis but afterwards continued to be reduced to the extent that by 2004, it had been reduced 25 percent from what it was at its peak. This represents 0.2 percent of Japan's GDP. However, within the OECD and the UN, calls are being heard for the developed countries to devote 0.7 percent of their GDP to ODA.)

As a high-level panel discussed recommendations for reforming the United Nations, Prime Minister Koizumi announced in September 2005 at the UN General Assembly Japan's desire to become a permanent member of the Security Council. Germany, India, and Brazil expressed similar desires and with Japan, the G4, as the group of four countries came to be known, lobbied the international community for support, but the United States and other countries opposed the expansion of the Security Council. China strongly opposed Japan's joining of the Security Council as a Permanent Member due to the history problem, symbolized by Prime Minister Koizumi's visits to the Yasukuni Shrine. A quick resolution to the Security Council problem appeared unlikely.

Japan's Asia diplomacy

In the above ways, in the wake of the international crisis of the 9/11 attacks Prime Minister Koizumi displayed leadership in strengthening the cooperative relationship with the United States and expanding Japan's role in international security affairs. Koizumi's diplomacy was characterized by its placing extraordinarily high attention on Japan–U.S. relations. No other country matched the importance of the United States in his eyes. Moreover, his diplomacy was different from the diplomatic styles of some of Koizumi's predecessors, who placed importance on the Japan–U.S. relationship but were also able to link it to their Asian diplomacy, such as Kishi Nobusuke (Southeast Asia and United States), Sato Eisaku (Vietnam and its neighbors during the Vietnam War and United States), and Nakasone Yasuhiro (South Korea, China, and United States).

At the time of the LDP presidential elections in April 2001, candidate Koizumi stated he would visit the Yasukuni Shrine on August 15 if he became prime minister. In fact, while he avoided going on August 15 (with the exception of his last year as prime minister, 2006), he visited the Yasukuni Shrine every year, explaining that he did so as a prayer for peace and not as an expression of his approval for Japan's war of aggression.

As mentioned above, Chinese leader Jiang Zemin's visit to Japan led to the worsening of Japanese public opinion toward China. Jiang's speeches, critical of Japan's past, invited their own reactions in Japan and an anti-China faction developed within Japan that opposed China's interference in Japanese domestic affairs. The argument was that giving in to China by taking a low profile would only emben it, visiting Yasukuni Shrine was a domestic issue, and China's criticism was not welcome. If the Japanese government just ignored China and continued unperturbed with the visits, China would eventually give up its opposition. These and other strong opinions were heard at the time in favor of visiting Yasukuni.

Rather than making China listen to Japan on this issue, the repeated visits by the prime minister to Yasukuni had the opposite effect, driving China away from Japan. Viewing the prime minister's visits to Yasukuni, where "A Class" war criminals convicted in the Tokyo Tribunals are interred, as official sanction for the war of aggression, China avoided summit meetings in Beijing and Tokyo and a constructive relationship between China and Japan failed to develop. In 2005, massive anti-Japanese rallies broke out in different places around China. This trend even spread to South Korea, where it had looked like reconciliation with Japan had finally occurred, and ended up harming Japan–South Korean relations.

Although Prime Minister Koizumi was seen as indifferent to Asia, he surprised everyone by traveling to North Korea, with which Japan does not have diplomatic relations, and met with Chairman Kim Jong Il, issuing the Pyongyang Declaration. Koizumi is unlike the more cautious Japanese politicians of the past. He was a new type of politician, willing to take risks on his own. The region still awaits North Korea joining the international community, which would help to stabilize the region. Japan's attempt at doing so is worthy of attention. However, for two reasons, Japan–North Korean negotiations were unsuccessful. The first has to do with the doubts surrounding the Japanese who were kidnapped by North Korea. For the longest time, North Korea denied the existence of the abduction problem, and when it finally admitted it and was presented the list, North Korean officials said that eight were already dead (five were later permitted to return to Japan). Japanese public opinion was incensed, and doubted the veracity of North Korea's statements. The second reason is the fact that North Korea's attempts at secretly developing nuclear weapons have become known. In May 2004, the prime minister revisited North Korea to request that the families of the abductees, who had already returned to Japan, be permitted to join their families in Japan. However, more questions emerged over the remains of those who had reportedly died in North Korea, and bilateral relations cooled again.

It was China that next took the lead in dealing with North Korea. China did not approve of the Bush administration's launching of the war in Iraq, and was joined by France, Germany, and Russia, among others. Afterwards, China accepted a U.S. request to bring North Korea to the table for trilateral talks (U.S.–China–N.K.) in April 2003, and then six-party talks (U.S., N.K., China, South Korea, Japan, and Russia) in August that year. Discussions have been held since then on an irregular basis on North Korea's abandoning its nuclear weapons program and directions for regional security. In August 2005, a vague agreement was signed between the United States and North

Korea on support for the building of a light water reactor in exchange for North Korea giving up its nuclear weapons program.

It is worthwhile noting that for the first time since the Opium Wars of the nineteenth century, or perhaps the Sino-Japanese War, the international relations of East Asia had returned to being China-centric. China's economic success of the past twenty-five years, beginning with Deng Xiaoping's economic reforms to the point where China is now being called the "factory of the world," has provided the foundation on which it can now play a new international role. As seen from its history, including the teachings of Sun Tzu, China originally was a country blessed with great political and diplomatic skills. That China is nearly ready to display its diplomatic style is apparent not only in its leadership in the case of North Korea but also in its attitude towards ASEAN. Particularly since the start of the Hu Jintao administration in 2003, China has sought to improve relations with neighboring countries and increase its visibility. Through the Hashimoto and Obuchi years, it was Japan that had played the role of being a bridge for cooperative relations in East Asia, but in the twenty-first century, it appears that it will be China that plays that role.

Historically, China was the hegemonic power in the region. There was no challenger to the China-led order. This sort of order is unlikely for the region in the future. Indeed, it is unclear what sort of order is emerging. On the one hand, East Asia is a part of the international relations of the world. The United States remains the sole superpower. In Asia, Japan is an important maritime nation and will likely continue to be strong, and India, next to China, is on the rise too. The middle powers and smaller states will likely not easily follow a hegemon and may seek to hedge against this more. The coming era should be one where freedom and pluralism are permitted.

There are some who warn that China will crash economically after the 2008 Olympics.[13] It is the Taiwan Strait problem that usually becomes the focus when talking about a Sino-U.S. clash. Taiwan's desire to "declare independence" and China's threat to "use force" to prevent this from happening have both increased in recent years. China expressed its rather strong feelings on the issue of Taiwanese independence when it launched missiles during a military exercise in March 1996, but toward Taiwan and the international community, China's message had the opposite effect. Since then, rather than apply direct pressure on Taiwan, China has emphasized diplomatic measures by asking the United States and Japan to restrict Taiwan's movements toward independence. The success of the appeals of the U.S. and Japanese governments to the Chen Shuibian administration to exercise restraint is one example. At the Japan–U.S. Security Consultative Committee (the so-called 2+2) meeting in February 2005, both governments called for a "peaceful resolution to the Taiwan Problem" and declared that the area was of interest to the Japan–U.S. Security Treaty. China opposed this declaration, calling it "interference in domestic affairs," and adopted an anti-secession law. It is probably necessary to recognize that there is no solution to the Taiwan problem, which began at the time of the Sino-U.S. agreement on Taiwan that there is "only one China" and that a "peaceful resolution" must be sought, other than maintenance of the status quo.

In East Asia, movements toward the building of a regional community are gradually forming. In this region, ASEAN, created during the Vietnam War by the countries near Vietnam, was first and has assisted the formation of other wider regional groupings, such as APEC, ARF, and the ASEAN+3 dialogue. Parallel to this have been movements, albeit to different degrees, toward the creation of Free Trade Areas. The experiences of the 1997 Asia financial crisis reminded states in the region of the reality of interdependence and the necessity of regional cooperation. The East Asia Vision Group, an advisory committee of the ASEAN+3 summit meeting, recommended in 2001 the establishment of an East Asia Summit to be held every other year. The first one was held in December 2005. Rather than trying to emulate the integration approach of the EU, this region is seeking to develop partial cooperation in functional areas and build on these successes.

The challenges facing Japanese diplomacy after the Cold War

The worldwide earthquake that was the end of the Cold War was followed by domestic earthquake in Japan when the "1955 System" came crashing down. The international and domestic orders on which postwar Japan was based for a long time both suddenly became fluid. Around the world, conflicts and wars became more common, and Japan was faced with numerous domestic and regional crises. Moreover, the bubble economy, of which Japan had been so proud in the 1980s, burst causing Japan to enter a long recession later known as the "Lost Decade." The favorable domestic and international environments that had blessed Japan for so long were lost as a result of the end of the Cold War and the basis of Japan's stability and prosperity was shaken.

Japanese tend to be a modest people even when things are going well, but they become downright dark and pessimistic when things do not go well. Quite common today is the discussion that Japan's demise is unavoidable due to the declining population and aging society. Yet, many countries in Europe which have less than half the population of Japan nevertheless raise their heads with pride, and as such it is strange to see the degree of pessimism in Japan due to a decline in its population of 130 million people.

However, there were many advances that also took place due to a sense of crisis and concern. Japanese diplomacy after the end of the Cold War was, for example, able in some instances to use the sense of crisis to break through old barriers and move ahead. Below are some examples that are especially noteworthy.

First was the Japan–U.S. alliance, which had been clearly necessary during the Cold War period. Rather than being allowed to die, the alliance was redefined to deal with new challenges and threats, being strengthened and expanded. As a result Japan did not panic during the crises in North

Korea or the Taiwan Strait, and has been able to gradually increase its role internationally without any drifting.

Second, it is important to note that Japan has actively participated in multilateral frameworks regionally and internationally, even helping to form certain institutions. Regionally, expanding on the 1977 Fukuda Doctrine, which lent support to the ASEAN region as a whole, Japan played a significant role in bringing prosperity to East Asia through a chain of economic cooperation with ASEAN, NIEs, China, and Vietnam. Japan helped the industrialization of East Asia through the three pillars of trade, foreign direct investment, and ODA, and was the country that most actively sought to help countries in the region affected by the 1997 Asia financial crisis.

Moreover, Japan enthusiastically supported the ARF, led by ASEAN. With Prime Minister Ohira's proposal as the basis, Japan, upon the end of the Cold War, raised the idea of the creation of a wider Asia-Pacific regional community, later known as APEC, with Australia. This was a wise effort by Japan, vulnerable as it is to the East–West and North–South divide, to shape the post-Cold War framework for the region.

Third, post-Cold War Japan greatly expanded its international role in security matters. Having experienced a defeat of its own during the Gulf War, it succeeded in passing the PKO Cooperation Bill in 1992 and sending the SDF on its first mission with the United Nations to Cambodia. As a result of the success of the Cambodia PKO mission, activities of this kind have come to be supported by the public under the name of *kokusai koken*, or "international contributions."

The 9/11 attacks happened in the first year of the twenty-first century, and the Koizumi cabinet enacted the anti-terrorism bill, sending the Maritime Self-Defense Forces to the Indian Ocean to participate in refueling operations. This action was taken both to support the war on terror in Afghanistan as well as to preserve stability in the Indian Ocean area. While Japan's military contribution is small compared to that of other countries, it is a significant step for a country that had strictly limited the operations of the SDF exclusively to the defense of Japan and has been praised by countries whose militaries are being supplied with fuel and water.

Moreover, when the U.S. led the coalition in attacking Iraq, the Koizumi administration did not hesitate to lend its support, enacting the Iraq Reconstruction Bill and sending both the Ground and Air Self-Defense Forces to Iraq. This was done to support humanitarian operations and the reconstruction of Iraq and provide other rear area support, and did not involve participating in combat operations. However, humanitarian operations of this sort are increasingly important around the world. The Bush administration highly praised Japan's participation, and Japan's efforts led to the strengthening of the Japan–U.S. alliance. This was particularly important as Japan was faced with a growing challenge from North Korea, which Japan sees as its primary threat due to its possession of nuclear weapons, missiles, as well as its having abducted Japanese citizens and sent spy and other suspicious ships into

Japanese waters. Japan strengthened its measures to prevent North Korea from abducting any more Japanese or sending its ships into Japan's territorial waters, but the problem of its nuclear weapons and missiles goes beyond Japan's own defense capabilities. As seen in its cooperation with the U.S. on missile defense, Japan is heavily reliant on the Japan–U.S. alliance.

Fourth, in general terms, Japanese diplomacy has been more proactive than in the past. While Japan still places the highest priority on its relationship with the United States, it has sought to greatly expand its relations with other countries. Particularly during the Hashimoto and Obuchi years, Japan actively pursued relations with many countries. Moreover, Prime Minister Obuchi put forward the concept of "human security" and took the initiative in banning landmines. Moreover, Prime Minister Koizumi strengthened Japan's role in international security, and undertook some personal diplomacy vis-à-vis North Korea, traveling there twice.

While strengthening the relationship with the United States to an all-time high, Prime Minister Koizumi's regular visits to the Yasukuni Shrine led to a worsening of relations with neighboring China and South Korea. The Abe and Fukuda administrations worked hard at repairing these two fractured relationships and were successful. Amid the reciprocal visits between Prime Minister Fukuda and Chinese President Hu Jintao, China supported Japan assuming a larger role in the United Nations, and expressed its willingness to cooperate in combating global warming, and in cooperating with Japan in the joint development in the East China Sea. Japan–China relations had recovered from the lowpoint of the anti-Japanese demonstrations in China in the spring of 2005.

This positive appraisal of Japan's diplomacy does not mean that there were no problems during the post-Cold War years. The biggest challenge was the decrease in domestic resources for its diplomacy caused by the long recession and the deficit during the 1990s. The budget for ODA, for example, declined by some 40 percent in the decade after 1997, and funds for diplomatic activities and the sponsoring of international conferences were similarly decreased. The Japanese public has turned inward as a result of the economic problems and is less willing to support international activities. At the turn of the century, there were some nationalists who decried Japan's loss of influence and increasingly began to criticize internationalism itself.

The problem is how the country's leadership will deal with this situation. Prime Minister Koizumi chose to revitalize the economy through going ahead with structural reform and privatizing the postal system, winning an historic victory in the September 2005 Lower House elections. Utilizing the two-thirds majority in the Lower House left by Koizumi, the subsequent Abe administration sought to undertake constitutional reform to exercize the right of collective self-defense, but instead ended up being defeated in the July 2007 Upper House elections, losing its majority to the opposition Democratic Party of Japan. The political instability caused by the divided Diet, in which the Lower House was controlled by the ruling coalition and the Upper House was controlled by the opposition parties, would act to limit the government in its diplomacy. Japan is faced with a situation now in which the domestic political foundations will need to be rebuilt following a change in government and a political realignment.

Notes

1 For changing interpretations of the constitutional peace clause in postwar history, see Nakamura Akira, *Sengo Seiji ni Yureta Kenpo Daikyujo* (Postwar Politics and Article 9 of the Constitution) (Tokyo: Chuo Keizaisha, 1996).

2 Teshima Ryuichi, *1991 Nen Nihon no Haiboku* (Japan's Defeat in 1991) (Tokyo: Shinchosha, 1993).

3 Don Oberdorfer, *The Two Koreas: A Contemporary History* (Reading: Addison-Wesley, 1997), particularly chaps. 9 and 10.

4 Yoichi Funabashi, *Asia-Pacific Fusion: Japan's Role in APEC* (Washington, D.C.: Institute for International Economics, 1995).

5 The author's interviews with government officials including Miyazawa Kiichi, Murata Ryohei, Kuriyama Shoichi, Owada Hisashi, Takeuchi Yukio, Nishimura Rokuzen, Fujita Kimio, Hasegawa Kazutoshi, Tanino Sakutaro, and Shinyo Takahiro. For the published transcripts of the Miyazawa interview, see *Kokusai Mondai* (International Affairs) 500 (November 2001). For more on the PKO bill, see Shinyo Takahiro, *Shin Kokurenron* (A New United Nations) (Osaka: Osaka University Press, 1995) and Tanaka, *Anzen Hosho*.

6 The following three diplomats who played important roles wrote memoirs of their experience. See Ikeda Tadashi, *Kanbojia Wahei e no Michi* (The Road to Peace in Cambodia) (Tokyo: Toshi Shuppan, 1996); Kono Masaharu, *Wahei Kosaku* (Peace-making) (Tokyo: Iwanami Shoten, 1999); Imagawa Yukio, *Kanbojia to Nihon* (Cambodia and Japan) (Tokyo: Rengo Shuppan, 2000).

7 These impressions were gained during discussions with officials and observers in China and Taiwan, and based on the author's observations during a trip to Xiamen (Amoy), China's largest city on the Taiwan Strait, and to the Taiwan Institute of Xiamen Univesity.

8 Funabashi Yoichi, *Alliance Adrift* (New York: Council on Foreign Relations, 1999). According to the author's interview with Hashimoto, his study of security matters was made possible by a secret initiative by a high foreign ministry official to hold regular meetings to discuss diplomatic and strategic matters with several LDP leaders, including Hashimoto. See Iokibe Makoto, *et al.* "Nihon Gaiko Intabyuu Series, 3: Hashimoto Ryutaro" (Interview Series on Japanese Diplomacy, vol 3: Hashimoto Ryutaro), parts 1–2; *Kokusai Mondai* (International Affairs) nos. 504–505 (March–April 2002).

9 Hosokawa resigned in April 1994 and the cabinet led by his successor, Hata Tsutomo, lasted a mere two months. The Murayama cabinet was formed in June 1994. For the new security policy process, see the above-mentioned books by Funabashi (*Alliance* Adrift) and Tanaka (*Anzen Hosho*). Also see Hashimoto Kohei, ed., *Nihon no Gaiko Seisaku Kettei Yoin* (Decision-making Factors in Japan's Foreign Policies) (Tokyo: PHP, 1999).

10 For more on this agenda, see Brian Bridges, *EC–Japanese Relations: In Search of a Partnership* (London: Royal Institute of International Affairs, 1992).

11 Author's interview with Hashimoto, *Kokusai Mondai*, nos. 504–5 (March and April 2002).

12 The proposal had been prepared by Sakakibara Eisuke, and his plan to establish an AMF did not include the United States, which made America suspicious of

Japan's intentions. Sakakibara wrote about this reaction related through an overseas midnight phone call that he received from an American counterpart who recognized Sakakibara had been planning to exclude the United States from the Asian Monetary Fund. Sakakibara Eisuke, *Nihon to Sekai ga Furueta Hi* (The Day Japan and the World Trembled) (Tokyo: Chuo Koronshinsha, 2000).

13 (This was written before the Beijing Olympics took place, in August 2008, and before the worldwide economic recession.) A more fundamental problem is how China, which continues as a communist state, will be able to adjust to the increasing demands for freedom and democracy. Another problem is how China, which is becoming a superpower in its own right, will interact with the United States. Not only neo-cons, but realists within the Pentagon argue that strategically, over the long term, in order for the United States to maintain its preeminence in world affairs, it cannot afford to permit the rise of a second major power. If China clashes head-on with U.S. thinking, both China's prosperity and the peace of the Asia-Pacific region would be lost.

Conclusion

What was postwar Japanese diplomacy?

Iokibe Makoto

What, in the end, was the essence of Japanese diplomacy in the postwar era? This chapter attempts to provide, in a systematic matter, an overview of the different aspects of Japanese diplomacy during the past six decades. In particular, after first looking at the three courses that faced Japan in the postwar—the social democratic approach, economics-first approach, and traditional nation-state approach—it then examines sixty years of Japanese diplomacy *in toto* and the role domestic politics played.

History: the rise and fall of modern Japan

The first non-Western state to successfully modernize

Japan is an island country in the seas off the Asian continent. It is situated on the outskirts of the Chinese cultural sphere, one of the most advanced civilizations from long ago. Needless to say, Japan has been much influenced by Chinese civilization. It is worth noting that Japan, at the same time, did not come under the control of past Chinese emperors and was able to maintain its sovereignty. This independence was due to the double functions that the oceans surrounding Japan possess. Namely, on the one hand, the oceans serve as a natural moat that protected Japan from foreign powers, particularly in the centuries prior to the advance of science and technology. Second, the oceans serve as a means of intercourse which allowed Japan to learn from foreign civilizations. Interacting with foreign cultures and learning from them while maintaining its independence would form a classic pattern in Japan's foreign relations. The high level of Japanese society's development and culture allowed Japan to be able to interact selectivity with China in this way.

Following the industrial revolution, Western civilization became the first world civilization in human history. The middle of the nineteenth century, when this unrivaled Western civilization began to extend its influence into East Asia, was also the time when the Chin Dynasty, which had enjoyed centuries of prosperity, was entering its period of decline. The response of the giant, China, to the challenge that the West represented was slow, but Japan, the small island nation, was forced to maneuver quickly, having had its era of seclusion ruptured by the coming of the Black Ships in 1853. Japan's response to Western civilization was similar to its response toward China over the years: namely, maintaining its independence while learning from the other stronger power. Japanese politics became divided between the "expel the barbarian" factions and the "open the country" advocates, with the former calling for the maintainance of autonomy vis-à-vis the West and the latter arguing for the need to learn from abroad. As discussed in the Introduction, in what Toynbee later described as Herodism, Meiji Japan learned the secrets of Western civilization while being able to protect itself from Western pressure. In this way, Japan was able to become the first non-Western country to successfully modernize. This was prewar Japan's historic role.

The demise of a military empire

In the wake of this success came an equally large fall. From the time of World War I, when the world was leaving the Age of Imperialism, anti-colonial nationalism was strengthening in Asia. From the perspective of Imperial Japan, which had gained territorial and other vested interests following its victories in the Sino-Japanese and Russo-Japanese wars, the endangerment of Japan's "legitimate" interests gained by treaties as seen in the anti-Japanese demonstrations and violence by Chinese were unlawful and repugnant acts. From the perspective of Japan's military elite, which was aware of the strength of the Western "haves" and sought to compete on equal footing with them, Japan was still a small, "have not" country. To do so, they felt it was necessary to continue to expand. From the time of the end of the Shogunate and the beginning of Meiji, Japan also suffered from the unequal treaties, but as it modernized, it continued to negotiate with the other Powers and resolved the issue peacefully. China should do so as well, Japanese believers in the importance of treaties argued. However, from the perspective of the Chinese, Japan's "legitimate interests" were not legitimate at all having been stolen against the will of the people of China. Chinese nationalism, which had been primarily directed against England, began to focus on Japan from 1928 at the time of the second dispatch of Japanese forces to Shandong.

Japan eventually was unable to end the war with China in the 1930s and continued to expand the fighting front. Needing more resources, it moved south into Indochina and Southeast Asia, which would eventually lead to war with the United States and Britain. At this time, Japan spoke of a "Greater Prosperity Sphere" and "All the World Becoming One State (under Japan's Guidance)," trying to change the international environment in its favor as the only military empire in Asia. Imperial Japan, after unlimited use of this military might, finally met defeat and destruction in 1945.

Occupation policy

The United States, which played the central role in the postwar disposition of Japan, had two policies toward Japan. The first one was that of President

Roosevelt, who sought complete victory over Japan along the lines of the January 1943 statement on "Unconditional Surrender" and place Japan under a direct military occupation in order to reform Japan at will. The second policy was that of Japan experts who, basing their policies on principles of equality as seen in the "Without Regard to Victor and Vanquished" phrase found in the Atlantic Charter, sought the eventual return of Japan to the international community of nations by using the Emperor and the civilian government in the ending of the war, the occupation, and democratic reforms. The former was the mainstream policy, but toward the end of the war after Roosevelt's death, the Potsdam Declaration was announced based on the recommendations of Under Secretary of State Grew and Secretary of War Stimson who represented the latter group. The Japanese government was barely able to take advantage of this less stringent set of demands following the dropping of the atomic bombs and the Soviet entry into the war when the emperor called for the ending of the war.

As a result, the occupation of Japan was an indirect one, by which MacArthur, as Supreme Commander for the Allied Powers, worked through the emperor and the Japanese government. The Potsdam Declaration did not call for the unconditional surrender of the Japanese state, only its "military forces." It was not a victors' peace, like that against Germany in World War I, in which the victors were free to decide its fate. Instead, Japan's surrender was based on the conditions expressed in the Potsdam Declaration.

The three political and diplomatic courses for postwar Japan

Two things can probably be said about postwar Japan's diplomatic posture based on the above history. First, Japan's postwar foreign policy followed the same approach that it had centuries ago towards Chinese civilization and in the previous century toward the Western Powers. In other words, by learning about the achievements in industry, technology, academics, and democratic institutions of the United States, which represented foreign civilization, Japan was able to pursue long-term independence in the postwar. The second thing that could be said about the postwar is that Japan was unhappy with its path to war in the 1930s and chose to pursue a completely different course. Japan employed its reaction to the international environment and focus on the military and the great destruction it brought upon itself as a lesson for the future. The postwar period leaned toward pacifism, anti-nationalism, and a passive form of international cooperation.

Amidst the rapid rebuilding of Japan's major cities, which were destroyed by the air raids, several visions for Japan's future and its political outlook were proposed. The main ones that ending up leading postwar were the following three: (1) social democracy; (2) economics-first; and (3) traditional nation-state. Postwar diplomacy and the respective courses and political climate at the time are described next.

(1) Social Democracy

The various forces of Socialism, which came of age in the wake of Liberalism from the Taisho to Showa eras and were repressed during the war, reemerged and expanded in the postwar and came to be known as the progressives/ reformists. They sought as national objectives for Japan "peace" and "democracy." They were not of one kind, and instead were made up of a variety of groups, such as the Communist Party, which called for revolution, the left wing of the Socialist Party, which recognized Marxism, and the moderate reformers, the right wing of the Socialist Party, which embraced socialism. In the April 1947 general elections, the Socialist Party did well and became the largest party. Katayama Tetsu, Nishio Suehiro, and others on the right wing of the Socialist Party became the center of a three-party coalition that including the reformists and conservatives. The Government Section of GHQ actively supported this coalition.

As the occupation policies of the United States began to turn in a more conservative direction with the start of the Cold War, the reformists strengthened their anti-American, anti-Establishment stance. They opposed the abandoning of Article 9 of the postwar constitution and the reliance on the United States, and expressed their opposition not only in the Diet but out in the streets as well. At the forefront of these efforts was the Socialist Party which called for "unarmed neutrality" in the area of diplomacy and security policies, opposing both the Japan–U.S. Security Treaty and the Self-Defense Forces. Seeing the future of "socialism" as just around the corner after "peace" and "democracy," this group opposed the conservatives and exerted a large influence in Japanese politics until around 1960.

(2) Economics-first

This course, led by Yoshida Shigeru, was critical of the focus on the military as seen in the prewar and instead sought to rebuild postwar Japan as an economic and trading state through industrial development and trade. With this goal in mind, Yoshida was cool toward early efforts to rearm Japan and instead sought to have the United States provide its security during the Cold War through the signing of the Japan–U.S. Security Treaty. Yoshida's group remade Japan into a pro-American state belonging to the Western camp in international politics, and domestically, fostered a liberal democracy. They sought a postwar Japan that would become an economic state that placed priority on economic recovery and prosperity. The realization of "security" and "prosperity" became the most important national goals for this group.

(3) Traditional nation-state

The traditional nation-state approach was lead by influential prewar politi- cians Hatoyama Ichiro and Kishi Nobusuke, among others. They believed it was a matter of course that postwar Japan, as a sovereign country, should have the military strength to deal with outside threats and called for "constitutional revision and rearmament." It can be said that the phrase "normal country," heard in recent years, actually had its start in the "traditional nation-state" position in the early postwar period. The politicians who traditionally adhered to this view were those who sought "autonomy" and "national power." After Yoshida's resignation in 1954, they joined with the second group in a conservative merger and came to control the government in the latter half of the 1950s. The result of this merger was the Liberal Democratic Party. Around the same time, the Right and Left wings of the Socialist Party also rejoined to make the Socialist Party the largest opposition party. This was known as the "1955 System," and it continued until 1993.

Japanese diplomacy in the postwar would develop through the intersection of the above three political streams.

Politics in the early occupation period

Japan lost its diplomatic rights with the start of the occupation. Only interaction with GHQ was permitted. The occupation, conducted over a long period in a controlled manner, would see at the end of it the fundamental reform of Japanese society based on the basic policies of "demilitarization" and "democratization." The complete revision of the Meiji Constitution and the numerous occupation reforms, all of which preceded the peace treaty, would reflect Japan's postwar reality and were done to create the necessary institutions. Because of this, the daily interaction with GHQ was an important act of "diplomacy."

The Japanese government in the early occupation period was led by prewar pro-British and pro-American diplomats Shidehara and Yoshida, but the main actor was not the Japanese government but GHQ itself. No matter who was in charge of the government, if the prime minister did not faithfully carry out the early occupation policies, he would not be allowed to continue much longer in office. Constitutional revision and many other occupation reforms were carried out by the two conservative administrations of Shidehara and Yoshida. These two prime ministers placed importance on negotiations at the top level with Supreme Commander MacArthur. While cooperating on democratization reforms, they were able to get from MacArthur his support in food supplies and aid, as well as in protecting the domestic peace.

The centrist coalition governments of Katayama of the Socialist Party, and Ashida of the Democratic Party, strongly believed in the need to pursue the democratization of postwar Japan and based their administrations on the support and advice from the "New Dealer" Kades, the deputy head of the Government Section of GHQ. This was the time when both GHQ and the Japanese government saw eye-to-eye on the need to pursue a reformist political agenda, namely the social democratic approach described above. If the forces of social democracy had truly demonstrated leadership and successfully held the reigns of government, it is likely that they would have become one of the two important axes of postwar Japanese politics, even if they did not actually become its mainstream.

In fact, however, the coalition government led by the Socialist Party lost its ability to govern and suffered serious ideological divisions within the party. Their problems necessitated intervention by the Government Section and they increasingly became unable to make any meaningful decisions.

The Yoshida Line becomes the mainstream amid Left–Right divisions in the 1950s

Both Kades and the progressive-conservative coalition lost their influence toward the end of 1948, and the Ashida government came to an end in October. As the Cold War deepened, it became possible for those calling for the economic reconstruction of Japan, namely the Yoshida Line, to come to the forefront. Yoshida had many young, elite bureaucrats with political ambitions run in the January 1949 elections where they won. Eventually, under Yoshida's tutelage, this group became the mainstream of postwar politics.

During the discussions on the peace treaty in January–February 1951, Yoshida resisted Dulles' call for Japan to undertake rapid rearmament and was able to take his time in slowly undertaking rearmament in a way consistent with civilian control and without drawing funds away unnecessarily from economic recovery. Dulles proposed a peace treaty that was non-punitive in nature which greatly put the Japanese at ease. As the occupation continued, U.S. views of Japan changed from that of a former enemy to one that was a new a partner in the Cold War. Because of this emerging realization, the Peace Treaty with Japan was a generous one but when only 49 countries signed it the result was a "majority peace" and not a "full peace," as the Soviet Union and some of its allies chose not to sign.

Prime Minister Yoshida signed the peace treaty and the Japan–U.S. Security Treaty, and aligned Japan as a strongly pro-American economic state that pursued only light rearmament as a member of the West. Relating this approach to the prewar, it was the *fukoku*, or "rich country" doctrine, only minus the "strong military" (*kyohei*). There was a widely held desire among the Japanese people in the postwar to recapture what they had lost as a result of the war, "security" and "prosperity." Yoshida's response to this desire was to maximize and deepen the relationship with the United States.

Yoshida made this decision for the following reasons. First, the United States was the only other superpower that could provide "security" to Japan, threatened as it was from the other superpower, the Soviet Union, during the Cold War. Moreover, at the time, the United States was the only superpower with any economic wherewithal, possessing as it did 45 percent of the world's GNP. As the founder of the IMF, GATT, World Bank, and other international economic organizations, it was the manager of the international trading system. Yoshida pursued Japan's "security" and "prosperity" by placing the relationship with the United States at the center of Japan's diplomatic posture and by "deepening Japan–U.S. relations."

This approach came to be called the "conservative mainstream." It pursued diplomacy with the Japan–U.S. relationship at its core, liberal democratic politics, and an economics-first approach that placed trade and industry above rearmament.

The Yoshida Doctrine without Yoshida

The Yoshida administration ended in late 1954. Succeeding Yoshida was Hatoyoma Ichiro, who called for "constitutional revision and rearmament." The U.S. and Japanese governments did not come to an agreement on rearmament at this point because despite the so-called "Hatoyama boom," there was little actual public support for "constitutional revision and rearmament." The Lucky Dragon incident in March 1954 had shifted public opinion toward pacifism and anti-nuclearism. In addition, through the wise counsel of Ambassador to Japan John Allison, rather than putting pressure on Japan to rearm, the United States adopted a policy of encouraging the stability of the domestic economy and society in Japan.

As a result, although the United States put pressure on Japan to rearm between 1950 and 1953 when the Korean War was in progress, Prime Minister Yoshida successful deflected those demands. Prior to the outbreak of the Korean War, and once again after 1954, the U.S. government placed priority on Japan's economic and political stability, and acquiesced in Japan's limited rearmament. While Hatoyama and Kishi both called for constitutional revision, not only did public opinion not support these calls, but the U.S. government was not really pushing it either. The mismatch between the U.S. and Japanese governments prevented full-blown rearmament and brought about the continuation of the "Yoshida Doctrine without Yoshida" in which Japan was rebuilt as an economic state.

The deepening of the Japan–U.S. relationship and expansion of Japan's diplomatic horizons

Diplomatic expansion beyond the United States

No matter how important relations with the United States were to Japan, it was of course not the only country with which Japan had to interact. It was an unnatural state of affairs when Japan did not have relations with some countries, including its large neighbors, China and the Soviet Union. The "expansion of Japan's diplomatic horizons," in which relations with those countries would be normalized and Japan could return to becoming a country acting on a truly global level, was another important diplomatic agenda. It became popular domestically, having the air of an independent approach vis-à-vis the United States, relations with which loomed exceedingly large for Japan.

Prime Minister Hatoyama was able to realize the restoration of relations with the Soviet Union, a task left over from Yoshida. While it was done by shelving the issue of the return of the Northern Territories, it made possible the restoration of relations with the other communist bloc countries in Eastern Europe as well as Japan's accession to the United Nations. Japan's diplomatic horizons expanded greatly.

The "deepening of Japan–U.S. relations" and the "expansion of Japan's diplomatic horizons" are not necessarily at odds with one another. Both were necessary for Japanese diplomacy after independence, and they were mutually reinforcing, as was demonstrated by Kishi's diplomacy.

Although expanding relations with Communist China was logically next on the agenda, the Kishi administration expanded relations not with the PRC, with which the U.S. opposed dealing, but with the countries of Southeast Asia, showing a strong willingness to resolve the problem of reparations with Indonesia and other countries. The Eisenhower administration positively evaluated Kishi's stance, and responded in kind by agreeing to make the Japan–U.S. Security Treaty more equal. The United States welcomed Japan's efforts to contribute to the development and stability of non-Communist Asia. For Japan, resolving the reparations problem and expanding its diplomatic horizons into Southeast Asia meant that the economic horizons of Japan, the economic state, would also expand because much of the reparations would be paid by providing Japanese products to those countries.

During the Kishi administration, the Foreign Ministry announced the "Three Principles of Japanese Foreign Policy." The first of the three principles, "cooperation with the Free World," was a roundabout way of emphasizing a pro-U.S. approach, which was generally unpopular domestically. "A member of Asia" was the declaration of a diplomatic program of expanding relations with the region in an attempt to overcome the loss of trust due to Japan's actions in World War II. The "UN-centric" approach was a statement of Japan's desire to pursue its foreign policy in accordance with universal values and legitimacy. These principles should be given credit for the attempt to introduce a more comprehensive approach to Japanese diplomacy amid the disproportionate importance of the relationship with the United States.

Gaining the support of the U.S. government, Kishi revised the security treaty without undertaking constitutional revision. The revision of the security treaty, done basically along the lines of Japan's desires, amended the problems of the old treaty and made the relationship a more equal one. Looking back, it is clear that only by revising the treaty was it possible to continue its effectiveness over the long-run, and for this reason it should be favorably evaluated. In addition, during this process, the LDP, which had been formed by cooperation between the economics-first group and the traditional nation-state believers, in fact became one party and a strong conservative ruling one at that. However, at the time, there was much opposition to Prime Minister Kishi's political stance and the opposition reformists fought back hard. In the 1960 security treaty crisis, as the ratification process of the new treaty was called, the leftists and the believers in the traditional nation-state clashed. As a result of both groups being politically damaged, the middle-of-the-road Yoshida approach reemerged, unscathed and indeed relatively strengthened. Ikeda and Sato, both loyal followers of Yoshida, would lead their administrations over the next decade, firmly establishing postwar Japan as an economic state after the uncertainty of the second half of the 1950s.

The formation of the economic state—the Ikeda administration

It was the Ikeda administration, following the 1960 security treaty crisis, that classically illustrated the synergy realized when pursuing the "deepening of the Japan–U.S. relationship" and the "expanding of Japan's diplomatic horizons." Ikeda visited the United States in June 1961. With the help of Japan expert and Ambassador to Japan Reischauer, he deepened the relationship with the United States, which had a fresher image now under a new president, John F. Kennedy. Next, Ikeda visited Western Europe in November 1962 and succeeding in making Japan a full member of GATT, the IMF, and OECD with the assistance of the United States, and spoke of the "Three Pillars of the Free World," Japan, Western Europe, and North America. Ikeda was one of the first people to see the trilateralism that was emerging among the developed countries of the world. He also visited the countries of Southeast Asia in November 1961 and again in September 1963, as he believed Japan had a responsibility to assist in the development of the region, deepening the relationship with them. Moreover, with China, he improved economic relations by separating political problems from economic questions.

In this way, the Ikeda administration expanded diplomatic relations on every front, characterized by an economic approach that emphasized mutual benefits. Domestically, Ikeda called for "income doubling" and led the high-growth period. In order to foster the international environment to pursue that, he expanded Japan's economic horizons. Japan's postwar path as an economic state dedicated to developing global trade was solidified during the Ikeda Years. The Yoshida Doctrine, after having faced the challenges it did in the latter half of the 1950s, reemerged in the 1960s and became the mainstream of postwar Japan.

The return of Okinawa—Japan–U.S. cooperation and the fruits of an economics-first approach

Prime Minister Sato Eisaku, who came to power amid the glow of the 1964 Tokyo Olympics and the shock of the Chinese nuclear test (which did not dim the Olympics), was a follower of Yoshida, but he placed more emphasis on high politics than did Ikeda. Sato sought, for example, the return of Okinawa, a national goal, which took all seven years of his administration to realize. During a visit to the United States in January 1965 he officially requested the return of Okinawa, and after that Sato's diplomacy focused on realizing that goal. Sato also signed the Korea–Japan Treaty of Friendship and supported the Park Chung-hee administration's attempt at rebuilding South Korea. Sato moreover worked at helping Indonesia in its path toward economic development as it began to move away from its anti-colonialism, pro-Communist China position after the September 30 (1965) coup. Relating to this, Sato worked toward establishing the Asia Development Bank in 1966, sponsored a Southeast Development Ministers Conference in Tokyo, and visited the countries of Southeast Asia and the Pacific in September and October 1967.

This economic form of Asian diplomacy was a reflection of the necessity to develop the foundations of the Japanese economy, which was continuing to grow throughout the 1960s, in this region as well. At the same time, Prime Minister Sato cooperated with the United States by supporting the unpopular Vietnam War, expressing interest in the security of the region, and economically aiding the countries around Vietnam. Because of these successive efforts, Sato was able to secure a promise from President Johnson during their meeting in November 1967 to decide on the timing of the return of Okinawa "within a few years,"and in November 1969, to gain from President Nixon the promise of Okinawa's return without nuclear weapons, on par with the mainland, in 1972.

The anti-Vietnam War and counter-culture movements of the latter half of the 1960s in America and Western Europe also reached Japan. The Sato administration won against the anti-American, anti-establishment radicals who caused chaos on the campuses, opposed the extension of the Japan–U.S. security treaty in 1970, and wanted to take back Okinawa, by force if necessary, when he deepened the relationship with the United States and peacefully realized the return of Okinawa. That diplomatic success in turn led to a domestic one—in the general elections at the end of 1969, the LDP won 300 seats (including those who joined the LDP after the election).

This was the moment when the merits of the pro-U.S. policy and economics-first approach of the Yoshida Doctrine bore fruit beyond everyone's expectations. It would probably be correct to view Japan's decision not to become a nuclear power when it announced the "Three Non-Nuclear Principles" as reflecting the overall approval with the Yoshida Doctrine. At the time of the 1960 security treaty crisis, anti-American nationalism was strong, but this nationalism appeared satisfied with Japan's economic advancements and by the return of Okinawa. Japan's GNP at this time even began to surpass that of some West European countries.

The crisis-filled 1970s: a test for Japan's diplomacy

Japan, the fragile blossom? The early 1970s

History likes to build up hopes and expectations, and then deflate them. At the end of the 1960s, the Japanese people, welcoming the predictions of Herman Khan (*The Emerging Japanese Superstate*) and others, only encountered difficulties in the 1970s.

In July 1971, President Nixon suddenly announced he was going to visit China, and in August he introduced the New Economic Policy (the so-called "dollar shock"). These two shocks were an attempt by Nixon and Kissinger to strengthen America's position in international politics and economy, as America had lost its predominance in those fields due to the wounds it received in Vietnam militarily, economically, and psychologically.

For Japan, this meant that it was meeting an international environment in the 1970s different from the one of the 1960s. Until the end of the 1960s, Japan was firmly protected by the United States in the Cold War, which permitted Japan to focus on its economy and trade and to grow economically. The warm affection shown by the United States as Japan's protector ended with the return of Okinawa. At the end of the 1960s, Japan was about to become the third strongest country economically. It had become too big to be protected any longer.

In 1972, the Sato cabinet proposed the establishment of an international exchange fund to promote cultural exchange. Foreign Minister Fukuda noted the perception gap that remained between Japan and the United States in their relations and explained the need for mutual understanding at the local level and grassroots exchanges. He also noted the need for such exchanges with Europe and Southeast Asia. Japan was finally responding to the fact that international relations were changing and the players multiplying.

After Sato had overcome the humiliation of the rapprochement between the United States and China while maintaining a pro-U.S. posture, the Tanaka Kakuei cabinet was able to move to a more autonomous diplomatic posture vis-à-vis the People's Republic of China. In 1972, the Tanaka administration succeeded in normalizing relations with the United States, something done ahead of the United States. With this, Japan was able overcome the feeling of isolation. However, the expression, "when it rains, it pours," certainly applies here. In October 1973, the oil crisis came with the outbreak of the fourth war in the Middle East. Domestically, a panic ensued in Japan. The period of high economic growth, which had lasted seventeen years continuously but was already showing signs of limitations, ended at this point, and the following year, Japan had negative growth.

The problems continued. During a visit to Southeast Asia in 1964, Prime Minister Tanaka met with anti-Japanese demonstrations in Bangkok and Jakarta. These numerous crises in the early 1970s not only weakened Japan–U.S. relations, they shook the foundations of Japan as an economic state and showed Japan as "a member of Asia" lacking any substance.

As Brzezinski wrote in his *Fragile Blossom*, postwar Japan was fundamentally fragile in that it possessed no natural resources and did not have the ability to truly provide for its own security. In times when the international system was stable due to the Japan–U.S. alliance and the free trading system, then all was well and good, but once the international system was thrown into turmoil, Japan was tossed about in the waves. This is probably the fate of trading states dependent on the international environment as Japan was. Moreover, while Japan was located in Asia, it was different from the other countries of Asia, having sought a Western identity and being a democracy with an advanced economy. Could Japan work well with Asia?

Japan faced domestic crises as well in the first half of the 1970s. Building on its economic success, the LDP continued to rule non-stop since its formation in 1955. Ironically, the rapid economic growth led to the birth of a new middle class and the diversification of Japanese society. Of course, this would lead to the growth in the number of political parties, such as the Democratic Socialist Party and the *Komeito*, and would begin to cause the long-term decline of the LDP and Socialist Party. During the 1970s, the LDP would lose seats under Prime Minister Tanaka, thought to be strong in elections, as a result of the public's unhappiness over his financial scandals. At the time of the general elections in 1976, which corresponded with the Miki cabinet, the LDP had already lost its majority in the Lower House. Reformist governors and mayors had by this time taken over the leadership of local governments and it looked like this reversal in fortunes meant that the days of the LDP-led administrations were numbered.

Overcoming the crises of the 1970s

Japan did not sink during the crises of the 1970s, however, and instead rebounded as an even stronger and more competitive economic power.

First, Japan asked the Arab countries to end their embargo on the export of oil to Japan and to lessen their other restrictions. From this point onward, Japan's Middle East policy was to continue a pro-American, pro-Israel posture while building friendly relations with the Arab countries. Faced with the twin problems of high inflation and a serious recession, Finance Minister Fukuda declared that Japan would have its economic woes under control in three years and announced a series of related policies to deal with the problems. The policies were not limited to just the financial and economic sector, but were directed at securing cooperation from labor unions as well as introducing energy conservation, as seen in the turning off of neon signs in Tokyo and throughout the country.

Most significant in the long run was the advancement in technology. Prior to the oil crisis, the Diet in 1972 (called the "Pollution Diet" for the focus of its deliberations at the time) passed strict environmental standards on pollution and other problems that had become serious due to Japan's high economic growth. It was shortly after the passage of these bills that the oil crisis hit, which meant that companies were doubly hit. As a result of their efforts in advancing new technologies, many companies developed fuel-efficient engines and energy sources that were low in pollution. It was during this time that Professor Ezra F. Vogel of Harvard University published his book *Japan as Number One*. As a result of these advancements, Japan's industrial production led the world in the 1980s.

The shocks of the oil crisis would stimulate Japanese society and resulted in Japan becoming an economic giant. This was helped by Japan playing a greater role globally as a member of the G7 summits, which began in 1975.

The rebounding of Japan's economy also led to a conservative swing in domestic politics toward the end of the 1970s. In the double elections held for both the Lower and Upper Houses in 1980 after Prime Minister Ohira's death, the LDP once again became the majority party and would continue as such until after the end of the Cold War.

Regional policy

Japan did not get angry and lash out after the anti-Japanese riots in 1974 in Southeast Asia, but instead, after careful reflection and numerous private and governmental studies, sought a new relationship with Asia. At the government level, Japan's response was seen three years later in the form of the Fukuda Doctrine. In a speech at the ASEAN summit in the Philippines in 1977, Prime Minister Fukuda declared that Japan would not become a military power and spoke of Japan's willingness to contribute to the economic development of all of Southeast Asia and to its social stability.

The need for Japan to give back more of its economic profits, which it had continued to rake in due to its growing competitiveness in exports and trade surpluses, became clear from this time. Over a three-year period beginning the following year, Japan doubled its ODA budget, and then over the next five years, doubled it again. Over the course of twenty years until the 1997 Asia financial crisis, Japan played an enormous role in transforming countries in Asia that had once been developing ones into newly industrialized economies through ODA, direct investment, and trade. In short, Japan's response to the anti-Japanese riots was to use its economic power, which had overcome the oil crisis and become that much stronger, to support the development of East Asia.

Although Japan had policies specific to each of the countries of Asia, it can be said that until the latter half of the 1970s, Japan did not possess a coherent regional policy. The Fukuda Doctrine was the first time for Japan to have a policy Southeast Asia, encompassing ASEAN and Indochina. In 1978, the Fukuda government signed a Treaty of Peace and Friendship with China's Deng Xiaoping, who finally was able to put an end to the Cultural Revolution, and the following year, Prime Minister Ohira signed an economic cooperation agreement with China. Since China had abandoned its claims to reparations in 1972, the economic cooperation agreement had a reparations-like aspect to it. However, more importantly, Ohira believed it worthwhile over the long-term to contribute economically to China's peaceful development in international society. Generally speaking, this was a policy of supporting China's growth into a responsible power, and in the case of Ohira, also reflected his realization of the necessity for Japan and China to cooperate and have friendly relations in the future. The Japanese government continued this approach over the coming decades.

In this way, Japan's regional policy was partly responsible for the continued economic development and cooperation between Japan, the NIEs, ASEAN, and China. During World War II, Japan attempted to expand its sphere of influence in a zero-sum manner, sacrificing the countries of Asia. In contrast, Japan's regional policy in the 1970s was plus-sum in nature, whereby Japan, as the stronger country economically, helped the less fortunate and supported the industrialization of developing countries for everyone's mutual benefit. In doing so, it slowed the spreading of the gap between rich and poor, haves and have-nots. It also led to the building of a foundation of "quiet reconciliation" between Japan and the countries of Southeast Asia after the war.

In addition, with the assistance of Okita Saburo, Prime Minister Ohira announced a regional policy covering a larger area known as the Pacific Basin Cooperation Concept. This was an idea to help forge East Asia, North America, and the Pacific into one Asia-Pacific region. From this the PECC emerged in 1980 made up of individuals from government and the private sector followed by APEC in 1989. This Asia-Pacific regionalism represented an attempt by Japan to forge a new identity, caught as it was between East and West in the Cold War and civilization-wise, as well as on the economic front, between North and South.

Diplomacy and security policy in the 1970s

Japan sought to pursue an autonomous diplomacy in the 1970s as the Cold War structure began to be shook up. For example, Prime Minister Tanaka was able to restore relations quickly between Japan and China, and Japan not only pursued its own diplomacy vis-à-vis the Arab countries in the wake of the oil shocks, but also sought to pursue "resource diplomacy" in order to secure natural resources for which it was heavily dependent on imports. It also attempted to break the stalemate in relations with the Soviet Union. This can be seen as the search by Japan, already an economic power due to its high economic growth, to become a political power on the world stage, particularly as the international framework was shaking. This was to be expected. However, Tanaka's autonomous diplomacy did not succeed. The anti-Japanese riots in Southeast Asia blocked it, as did the United States, in a different way. Amid the economic crisis and his personal scandals, Prime Minister Tanaka lost the ability to govern effectively.

Fukuda and Ohira, who pursued close relations with the United States while seeking a mutually profitable relationship with Asia, were much more successful that those attempting blatant autonomous diplomacy. Regarding Japan's economic diplomacy with Southeast Asia, Japan had built up a certain amount of capital vis-à-vis the countries of the region after participating in the 1954 Colombo Plan and supporting Indonesia's shift in 1965 to its development path. In the wake of America's departure from the region, Japan, using an economic approach, was able to extend its type of diplomacy in the region in a way that would promote regional development and stability. Prime Minister Fukuda spoke of a "comprehensive diplomacy" and Prime Minister Ohira showed that Japan was a "Member of the West" by strengthening its cooperation with the Carter administration as it was dealing with the crisis in Iran and the Soviet invasion of Afghanistan. Regional policy was furthered while maintaining the balance between the deepening of Japan–U.S. relations and the expansion of Japan's diplomatic horizons.

It is worth looking at the security policy in the 1970s, which is like the other side of the coin to the economic approach. As the 1970s began, Defense Agency Director General Nakasone called for an "autonomous defense" posture and made it seem that the economic power Japan was now choosing the route of becoming a military power. In fact, it can be said that the 1970s, which was witnessing the downsizing of the U.S. military in Asia, was the second time that the "normal state" argument began to be heard, the first being around the time of the Korean War. However, actual security policy did not head in the direction of a military force capable of defending Japan completely, but instead stopped at the Basic Defense Capability concept that Vice Minister of Defense Kubo Takuya had proposed. Namely, under the Japan–U.S. Security Treaty that had been extended after 1970, Japan would rely on the United States for deterrence, while Japan itself would build its military strength to a level that would be able to deny the enemy its objective were it to attack Japan. This approach clarified that Japan would limit its strength primarily to its own defense and would not become a military or nuclear power.

Japan could probably be mocked for its decision in the 1970s not to possess nuclear weapons and not to become an independent military power. However, this decision was of great importance for Japan and the region as a whole. While declaring that Japan would not become a military power, the direction of Fukuda Doctrine's regional economic development approach was set by the above security policy. The Yoshida Doctrine did not end during the crises of the 1970s. Indeed, its value was reaffirmed and it would be further pursued longer.

What also needs to be pointed out is that Japan's postwar views on the economy spread to East Asia. From the end of the Vietnam War until the beginning of the twenty-first century, East Asia was able to focus on the economy without any wars breaking out. Until the end of the Cold War, Japan was the only developed country that was also a democracy. In that sense, Japan was isolated. However, from then on, South Korea and other countries in East Asia followed the same path, and began to pursue democratization. It is clear that numerous societies in East Asia are becoming more like Japan, democratic, stable, and developed.

The peak of the economic state: the 1980s

The New Cold War

The Cold War was a long exercise in preventing the tensions existing between the U.S. and Soviet camps from becoming a hot war. In retrospect, the Cold War gradually settled down into a stable system. However, the change from a "thaw" to "détente" to the end of the Cold War did not occur in a smooth progression. Instead a period of renewed tension was found in between. In the first half of the 1970s, the United States pursued détente with both the Soviet Union and China and the tensions of the Cold War receded, but in the latter half there were signs that the Cold War was starting again. Cold War history therefore can be seen as moving between both tension and the relaxation of the tension.

Following its intervention in the Angolan civil war in 1976, the Soviet Union sought to extend its influence abroad by using its military might, which had reached parity with the United States (which was scaling down after Vietnam as the Soviet Union was increasing its strength). As the view of the Soviet Union as a threat grew, it invaded Afghanistan, drawing the strong condemnation of the United States and the West. In 1980, Reagan was elected president of the United States, having called for confrontation with the Soviet Union, which he described as the "Evil Empire." The first half of the 1980s became known as the "New Cold War."

Success brings other problems

The threat posed by the communist Soviet Union happened to coincide with the rebirth of the Japanese economy and would bring about a conservative shift in Japanese politics. Having overcome the economic crises of the 1970s, the Japanese economy boasted a competitive might unrivaled by the other developed countries. In 1980, Japan represented 10 percent of the world's GNP and began to be called the "10 percent country (*ichiwari kokka*)." It went up even further to 15 percent in the 1980s. This was the strength of Japan's economy at the time. The decade of the 1980s was the most prosperous period in Japan's history, and the one in which Japan had the largest economic impact on the world's economy.

In situations like this, when a society is at its peak, it is easy to become relaxed, complacent, and greedy. It is surprisingly difficult to continue "prosperity." At the same time, it is also necessary to be prepared for the international reaction to such a strong economy, which causes economic friction and other problems. On the eve of the 1980s, Prime Minister Ohira established nine different study groups to consider the question of friction and other issues over the long range. The timing could not have been better.

Following the economic successes of the 1980s, it was necessary to establish other national goals. The expansion of Japan's international role and enhancing the livelihoods of the people were two such goals. These are two essential issues that are necessary for Japan, which was modernized in a top-down fashion and became a developed country.

Nakasone diplomacy

Prime Minister Nakasone Yasuhiro, who entered office in November 1982, visited the United States after traveling to South Korea in January 1983 in order to resolve some of the economic cooperation problems that existed between Japan and its neighbor. Cold war warrior Reagan could not but be pleased that his two alliance partners in Asia were trying to repair the damage in their relationship. Prime Minister Nakasone also worked to strengthen the Japan–U.S. relationship, which had not gone well during the cabinet of Suzuki Zenko, and as a result, the "Ron–Yasu" special friendship was built.

As seen when he took the lead at the May 1983 Williamsburg Summit in discussing global security issues, Prime Minister Nakasone's desire to see Japan, having become an economic power, play a larger role in international security got a lot of people's attention. He was a presidential prime minister, exercising leadership in a top-down fashion, as seen in his success in privatizing Japan Railways and other public companies.

Nakasone's diplomacy had as its core the deepening of the Japan–U.S. relationship, but this did not mean it was done at the expense of relations with Asia. Nakasone was able to build an especially good relationship with Chinese leader Deng Xiaoping, and also successfully visited Southeast Asia. The place where Nakasone most showed off his diplomatic flair was the G7 Summit in Tokyo in May 1986. Economic friction had been increasing due to the Japanese economy becoming stronger and stronger and a sense of discord had been building. However, the summit ended successfully for Nakasone because the Maekawa Report, released the month before, gave hope to the representatives of the other G7 countries that the problems would be resolved through economic structural changes. A month after the summit, Nakasone held elections for both the Lower and Upper Houses, and the LDP won its largest victory since the days of Sato.

It would not be incorrect to say that the period of the Nakasone administration was the peak of postwar Japanese diplomacy, but at the same time, it would be difficult to argue that Japan moved from being an economic power to a truly international one. There were some developments in the manner and level of cooperation in the Japan–U.S. alliance, but it was not a large expansion of its actual role on the security front. Nakasone's diplomacy was characterized by personal relations at the top level, but it has apparently proved difficult to institutionalize and sustain new relationships.

After the Plaza Agreement in 1985, Japan's economic power greatly expanded through direct investment abroad by Japanese companies, which began buying famous properties and brand items. However, there was no clear and comprehensive vision on how the extra wealth should be used. As a result, Japan's future became tied to the bubble economy.

International developments after the Cold War and Japanese diplomacy

The end of the bipolar order and the repeat of "geography and history"

With the coming down of the Berlin Wall in the fall of 1989, the Communist bloc of Eastern Europe also came crashing down with amazing speed.

Earlier that year in January in Japan, another age had come to an end. The Showa Emperor died, and a new era, called Heisei, had begun. While not the same as when General Nogi and his wife committed suicide on the occasion of the Meiji Emperor's passing nearly eighty years before, several people who represented Japan in different fields also by chance passed away the same year as Hirohito—Matsushita Konosuke, Biku Hibari, Tezuka Naoshi. In July 1989, the LDP lost for the first time in the Upper House elections, signaling the beginning of the end of the 1955 system.

The international environment and the domestic situation were very much linked. The end of the Cold War greatly impacted both the international system and Japan. Regarding the changes internationally, two competing things occurred. On the one hand, the end of the Cold War meant the end of the Soviet and Communist system as well as the end of the bipolar world, managed by the United States and the Soviet Union. The end of the Cold War also brought to the surface the numerous historical and other problems that existed in different regions that had been stifled over the years. Ethnic conflicts in the former Soviet Union and Yugoslavia, for example, exploded and the various dilemmas of geography and history reappeared. After the bipolar world, a new one emerged where countless nations and ethnic groups as well as religions all argued their identity.

U.S.-led globalization

On the other hand, the victor in the Cold War was the Western camp centered on the United States. Liberal democracy, not communism or socialism, became the leading approach in the post-Cold War period. Moreover, the prestige of market liberalism, the mainstay of economic principles since the 1980s, rose with the West's victory in the Cold War. America, as the only superpower, called for a "New World Order" at the time of the Gulf Crisis and War, but due to domestic economic problems of its own, its international involvement had to be limited, as seen by the defeat of its President Bush in the presidential elections of 1992. The new president, Clinton, sought to relieve the United States of the burdens left over from the Cold War and focus on the domestic economy. America's involvement in international affairs in the 1990s was more a response to specific situations than a creative, sustainable policy. What helped the international order most was the completion of the Uruguay Round of the GATT in late 1993 and the start of a comprehensive trading system known as the WTO in January 1995.

The end of the Cold War stimulated U.S.-led globalization from an unexpected place. After the Cold War, several advanced military technologies, for which the Pentagon had spent much money over the years, were made available to the civilian sector and became widely used. One area was IT. The U.S. -led IT revolution saw the inexpensive flow of lots of information across borders, further pushing along globalization. At the same time, Microsoft led the rebirth of the U.S. economy. In the 1980s, Japan's industrial production led the world economy, but in the 1990s, the United States, which had switched to digital information technologies, recovered its leading role.

In other words, the world after the Cold War saw on the one hand increasing divisions along ethnic, religious, and regional lines, while on the other hand, witnessing globalization move forward, pulled by the U.S. IT revolution like a train by an engine. Both trends would impact the post-Cold War world, and greatly shake up the international order.

Japan–U.S. relations adrift after the Cold War

These changes at the international level impacted Japan significantly. First, globalization and the U.S. strategy to break away from the legacy of the Cold War changed Japan's security, economic, diplomatic, and political environment in the 1990s. The American policy of protecting Japan and giving it special consideration as part of its security policy vis-à-vis the Soviet Union during the Cold War quickly decreased. The degree of U.S. criticism of Japan's lack of contribution to the Gulf War was something not seen before during the Cold War. Japan's level of cooperation was constantly seen "as too little, too late." Not one voice of praise was heard when Japan raised taxes to pay for a $13 billion financial contribution.

At the beginning of the Clinton administration, there were even those who viewed Japan as the main threat. Since traditional security threats had lessened for the United States, it was Japan that was seen as the biggest problem for the United States in economic security. In order to reduce Japan's trade surpluses, the United States brazenly called for numerical targets in numerous areas. It was premised on the Japanese economy being so strong, and thus the need for political pressure on Japan.

Ironically, this view was already wrong in 1993 when the Clinton administration began. Japan's bubble economy had already burst, and Japan had entered a recession. In contrast, the United States had begun to recapture its commanding role in the international economy due to the success of its IT revolution. Despite the reversal in the economic fortunes of Japan and the United States, the Clinton administration continued to put political pressure on Japan through the summer of 1995. Within the Japanese elite, which had been essentially pro-American, there were elements which were now becoming anti-American, or worse, starting to hate the U.S.

The "Lost Decade"

More than this change, however, the biggest problem for Japan was the fact it was late in joining the U.S.-led IT revolution and globalization. The more Japan resisted what it felt was improper political pressure from the United States, the less it saw the changes to the market that were in fact taking place in the wake of these new technologies and products. As a result, it fell behind and hurt itself in the end. Among the Japanese, a defensive sort of economic nationalism was being felt more, made up, on the one hand, of a haughtiness that was responsible for the successes of the 1980s, and on the other, a sense of loss or despair in light of the non-stop challenges of the 1990s. Japan was not able to keep up with the international changes. Some of its pioneering companies made incorrect strategic choices about the direction of future technologies. The 1990s for the Japanese economy was indeed the "Lost Decade."

This was related to the problem of not being able easily to change the inefficiencies of the vested interests and oligopoly of the so-called "iron triangle" relationship between politicians, the bureaucracy, and big business. Having succeeded through "modernization from above," Japan had imposed many restrictions on the market economy, which is supposed to be guided by free competition. As a result, a closed structure remained in which interests were divided up and protected by the bureaucrats, much like escort ships on a potentially perilous sea. This made a quick response to the IT revolution and globalization difficult.

In light of this, it can be said that the traditional strength of Japan—sensitive to the changes in the world and able to learn from the world—does not apply to all periods. In the Meiji period and in the postwar, when Japan had to start from scratch again in the wake of destruction or in light of some danger, Japan rebounded quickly. However, in both the prewar and postwar eras, Japan succeeded perhaps too well, and psychologically became so self-focused that it became easy for it to make mistakes internationally.

Of course, it was not only Japan that was faced with the tsunami that globalization represented. There were some rapidly advancing countries in East Asia that saw this as an opportunity to further advance and succeeded in doing so, but there were also many countries which had even greater problems than Japan in dealing with globalization. As the new phrase "digital divide" suggests, there were some countries which were able to ride the wave of the IT revolution and globalization and others which sank. Because everyone followed the doctrine of the new liberal market economy in the 1980s and 1990s, there was no recognition of the need to redistribute wealth. Some of this inflated wealth caused by globalization was invested in short-term international financial trading, becoming one of the main reasons for the 1997 Asia financial crisis. Moreover, it would be hard to deny that the lack of fairness internationally, symbolized by the imbalance between hopelessly bankrupt countries and those strong and wealthy, was one of the breeding grounds of terrorism.

Participation in international security activities

It probably would be incorrect to say, however, that Japan just sat by and did nothing during the "Lost Decade" in the face of numerous crises that occurred. It is important that Japan in the 1990s, as it had in the 1970s, undertook new steps to deal with the crises it faced. After the trials of the Gulf Crisis

and War, Japan passed a UN PKO law in 1992 to allow its SDF to participate in overseas peacekeeping operations, and participated in PKO for the
first time in Cambodia the following year. Having made major diplomatic
contributions to the Cambodian peace process, Japan participated in the
UNTAC mission headed by Akashi Yasushi which led to the successful
holding of the elections throughout Cambodia in 1993.

The peaceful conclusion to the Cambodian civil war and the success in
rebuilding Cambodia changed Japanese thinking. Until then, the Japanese
public was against the dispatch of the SDF abroad, but opinion changed to a
majority in favor of it. In addition, the Japanese public began to support
revision of Article 9 of the Constitution. This change was not brought about
by the views of nationalists who traditionally argued that the postwar Constitution was an "imposed one." Rather, the change was led by the believers
in international cooperation who felt that constitutional revision was necessary to permit the dispatch of the SDF for the sake of international peace
without any domestic problems. Moreover, the Socialist Party, which had led
the debate during the postwar in favor of staunchly protecting the constitution, saw its leader, Murayama Tomiichi, who had become prime minister in
1994, recognize both the SDF and the Japan–U.S. Security Treaty. The main
points of contention, namely basic defense and security policies, between the
conservatives and reformists officially disappeared with this decision. In other
words, after the harsh experiences of the Gulf War, the Japanese government
decided to participate in UN-led peacekeeping operations and was able to
gradually gain the support of the public and over the years that of the opposition parties as well to a certain extent.

The redefinition of the Japan–U.S. Security Treaty

The experiences of the Gulf War made the supporters of close Japan–U.S.
relations nervous that the alliance was in danger. In 1994, when the North
Korean nuclear issue emerged, the United States prepared for war with the
regime of Kim Il Sung. If the Japanese government failed to assist in the
North Korean crisis, repeating its indecisiveness and inaction at the time of
the Gulf War, there likely would have been calls in the U.S. Congress and
elsewhere to end the Japan–U.S. alliance. In that case, Japan would have been
unable to deal with the North Korean nuclear threat alone as it had pursued
an "exclusive self-defense" posture and a "non-nuclear" policy throughout
the postwar. The dual external problems of North Korea and the Taiwan
Strait and the internal problem of bases in Okinawa and frictions with the
local residents both showed the importance as well as the fragility of the
Japan–U.S. alliance once again leading to the joint statement between
Hashimoto and Clinton on redefining the bilateral alliance. The declaration
spoke of the alliance as a "stabilizer" for the Asia-Pacific region, going
beyond simply the defense of Japan and areas surrounding Japan. In 1997,
the Japan–U.S. Guidelines for Security Cooperation were agreed on, laying

out the joint response for regional security. The Japan–U.S. alliance not only was extended after the end of the Cold War, but its scope was expanded and its contents strengthened as well.

In 1995, the myth that Japanese society was safe came crashing down with the Hanshin–Awaji Earthquake in Kobe and the *Aum Shinrikyo* terrorist attack in Tokyo. Subsequently, Japan's coastal areas were repeatedly violated by North Korean spy ships and it was learned that its citizens had been abducted by trained agents over the past few decades. The Japanese public finally came to understand just how defenseless they had let themselves become, and the Japanese government began to take specific measures to deal with protecting the sovereignty of the country and its people, including the passage of the Contingency Laws (*Yuji Hosei*) in 2003. In summary, amid the crises of the postwar period, Japan responded on three levels—(1) participation in international security missions under the UN; (2) expansion of the Japan–U.S. alliance; and (3) strengthening of Japan's own capabilities.

Historically speaking, there is a stark contrast between prewar and postwar Japan–U.S. relations. The relationship in the prewar was one of both friendship and rivalry, ending in the destruction in World War II. In the postwar, both countries restored their friendly relations and Japan was able to recover economically, but from the 1970s through the early 1990s, the two countries faced a difficult period of economic friction. Fortunately, despite this friction, the bilateral alliance remained strong. No sooner had the economic friction ended when Japan was faced with several domestic and international crises. During this time, the Japan–U.S. relationship actually deepened, which shows how much the relationship matured over the years.

The end of the Yoshida Doctrine

The Yoshida Line, which sought the development of Japan as an economic state under the framework of the Japan–U.S. alliance, continued throughout the Cold War as Japan's policy. Known as the "Yoshida Doctrine," it had an unbelievably long life and would essentially continue in the post-Cold War period as well. However, as security crises multiplied in the 1990s, the types of responses needed caused the proponents of the Yoshida Doctrine to debate its contemporary relevance divide into two positions. One group that continued to adhere to the approach by which Japan would continue as a peaceful economic state cooperating internationally. The other view emphasized the importance of the Japan–U.S. alliance, and called for the revision of the constitution and the exercise of the right to collective self-defense. They see Japan and the United States working together to maintain the international order.

The former group, possessing a liberal internationalist bent and believing in peaceful development, argue that Japan in the post-Cold War period should play a "global civilian power" role (so called by Funabashi Yoichi). The latter group is comprised of "realists" and believes that in order to defend Japan and preserve the international order it is necessary for Japan to actively participate in security matters. They argue that Japan should place the Japan–U.S. alliance, as a maritime alliance, at the center of its security policy and that Japan should play a larger security role internationally. The debate on the need for Japan to become a "normal state" and for the spell of "one-country pacifism" over Japan to be broken reflects this view.

As seen in the passage of the PKO Cooperation Bill by Prime Minister Miyazawa, an adherent of the former view, when it comes to cooperation in PKO under the UN, both groups are able to cooperate. However, the two groups split on the issue of SDF participation as combat troops in a multinational force or for joint activities with the U.S. beyond the scope of the defense of Japan.

Following the terrorist attacks on September 11, 2001, Japan's international involvement grew even further on the security front. Prime Minister Koizumi passed a new bill to allow for the dispatch of the SDF to the Indian Ocean and Iraq. The UN resolution was used as the justification for it but it in fact led to the strengthening of the Japan–U.S. alliance. The belief that Japan should limit its role to that of a civilian power was seen in the clear opposition to the SDF's participation in combat. The SDF was dispatched, but its work was limited to rear-area support and reconstruction within the existing constitutional framework. However, the fact is that it is increasingly becoming difficult to separate Japan's defense from that of the rest of the world, and the trend of Japan sharing a larger burden of international security cannot be ignored.

The unresolved problems of the wartime era

Curiously, the problems of Japan's role in World War II resurfaced *after* the end of the Cold War in the 1990s. One wonders why it was not immediately after the war, but now, long after those responsible for it are gone, that the question of war responsibility resurfaces. Usually, problems arising from wars between states are handled through reparations and a peace treaty. At the time of the peace treaty, the United States and several other countries renounced their claims for reparations. For the countries of Asia which were paid reparations, it was done in a way that would not impede Japan's economic recovery. Overall, Japan was treated quite generously as a part of U.S. policy in the Cold War.

That was probably good for Japan, at least in the beginning. However, the Cold War ended up freezing the issue of Japan's war responsibility because after the diplomatic settlement the people of Asia, who suffered Japan's invasion and domination, were left with bitter feelings. Even if they could forget, they had trouble forgiving. It is often said that time heals all wounds, but for the people in Asia, they were busy just trying to get by after the war and so it was not until much later in their lives, after their country had reached a certain level of development and prosperity and their confidence and self-pride had returned, when they were faced with their feelings of the surpressed past.

Is reconciliation possible? Japan's style of reconciliation can be seen most clearly in its relations with Southeast Asia. Reparations or economic cooperation agreements used in place of reparations were signed during the 1950s. At times, representatives of the Japanese government would offer their apologies. In the 1960s, Japan increased its level of economic involvement in Southeast Asia, particularly in the countries impacted by the Vietnam War. However, it became apparent at the time of the 1974 anti-Japanese riots that the reconciliation of the hearts and minds had in fact not really been furthered.

Japan in Asia

The change came after the announcement of the Fukuda Doctrine, mentioned above. Recovering from the oil shock, the Japanese economy increased its involvement by raising the levels of the Asian economies, helping them to become the exporters of industrial products. Even if the people of Southeast Asia had not forgotten the war, they pardoned postwar Japan, which had become a peaceful economic state and continued to contribute to their economic development and did not overly question the past. This sort of quiet reconciliation continued until the end of the twentieth century.

Anti-Japanese sentiment is both deep and strong in Korea, which Japan colonized between 1910 and 1945. However, in October 1998, South Korean President Kim Dae Jung called for a "historical reconciliation." While the style of reconciliation was different from that of Southeast Asia, the contributing factors were the same. President Kim's decision to work with Japan in moving toward the future was based on his high praise of postwar Japan's "peaceful development," "democratization," and its aid programs toward poorer countries, including South Korea.

Problems with China, the scene of a longer and larger path of destruction, remain. While there have been movements toward reconciliation over the years along the same principles as those of Southeast Asia and South Korea, issue that has done most to prevent bilateral relations achieving the same level as that with Japan's other Asian neighbors has been the history problem. Chinese Premier Zeming's November 1998 trip to Japan became an opportunity to criticize Japan's past. Prime Minister Koizumi's repeated visits to the Yasukuni Shrine complicated the working relationship between the two governments. In 2005, anti-Japanese riots occurred in China, and the Chinese government undertook diplomatic initiatives to block Japan's bid for a permanent seat on the UN Security Council. Rather than being partners in East Asia, there are clear signs that Japan and China are becoming rivals. This will make Japan's diplomacy in the coming years difficult, particularly if China, in this new century, is attempting to recover its position as the middle kingdom in East Asia.

Issues for Japanese diplomacy in the twenty-first century

Throughout the postwar, Japanese diplomacy did not lose sight of the essential needs and desires of the people. Pursuing peaceful development with a focus on the economy, Japan established a democracy domestically and built a fair and rich society where the divide between rich and poor is probably the smallest anywhere in the world. It also contributed to the economic development of the neighboring countries of East and Southeast Asia. The results of this civilian power were made possible only by the existence of the free-trade system and market economies of the postwar led by the United States and supported by countries like Japan. Moreover, under its peace constitution, postwar Japan avoided becoming a participant in military conflicts, because it enjoyed the protection of *Pax Americana* for its security. This legacy was the fruit of the strategic choice made by Yoshida, and it continued until after the end of the Cold War.

However, over the years, Japan's diplomacy has lacked the ideals and principles to produce a new international order, the strength to pursue it, the logic and expressiveness to move the world, and the people who have the personality and prestige to fight for it.

However, such qualities are held by the powers that have the ability to reshape the international environment on their own. One might think Japan, having tried this approach in the prewar with the Greater East Asia Co-Prosperity Sphere, cannot hope to try it again. Yet, it may be more a question of degree and balance. Both those countries that want to control and change the international order in their own image and those that do absolutely nothing to shape it and just comform to their environment, are problems. Believers in peaceful cooperation who have lost their sense of autonomy and pride will actually cause an opposite trend to emerge. At the start of the twenty-first century, Japan has increasingly sought to assert its views vis-à-vis its neighbors. Postwar Japan's decision in the past to pursue peaceful development and international cooperation brought much success.

But this success does not mean that Japan itself should refrain from trying to influence the world by its words and ideas. Just because it does not have military power does not mean it cannot undertake effective diplomacy. In short, Japan's problems today are its lack of confidence in its own style, and the ability to express it.

It goes without saying that the difficulty Japan has had in demonstrating a healthy proactive policy in the postwar came from its reflection, amid the shock of having lost the war, on the extreme activism it undertook in the prewar and wartime periods.

In addition, Japan's reluctance to play a more proactive role was also done in order for a poor, defeated country to avoid the wrath of other countries and focus on its own recovery. However, even after it recovered and had become strong again, Japanese diplomacy did not become proactive. There were two reasons for this, one systemic, and the other related to staffing.

Compared to the prewar, the powers of the prime minister in postwar Japan have been increased, with the related diplomatic powers in the hands of the prime minister. However, each of the postwar prime ministers lacked the staff to conduct effective diplomacy at his official residence (*kantei*). Until not too long ago, there was only one person sent from the Foreign Ministry to the *kantei* to act as the prime minister's secretary. The prime minister, figuratively speaking, was a commander without a command staff. As a result, diplomacy was primarily conducted by the bureaucracy at Kasumiga-seki. At the minimum, if the Foreign Ministry did not prepare anything for review, discussion, or decision, there was very little the prime minister's office could do.

The Foreign Ministry, on the other hand, had as its head a foreign minister appointed by the prime minister. Under the foreign minister was the vice minister (*jimu jikan*) and two counselors (*jimu shingikan*). In fact, the ministry is a structure divided between regional offices and functional ones. Neither the minister nor the vice minister has his own command staff. In the prewar, as problems multiplied in its foreign policy, a policy affairs division (*seimukyoku*) was established above the regional and functional areas to develop a new comprehensive policy. During the Cold War, however, the Japan–U.S. Security Treaty in some ways reflected the policy affairs division in the ministry, with the Treaty Division (*Joyakukyoku*) and North American Affairs Division (*Hokubeikyoku*) the most powerful offices in the ministry. After the end of the Cold War, as the problems and challenges multiplied, a Foreign Policy Bureau (*Sogo Gaiko Seisakukyoku*) was created and hopefully will serve as a sort of command staff for Japanese diplomacy. (In contrast, the U.S. govern-ment created the Policy Planning Staff under the Secretary of State as early as 1947 when the Cold War was emerging.)

The recognition that a staff of this kind was needed within the *kantei* was emphasized during the time of the Nakasone cabinet, and as part of the administrative reforms undertaken during the Hashimoto cabinet, and as a result the *kantei*'s diplomatic policy functions were gradually strengthened. During the Koizumi cabinet, not only was the prime minister's residence rebuilt, but the powers of the *kantei* were strengthened to an unprecedented level. Nevertheless, the *kantei* still does not possess the staff to conduct high-level diplomacy. The biggest problem related to this is the lack of people with diplomatic know-how.

With the exception of Shidehara, Yoshida, and Ashida during the Occu-pation, who were all former diplomats, the postwar prime ministers, other than Miyazawa and Nakasone, were unable to speak English freely. Of course, they are free to use Japanese and have it translated. The problem is, however, that Japanese politicians like a shared international perspective and the ability to deal with the world's problems.

Most of the leaders of other countries, on the other hand, including those from developing countries, have been educated at American and Eur-opean universities and are an international elite complete with language skills and a common intellectual background. In contrast, Japanese politicians are products of domestic universities, with only the ability to speak and think locally.

In this day and age, as the world gets smaller and smaller, it is necessary for Japanese officials, and leaders in the private sector, especially those involved in politics and diplomacy, to have international experience, to be able to compete internationally, and to have a shared understanding of important issues in order to be able to pursue Japan's national interests and make their points effectively. Only when such a group of individuals is working in the *kantei* will Japanese diplomacy be able to have the gift of imagination to move international affairs. Japan's diplomacy in the twenty-first century will likely be shaped by the ability to repair the institutional and personnel problems it has traditionally faced.

Index